Cultural Anthropology

Cultural Anthropology

A PERSPECTIVE ON THE HUMAN CONDITION

FOURTH EDITION

Emily A. Schultz
Beloit College

Robert H. Lavenda
St. Cloud State University

Mayfield Publishing Company

Mountain View, California

London • Toronto

Library of Congress Cataloging-in-Publication Data
Schultz, Emily A.
    Cultural Anthropology : a perspective on the human condition /
Emily A. Schultz, Robert H. Lavenda. — 4th ed.
        p.   cm.
    Includes bibliographical references and index.
    ISBN 1-55934-859-3
    1. Ethnology.   I. Lavenda, Robert H. II. Title.
GN316.S38 1998
306—dc21   97-9019
                                                                        CIP

Manufactured in the United States of America
10 9 8 7 6 5 4 3

Mayfield Publishing Company
1280 Villa Street
Mountain View, California 94041

Sponsoring editor, Janet M. Beatty; production editor, Lynn Rabin Bauer; manuscript editor, Dale Anderson; design manager, Susan Breitbard; text and cover designer, Joan Greenfield; cover photograph, © Nicholas DeVore/Tony Stone Images; art editor, Robin Mouat; illustrators, Judith Ogus, Alice and William Thiede, John and Judy Waller; manufacturing manager, Randy Hurst. The text was set in 9/12 Stone Serif by ColorType and printed on 45# Chromatone Matte, PMS 259, by Banta Company.

For Daniel and Rachel

Preface

Anthropology is no longer about the strange customs of exotic peoples (if it ever really was). Today, anthropology examines broad and complex issues about human cultures, including how cultural creativity, human agency, and material constraint shape human cultural traditions. While recognizing the importance of each of these factors, however, we do not reduce human culture to any one of them. We recognize that human experience of the world is fundamentally ambiguous. Human beings work to resolve that ambiguity through interaction with various aspects of the material world, including each other. Because ambiguous experiences can always be resolved in more than one way, individuals and groups must choose some interpretations rather than others simply to get on with living. As a result, human beings cannot avoid participating in the construction and reconstruction of cultural practices. Cultural practices that work become part of local traditions that serve as resources on which people can draw when faced with ambiguities in the future. However, the power struggles that go on in all societies always shape decisions about what works and what does not, further complicating the relationship between what people do and what "ecology" or "economics" or "rationality" is thought to require. The result is the tremendous variety of culturally constructed ways of life, none of which can easily be explained as the inevitable outcome of a single shaping force. Our book aims to show how human agents use cultural creativity to cope with the material constraints that circumscribe all human life.

WHAT'S NEW IN THE FOURTH EDITION

1. All chapters have been edited with an eye to streamlining and improving readability and accessibility. The text is more concise and easier to teach from.

2. The text is now divided into five parts. Part I, The Tools of Cultural Anthropology, consists of three introductory chapters on the concept of culture, ethnographic fieldwork, and a historical approach to anthropological explanations of cultural diversity. Part II, The Resources of Culture, highlights the key dimensions and products of human creativity: language; cognition; play, art, myth, and ritual; and worldview. Part III, The Organization of Material Life, consists of two chapters that treat the ways human cultural creativity is channeled and circumscribed by political and economic constraints. Part IV, Systems of Relationships, looks at the organization of human interdependence. Chapters about kinship, marriage and the family, and what's beyond kinship allow us to emphasize how people make use of cultural resources as they struggle to pursue their personal projects within contexts of political and material constraints. This allows us to emphasize the ways people everywhere exercise agency, creating "imagined communities" based on kinship, ethnicity, or nationality as strategies for domination, resistance, or accommodation to contending political, economic, and social structures. Part V, From Local to Global, concludes the text by asking students to contemplate the globalizing context in which all human beings live at the end of the twentieth century, as well as the ever-intensifying political, economic, and cultural forces with which all contemporary societies must cope. Each part has its own introduction, which allows students better to understand the logic that guides the book.

3. The emphasis on the way humans use culture to adapt to and transform the world has been strengthened and more thoroughly integrated throughout.

4. We have reorganized the chapters. The first two parts remain the same. They are followed now by

Social Organization and Power and Making a Living. By placing these chapters before the chapters that address the organization of human interdependence, we are able to emphasize more strongly the political and material constraints on people in creating social relations.

While every chapter has been revised—most substantially—some chapters have seen particularly noteworthy changes:

- *Chapter 2: Culture and the Human Condition.* This chapter contains a new discussion of Rick Potts' "monolith of culture," which we believe successfully demystifies the supposed "all or nothing" paradox of the evolution of human culture. We have revised and strengthened the discussion of agency and addressed the deterritorialization of culture in the contemporary world.

- *Chapter 5: Language.* Material on formal linguistics has been shortened, and there is much greater emphasis on discourse and language as practice. Ethnopragmatics and heteroglossia are discussed and illustrated with new ethnographic examples. Our earlier discussion on African American English is updated in the context of an enlarged discussion of pidgins and creoles, and we now include an In Their Own Words selection about the Ebonics controversy in the Oakland, California, public schools.

- *Chapter 9: Social Organization and Power.* In addition to its new placement, this chapter contains new material on domination and hegemony and anthropological approaches to the study of nationalism.

- *Chapter 10: Making a Living.* This chapter is also in a new position in the order of chapters. It contains revised and updated discussions of economic anthropology, as well as a new consideration of political and social implications of storage.

- *Chapter 11: Kinship.* We have added a discussion of kinship institutions, such as adoption, based on nurturance. There is an expanded discussion of supernumerary sexes and genders. We have tried to strike a balance between recognizing the past achievements and new directions in anthropological studies of kinship.

- *Chapter 12: Marriage and the Family.* This chapter contains a new section comparing bridewealth and dowry. There are revised and expanded discussions comparing sexuality cross-culturally, new reproductive technologies and their effects on child custody in the United States, and new materials on gay and lesbian families of choice.

- *Chapter 14: The World System.* The section on Amazonian Indians has been updated. Discussions of colonialism and peasant resistance have been revised. We have added material from the work of John and Jean Comaroff on missionary activity in Africa as well as a new section on globalization.

FEATURES AND LEARNING AIDS

- *Material on gender and feminist anthropology is featured throughout the text.* Discussions of gender are tightly woven into the fabric of the book, and include (for example) material on supernumerary sexes and genders (such as Sambia kwolu-aatmwol and male and female berdaches in Native North America), varieties of human sexual practices, language and gender, dance and gender politics, and women and colonialism. Extensive material on gender is found in the chapters on Language; Cognition; Play, Art, Myth, and Ritual; Social Organization and Power; Making a Living; Kinship; Marriage; and The World System.

- *We take an explicitly global approach in the text.* We systematically point out the extent to which the current sociocultural situation of particular peoples has been shaped by their particular histories of contact with world capitalism and their degrees of incorporation in it. Cultures cannot be studied outside the broader context that shapes people's lives.

- *New voices, including those of indigenous peoples, anthropologists, and nonanthropologists, are presented in the text in commentaries called* In Their Own Words. These short commentaries provide alternative perspectives—always interesting and sometimes controversial—on topics featured in the chapter in which they occur.

◆ *EthnoProfiles*. These text inserts provide a consistent, brief information summary for each society discussed at length in the text. They emerged from our sense as instructors that students could not be expected to know readily where the different societies anthropologists talk about are located, nor how many people might be involved. Each EthnoProfile includes data on the location of the society, the nation it is in, the population, the environment, the livelihood of the people, their political organization, and a source for further information. Each EthnoProfile also contains a map of the area in which the society is found. They are not intended to be a substitute for reading ethnographies or for in-class lectures, nor are they intended to reify the "people" or "culture" in question. Their main purpose is to provide a consistent orientation for the reader.

◆ *Additional learning aids.* Key terms are boldfaced in the text and defined in a running glossary on the page where they appear. Each chapter ends with a list of the key terms in the order they appear in the text, a numbered chapter summary, and annotated suggested readings. Maps are featured extensively throughout the text.

◆ *In our discussions, we have tried to avoid being omniscient narrators by making use of citations and quotations in order to indicate to students where anthropological ideas come from.* In our view, even first-year students need to know that an academic discipline like anthropology is constructed by the work of many people; no one, especially not textbook authors, should attempt to impose a single voice on the field. We have avoided, as much as we could, predigested statements that students must take on faith. We try to give them the information they need to reach the conclusions.

◆ *A Study Guide* written with Margaret Rauch, Emerita Director of the Academic Learning Center at St. Cloud State University. This Study Guide is unusual in that Dr. Rauch poured into it her many years of experience in helping students learn to study and succeed at the university. It is filled with hints and suggestions on improving study skills, strategies for studying this text, organizing information, writing essay exams, taking multiple-choice exams, and much more. Any student, even the best-prepared, will find the information and strategies in the Study Guide valuable. Each chapter in the Study Guide also contains a key terms review, sample multiple-choice questions, and an innovative Arguing Anthropology section with a pair of questions for students to consider arguing about with their friends.

◆ *An Instructor's Manual* with test-bank questions, chapter outlines, supplemental activities, and film suggestions. The test bank questions are also available on computer disk for IBM-compatible and Macintosh computers. Instructors can select, add, or edit questions, randomize the question order for each exam and the answer order for each question, and print tests that meet the needs of their classes.

We take students seriously. In our experience, although students may sometimes complain, they are also pleased when a course or a textbook gives them some credit for having minds and being willing to use them. We have worked hard to make this book readable and to present anthropology in its diversity, as a vibrant, living discipline full of excitement, contention, and intellectual value. We do not run away from the meat of the discipline with the excuse that it's too hard for students. Our collective teaching experience has ranged from highly selective liberal arts colleges to multi-purpose state universities, to semi-rural community colleges. We have found students at all of these institutions willing to be challenged and make an effort when it is clear to them that anthropology has something to offer, whether intellectual, emotional, or practical. It is our hope that this book will be a useful tool in challenging students and convincing them of the value of anthropology as a way of thinking about, and dealing with, the world in which they live.

ACKNOWLEDGMENTS

We would like to thank Jan Beatty, our editor at Mayfield, for her confidence, support, advice, and sure eye. We appreciate her eagerness to publish both this book and the anthropology book. It has been a great pleasure to work with her and the superb production team at Mayfield, especially Lynn Rabin Bauer, once again, production editor extraordinaire. We would also like to acknowledge the contributions of our exceptional copyeditor Dale Anderson. To all authors we wish such a copyeditor. Our thanks as well to art editor Robin Mouat, permissions editor Martha Granahan, and editorial assistant Pam Lucas.

We continue to be impressed by the level of involvement of the reviewers of this manuscript. Our reviewers seem to recognize how important they are not only to us, to the authors of textbooks, but to the users of textbooks—students and colleagues both. They also recognize that authors may have more than time invested in their work. We have found that, even when we didn't follow their suggestions, their work caused us to think and rethink the issues they raised. We would like therefore to recognize Ana M. Alonso, University of Arizona; Kathleen Barlow, University of Min-

nesota; Jill Brody, Louisiana State University; Jeffrey H. Cohen, Texas A & M University; Martha Kaplan, Vassar College; Richard Moore, Ohio State University; Amy Mountcastle, William Patterson College and Rutgers University; Susan Rasmussen, University of Houston; Kathleen M. Stemmler, Northern Arizona University; and Mahir Saul, University of Illinois.

We owe a special and profound debt to Ivan Karp, who has been our most important source of intellectual stimulation and support throughout this project.

We have found that textbook writing is a particularly solitary occupation, and that means that our children, Daniel and Rachel, have had to get used to our spending an awful lot of time reading, taking notes, writing, revising, and attending to a seemingly unending stream of details. For a host of reasons, it is for our children and the future in which they will live that we undertook this project. As they read what we have written, we hope that they come to understand why.

Contents in Brief

Contents

---

8   WORLDVIEW 153

Part III: The Organization of Material Life 177

9   SOCIAL ORGANIZATION AND POWER 179

---

10   MAKING A LIVING 206

Part IV: Systems of Relationships 231

11   KINSHIP 233

15   ANTHROPOLOGY IN EVERYDAY LIFE   337

EthnoProfiles

1

The Anthropological Perspective

n early 1976, we (Emily Schultz and Robert Lavenda) traveled to northern Cameroon, in western Africa, to study social relations in the town of Guider, where we rented a small house. In the first weeks we lived there, we enjoyed spending the warm evenings of the dry season reading and writing in the glow of the house's brightest electric fixture, which illuminated a large, unscreened veranda. After a short time, however, the rains began, and with them appeared swarms of winged termites. These slow-moving insects with fat, two-inch abdomens were attracted to the light on the veranda, and we soon found ourselves spending more time swatting at them than reading and writing. One evening, in a fit of desperation, we rolled up old copies of the international edition of *Newsweek* and began an all-out assault, determined to rid the veranda of every single termite.

The rent we paid for this house included the services of a night watchman. As we launched our attack on the termites, the night watchman suddenly appeared beside the veranda carrying an empty powdered milk tin. When he asked if he could have the insects we had been killing, we were a bit taken aback but warmly invited him to help himself. He moved onto the veranda, quickly collected the corpses of fallen insects, and then joined us in going after those termites that were still airborne. Although we became skilled at thwacking the insects with our rolled-up magazines, our skills paled beside those of the night watchman, who simply snatched the termites out of the air with his hand, squeezed them gently, and dropped them into his rapidly filling tin can. The three of us managed to clear the air of insects in about ten minutes. We offered the night watchman our kill, which he accepted politely. He then returned to his post, and we returned to our books.

The following evening, soon after we took up our usual places on the veranda, the watchman appeared at the steps bearing a tray with two covered dishes. He explained that his wife had prepared the food for us in exchange for our help in collecting termites. We accepted the food and carefully lifted the lids. One dish contained *nyiri,* a stiff paste made of red sorghum, a staple of the local diet. The other dish contained another pasty substance with a speckled, salt-and-pepper appearance, which we quickly deduced was termite paste prepared from the previous night's kill.

The night watchman waited at the foot of the veranda steps, an expectant smile on his face. Clearly, he did not intend to leave until we tasted the gift he had brought. We looked at each other. We had never eaten insects before or considered them edible in the North American, middle-class diet we were used to. To be sure, "delicacies" like chocolate-covered ants exist, but such items are considered by most North Americans to be food fit only for eccentrics. However, we understood the importance of not insulting the night watchman and his wife, who were being so generous to us. From our training, we knew that insects were a favored food in many human societies and that eating them brought no ill effects. With the watchman still standing there, smiling, waiting to see what we would do, we reached into the dish of *nyiri,* pulling off a small amount. We then used the ball of *nyiri* to scoop up a small portion of termite paste, brought the mixture to our mouths, ate, chewed, and swallowed. The watchman beamed, bid us goodnight, and returned to his post. We looked at each other in wonder. The sorghum paste had a grainy tang that was rather pleasant, and the termite paste tasted mild, like chicken, not unpleasant at all. We later wrote to our families about this experience. When they wrote back, they described how they had recounted the details of our meal to a friend who was a home economist. Her response contained no shock whatsoever. She simply commented that termites are a good source of clean protein.

WHAT IS ANTHROPOLOGY?

Some of the central elements of the anthropological experience can be found in this anecdote. Anthropologists want to learn about as many different human ways of life as they can. Whether the people they come to know are members of their own society, live on a different continent, or must be recreated from traces of the life they lived hundreds or thousands of years ago, anthropologists are sometimes exposed to practices that startle them. However, as they take the risk of getting to know such ways of life better, they are often treated to the sweet discovery of familiarity. This shock of the unfamiliar becoming familiar—as well as the familiar becoming unfamiliar—is something anthropologists come to expect and is one of the real pleasures of the field. In this book, we share aspects of the anthropological experience in the hope that you, too, will come to find pleasure, insight, and self-recognition from an involvement with the unfamiliar.

Anthropology can be defined as the study of human nature, human society, and the human past (cf. Greenwood and Stini 1977). It is a scholarly discipline that aims to describe in the broadest possible sense what it means to be human.

Anthropologists are not alone in focusing their attention on human beings and their creations. Human biology, literature, art, history, linguistics, sociology, politics, economics—all these scholarly disciplines, and many more—concentrate on one or another aspect of human life. Anthropology is unique because it draws on the findings of these other disciplines and attempts to fit them together with its own data in order to understand how human biology, economics, politics, religion, and kinship collectively shape one another to make human life what it is. That is, anthropology is **holistic**; holism is a central feature of the anthropological perspective.

To generalize about human nature, human society, and the human past requires evidence from the widest possible range of human societies. Thus, in addition to being holistic, anthropology is a **comparative** discipline. It is not enough, for example, to observe only our own social group, discover that we do not eat insects, and conclude that human beings as a species do not eat insects. When we compare human diets in different societies, we discover that insect eating is quite common and that our North American aversion to eating insects is nothing more than a dietary practice specific to our own society.

Anthropologists try to come up with generalizations about what it means to be human that are valid across space and over time. The field for comparison includes all human societies as well as all periods of the human past, from the emergence of humanlike primates some 5 million years ago to the present time. For this reason, anthropology also examines the biological evolution of the human species over time, including the study of human origins and genetic variety and inheritance in living human populations.

If evolution is understood broadly as change over time, then human societies and cultures may also be understood to have evolved from prehistoric times to the present. One of anthropology's most important

contributions to the study of human evolution has been to emphasize the critical differences that separate *biological evolution* (which concerns attributes and behaviors passed on by genes) from *cultural evolution* (which concerns beliefs and behaviors that are *not* passed on by genes but are transmitted through teaching and learning). Later chapters will provide a more detailed discussion of the differences between these two modes of evolution; however, we wish to point out here that the human species, human societies, and human cultures all change over time. Because anthropologists are interested in documenting and explaining these changes, the anthropological perspective is **evolutionary** at its core.

THE CONCEPT OF CULTURE

A consequence of human evolution that had the most profound impact on human nature and human society was the emergence of **culture**, which can be defined as sets of learned behavior and ideas that human beings acquire as members of society. Human beings use culture to adapt to and transform the world in which we live.

Culture makes us unique among living creatures. Human beings are more dependent than any other species on learning for survival because we have no instincts that automatically protect us and help us find food and shelter. Instead, we have come to use our large and complex brains to learn from other members of society what we need to know to survive. Learning

anthropology The study of human nature, human society, and the human past.

holistic A characteristic of the anthropological perspective that describes how anthropology tries to integrate all that is known about human beings and their activities at the highest and most inclusive level.

comparative A characteristic of the anthropological perspective that requires anthropologists to consider similarities and differences in as wide a range of human societies as possible before generalizing about human nature, human society, or the human past.

evolutionary A characteristic of the anthropological perspective that requires anthropologists to place their observations about human nature, human society, or the human past in a temporal framework that takes into consideration change over time.

culture Sets of learned behavior and ideas that human beings acquire as members of society. Human beings use culture to adapt to and to transform the world in which we live.

is a primary focus of childhood, which is longer for humans than for any other species.

In the anthropological perspective, the concept of culture is central to explanations of why human beings are what they are and why they do what they do. Anthropologists have frequently been able to show that members of a particular social group behave in a particular way *not* because the behavior was programmed by their genes, but because they observed other people and copied what they did. For example, North Americans typically do not eat insects, but this behavior is not the result of genetic programming. Rather, North Americans have been told as children that eating insects is disgusting, have never seen any of their friends or family eat insects, and do not eat insects themselves. As we discovered personally, however, insects can be eaten by North Americans with no ill effects. Thus, this difference in social behavior can be explained in terms of culture rather than biology.

Interestingly, anthropologists have been able to demonstrate the power of culture precisely because they are also knowledgeable about human biology. Scholars who are trained in both areas, as has been traditional in many North American anthropology programs, understand how genes and organisms work and are acquainted with comparative information about a wide range of human societies. As a result, they are more realistic in evaluating the ways that biology and culture contribute to any particular form of human behavior. Indeed, most anthropologists reject explanations of human behavior that force them to choose between biology and culture as the cause. Instead, they prefer to emphasize that human beings are **bicultural organisms.** Our genetically guided biological makeup, including our brain, nervous system, and anatomy, makes us organisms capable of creating and using culture. Without these biological endowments, human culture as we know it would not exist. At the same time, our survival as biological organisms depends upon learned cultural traditions that help us find food, shelter, and mates and that teach us how to rear our offspring. This is because our biological endowment, rich as it is, does not provide us with instincts that would automatically take care of these survival needs. Human biology makes culture possible; human culture makes human biological survival possible.

Anthropologists sometimes distinguish between Culture (with a capital C) and cultures (plural with a lowercase c). *Culture* is used to describe an attribute of the human species as a whole—its members' ability to create and to imitate behaviors and ideas that promote the survival of our species in the absence of highly specific genetic programming. By contrast, *cultures* refer to particular traditions of learned behavior and ideas that belong to specific groups of human beings. Anthropologists like E. B. Tylor first used the concept of culture in this way in the late nineteenth century. They questioned the accepted understanding of culture as refinement or cultivated good taste that some people had and others did not. From then until now, the concept of culture has been applied to the traditions of all members of any human society. Each tradition may be called a separate culture, although the boundaries separating one culture from another are often not easy to draw.

The human species as a whole can be said to have *Culture* as a defining attribute, but anthropologists and other human beings have access only to particular human cultures. Ordinarily, anthropologists gain information about specific cultures by making direct contact with some other, particular way of life. Whether living with a group of Fulbe in northern Cameroon, excavating an ancient Aztec site in Mexico, or studying the differences between men's and women's speech in Alabama, anthropologists must shift their perspectives away from the ones with which they are most familiar. Anthropologists who study chimpanzees or gorillas in the wild or who attempt to reconstruct the ways of life of the fossilized ancestors of modern human beings and apes push the boundaries of our understanding of what it means to be human. The results of their work, as later chapters will demonstrate, frequently require us to reevaluate our common-sense notions about who we are. The experience of being "in the field" is central to modern anthropology and contributes profoundly to the anthropological perspective. All anthropology comes back to the mental, emotional, and physical experience of direct contact with a frequently unfamiliar world.

THE CROSS-DISCIPLINARY DISCIPLINE

Because the goal of anthropology is to describe what it means to be human, the discipline is extraordinarily diverse. At any given yearly meeting of the American Anthropological Association (the professional society

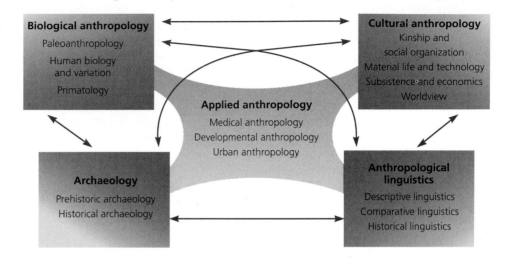

FIGURE 1.1 In the United States, anthropology is traditionally divided into four specialties: biological anthropology, cultural anthropology, anthropological linguistics, and archaeology. Applied anthropology draws on information provided by the other four specialties.

Anthropology
The integrated study of human nature, human society, and human history.

Biological anthropology
Paleoanthropology
Human biology and variation
Primatology

Cultural anthropology
Kinship and social organization
Material life and technology
Subsistence and economics
Worldview

Applied anthropology
Medical anthropology
Developmental anthropology
Urban anthropology

Archaeology
Prehistoric archaeology
Historical archaeology

Anthropological linguistics
Descriptive linguistics
Comparative linguistics
Historical linguistics

to which most anthropologists belong), you will find research papers presented on such topics as the size and shape of the teeth of fossilized primates believed to be ancestral to modern human beings, patterns of marriage and divorce in Europe, biological and social factors involved with AIDS in different cultural settings, traditional food-getting activities in Africa, and mat making in Polynesia. Because of its diverse interests, anthropology does not easily fit into any of the standard academic classifications. The discipline is usually listed as a social science, but it spans the natural sciences and the humanities as well.

Figure 1.1 brings some order to the variety of interests found under the anthropological umbrella. At the most inclusive level, we may think of anthropology as the integrated (or holistic) study of human nature, human society, and the human past. This commitment to holism is reflected in many university departments of anthropology whose faculty and courses try to represent a full range of anthropological subfields. Traditionally, North American anthropology has been divided into four such subfields: biological anthropology, cultural anthropology, anthropological linguistics, and archaeology.

Biological Anthropology

The first, and oldest, specialty within anthropology is called **biological** (or **physical**) **anthropology**. Biological anthropologists are most interested in looking

at human beings as living organisms in order to discover what makes us different from or similar to other animals.

In the nineteenth century, when anthropology was developing as an academic field, physical anthropology flourished. Interest in this field was a by-product of centuries of exploration. Western Europeans had found tremendous variation in the physical appearance of peoples around the world and had long tried to make sense of these differences. Physical anthropologists invented a series of elaborate techniques to measure different observable features of human populations, including skin color, hair type, body type, and so forth. Their goal was to find scientific evidence that would allow them to classify all the peoples of the world into a set of unambiguous categories based on distinct sets of biological attributes. Such categories were called **races**, and many physical anthropologists were convinced that clear-cut criteria for racial classification would be discovered if careful measurements were made on enough people from around the world.

---

biocultural organisms Organisms (in this case, human beings) whose defining features are codetermined by biological and cultural factors.

biological anthropology (or **physical anthropology**) The specialty of anthropology that looks at human beings as biological organisms and tries to discover what characteristics make us different from other organisms and what characteristics we share.

races Social groupings that allegedly reflected biological differences.

Of course, this early research in physical anthropology did not take place in a social and historical vacuum. The very peoples whom physical anthropologists were trying to assign to racial categories were in most cases non-European peoples who were coming under increasing political and economic domination by expanding European and European American capitalist societies. These peoples differed from "white" Europeans not only because of their darker skin color but also because of their unfamiliar languages and customs and because, in most cases, they possessed technologies that were no match for the might of the industrialized West. As a result, racial membership was understood to determine not just outward physical attributes of groups but their mental and moral attributes as well. Races were ranked in terms of these attributes. Not surprisingly, "white" Europeans and North Americans were seen as superior, and the other races were seen to represent varying grades of inferiority. In this way, the first physical anthropologists helped develop theories that would justify the social practice of **racism:** the systematic oppression of members of one or more socially defined "races" by another socially defined "race" that is justified in terms of the supposed inherent biological superiority of the rulers and the supposed inherent biological inferiority of those they rule.

As time passed, research techniques in physical anthropology improved. Physical anthropologists began to measure numerous internal features of populations, such as blood types, that they added to their calculations. They learned a tremendous amount about physical variation in human beings. Indeed, they discovered that the external traits traditionally used to identify races, such as skin color, did not correlate well with other physical and biological traits. The more they learned about the biological attributes of human populations, the more they realized that races with distinct and unique sets of such attributes simply did not exist.

By the early twentieth century, some anthropologists and biologists concluded that the concept of "race" did not reflect a fact of nature but was instead a cultural label invented by human beings to sort people into groups. Anthropologists like Franz Boas, for example, who in the early 1900s founded the first department of anthropology in the United States, had long been uncomfortable with racial classifications in anthropology. Boas and his students devoted much energy to debunking racist stereotypes, using both their knowledge of biology and their understanding of culture. As the discipline of anthropology developed in the United States, students were trained in both human biology and human culture to provide them with the tools to fight racial and ethnic stereotyping.

Rejecting the racial thinking of the nineteenth century, many modern anthropologists who study human biology prefer to call themselves **biological anthropologists** (Figure 1.2). They no longer study "race" and instead pay attention to patterns of variation within the human species as a whole.

Some biological anthropologists work in the fields of **primatology** (the study of the closest living relatives of human beings, the nonhuman primates), **paleoanthropology** (the study of fossilized bones and teeth of our earliest ancestors), and human skeletal biology (measuring and comparing the shapes and sizes—or morphology—of bones and teeth using skeletal remains from different human populations). Newer specialties focus on human adaptability in different ecological settings, on human growth and development, or on the connections between a population's evolutionary history and its susceptibility to disease. Forensic anthropologists use their knowledge of human skeletal anatomy to aid law enforcement and human rights investigators. Molecular anthropologists trace chemical similarities and differences in the immune system, an interest that has recently led into active work on AIDS. Moreover, new analytic techniques such as biostatistics, three-dimensional imaging, and electronic communication and publishing have revolutionized the field. In all these ways, biological anthropologists can illuminate what makes human beings similar to and different from one another, other primates, and other forms of life (Boaz and Wolfe 1995; Weinker 1995).

Whether they study human biology, primates, or the fossils of our ancestors, biological anthropologists clearly share many methods and theories used in the natural sciences—primarily biology, ecology, chemistry, and geology. What tends to set biological anthropologists apart from their nonanthropological colleagues is the holistic, comparative, and evolutionary perspective that has been part of their anthropological training. That perspective reminds them always to consider their work as only part of the overall study of human nature, human society, and the human past.

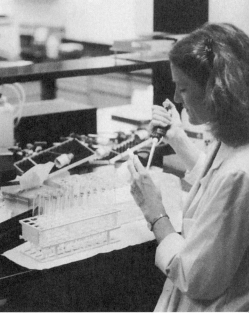

FIGURE 1.2 Some biological anthropologists are primatologists, such as Barbara Smuts (left), who studies olive baboons in Kenya. Other biological anthropologists, such as Carol Worthman (right), study human biological variation in a laboratory.

Cultural Anthropology

The second specialty within anthropology is **cultural anthropology**, which is sometimes called *sociocultural anthropology, social anthropology,* or *ethnology.* Once anthropologists realized that racial biology could not be used to explain why everyone in the world did not dress the same, speak the same language, pray to the same god, or eat insects for dinner, they knew that something else must be responsible for these differences. They suggested that this "something else" was culture: sets of learned behavior and ideas that human beings acquire as members of society. Because people everywhere use culture to adapt to and transform the wider world in which we live, the field of cultural anthropology is vast.

Cultural anthropologists tend to specialize in one or another domain of human cultural activity (Figure 1.3). Some study the ways human beings organize themselves to carry out collective tasks, whether economic, political, or spiritual. This focus within cultural anthropology bears the closest resemblance to the discipline of sociology, and from it has come the identification of anthropology as one of the social sciences. In fact, sociology and anthropology developed during the same period and share similar interests in social organization.

---

racism The systematic oppression of one or more socially defined "races" by another socially defined "race" that is justified in terms of the supposed inherent biological superiority of the rulers and the supposed inherent biological inferiority of those they rule.

biological anthropologists Anthropologists who specialize in the study of patterns of biological variation within the human species as a whole.

primatology The study of nonhuman primates, the closest living relatives of human beings.

paleoanthropology The search for fossilized remains of humanity's earliest ancestors.

cultural anthropology The specialty of anthropology that shows how variation in the beliefs and behaviors of members of different human groups is shaped by sets of learned behavior and ideas that human beings acquire as members of society, that is, by culture.

FIGURE 1.3 Emily Schultz interviews a resident of Guider in northern Cameroon. Cultural anthropologists talk to many people, observe their actions, and participate as fully as possible in a group's way of life.

One important factor that first differentiated anthropology from sociology was the anthropological interest in comparing different forms of human social life. In the racist framework of nineteenth- and early-twentieth-century European and North American societies, some people viewed sociology as the study of "civilized" industrial societies and labeled anthropology as the study of all other societies, lumped together as "primitive." But modern anthropologists are concerned with studying *all* human societies, and they reject the labels "civilized" and "primitive" for the same reason they reject the term "race." Today, anthropologists do research in urban and rural settings around the world and among members of all societies, including their own.

Anthropologists discovered that people in many non-Western societies do not organize bureaucracies or churches or schools, yet they still manage to carry out successfully the full range of human activity because they have developed the institution called *kinship,* organizing themselves into social groups whose members are all considered "relatives." The study of kinship has become highly developed in anthropology and remains a focus of interest today. In addition, anthropologists have described a variety of nonkin forms of social organization that can be found outside the Western world. These include secret societies, age sets, and numerous forms of complex political organization, including states. In recent years, cultural anthropologists have studied contemporary issues of gender and sexuality, transnational labor migration, and the post Cold War resurgence of ethnicity and nationalism around the globe.

Cultural anthropologists have investigated the patterns of material life found in different human groups. Among the most striking are worldwide variations in clothing, housing, tools, and techniques for getting food and making material goods. Some anthropologists specialize in the study of technologies in different societies or in the evolution of technology over time. Those interested in material life also describe the natural setting for which technologies have been developed and analyze the way technologies and environments shape each other. Others have investigated the way non-Western people have responded to the political and economic challenges of colonialism and the capitalist industrial technology that came with it. Many are currently tracing the effects of cybertechnology on the social and cultural life of populations both inside and outside the West.

As cultural anthropologists have become increasingly aware of the sociocultural influences that stretch across space to affect local communities, they have also become sensitive to those that stretch over time. As a result, many contemporary cultural anthropologists make serious efforts to place their cultural analyses in detailed historical context. Anthropologists who do comparative studies of language, music, dance, art, poetry, philosophy, religion, or ritual share many of the interests of specialists in the disciplines of fine arts and humanities.

FIELDWORK Cultural anthropologists, no matter what their area of specialization, ordinarily collect their data during an extended period of close involvement with

IN THEIR OWN WORDS

Anthropology as a Vocation: Listening to Voices

James W. Fernandez (Ph.D., Northwestern University) is a professor of anthropology at the University of Chicago. He has worked among the Fang of Gabon and among cattle keepers and miners of Asturias, Spain. This is an excerpt from an essay about the anthropological vocation.

For me, the anthropological calling has fundamentally to do with the inclination to hear voices. An important part of our vocation is "listening to voices," and our methods are the procedures that best enable us to hear voices, to represent voices, to translate voices.

By listening carefully to others' voices and by trying to give voice to these voices, we act to widen the horizons of human conviviality. If we had not achieved some fellow feeling by being there, by listening carefully and by negotiating in good faith, it would be the more difficult to give voice in a way that would widen the horizons of human conviviality. Be that as it may, the calling to widen horizons and increase human conviviality seems a worthy calling—full of a very human optimism and good sense. Who would resist the proposition that more fellow feeling in the world is better than less, and that to extend the interlocutive in the world is better than to diminish it?

At the same time, there is a paradox here, one that demands of us a sense of proportion. Although the anthropologist is called to bring diverse people into intercommunication, he or she is also called to resist the homogenization that lies in mass communication. We are called by our very experience to celebrate the great variety of voices in the human chorus. The paradox is that we at once work to amplify the scale of intercommunication—and in effect contribute to homogenization—while at the same time we work to insist on the great variety of voices in communication. We must maintain here too a sense of proportion. We must recognize the point at which wider and wider cultural intercommunication can lead to dominant voices hidden in the homogenizing process. Human intercommunication has its uses and abuses.

Source: Schultz and Lavenda 1990, 14–15.

the people in whose language or way of life they are interested. This period of research is called **fieldwork**, and its central feature is the anthropologists' involvement in the everyday routine of those among whom they live. People who share information about their culture and language with anthropologists have traditionally been called **informants**; however, anthropologists use this term less today and prefer to describe these individuals as *respondents, teachers,* or *friends* because these terms emphasize a relationship of equality and reciprocity. Fieldworkers gain insight into another culture by participating with members in social activities and by observing those activities as outsiders. This research method is known as participant-observation, which is central to cultural anthropology—and to human interaction in general.

Cultural anthropologists write about what they have learned in scholarly articles or in books and sometimes document the lives of their research subjects on film. An **ethnography** is a description of a particular culture; **ethnology** is the comparative study of two or more cultures. Thus, cultural anthropologists who write ethnographies are sometimes called *ethnographers,* and anthropologists who compare ethnographic information on many different cultures are sometimes called *ethnologists.*

Anthropological Linguistics

Perhaps the most striking cultural feature of our species is **language:** the system of arbitrary vocal symbols we use to encode our experience of the world and of one another. People use language to talk about all areas of

---

fieldwork An extended period of close involvement with the people in whose language or way of life anthropologists are interested, during which anthropologists ordinarily collect most of their data.
informants People in a particular culture who work with anthropologists and provide them with insights about their way of life. Also called *respondents, teachers,* or *friends.*
ethnography An anthropologist's written or filmed description of a particular culture.
ethnology The comparative study of two or more cultures.
language The system of arbitrary vocal symbols we use to encode our experience of the world and of one another.

their lives, from material to spiritual, which means that language is the main carrier of important cultural information. Many early anthropologists were the first people to transcribe non-Western languages and to produce grammars and dictionaries of those languages. Contemporary linguistic anthropologists and their counterparts in sociology (called *sociolinguists*) study the way language differences frequently correlate with differences in gender, race, class, or ethnic identity. Some have specialized in studying what happens when speakers are fluent in more than one language and must choose which language to use under what circumstances. Others have written about what happens when speakers of unrelated languages are forced to communicate with one another, producing languages called *pidgins*.

In all these cases, anthropological linguists seek to understand language in relation to the broader cultural, historical, or biological contexts that make it possible. **Anthropological linguistics** has become so highly developed that it is traditionally considered a separate subfield of anthropology. Modern anthropo-logical linguists are trained in both linguistics and anthropology, and many cultural anthropologists also receive linguistics training as part of their professional preparation.

Archaeology

Archaeology, another major specialty within anthropology, is a cultural anthropology of the human past involving the analysis of material remains. Through archaeology, anthropologists discover much about human history, particularly prehistory, the long stretch of time before the development of writing. Archaeologists look for evidence of past human cultural activity, such as postholes, garbage heaps, and settlement patterns. Depending on the locations and ages of sites they are digging, archaeologists may also have to be experts on stone-tool manufacture, metallurgy, or ancient pottery. Because archaeological excavations frequently uncover remains such as bones or plant pollen, archaeologists often work in teams with other scientists who specialize in the analysis of these remains.

FIGURE 1.4 Some applied anthropologists use their knowledge and skills in skeletal identification. In February 1994, forensic anthropologist Clyde Snow investigated the death of peasants following the Mexican army's battle with the Emiliano Zapata Liberation Army in the Mexican state of Chiapas.

Archaeologists' findings complement those of paleoanthropologists. For example, archaeological information about successive stone-tool traditions in a particular region may correlate with fossil evidence of prehistoric occupation of that region by ancient human populations. Archaeologists can use dating techniques to establish ages of artifacts and create distribution maps of cultural artifacts that allow them to make hypotheses about the age, territorial ranges, and patterns of sociocultural change in ancient societies. Tracing the spread of cultural inventions over time from one site to another allows them to hypothesize about the nature and degree of social contact between different peoples in the past. The human past that they investigate may be quite recent: Some contemporary archaeologists dig through layers of garbage deposited by human beings within the last two or three decades, often uncovering surprising information about modern consumption patterns.

Applied Anthropology

Applied anthropologists use information gathered from the other anthropological specialties to solve practical cross-cultural problems (Figure 1.4). Some may use a particular culture's ideas about illness and health to introduce new public health practices in a way that makes sense to and will be accepted by members of that culture. Other applied anthropologists may use knowledge of traditional social organization to ease the problems of refugees trying to settle in a new land. Still others may use their knowledge of traditional and Western methods of cultivation to help farmers increase their crop yields. Given the growing concern throughout the world with the effects of different technologies on the environment, this kind of applied anthropology holds promise as a way of blending Western science and non-Western tradition in order to create sustainable technologies that minimize pollution and environmental degradation.

Although many anthropologists believe that applied work can be done within any of the traditional four fields of anthropology, increasing numbers in recent years have come to view applied anthropology as a separate field of professional specialization (see Figure 1.1). More and more universities in the United States have begun to develop courses and programs in applied anthropology.

THE USES OF ANTHROPOLOGY

Why take a course in anthropology? An immediate answer might be that human fossils or ancient potsherds or the customs of faraway peoples inspire a fascination that is its own reward. But the experience of being dazzled by seemingly exotic places and peoples carries with it a risk. As you become increasingly aware of the range of anthropological data, including the many options that exist for living a satisfying human life, you may find yourself wondering about the life you are living. Contact with the unfamiliar can be liberating, but it can also be threatening if it undermines your confidence in the absolute truth and universal rightness of your previous understanding of the way the world works.

The modern world is becoming increasingly interconnected. As people from different cultural backgrounds come into contact with one another, learning to cope with cultural differences becomes crucial. Anthropologists experience both the rewards and the risks of getting to know how other people live, and their work has helped to dispel many harmful stereotypes that sometimes make cross-cultural contact dangerous or impossible. Studying anthropology may help prepare you for some of the shocks you will encounter in dealing with people who look different from you, speak a different language than you, or do not agree that the world works exactly the way you think it does.

Anthropology involves learning about the kinds of living organisms human beings are, the various ways we live our lives, and how we make sense of our experiences. Studying anthropology can equip you to deal with a different culture in a less threatened, more tolerant manner. You may never be called on to eat termite paste. Still, you may one day encounter a situation in which none of the old rules seem to apply. As you struggle to make sense of what is happening, what you learned in anthropology class may help you relax and dare to try something totally new to you. If you

---

anthropological linguistics The specialty of anthropology concerned with the study of human languages.

archaeology A cultural anthropology of the human past involving the analysis of material remains left behind by earlier human societies.

applied anthropologists Specialists who use information gathered from the other anthropological specialties to solve practical cross-cultural problems.

do so, perhaps you too will discover the rewards of an encounter with the unfamiliar that is at the same time unaccountably familiar. We hope you will savor the experience.

Key Terms

anthropology	primatology
holistic	paleoanthropology
comparative	cultural anthropology
evolutionary	language
culture	fieldwork
biocultural organisms	informants
biological anthropology	ethnography
(physical anthropology)	ethnology
races	anthropological linguistics
racism	archaeology
biological anthropologists	applied anthropologists

Chapter Summary

1. Anthropology is a scholarly discipline that aims to describe in the broadest sense what it means to be human. To achieve this aim, anthropologists have developed a perspective on the human condition that is holistic, comparative, and evolutionary.

2. Because human beings lack instincts that automatically promote our survival, we must learn from other members of our society what we need to know to survive. For this reason, the concept of culture is central to the anthropological perspective.

3. Most anthropologists emphasize that human beings are biocultural organisms whose biological makeup allows us to make and use culture. As a result, human beings have produced a tremendous variety of distinct cultural traditions.

4. Anthropology is a field-based discipline. All subdivisions of anthropological research bring anthropologists into contact with some particular way of life.

5. In the United States, anthropology is usually considered to have four major specialties: bio-

logical anthropology, cultural anthropology, anthropological linguistics, and archaeology. Some anthropologists consider applied anthropology to be a separate subfield of professional specialization.

6. Biological anthropology began as an attempt to classify all the world's populations into different races, an undertaking that some people used to justify the social practice of racism. By the early twentieth century, however, most anthropologists had rejected racial classifications as scientifically unjustifiable. From the time of Franz Boas and his students, anthropologists have used information about human biology and human culture to debunk racist stereotypes.

7. Modern anthropologists who are interested in human biology include biological anthropologists, primatologists, and paleoanthropologists. Cultural anthropologists study human diversity by focusing on sets of learned behaviors and ideas that human beings acquire as members of different societies. Because anthropology is comparative, research is done in Western and non-Western settings alike. Anthropological linguists study linguistic diversity in different human societies, relating various forms of language to their cultural contexts.

8. Through fieldwork, cultural anthropologists gain insight into another culture both by participating with their informants in social activities and by observing those activities as outsiders. Ethnographies are published accounts of what was learned during fieldwork. Ethnology involves comparing ethnographic information from two or more different cultures.

9. Archaeology is a cultural anthropology of the human past, but the material remains archaeologists recover can be of value to biological and cultural anthropologists. Archaeologists' interests range from research in human origins to what twentieth-century garbage dumps can tell us about the recent past.

10. Applied anthropologists use information gathered from the other anthropological specialties to solve practical cross-cultural problems in such areas as health care and economic development.

11. The study of human diversity may be threatening if it undermines your confidence in the truth and

rightness of your own way of life. Yet it can also be liberating, enabling you to cope more realistically and tolerantly with people whose appearance or behavior is unfamiliar to you.

Suggested Readings

Ashmore, Wendy, and Sharer, Robert J. 1996. *Discovering our past: A brief introduction to archaeology.* 2d ed. Mountain View, CA: Mayfield. *An engaging introduction to the techniques, assumptions, interests, and findings of modern archaeology.*

Barrett, Richard A. 1984. *Culture and conduct: An excursion in anthropology.* Belmont, CA: Wadsworth. *A short, well-written introduction to some of the most interesting questions in contemporary anthropology.*

Feder, Kenneth L. 1996. *Frauds, myths and mysteries: Science and pseudoscience in archaeology.* 2d ed. Mountain View, CA: Mayfield. *An entertaining and informative exploration of fascinating frauds and genuine archaeological mysteries that also explains the scientific method.*

Freilich, Morris. 1983. *The pleasures of anthropology.* New York: New American Library, Mentor Books. *A wide-ranging collection of accessible articles arranged into eight sections. Most are from the 1960s to the early 1980s, but some enduring classics are also reprinted. All are a pleasure to read and are thought provoking.*

Johanson, Donald, and Maitland Edey. 1981. *Lucy: The beginnings of humankind.* New York: Simon and Schuster. *A well-written, exciting introduction to one aspect of biological anthropology: human origins. This book reads like a good thriller and is highly recommended.*

PART I

The Tools of Cultural Anthropology

This section introduces the basic principles and methods of cultural anthropology. The first of these is the concept of culture, arguably anthropology's most important contribution to the understanding of human beings. The concept of culture has anchored an anthropological perspective that illuminates the human condition in new and powerful ways. In order to study human cultures, anthropologists have long favored research methods that bring them into direct contact with specific groups of people for extended periods of time. We will explore the rewards and the challenges of learning about human cultures in this way. The final chapter in this section examines how anthropologists have historically attempted to make sense of human cultural diversity by developing various ways to classify forms of human society.

2 ✺

Culture and the Human Condition

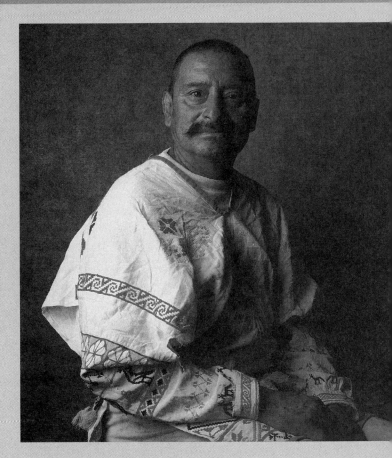

The human condition is distinguished from the condition of other living species by **culture.** Other living species learn, but the extent to which human beings depend upon learning is unique in the animal kingdom. Because our brains are capable of open symbolic thought and our hands are capable of manipulating matter powerfully or delicately, we penetrate the wider world more deeply than any other species.

Culture is not reinvented by each generation; rather, we learn it from other members of the social groups we belong to, although we may later modify this heritage in some way. Therefore, culture is shared as well as learned. Many things we learn, such as table manners and what is good to eat and where people are supposed to sleep, are never explicitly taught but rather are absorbed in the course of daily practical living: This kind of cultural learning is sometimes called *habitus*. And cultural traditions often encompass the varied knowledge and skills of many different individuals. For example, Saturn 5 rockets are part of North American culture, and yet no individual North American could build one from scratch.

The boundaries around a cultural tradition are always fuzzy, being determined not only by the customs of that tradition but also by how different those customs are from someone else's. Furthermore, customs in one domain of culture may contradict customs in another domain, as when religion tells us to share with others and economics tells us to look out for ourselves alone. Nevertheless, people in most societies somehow ordinarily manage to keep such contradictions from getting out of control. So culture can also be understood as "established ways of bringing ideas from different domains together" (Strathern 1992, 3).

Just as the transmission and enriching of cultural traditions depend on culture being shared, so too human survival depends on culture. Apart from sucking, grasping, and crying, human newborns have no instincts, or innate responses, to ensure their survival; even those elementary responses fade after a few weeks, and they must be replaced by learned responses. Our dependence on culture is total. Without it, we cannot survive as biological organisms (Figure 2.1).

Finally, culture is symbolic. A **symbol** is something that stands for something else. The letters of the alphabet, for example, symbolize the sounds of spoken language. There is no necessary connection between

FIGURE 2.1 Of all living organisms, humans are the most dependent upon learning for their survival. From a young age, girls in northern Cameroon learn how to carry heavy loads on their heads.

the shape of a particular letter and the speech sound it represents. Indeed, the same or similar sounds are represented symbolically by very different letters in the Latin, Cyrllic, Hebrew, Arabic, and Greek alphabets, to name but five. Even the sounds of spoken language are symbols for meanings a speaker tries to express. The fact that we can translate from one language to another suggests that the same or similar meanings can be expressed by different spoken symbols in different languages. But language is not the only domain of culture that depends on symbols. Everything we do in society has a symbolic dimension, from how we conduct ourselves at the dinner table to how we bury the dead. It is our heavy dependence on symbolic learning that sets human culture apart from the apparently nonsymbolic learning on which other species rely.

Culture, then, is learned, shared, adaptive, and symbolic. And the contemporary human capacity for cul-

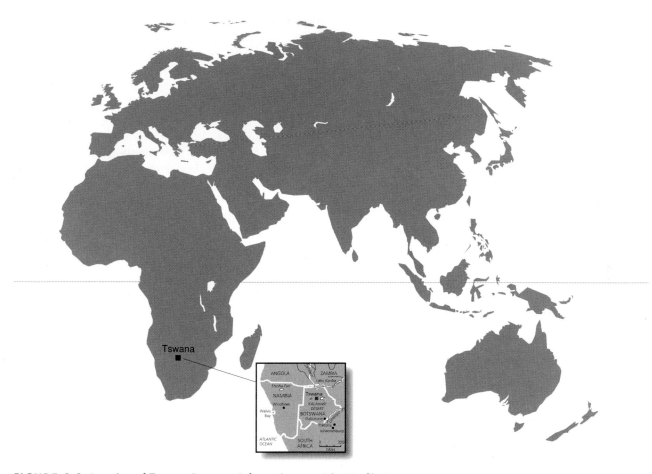

FIGURE 2.2 Location of Tswana. For more information, see EthnoProfile 2.1.

ture has also evolved, over millions of years. Culture's beginnings can be glimpsed among the Japanese macaques who invented the custom of washing sweet potatoes and among wild chimpanzees who invented different grooming postures or techniques to crack open nuts or to gain access to termites or water (Boesch-Ackerman and Boesch 1994; Wolfe 1995, 162–63). Our apelike ancestors surely shared similar aptitudes when they started walking on two legs over 5 million years ago. By 2.5 million years ago, their descendants were making stone tools. Thereafter, our hominid lineage gave birth to a number of additional species, all of whom depended on culture more than their ancestors had. By the time *Homo sapiens* appeared some 200,000 years ago, a heavy dependence on culture had long been a part of our evolutionary heritage.

Thus, as Rick Potts puts it, "an evolutionary bridge exists between the human and animal realms of behavior. . . . Culture represents continuity" (1996, 197). Potts urges us to think of the modern human capacity for culture not as a uniform monolith, but rather as a structure whose various pieces were added at different times in our evolutionary past (Figure 2.3). The foundation of culture, he proposes, contains five elements: (1) *transmission*, copying behavior by observation or instruction; (2) *memory*, because traditions cannot develop unless the new behavior is remembered; (3) *reiteration*,

---

culture Sets of learned behavior and ideas that humans acquire as members of society. Humans use culture to adapt to and transform the world in which we live.
symbol Something that stands for something else.

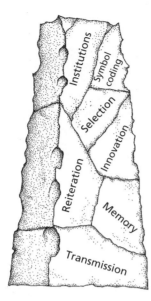

FIGURE 2.3 The modern human capacity for culture did not appear all at once; rather, the various pieces that make it up were added at different times in our evolutionary past.

the ability to reproduce or imitate behavior or information that has been learned; (4) *innovation,* the ability to invent new behaviors, and (5) *selection,* the ability to select which innovations to keep and which to discard. Monkeys and apes possess many of these elements to varying degrees, which is why they can be said to possess simple cultural traditions. Certainly our earliest hominid ancestors were no different.

Apes apparently also possess the rudiments of *symbolic coding,* a capacity our ancestors also undoubtedly possessed. But new species can evolve new capacities not found in their ancestors. This occurred in the human past when our ancestors first developed a capacity for *complex symbolic coding,* including the ability to communicate freely about the past, the future, and the invisible. This ability distinguishes human language, for example, from the vocal communications systems of apes (see Chapter 5). We have used our complex symbolic abilities, moreover, to create complex and variable forms of social organization, also unique to our species. As a result, for *Homo sapiens,* culture has become "the predominant manner in which human groups vary from one another . . . it *swamps* the biological differences among populations" (Marks 1995, 200). We are truly biocultural organisms.

EXPLAINING THE HUMAN CONDITION AND CULTURE

Dualistic Explanations

What is the world like? And what is the human condition within the world? Not only anthropologists but members of all societies pose questions like these. And all societies develop their own answers. If asked what they believe about human nature, for example, many North Americans would answer that human nature has two parts: sometimes called *mind* and *matter, soul* and *body,* or *spirit* and *flesh.* The belief that human nature, or reality as a whole, is made up of two radically different forces is called **dualism.** Dualistic thinking is deeply rooted in Western thought; for millennia, people have debated the importance of each half of our nature. Perhaps the oldest attempt to resolve this debate can be traced to the ancient Greek philosopher Plato.

Plato divided all reality into mind and matter: Mind is higher and finer and belongs to the celestial realm of ideal forms; matter is lower and cruder and corruptible, belonging to the earthly realm. Human nature is dualistic because each person is made up of an earthly material body inhabited by a mind whose true home is the realm of ideal forms. According to Plato, the drama of human existence consists of the internal struggle between the body, drawn naturally to base, corruptible matter, and the mind or soul, drawn naturally to pure, unchanging forms. Christian theology later incorporated the view that each human being consists of a soul that seeks God and a physical body that is tempted by the material world. This view of earthly life as a struggle between flesh and spirit is sometimes called *conflict dualism.*

The Platonic and Christian theories of human nature argue that although human beings are equipped with material bodies, their true nature is spiritual, not material; the body is a material impediment that frustrates the full development of the mind or spirit. This view is known as **idealism.** Platonic idealism was the source of the pre-Darwinian notion that all the members of any living species were imperfect material embodiments of a distinct natural kind whose ideal form, or essence, existed eternally in the celestial realm.

However, it is equally possible to make the contrary argument: that matter—the material activities of our physical bodies in the material world—constitutes the essence of human nature. From this perspective, human existence becomes the struggle to exercise our physicality as fully as we can; to put spiritual values above bodily needs would go against human nature. People would not seek spiritual salvation, it is sometimes argued, if their material needs were satisfied. This view is known as **materialism.**

Reductionism is the attempt to explain something complex by showing that complexity is *nothing but* the outcome of simpler causal forces. Idealists are reductionists because they claim that human nature is nothing but mind or spirit; materialists are reductionists because they claim that human nature is nothing but the product of genes or anatomy or biology. Reductionism is a form of **determinism.** Consequently, idealism and materialism are often called *deterministic theories.*

Although both idealism and materialism have been defended since the time of the pre-Socratic Greeks, Western materialism gained more support during the seventeenth-century Enlightenment, and was reinforced as the Industrial Revolution got underway later. As a result, materialist views of the human condition gradually replaced idealist views among scientists and the highly educated.

The nineteenth century was the great century of evolutionary thought in the Western world, and Charles Darwin was probably its most famous evolutionary thinker. Darwin was not the first to argue that change over time was the rule for biological species. Darwin's innovation was to propose a materialist explanation for such change. Natural selection is a two-step, random material process in which organisms possessing varied material traits are "tested" by forces of the material environment in which they live and, if they pass this environmental test and survive, then transmit those traits to later generations. There is no need for mind or spirit or God in this process. The material world, if left to its own devices, automatically improves the various living species by fitting them ever more perfectly into their respective environments.

Long before Darwin wrote about the origin of species through natural selection, other Western thinkers had speculated about the evolution of human society. Indeed, the expression "survival of the fittest," long associated with Darwin, was first used by his contemporary, Herbert Spencer, whose main interest was the evolution of society. Spencer believed that competition was the driving force of evolution and that it would inevitably produce a better world if allowed to operate without interference. Thus, social inequality and the suffering of the poor, however unjust or cruel they might appear, must be understood as the best of all possible social arrangements. Attempts to tamper with these arrangements go against evolutionary destiny and are doomed to failure.

Spencer's belief that social competition promoted the survival of the fittest contributed to a perspective called *biological determinism,* which was responsible for the racist classifications of human groups by nineteenth-century anthropologists and sociologists. Biological determinists claim that complex human social life is nothing more than the by-product of the simpler actions of many individual human beings who are simply following the dictates of their genes or hormones.

Other materialists subscribe to a second form of materialist reductionism called *environmental determinism.* Environmental determinists argue that the important material forces that shape our lives exist outside our bodies in the surrounding natural world. Rich soil, a temperate climate, too little rainfall, or the absence of domesticable animals are examples of environmental forces that shape human societies and determine forms of social organization, political arrangements, and religious beliefs.

For the followers of Karl Marx, social forces play a critical role. The collective material actions of people in society, shaped by the interests of the dominant class, are responsible for the human condition at any point in history. Progress is still possible, indeed inevitable, as historical necessity works itself out. Marx and his followers believe, however, that progress comes only through revolution. The old and the worse have

---

dualism The philosophical view that reality consists of two equal and irreducible forces.

idealism The philosophical view (dating back at least as far as Plato in Western thought), that ideas—or the mind that produces such ideas—constitute the essence of human nature.

materialism The philosophical view that the material activities of our physical bodies in the material world constitute the essence of human nature.

reductionism The philosophical view that explains all evidence in terms of (or "reduces" it to) a single set of explanatory principles.

determinism The philosophical view that one simple force (or a few simple forces) causes (or determines) complex events.

to be overthrown forcibly to make way for the new and the better. This view is known as *historical materialism*.

An extreme idealist reaction against materialist thinking is called *cultural determinism*. Cultural determinists argue that the ideas, meanings, beliefs, and values that people learn as members of society are the determining agents of the human condition. In this view, "you are what you learn." Optimistic versions of cultural determinism place no limits on the abilities of human beings to be or do whatever they want. This perspective became very popular among many anthropologists in the 1940s and 1950s, who held out the hope that, if human nature is infinitely malleable, then human beings can mold themselves into the kinds of people they want to be. Pessimistic versions of cultural determinism rule this out: "You are what you learn" becomes "you are what you are conditioned to be," something over which you have no control. In this view, human beings are passive creatures who have no choice but to do what their culture tells them to do.

Holistic Explanations

Materialists and idealists have battled with one another for centuries. To some observers, this unresolvable conflict is rooted in the dualistic view of human nature on which it is based. Many anthropologists have long argued that there is yet another point of view on the human condition that is less distorting than dualism and less simplistic than materialism or idealism. The anthropological point of view called **holism** assumes that no sharp boundaries separate mind from body, body from environment, individual from society, my ideas from our ideas, or their traditions from our traditions. Rather, holism assumes that mind and body, body and environment, and so on, interpenetrate each other and even define each other. From a holistic perspective, attempts to divide reality into mind and matter at most isolate and pin down certain aspects of a process that, by its very nature, resists isolation and dissection. Anthropologists who have struggled to develop this holistic perspective on the human condition have made a contribution of unique and lasting value. Holism holds great appeal for those who seek a theory of human nature that is rich enough to do justice to its complex subject matter.

One traditional way of expressing the holistic insight is to say that the whole (that is, a human being, a society, a cultural tradition) is greater than the sum of its parts. Individual human organisms are not just *x* percent genes and *y* percent culture added together. Rather, human beings are what they are because the mutual shaping of genes and culture has produced something new, something that cannot be reduced to the materials used to construct it. Similarly, a society or a culture is not just the sum of the behaviors of its individual members. Instead, human beings living in groups become different kinds of creatures. They are so deeply affected by shared cultural experiences that they become different from what they would have been had they matured in isolation. Clifford Geertz notes that human beings raised in isolation would be neither failed apes nor "natural" people stripped of their veneer of culture; they would be "mental basket cases" (1973, 40). Indeed, we have discovered that human beings subjected to isolation do not behave in ways that appear recognizably human. Social living and cultural sharing are necessary for individual human beings to develop what we recognize as a *human* nature.

We can enrich our understanding of the relationships among the parts that make up a whole by approaching those relationships in a dialectical manner. **Dialectical relationships** refer to a network of cause and effect, in which the various causes and effects affect each other. A dialectical approach to the human condition, therefore, emphasizes that biology and culture are neither separable nor antithetical nor alternatives, but complementary to one another. Lewontin, Rose, and Kamin observe that all causes of the behavior of organisms "are simultaneously social and biological . . . chemical and physical" (1984, 282). Put another way, the properties of parts and wholes *codetermine* one another. This was what we meant by stating in Chapter 1 that anthropologists see human nature as *biocultural*.

We are proposing a holistic and dialectical view of human nature, a view that rejects dualism and reductionism. Dialectical holism is based on the view that human beings are open systems, and that the wider world, the environment, is also open to modification by the objects (including people) that inhabit it. For human beings, part of the wider world is human society, so human society too must be considered an open system. Figure 2.4 offers a comparison of this holistic perspective with the other alternatives discussed so far.

In the late twentieth century, scientists have become increasingly aware that the codetermination of organisms and environment involves information as

FIGURE 2.4 Perspectives on the human condition.

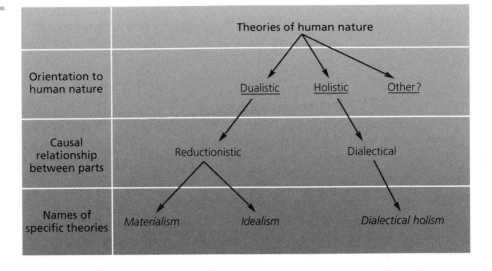

	Theories of human nature
Orientation to human nature	Dualistic Holistic Other?
Causal relationship between parts	Reductionistic Dialectical
Names of specific theories	*Materialism* *Idealism* *Dialectical holism*

well as matter. The transformation of signals from the wider world into information that an organism can process and the exchange of information between organisms are usually what we are referring to when we talk about learning.

Of all living organisms, human beings are the most dependent upon learning for survival, and what we learn concerns both the physical and social environments in which we live. We tend to think of learning primarily as a mental process, a capacity of mind. However, a holistic, dialectical view of the human condition would describe human beings as creatures whose bodies, brains, actions, and thoughts are equally involved in learning, codetermining one another. The result of their constant association is a human nature embedded in a wider world that also helps to define the human condition. A most important aspect of that wider world, which shapes us and is shaped by us, is culture.

CULTURAL DIFFERENCES

The same objects or events frequently mean different things to people in different cultures. In fact, what counts as an object or event in one tradition may not be recognized as such in another. This powerful lesson of anthropology was illustrated by the experience of some Peace Corps volunteers working in southern Africa.

In the early 1970s, the Peace Corps office in Botswana was concerned by the number of volunteers who seemed to be "burned out," failing in their assignments, and increasingly hostile to their Tswana hosts. (See EthnoProfile 2.1: Tswana.) The Peace Corps asked American anthropologist Hoyt Alverson, who was familiar with Tswana culture and society, for advice. Alverson (1977) discovered that one major problem the Peace Corps volunteers were having involved exactly this issue of similar actions having very different meanings. The volunteers complained that the Tswana would never leave them alone. Whenever they tried to get away and sit by themselves for a few minutes to have some private time, one or more Tswana would quickly join them. This made the Americans angry. From their perspective, everyone is entitled to a certain amount of privacy and time alone. To the Tswana, however, human life is social life; the only people who want to be alone are witches and the insane. Because these young Americans did not seem to be either, the Tswana who saw them sitting alone naturally assumed that there had been a breakdown in hospitality and that the volunteers would welcome some company. Here, one behavior—a person walking out into a field and

---

holism A perspective on the human condition that assumes that mind and body, individuals and society, and individuals and the environment interpenetrate and even define one another.

dialectical relationships A network of cause and effect in which the various causes and effects affect each other.

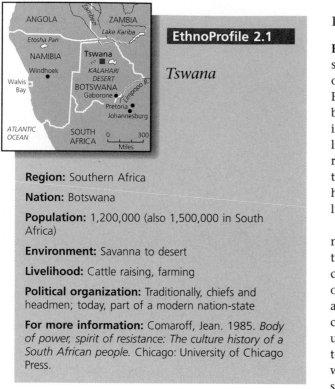

EthnoProfile 2.1

Tswana

Region: Southern Africa

Nation: Botswana

Population: 1,200,000 (also 1,500,000 in South Africa)

Environment: Savanna to desert

Livelihood: Cattle raising, farming

Political organization: Traditionally, chiefs and headmen; today, part of a modern nation-state

For more information: Comaroff, Jean. 1985. *Body of power, spirit of resistance: The culture history of a South African people.* Chicago: University of Chicago Press.

sitting by himself or herself—had two very different meanings.

Even within a single culture, the meaning of an object or an action may differ depending on the context. Quoting philosopher Gilbert Ryle, anthropologist Clifford Geertz notes that there is a world of difference between a wink and a blink, as anyone who has ever mistaken one for the other has undoubtedly learned (Geertz 1973, 6).

Thus, human experience is inherently ambiguous. To resolve the ambiguity, experience must be interpreted. Human beings turn to their own cultural traditions in search of an interpretation that makes sense and is coherent. They do this daily as they go about life among others with whom they share traditions. But this interpretive activity does not cease at the boundary of their own culture. Self and other need not belong to the same society or share the same traditions, and yet this interpretive activity continues. Serious misunderstandings may arise when two individuals are unaware that their ground rules differ. At this point, the concepts of ethnocentrism and cultural relativism become relevant.

Ethnocentrism

Ethnocentrism is the term anthropologists use to describe the opinion that one's own way of life is natural or correct, indeed the only way of being fully human. Ethnocentrism is one solution to the inevitable tension between one cultural self and another cultural self. It is a form of reductionism; it reduces the other way of life to a distorted version of one's own. If our way is right, then their way can only be wrong. At best, their truth is a distorted truth; at worst, it is an outright falsehood. (Of course, from their perspective, our way of life may seem to be a distortion of theirs.)

The members of one tradition may go beyond merely interpreting another way of life in ethnocentric terms. They may decide to do something about the discrepancies they observe. They may conclude that the other way of life is wrong but not fundamentally evil and that the members of the other group need to be converted to their own point of view. If the others are unwilling to change their ways, however, the failed attempt at reduction may enlarge into an active dualism: we versus they, civilization versus savagery, good versus evil. The ultimate result may be war and *genocide*—the deliberate attempt to exterminate an entire group based on race, religion, national origin, or other cultural features.

The Cross-Cultural Relationship

Is it possible to avoid ethnocentric bias? A holistic approach to relationships between ourselves and others, both across and within cultural traditions, holds promise. This approach views cross-cultural relationships as not being fundamentally different from intracultural relationships. Although cross-cultural relationships are often much more difficult to negotiate because the people involved have so much to learn about each other, they are possible. Like all human relationships, they affect all parties involved in the encounter, changing them as they learn about each other.

This sort of interwoven learning experience is common to all human relationships, but it is potentially much more radical when it involves parties from different cultural backgrounds. People from another culture may help you see possibilities for belief and action that are drastically at odds with everything your tradition considers possible. By becoming aware of these un-

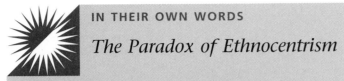

IN THEIR OWN WORDS

The Paradox of Ethnocentrism

Ethnocentrism is usually described in thoroughly negative terms. As Ivan Karp points out, however, ethnocentrism is a more complex phenomenon than we might expect.

Anthropologists usually argue that ethnocentrism is both wrong and harmful, especially when it is tied to racial, cultural, and social prejudices. Ideas and feelings about the inferiority of blacks, the cupidity of Jews, or the lack of cultural sophistication of farmers are surely to be condemned. But can we do without ethnocentrism? If we stopped to examine every custom and practice in our cultural repertoire, how would we get on? For example, if we always regarded marriage as something that can vary from society to society, would we be concerned about filling out the proper marriage documents, or would we even get married at all? Most of the time we suspend a quizzical stance toward our own customs and simply live life.

Yet many of our own practices are peculiar when viewed through the lenses of other cultures. Periodically, for over fifteen years, I have worked with and lived among an African people. They are as amazed at our marriage customs as my students are at theirs. Both American students and the Iteso of Kenya find it difficult to imagine how the other culture survives with the bizarre, exotic practices that are part of their respective marriage customs. Ethnocentrism works both ways. It can be practiced as much by other cultures as by our own.

Paradoxically, ethnographic literature combats ethnocentrism by showing that the practices of cultures (including our own) are "natural" in their own setting. What appears natural in one setting appears so because it was constructed in that setting—made and produced by human beings who could have done it some other way. Ethnography is a means of recording the range of human creativity and of demonstrating how universally shared capacities can produce cultural and social differences.

This anthropological way of looking at other cultures—and, by implication, at ourselves—constitutes a major reason for reading ethnography. The anthropological lens teaches us to question what we assume to be unquestionable. Ethnography teaches us that human potentiality provides alternative means of organizing our lives and alternative modes of experiencing the world. Reading ethnographies trains us to question the received wisdom of our society and makes us receptive to change. In this sense, anthropology might be called the subversive science. We read ethnographies in order to learn about how other peoples produce their world and about how we might change our own patterns of production.

Source: Karp 1990, 74–75.

suspected possibilities, you become a different person. People from the other culture are likely to be affected in the same way. None of you will be the same again.

Cross-cultural learning is at once enormously hopeful and immensely threatening; once it occurs, we can no longer claim that any single culture has a monopoly on truth. Although this does not mean that the traditions in question must therefore be based entirely on illusion or falsehood, it does mean that the truth embodied in any cultural tradition is bound to be partial, approximate, and open to further insight and growth.

Cultural Relativism

Anthropologists must come to terms with the consequences of cross-cultural learning as they do their fieldwork. One result has been the formulation of the

concept of **cultural relativism.** Definitions of cultural relativism have varied as different anthropologists have tried to draw conclusions based on their cross-cultural experience. One definition that attempts a holistic approach is: "[Cultural relativism involves] understanding another culture in its own terms sympathetically enough so that the culture appears to be a coherent and meaningful design for living" (Greenwood and Stini 1977, 182).

According to this definition, the goal of relativism is understanding. For example, cultural relativism demands that we try to understand how *genocide,* the

ethnocentrism The opinion that one's own way of life is natural or correct and, indeed, is the only true way of being fully human.
cultural relativism Understanding another culture in its own terms sympathetically enough so that the culture appears to be a coherent and meaningful design for living.

FIGURE 2.5 Was the Holocaust due to the perversion of German morality by a charismatic madman who wished to rule the world, or was it rooted in long-standing social, historical, and cultural patterns?

attempt by one social group to exterminate another, could develop in a society. Recent episodes involving ethnic cleansing in the former Yugoslavia or Rwanda prove, tragically, that genocide did not end with the defeat of Nazi Germany in World War II. Examination of the Nazi example, however, may offer insight into these more recent episodes.

The Nazi attempt to exterminate the Jews, called the *Holocaust,* was conceived and implemented in German society in the middle twentieth century (Figure 2.5). Knowledge about German culture in particular (including its history) and European culture in general (including the history of anti-Semitism and the rise of fascism outside Germany) can help us understand these events. An explanation based on this knowledge implies that the Holocaust was not a momentary aberration brought on by a handful of madmen who managed to seize power in Germany for a few years and implement policies totally at odds with German culture and history. Rather, the Holocaust was intimately related to certain cultural patterns and historical processes that are deeply rooted in German, and European, society.

Therefore, to understand the Holocaust from a relativistic point of view, we must ask why the Nazis were able to achieve power and why Jews were chosen as scapegoats. Answering these questions involves inves-tigating the historical roots of anti-Semitism and nationalism in Germany. Moreover, the success of the Nazis in achieving their program cannot be explained in terms of German culture and society alone. Such boundaries are never clear, and it is unlikely that so many Jews would have died without the overt and covert assistance rendered Germany by the other countries of Europe. Even the United States is implicated because the American government refused to accept Jews as political refugees and, as a result, helped deliver them into the hands of their enemies.

This relativistic understanding accomplishes several things. It makes the Holocaust comprehensible and even coherent. It reveals, to our horror, how the persecution and murder of human beings can appear perfectly acceptable when placed in a particular context of meaning. One thing that this relativistic understanding does not do, however, is allow us to excuse or condemn the Nazis for what they did on the grounds that it was all due to their culture. For many people, a deterministic interpretation would be preferable: For some, it would absolve Germans of any blame because they had no choice but to do what German culture dictated; for others, it would absolve non-Germans of blame—after all, if German culture had led to the Holocaust, then responsibility for its horrors would lie squarely on the German people.

These attempts to contain the evil of Nazi Germany by placing blame on one or another group of people are understandable. After all, the active, leading roles were played by Germans, in particular by members of the Nazi party. But to leave matters here is to give an incomplete account of a complex historical phenomenon. And to call the incomplete account "relativistic," as some critics have done, is to vulgarize the holistic understanding of cultural relativism that makes a complex historical explanation possible.

To accept the argument that their culture made them do it is to accept cultural determinism. Cultural determinism requires us to accept three assumptions about human nature and human society: first, that cultures have neat boundaries between them and are sealed off from one another; second, that every culture offers people only one way to interpret experience, that cultures are monolithic and permit no variety, harbor no contradictions, and allow no dissent; and third, that people living in these closed cultural worlds are passively molded by culture, helpless to resist indoctrination into a single worldview, and incapable of inventing alternatives to that view.

All three assumptions, however, are belied by human experience. Cultures are not sealed off from one another. Their boundaries are fuzzy; their members exchange ideas and practices. Cultures are not monolithic. Even without the alternatives introduced from the outside, every culture offers a variety of ways to interpret experience, although official sanction may be given only one. Finally, human beings are not passive lumps shaped unresistingly to fit a single cultural mold. There is no such thing as a single cultural mold in a society acquainted with variety, and in a society where options exist, choices must be made.

In fact, abundant evidence suggests that German society in the middle twentieth century did not conform to the sealed-off, monolithic model. Germany was not closed to the rest of the world. Moreover, German cultural tradition had more than one strand. There were, after all, Germans who resisted Nazism, sometimes at the cost of their lives, such as Hans and Sophie Scholl, who rallied German university students against the Nazis in 1943. They, too, drew on German tradition to justify their choices, suggesting that there was (and is) more to German culture than those aspects that the Nazis made use of. And this suggests that the recognition of evil is not simply a matter of condemning what your culture teaches you to condemn.

Understanding something is not the same as approving of it or excusing it. Often we are repelled by unfamiliar cultural practices when we first encounter them. Sometimes when we understand these practices better, we change our minds. We may conclude that the practices in question are more suitable for the people who employ them than our own practices would be. We might even recommend that they be adopted in our own society. But the opposite may also be the case. We may understand perfectly the cultural rationale behind such practices as slavery, infanticide, headhunting, or genocide—and still refuse our approval. We may not be persuaded by the reasons offered to justify these practices, or we may be aware of alternative arrangements that could achieve the desired outcome using less drastic methods. Moreover, it is likely that any cultural practice with far-reaching consequences for human life will have critics as well as supporters within the society where it is practiced. This is certainly the case in American society, which is far from achieving moral consensus on such sensitive topics as abortion, capital punishment, or nuclear weapons.

Cultural relativism makes moral reasoning more complex. It does not, however, require us to abandon every value our own society has taught us. Our culture, like every other culture, offers us more than one way of evaluating experience. Exposure to the interpretations of an unfamiliar culture forces us to reconsider the possibilities our culture recognizes in light of new alternatives and to search for areas of intersection as well as areas of disagreement. What cultural relativism does discourage is the easy solution of refusing to consider alternatives from the outset. It also does not free us from sometimes facing difficult choices between alternatives whose rightness or wrongness is less than clear-cut. In this sense, "cultural relativism is a 'tough-minded' philosophy" (Herskovits 1973, 37).

CULTURE, HISTORY, AND HUMAN AGENCY

The human condition is rooted in time and shaped by history. As part of the human condition, culture is also historical, being worked out and passed on from one

IN THEIR OWN WORDS

Culture and Freedom

Finding a way to fit human agency into a scientific account of culture has never been easy. Hoyt Alverson describes some of the issues involved.

One's assumptions concerning the existence of structure in culture, or the existence of freedom in human action, determine whether one believes that there can be a science of culture or not. Note that the possibility of developing a science of culture has nothing to do with the use of mathematics, the precision of one's assertions, or the elegance of one's models. If a phenomenon actually has structure, then a science of that phenomenon is at least conceivable. If a phenomenon exhibits freedom and is not ordered, then a science of that phenomenon is inconceivable. The human sciences, including anthropology, have been debating the issue of structure versus freedom in human cultural behavior for the past two hundred years, and no resolution or even consensus has emerged.

Some persuasive models of culture, and of particular cultures, have been proposed, both by those working with scientific, universalist assumptions, and by those working with phenomenological, relativistic assumptions.

To decide which of these approaches is to be preferred, we must have a specific set of criteria for evaluation. Faced with good evidence for the existence of both structure and freedom in human culture, no coherent set of criteria for comparing the success of these alternative models is conceivable. The prediction of future action, for example, is a good criterion for measuring the success of a model that purports to represent structure: it must be irrelevant to measuring the success or failure of a model that purports to describe freedom. For the foreseeable future, and maybe for the rest of time, we may have to be content with models that simply permit us to muddle through.

Source: Alverson 1990, 42–43.

---

generation to the next. As paleoanthropologists have shown, the human species is itself a product of millions of years of evolution. Hence, human history is an essential aspect of the human story.

Anthropologists sometimes disagree about how to approach human history. Nineteenth-century thinkers such as Herbert Spencer argued that the evolution of social structures over time was central to the study of the human condition. Other anthropologists, sensitive to the excesses of people like Spencer, were not interested in change over time. In the 1930s, A. R. Radcliffe-Brown justified this lack of interest by pointing out that, in societies without written records, knowledge about past life is nonexistent; any attempt to reconstruct such past life would be an unfounded attempt at "conjectural history."

Other anthropologists had no interest in history for a different reason. Western capitalist culture, with its eye on the future and its faith in progress, has had little use for the past. It is therefore no wonder that some anthropologists built clockwork models of social structures that could be trusted to run reliably without "losing time." In these models, human beings and societies are both likened to machines. If a living organism is used as the model of society, and if organisms are nothing but machines, then a machine model of society, with individuals as robotlike moving parts, is not at all farfetched. A holistic and dialectical approach to human history, however, rejects these clockwork models. Culture is part of our biological heritage. Our biocultural heritage has produced a living species that uses culture to surmount biological and individual limitations. The result has been the emergence of creatures who are capable of studying themselves and their own biocultural evolution.

This realization, however, raises another question: Just how free from limitations are humans? Opinion in Western societies often polarizes around one of two extremes: Either we have *free will* and may do just as we please, or our behavior is completely determined by biology or society. Many social scientists, however, are convinced that a more realistic description of human freedom was offered by Karl Marx, who wrote, "Men [sic] make their own history, but they do not make it just as they please; they do not make it under circumstances chosen by themselves, but under circumstances

FIGURE 2.6 People regularly struggle, often against great odds, to exercise some control over their lives. Students in Belgrade, protesting against election fraud in December, 1996, defy a police warning and march against the government of Serbian President Slobodan Milosevic.

directly encountered, given and transmitted by the past" (1963, 15). That is, people regularly struggle, often against great odds, to exercise some control over their lives. Human beings active in this way are called *agents* (Figure 2.6). Human agents cannot escape from the cultural and historical context within which they act. However, we must frequently select a course of action when the "correct" choice is unclear and the outcome uncertain. Some anthropologists even liken human existence to a mine field that we must painstakingly try to cross without blowing ourselves up. It is in such contexts, with their ragged edges, that human beings make interpretations, formulate goals, and set out in pursuit of them. A holistic, dialectical approach to the human condition recognizes the existence and importance of human agency.

THE PROMISE OF THE ANTHROPOLOGICAL PERSPECTIVE

The anthropological perspective on the human condition is not easy to maintain. It forces us to question the common-sense assumptions with which we are most comfortable. It only increases the difficulty we encounter when faced with moral and political decisions. It does not allow us an easy retreat to ethnocentrism when the going gets rough. For once we are exposed to the kinds of experience that the anthropological undertaking makes possible, we are changed—for better or worse. We cannot easily pretend that these new experiences never happened to us. Once we have had a genuine glimpse of the other, seen his or her full humanity, there is no going back, except in bad faith.

So, anthropology is guaranteed to complicate your life. Nevertheless, the anthropological perspective can give you a broader understanding of human nature and the wider world, of society, culture, and history and thus help you construct more realistic and authentic ways of coping with those complications.

Key Terms

culture	determinism
symbol	holism
dualism	dialectical relationships
idealism	ethnocentrism
materialism	cultural relativism
reductionism	

Chapter Summary

1. Culture distinguishes the human condition from the condition of other living species. Culture is learned, shared, adaptive, and symbolic. It did not emerge all at once but evolved over time.

2. The belief that human nature has two parts is known as dualism. Mind-matter dualism is deeply rooted in Western thought, dating back to such figures as Plato.

3. Idealism reduces human nature to ideas or the mind that produces them. Materialism reduces human nature to genes, hormones, or biology. Biological determinism, environmental determinism, and historical materialism are all forms of materialist determinism.

4. The most extreme position against the various forms of materialist reductionism, cultural determinism argues that the ideas, meanings, beliefs, and values that people learn in society determine their behavior. Optimistic versions of cultural determinism hold out the hope that we can change these determining agents and make ourselves whatever we want to be. Pessimistic versions conclude that "you are what you are conditioned to be," something over which you have no control.

5. In preference to dualism, anthropologists have suggested holism, which assumes that objects and environments interpenetrate and even define each other. Thus, the whole is more than the sum of its parts. Human beings and human societies are open systems that cannot be reduced to the parts that make them up. Holism is dialectical rather than deterministic: The parts and the whole mutually define, or codetermine, each other. This book adopts a holistic and dialectical approach to human nature, human society, and human history.

6. Because human experience is often ambiguous, adaptation requires cultural interpretation, which is a constant, necessary process, whether it is an attempt to understand people or symbols within one's own culture or those of another culture.

7. Ethnocentrism is a form of reductionism. Anthropologists believe it can be countered by a commitment to cultural relativism, an attempt to understand the cultural underpinnings of behavior. Cultural relativism makes moral decisions more difficult because it requires us to take into account many things before we make up our minds. Cultural relativism does not require us to abandon every value our society has taught us; however, it does discourage the easy solution of refusing to consider alternatives from the outset.

8. Human history is an essential aspect of the human story, a dialectic between biology and culture. Culture is worked out over time and passed on from one generation to the next. Because human beings have the power to act in their own interests, the story of our species also involves human agency.

Suggested Readings

Gamst, Frederick, and Edward Norbeck. 1976. *Ideas of culture: Sources and uses.* New York: Holt, Rinehart and Winston. *A useful collection of important articles about culture. The articles are arranged according to different basic approaches to culture.*

Garbarino, Merwyn S. 1977. *Sociocultural theory in anthropology: A short history.* New York: Holt, Rinehart and Winston. *A short (114-page) chronological consideration of the development of anthropological thought. Evenhanded and clear.*

Geertz, Clifford. 1973. Thick description: Towards an interpretive theory of culture; The impact of the concept of culture on the concept of man. In *The interpretation of cultures.* New York: Basic Books. *Two classic discussions of culture from a major figure in American anthropology. These works have done much to shape the discourse about culture in anthropology.*

Marks, Jonathan. 1995. *Human biodiversity.* New York: Aldine. *Marks is a biological anthropologist with a strong commitment to a biocultural approach to human nature. This book is an excellent introduction to biological anthropology.*

Voget, Fred. 1975. *A history of ethnology.* New York: Holt, Rinehart and Winston. *A massive, thorough, and detailed work. For the student seeking a challenging read.*

3

Ethnographic Fieldwork

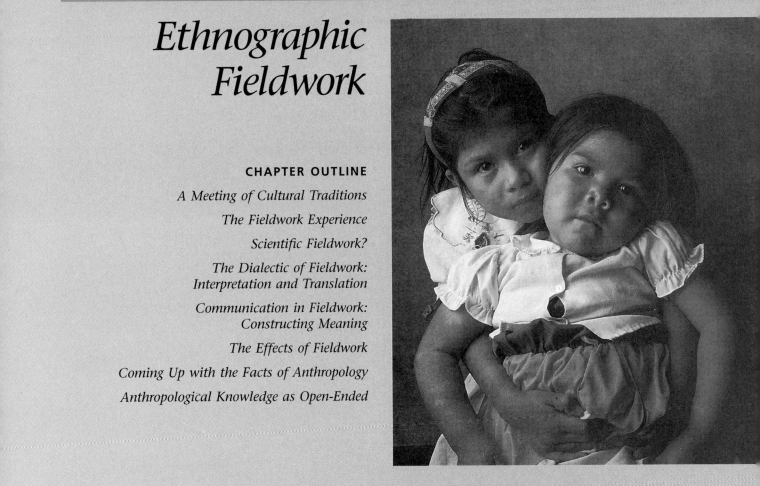

Roger Lancaster is an anthropologist who worked extensively in a Nicaraguan working-class neighborhood during the 1980s (Figure 3.1; see EthnoProfile 3.1: Managua). In June 1985, he went to Don Pablo's *tienda popular* (a "popular store" that carried government-subsidized food basics) to buy a chicken. On his way into the store, he was stopped by a drunken old man who wanted to talk. They exchanged greetings in Spanish and then the old man "uttered a string of vowels and consonants that proved entirely unintelligible." Lancaster explained in Spanish that he did not understand what the man was saying, and then entered the store to buy chicken. He relates the rest of the encounter:

> I was trying to decide how large the chicken should be when the drunk old man appeared in the doorway, waving his arms and raving that he had caught an agent of the CIA trying to spy on Nicaragua. "*¡La CIA!*" he kept shouting. I turned and realized he was talking about me. . . .
>
> Now it was Don Pablo's turn to speak. "Now what makes you think this *joven* [youth] is CIA?" "Because," replied the old man with a flourish of cunning, "I spoke to him in English, and he pretended that he didn't understand what I was saying! Now why else would he do that unless he were trying to conceal his nationality? And why would he conceal his nationality unless he were trying to hide something? He must be CIA. Arrest him!"
>
> I was growing concerned because the old man was now blocking the doorway, and it would scarcely have been appropriate for me to push my way past him. I was trying to figure out how to prevent this from becoming an even more unpleasant scene when Don Pablo's wife walked over to the meatbox, pulled out a chicken, and asked me if it were acceptable. I said that it was, and she put it on the scales. "Two and a half pounds," she observed, and then turned to address the old man. With an air of authority, she announced, "Listen, compañero, this isn't a spy from the CIA. This is Róger Lancaster, a friend of Nicaragua from the United States. He's an anthropology student at the University of California at Berkeley—not Los Angeles, there's another one in Berkeley, which doesn't have a basketball team. He's working on his doctoral dissertation, and he's here studying the role of religion in our revolution, especially the Popular Church. When he goes back, he's going to tell the truth about Nicaragua, and our revolution, and it will be good for us."

FIGURE 3.1 A working-class neighborhood in Nicaragua.

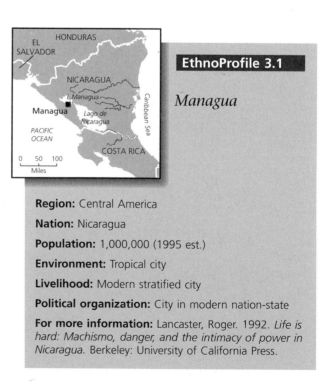

EthnoProfile 3.1

Managua

Region: Central America

Nation: Nicaragua

Population: 1,000,000 (1995 est.)

Environment: Tropical city

Livelihood: Modern stratified city

Political organization: City in modern nation-state

For more information: Lancaster, Roger. 1992. *Life is hard: Machismo, danger, and the intimacy of power in Nicaragua.* Berkeley: University of California Press.

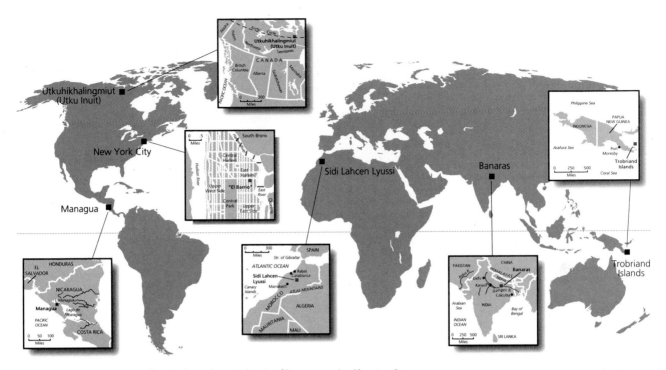

FIGURE 3.2 Locations of societies whose EthnoProfiles appear in Chapter 3.

I listened with amazement. I had never been in-side the popular store before, and I didn't even know either the proprietor or his wife by their names. I had seen them only in passing, and we had never been in-troduced. Yet here was Doña Carmen, accurately de-scribing my credentials and my research topic. Gossip moves quietly but quickly on the streets of the neigh-borhoods. (Lancaster 1992, 76)

A MEETING OF CULTURAL TRADITIONS

By deliberately bringing together people from differ-ent cultural traditions, ethnographic **fieldwork** makes such misunderstandings, understandings, and surprises likely. It is through encounters like this, and through many others, that fieldwork generates much of what anthropologists come to know about people in other societies.

Gathering data while living for an extended pe-riod in close contact with members of another soci-ety is called **participant-observation.** Anthropologists also gather data by consulting archives and previ-ously published literature relevant to their research. But participant-observation, which relies on face-to-face contact with people as they go about their daily lives, was pioneered by cultural anthropologists and re-mains characteristic of anthropology as a discipline. Participant-observation allows anthropologists to in-terpret what people say and do in the wider context of social interaction and cultural beliefs and values. Some-times they administer questionnaires and psychologi-cal tests as part of their fieldwork, but they would never rely solely on such methods because such information alone cannot be contextualized and may be highly

---

fieldwork An extended period of close involvement with the people in whose language or way of life an anthropologist is interested, during which anthropologists ordinarily collect most of their data.
participant-observation The method anthropologists use to gather information by living as closely as possible to the people whose culture they are studying while participating in their lives as much as possible.

misleading. Participant-observation is perhaps the best method available to scholars who seek a holistic understanding of culture and the human condition.

THE FIELDWORK EXPERIENCE

For most cultural anthropologists, ethnographic fieldwork is the experience that characterizes the discipline. Anthropologists sometimes gain field experience as undergraduates or early in their graduate studies by working on research projects or in field schools run by established anthropologists. For most anthropologists, an extended period of fieldwork is the final phase of formal training. Most anthropologists hope to return frequently to the field throughout their careers.

During graduate school, beginning anthropologists usually decide where they wish to do their research and on what topic. Next, they work to obtain funding for their research. In the United States, this generally requires submitting grant proposals to private foundations or government agencies. Some anthropologists have begun to pay for their research themselves by getting a job in the area where they want to do fieldwork or by supplementing small grants out of their own pockets.

Once funding is secured, the anthropologist must get permission to carry out research in the region chosen. For research outside the United States, this means contacting the government of the country where the research site is located or a research center or local university or both. If the research project is approved, the researcher establishes professional ties with local scholars and institutions while the project is under way. In many countries, such professional affiliation is required by law. Anthropologists view this affiliation as a significant part of their fieldwork. Colleagues at the institution can provide useful contacts, information, and shoptalk. Anthropologists must also consider what they can give to the people and the nation hosting them. The least they can do is share their work with host colleagues.

Living conditions in the field depend both on the nature of the host society and the kind of research being undertaken. Participant-observation requires living as closely as possible to the people whose culture you are studying. Anthropologists who work among remote peoples in rain forests, deserts, or tundra may

EthnoProfile 3.2

Blackston

Region: North America
Nation: United States
Population: 100,000
Environment: Urban ghetto
Livelihood: Low-paying full-time and temporary jobs, welfare
Political organization: Lowest level in a modern nation-state
For more information: Valentine, Bettylou. 1978. *Hustling and other hard work.* New York: Free Press.

need to bring along their own living quarters. In other cases, an appropriate house or apartment in the village, neighborhood, or city where the research is to be done becomes the anthropologist's home.

In any case, living conditions in the field can themselves provide major insights into the culture under study. This is powerfully illustrated by the experiences of Charles and Bettylou Valentine, whose field site was a poor neighborhood they called *Blackston,* located in a large city in the northern United States. (See EthnoProfile 3.2: Blackston.) The Valentines lived for the last field year on one-quarter of their regular income; during the final six months, they matched their income to that of welfare families:

> For five years we inhabited the same decrepit rat- and roach-infested buildings as everyone else, lived on the same poor quality food at inflated prices, trusted our health and our son's schooling to the same inferior institutions, suffered the same brutality and intimidation from the police, and like others made the best of it by some combination of endurance, escapism, and fighting back. Like the dwellings of our neighbors, our home went up in flames several times, including one disaster caused by the carelessness or ill will of the city's 'firefighters.' For several cold months we lived and worked in one room without heat other than what a cooking stove could provide, without hot water or windows, and with only one light bulb. (C. Valentine 1978, 5)

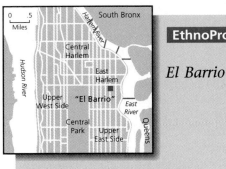

EthnoProfile 3.3

El Barrio

Region: North America

Nation: United States (New York City)

Population: 110,000 (1990 census)

Environment: Urban ghetto

Livelihood: Low-paying full-time and temporary jobs, selling drugs, welfare

Political organization: Lowest level in a modern nation-state

For more information: Bourgois, Philippe. 1995. *In search of respect: Selling crack in el Barrio.* Cambridge: Cambridge University Press.

Not all field sites offer such a stark contrast to the middle-class backgrounds of many fieldworkers, and indeed some can be almost luxurious. But physical and mental dislocation and stress can be expected anywhere. People from temperate climates who find themselves in the tropics have to adjust to the heat; fieldworkers in the Arctic have to adjust to the cold. In hot climates especially, many anthropologists encounter plants, animals, insects, and diseases with which they have had no previous experience. In any climate, fieldworkers need to adjust to local water and food.

In addition, there are the cultural differences—which is why the fieldworkers came. Yet the immensity of what they will encounter is difficult for them to anticipate. Initially, just getting through the day—finding a place to stay and food to eat—may seem an enormous accomplishment; but there are also data to gather, research to do!

Sometimes, however, the research questions never become separate from the living arrangements. Philippe Bourgois, who studied drug dealers in East Harlem in New York City, had to learn to deal not only with the violence of the drug dealers but also with the hostility and brutality that white police officers directed toward

him, a white man living in *el Barrio*. (See EthnoProfile 3.3: *El Barrio*.) His experiences on the street pressed him to consider how the situation he was studying was a form of what he calls "inner-city apartheid" in the United States (Bourgois 1995, 32).

Early in their stay, it is not uncommon for fieldworkers to feel overwhelmed. With time, however, they discover that the great process of human survival begins to assert itself: They begin to adapt. The rhythms of daily activity become familiar. Their use of the local language improves. Faces of the local inhabitants become the faces of neighbors. Incredibly, the time comes when they are able to turn their attention to the research questions that brought them there.

SCIENTIFIC FIELDWORK?

When anthropology began to take on its own identity as an intellectual discipline during the nineteenth century, it aspired to be scientific. Anthropology still aims to be scientific in its study of human nature, human society, and human history. However, twentieth-century scientists and philosophers have grown increasingly aware that the traditional scientific method followed in the physical sciences is only one way of doing science.

The Positivist Approach

The traditional method of the physical sciences, which early social scientists tried to imitate, is now often called *positivistic science*. Its proponents based their view of science on a set of principles most fully set out in the writings of a group of influential thinkers known as positivists, who were active in the late nineteenth and early twentieth centuries. Today, **positivism** is a label for a particular way of looking at and studying the world scientifically.

First of all, positivists are materialists. They hold that reality can be known through the five senses (sight, smell, touch, hearing, and taste). Second, positivists separate facts from values. For them, facts relate to the

---

positivism The view that there is a reality "out there" that can be known through the senses and that there is a single, appropriate set of scientific methods for investigating that reality.

nature of physical, material reality—what *is*—and values are speculation about what *ought to be*. To the positivist, scientific research into subatomic structure, genetic engineering, in vitro fertilization, or human sexual response is all part of a disinterested quest for knowledge, a quest that cannot be compromised simply because it offends some people's moral or political sensibilities. Truth remains the truth, whether people like it or not, whether it conforms to their idea of what is good and proper or not. These examples illustrate a third point about positivism: the belief that a single scientific method can be used to investigate any domain of reality, from planetary motion to chemical reactions to human life. Their hope is that all scientific knowledge will ultimately be unified.

The traditional goal of the positivist program has been to produce **objective knowledge**, knowledge about reality that is true for all people in all times and places. Positivist science has been viewed as the route to that objective knowledge, providing theories that are true because they describe the way the world is, independent of its meaning for human groups. For the positivist, there is a single structure to reality, and science can lay it bare.

Applying Positivist Methods to Anthropology

For the positivist, the prototypical research scenario involves a physical scientist in a laboratory. This prototype creates obstacles for those who study human life by means of participant-observation in a natural setting. Early cultural anthropologists were aware of these obstacles, and they tried to devise ways to get around them. Their first step was to approximate lab conditions by testing hypotheses in different cultural settings. These settings were carefully selected to exhibit naturally the same range of variation that a laboratory scientist could create artificially. As a result, the field could be seen as a living laboratory. Each research setting would correspond to a separate experimental situation, a method called *controlled comparison*. Margaret Mead used this method in the 1930s, when she studied four different societies in an attempt to discover the range and causes of gender roles (Figure 3.3).

Positivist anthropologists were encouraged by the enormous successes that the physical scientists had attained by following these principles. They were convinced that a similar commitment on their part would help them unlock the secrets of human social life. In fact, fieldworkers committed to the positivistic view of anthropology did learn a great deal. Research carried out from the middle of the nineteenth century through the middle of the twentieth century was clearly superior to much of the slipshod, impressionistic writing on other cultures that had preceded it. For decades, anthropologists following this research program traveled into the remote corners of the world. They recorded as accurately as they could the ways of life of peoples their contemporaries had neither heard of nor cared to know. Their research was systematic and accurate—and sometimes insensitive.

What does it mean to accuse scientists of insensitivity? Positivist scientists regard the behavior of human beings as no different from the behavior of rocks or molecules, which have no thoughts or feelings, no freedom or dignity. Anthropologists can be charged with insensitivity when their reports treat their human subjects as if they, too, lacked thoughts, feelings, freedom, and dignity. These anthropologists often developed close personal ties to the people whose lives they studied. Many anthropologists became their friends and advocates, defending their full humanity to outsiders and sometimes intervening on behalf of these people with the government. But in their books and articles, those same anthropologists felt compelled to write as though they had been invisible in the village, recording and analyzing data objectively, like machines, with no human connection to the subjects. The charge of insensitivity is troubling, for the subject matter of the social sciences differs in one major respect from that of all the physical sciences: It involves human beings who belong to the same species (and possibly to the same society) as the scientists themselves. Scientists experience their own inner consciousness, have their own thoughts and feelings. If the subjects of their study are also human beings, how can scientists justify denying to those human subjects the same "inner life" they claim for themselves?

Generations of anthropologists have attempted scientific fieldwork in the spirit of positivism. But more recently, cultural anthropologists have been developing new ways of writing about their cross-cultural experiences that reject the pose of total objectivity and instead focus on the ways they and their informants use culture to construct their interpretations of the world and of each other.

FIGURE 3.3 Participant-observation has long been a hallmark of research in cultural anthropology, whether in the 1920s with Margaret Mead in Samoa (left) or in the 1980s and 1990s with Sharon Hutchinson among Nuer in Sudan (right).

Anthropologists are also more aware that even those who tried the hardest to do positivistic fieldwork often gained some of their deepest insights in ways not recognized by the positivist program. Was that a wink or just an involuntary blink? Interpretations of ambiguous signals are inevitably influenced by assumptions about the way the world works. Thus, the particular assumptions of positivist science must have contributed to the creation of the knowledge that positivist fieldworkers offer as a result of their labors; different observers working from different assumptions would have produced different knowledge.

Consider the fieldwork of Annette Weiner in the Trobriand Islands carried out in the 1970s, nearly sixty years after Bronislaw Malinowski did his original and celebrated fieldwork there. Weiner and Malinowski were anthropologists of different nationalities and different sexes working in different villages with different informants during different historical periods. Weiner made an important contribution to our understanding of Trobriand life by describing and explaining activities involving Trobriand women's "wealth" that were absolutely central to the continued healthy functioning of Trobriand life—but about which Malinowski

---

objective knowledge Knowledge about reality that is absolute and true.

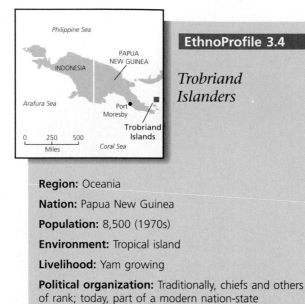

EthnoProfile 3.4

Trobriand Islanders

Region: Oceania

Nation: Papua New Guinea

Population: 8,500 (1970s)

Environment: Tropical island

Livelihood: Yam growing

Political organization: Traditionally, chiefs and others of rank; today, part of a modern nation-state

For more information: Weiner, Annette. 1988. *The Trobrianders of Papua New Guinea.* New York: Holt, Rinehart and Winston.

had written nothing (see Chapter 10). Weiner might have published her findings by declaring that Malinowski had got it wrong. But this route did not appeal to her, primarily because, as she puts it, he got so very much right. Malinowski's own preoccupations led him to write about aspects of Trobriand life different from those that interested Weiner. As a result, he left behind a portrait of Trobriand society that Weiner later felt obliged to correct. Nevertheless, Weiner found that much of Malinowski's work remained valid and insightful in her day. She quoted long passages from his ethnographies in her own writings about the Trobriands, in tribute to him (see Weiner 1976, 1988; see also EthnoProfile 3.4: Trobriand Islanders).

Anthropologists have increasingly recognized that a sound scientific study of human beings requires viewing our involvement with them not as a necessary evil but as central to our method. If those we study are as human as ourselves, then scientific accuracy demands that we treat them as human beings. Field methods and knowledge are thus intimately connected. In cultural anthropology, a person studies other persons, subjects study other subjects. Is fieldwork just one person's

subjective impressions of other people? No, because the fieldwork experience is a dialogue, not a solitary activity. Not only are anthropologists trying to figure out the locals, the locals are also trying to figure out the anthropologists.

It is not just the humanity of the informants that must not be overlooked; anthropologists must remember that they themselves are people. Understanding the way of life of another human society "requires interpretation, imagination, insight, perceptivity, human sympathy, humility, and a whole series of qualities—human qualities. It requires, fundamentally, that the student be himself or herself a human person" (W. Smith 1982, 68). Despite its difficulties, fieldwork offers the fullest encounter possible between anthropologists and a group of human beings whose way of life interests them. For these reasons, we will pay particular attention in the remainder of this chapter to the unique requirements, and opportunities, offered by fieldwork in cultural anthropology.

To gather data about a culture, anthropologists are obliged to interact closely with the sources of that data: their **informants.** As a result, field data are not subjective but *intersubjective:* They are the product of long dialogues between researcher and informant (Figure 3.4). These dialogues are often patient and painstaking collaborative attempts to sort things out, to piece things together. When successful, the outcome is a new understanding of the world that both anthropologist and informant can share. Recognizing the humanity of one's informants in this way is not trying, through sheer imagination, to reproduce the psychological states of those informants—which is what positivists often accuse their critics of doing. Such an imaginative effort, assuming it is possible, is solitary, whereas fieldwork is a dialogue. The focus of fieldwork is the range of **intersubjective meanings** that informants share. Fieldworkers can come to understand these meanings by sharing activities and conversations with their informants. This is what participant-observation is all about.

Reflexivity

The intersubjective meanings on which informants rely are public, not private. Informants take them for granted, but they may not be obvious to an outsider. In order to make these meanings explicit, anthropologist and informant together must occasionally step

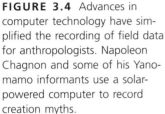

FIGURE 3.4 Advances in computer technology have simplified the recording of field data for anthropologists. Napoleon Chagnon and some of his Yanomamo informants use a solar-powered computer to record creation myths.

back from the ordinary flow of daily life and examine them critically. They must think about the way members of the culture normally think about their lives. This thinking about thinking is known as **reflexivity**; thus, fieldwork in cultural anthropology is a reflexive experience. Both anthropologists and their informants have important reflexive roles to play in fieldwork. Anthropological theory has come to acknowledge this reflexivity, recognizing it as the least distorting path to knowledge about human social life. The best ethnographies have always been reflexive, whether they were done in 1937 or 1997 and whether or not the ethnographers realized it.

The commitment to reflexivity has had far-reaching implications for the ways anthropologists carry out their research. Fieldworkers do not merely participate and observe and let it go at that. They are scientifically obligated to make public the way in which they gather data. Some anthropologists have argued that they must also share their conclusions with their informants and include their informants' reflections on those conclusions in their published ethnographies. Let us look at one attempt to maximize reflexivity in a published ethnography. Charles Valentine (1978, 7–8) notes that his wife, Bettylou Valentine, persuaded several of her

informants People in a particular culture who work with anthropologists and provide them with insights about their way of life. Also called *teachers* or *friends*.
intersubjective meanings The shared, public symbolic systems of a culture.
reflexivity Critically thinking about the way one thinks; reflecting on one's own experience.

informants to comment on her manuscript before publication. She visited them for lengthy discussions and found that, in general, they agreed with her conclusions. In the published volume, Valentine states her own conclusions, based on her own research and analysis. She also allows her informants a voice, permitting them, in a final chapter, to state where and why they disagree with her. Valentine's ethnography presents a vivid example of the open-endedness of the dialogue between anthropologist and informant: No single interpretation of human experience is final. This kind of mutual reflexivity is at the heart of anthropological knowledge.

THE DIALECTIC OF FIELDWORK: INTERPRETATION AND TRANSLATION

Fieldwork is a risky business. Fieldworkers not only risk offending their informants by misunderstanding their way of life, they also face the shock of the unfamiliar and their own vulnerability. Indeed, they must embrace this shock and cultivate this vulnerability if they are to achieve any kind of meaningful understanding of their informants' culture.

In the beginning, fieldworkers can be reassured by some of the insights that anthropological training has provided. Basic to these is the working assumption of *pan-human rationality*. Over a century of research in biological anthropology has demonstrated that all human beings are members of the same biological species. This means that with regard to such human potentialities as intelligence, we should expect to find the same range of variation in all human groups. We can therefore resist ethnocentric impulses by recalling "that if what we observe appears to be odd or irrational, it is probably because we do not understand it and not because it is a product of a 'savage' culture in which such nonsense is to be expected" (Greenwood and Stini 1977, 185).

Interpreting Actions and Ideas

The problem becomes how to interpret our observations. But what exactly does **interpretation** involve? Jean Paul Dumont offers the following suggestion: "Interpretation . . . can refer to three rather different matters: an oral recitation, a reasonable explanation, and a transla-

tion from another language. . . . In all three cases, something foreign, strange, separated in time, space or experience is made familiar, present, comprehensible: something requiring representation, explanation or translation is somehow 'brought to understanding' — is interpreted" (1978, 4, quoting Palmer).

How does one go about interpreting the actions and ideas of other human beings? We need a form of interpretation that does not turn our informants into objects. That is, we need a form of interpretation based on reflexivity rather than objectivity. Paul Rabinow suggests that what we require has already been set forth in the philosophy of the French thinker Paul Ricoeur: "Following Ricoeur, I define the problem of hermeneutics (which is simply Greek for "interpretation") as 'the comprehension of self by the detour of the comprehension of the other.' It is vital to stress that this is not psychology of any sort. . . . The self being discussed is perfectly public. . . . [It is] the culturally mediated and historically situated self which finds itself in a continuously changing world of meaning" (Rabinow 1977, 5–6). For the anthropologist in the field, then, interpretation becomes a task of coming to comprehend the *cultural self* by the detour of comprehending the *cultural other*. In other words, the anthropologist's understanding of the cultural other is intersubjectively constructed, using elements drawn from the cultural systems of anthropologist and informant alike. As we come to grasp the meaning of the other's cultural self, we simultaneously learn something of the meaning of our own cultural identity.

Learning to understand what makes other people tick may seem plausible among people from the same culture. After all, members of the same culture share at least some of the same intersubjective symbolic language and therefore have at least some foundation on which to build. But the anthropologist doing fieldwork in another culture and his or her informants cannot be assumed to share such a language. On what can they build their intersubjective understanding? The gulf between self and other may seem unbridgeable in this context. Yet anthropologist and informant engaged in participant-observation do share something: the fieldwork situation itself.

Anthropologist and informant find themselves in physical proximity, observing and discussing the same material activities. At first, they may talk past one another, as each describes these activities from a different

The Situation of the Brazilian Anthropologist

Contemporary anthropologists come from many places other than Europe or the United States. Anthropologist Roberto da Matta explores what it means for him to be a Brazilian anthropologist working in Brazil.

In order to grasp deep motivations in ethnographic styles, one has to deal with how natives are represented as "others"—as different, as distinct—in divergent national contexts. In Brazil, the "other" is incarnated by a small native population, scattered in the empty Amazon and Central Brazil, a population generically called by the name, "Índio" (Indian). But the "Indian" is not alone, for with the category "Negro" they form the basis of a singular and intriguing view of the immediate human diversity for Brazilians. The "Negro" (who is fundamentally the ex-slave) is an intrinsic element of Brazilian social structure, haunting with his massive presence the "whiteness" of a bourgeois lifestyle. The "Indian" is an out-

sider, giving rise to the romantic fantasies of the noble savage who has to be either isolated and protected from the evils of civilization or be eliminated from the national landscape for incapacity to take part in modern progress.

In this context, to be with "Indians" is, for a Brazilian anthropologist, more than having the opportunity of living with another humanity. It is also to have the privilege of getting in touch with a mythical other. And by doing so, have the honor of being the one to overcome all manner of discomforts in order to describe a new way of life in the midst of Brazilian civilization. Thus, for Brazilian anthropologists, "to be there" is also an opportunity of being a *witness* to the way of life of a different society. This is particularly true when that way of life runs the risk of succumbing to a contact situation that is brutally unequal in political terms.

Source: da Matta 1994, 122–23.

perspective using a different language. However, all cultures and languages are open enough to entertain a variety of viewpoints and a variety of ways to talk about them. Continued discussion allows anthropologist and informant to search for areas of intersection for understanding and describing the same behavior. Any intersection, however small, can form the foundation on which anthropologist and informant may then build a new intersubjective symbolic language. This process of building a bridge of understanding between self and other is what Rabinow refers to as "the dialectic of fieldwork" (1977, 39).

The Dialectical Process

Both fieldworker and informant begin with little or nothing in the way of shared experience that could allow them to figure one another out with any accuracy. But if they are motivated to make sense of one another and willing to work together, steps toward understanding and valid interpretation—toward recognition—can be made.

For example, traditional fieldwork often begins with collecting data on kinship relations in the host

society. A trained anthropologist comes to the field with certain ideas about kinship in mind. These ideas derive in part from the anthropologist's own experience of kinship in his or her own culture. They are also based on research and theorizing about kinship by other anthropologists. As the fieldworker begins to ask kinship questions of informants, he or she may discover that the informants have no word in their language that accurately conveys the range of meaning carried by the term *kinship*. This does not mean that the anthropologist must give up. Rather, the anthropologist must enter into the dialectic process of interpretation and translation.

This process works something like this. The anthropologist poses a question about kinship using the term in the informants' language that seems to come closest to kinship in meaning. The informants do their best to interpret the anthropologist's question in a way that makes sense to them. That is, each informant has to be reflexive, thinking about how people in his or her society think about a certain domain of experience.

interpretation The process of bringing to understanding.

Having formulated an answer, the informant responds to the anthropologist's question in terms he or she thinks the anthropologist will understand. Now it is the anthropologist's turn to interpret this response, to decide whether it carries the kind of information he or she was looking for.

Translating

In the dialectic of fieldwork, both anthropologist and informant are active agents. Each party tries to figure out what the other is trying to say. If there is goodwill on the part of both, each party also tries to provide responses that make sense to the other. As more than one anthropologist has remarked (see, for example, Crick 1976; Rabinow 1977), anthropological fieldwork is **translation.** Moreover, the informant is just as actively engaged in translation as the anthropologist. As time passes and the partners in this effort learn from their mistakes and successes, their ability to communicate increases. Each participant learns more about the other: The anthropologist gains skill at asking questions that make sense to the informant, and the informant becomes more skilled at answering those questions in terms relevant to the anthropologist. The validity of this ongoing translation is anchored in the ongoing cultural activities in which both anthropologist and informant are participant-observers.

The Dialectic between Self and Other

Out of this mutual activity comes knowledge about the informant's culture that is meaningful to both anthropologist and informant. This is new knowledge. And this is what dialectical holism is all about: The whole (knowledge about the culture) is more than the sum of its parts (the anthropologist's knowledge and the informant's knowledge). Knowledge of the culture arises out of the collaboration of anthropologist and informant, who create a world, usually thin and fragile, of common understandings and experiences.

It is possible to argue that all learning about another human being is the result of a dialogue between self and other. We have suggested that informants are equally involved in this dialogue and may end up learning as much or more about anthropologists as anthropologists learn about them. But it is important to emphasize that in field situations, the dialogue is initiated by anthropologists. Anthropologists come to the field with their own sets of questions, which are determined not by the field situation but by the discipline of anthropology itself (see Karp and Kendall 1982, 254). Furthermore, when anthropologists are finished with a particular research project, they are free to break off the dialogue with informants and resume discussions with fellow professionals. The only link between these two sets of dialogues—between particular anthropologists and the people with whom they work and among anthropologists in general—are the particular anthropologists themselves.

Professional colleagues have relied on fieldworkers to speak for informants, traditionally assuming that informants would not speak for themselves. In recent years, members of indigenous societies have begun to speak powerfully on their own behalf, as political advocates for their people. However, language barriers still often prohibit informants from speaking to an audience of professional scholars on complex topics, nor are their interests usually the same as those of professional scholars. Fieldwork therefore involves differences of power and places a heavy burden of responsibility on researchers. Anthropologists feel strongly that their informants' identities should be protected. The need for protection is all the greater when informants belong to marginal and powerless groups that might suffer retaliation from more powerful members of their society. However, because some informants wish to express their identity and their ideas openly, anthropologists have experimented with forms of ethnographic writing in which they serve primarily as translators and editors of the voices and opinions of individual informants (see, for example, Keesing 1983; Shostak 1981). Increasingly, anthropologists working in their own societies write about their fieldwork both as observers of others and as members of the society they are observing (see, for example, Foley 1989; Kumar 1992).

COMMUNICATION IN FIELDWORK: CONSTRUCTING MEANING

Meaning in culture is never fully self-evident; rather it is constructed by those who communicate, negotiated between them, sometimes with great difficulty. Nowhere is the problematic nature of human commu-

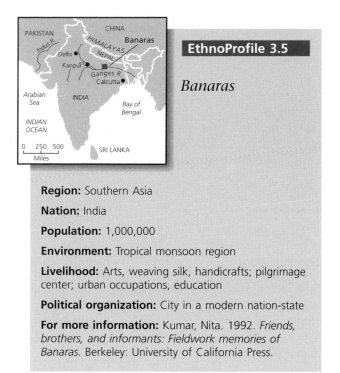

EthnoProfile 3.5

Banaras

Region: Southern Asia

Nation: India

Population: 1,000,000

Environment: Tropical monsoon region

Livelihood: Arts, weaving silk, handicrafts; pilgrimage center; urban occupations, education

Political organization: City in a modern nation-state

For more information: Kumar, Nita. 1992. *Friends, brothers, and informants: Fieldwork memories of Banaras.* Berkeley: University of California Press.

nication more obvious than in anthropological fieldwork. Finding informants and establishing rapport with them has always been seen as an indispensable first step, but there are no foolproof procedures that guarantee success. Nita Kumar is an anthropologist from Delhi, India, who chose to do research in a region of India very different from the one where she grew up: "Banaras was such a mystery to me when I arrived there in 1981 ironically *because* I was an Indian and expected to have a privileged insight into it. In fact, from Banaras I was *thrice* removed: through my education and upbringing, than which there is no greater molder of attitudes; by language and linguistic culture; and by region and regional culture" (1992, 15). (See EthnoProfile 3.5: Banaras.) Although her social connections smoothed the way for her in official circles, she had no special advantage when trying to make contact with the artisans in Banaras whose way of life interested her.

In her fieldwork memoir, *Friends, Brothers, and Informants,* Kumar shares the four failed attempts she made to contact weavers. The first time, the weavers turned out to have well-established ties to rickshaw pullers and taxi drivers who regularly brought tourists to visit their shop and buy souvenirs. Not wishing to

become just another business contact, she left. Her second contact was with the Muslim owner of a weaving establishment whose suspicions of her motives caused her to turn elsewhere. Her third attempt was made through a sari salesman who took her to a market where silk weavers sold their wares. Unfortunately for her, he would periodically announce to all assembled who she was and invite weavers to come up and speak with her, a procedure she found deeply embarrassing. Her fourth attempt followed the accidental discovery that two members of a family selling firecrackers were also weavers. When she was invited to see one brother's loom, however, she grew "uncomfortable with all the obvious evidence of bachelor existence and their readiness to welcome me into it. . . . I just went away and never came back" (99). On her fifth attempt, she was introduced by a silk-yarn merchant to weavers living in a government-subsidized housing project next to his house. In the home of a weaver named Shaukatullah, surrounded by members of his family, she finally found a setting in which she felt welcome and able to do her work. "In a matter of weeks I was given the status of a daughter of Shaukatullah" (105). That status of daughter was not only important to her research, but it was also a congenial status to her, one with which she was familiar.

Jean Briggs is an anthropologist who was also adopted by a family of informants. Briggs worked among the Utkuhikhalingmiut (Utku, for short), an Inuit (Eskimo) group in Alaska. (See EthnoProfile 3.6: Utkuhikhalingmiut [Utku Inuit].) There were several steps her informants took in order to figure her out once she took on the role of daughter in the home of her new "father," Inuttiaq, and "mother," Allaq: "From the moment that the adoption was settled, I was 'Inuttiaq's daughter' in the camp. [They] drilled me in the use of kin terms appropriate to my position, just as they drilled [Inuttiaq's] three-year-old daughter, who was learning to speak" (Briggs 1980, 46). The context of their interactions had clearly changed as a result of the adoption, and Briggs's family had new expectations both of Briggs and of themselves: "Allaq, and especially Inuttiaq . . . more and more attempted to assimilate me into a proper adult parent-daughter relationship. I was ex-

---

translation In anthropological fieldwork, the process of learning to describe one culture in terms that can be understood by members of another culture.

EthnoProfile 3.6

*Utkuhikhalingmiut
(Utku Inuit)*

Region: North America

Nation: Canada (Northwest Territories)

Population: 35

Environment: Tundra

Livelihood: Nomadic fishing, hunting, gathering

Political organization: Communal

For more information: Briggs, Jean. 1989. Kapluna daughter: Adopted by the Eskimo. In *Conformity and conflict: Readings in cultural anthropology.* 7th ed., edited by J. Spradley and D. McCurdy, Glenview, IL: Scott, Foresman & Co., 44–62.

pected to help with the household work . . . and I was expected to obey unquestioningly when Inuttiaq told me to do something. . . . Inevitably, conflicts, covert but pervasive, developed" (47).

Briggs found herself feeling increasingly uncomfortable and began to analyze her situation. She began to realize that part of the problem had to do with differences between her ideas of how parents ought to relate to their daughters and Utku beliefs on these matters. She also experienced contradictions between her roles as daughter and anthropologist. The dialectic of fieldwork brought sharply to awareness—aided in the construction of—her understanding of the meaning of those roles in her own culture.

Briggs was not the only person who had to be reflexive. Her Utku informants were forced to reconsider how they had been dealing with her since her arrival. As she was able to reconstruct it, their understanding of her went through three stages. At first, her informants thought she was strange, anomalous. After her adoption, they saw her as educable. But when the communication breakdown occurred, they concluded that she was "uneducable in important ways . . . a defective person" (60–61). Either her informants could find

no further way of making clear what was expected of her, or else it became obvious to them that she was unwilling to do what she knew they expected of her. Either conclusion on their part might have meant the end of Briggs's fieldwork were it not for the timely intervention of a third party. An Utku woman, who knew both Briggs and her adoptive family, was able to explain to Briggs's informants the aspects of her behavior that had been most distressing.

THE EFFECTS OF FIELDWORK

The Effect of Fieldwork on Informants

Because informants play active roles in fieldwork, it is appropriate to discuss the role of informant in more detail. Many fieldworkers have long considered *informant* to be a term of respect for those who agree to try to explain their way of life to an anthropologist. Unfortunately, the term has taken on a sinister connotation in recent years as law enforcement professionals have used it to describe those who betray their partners in crime. Consequently, some anthropologists have searched for a new term—*teacher* or *friend,* for example—that might be free of taint, although no alternatives have yet gained widespread acceptance. Regarding the term *informant,* Rabinow observes: "The present somewhat nasty connotations of the word do apply at times, but so does its older root sense 'to give form to, to be the formative principle of, to animate.' . . . The informant gives external form to his own experiences, by presenting them to meet the anthropologist's questions, to the extent that he can interpret them" (1977, 153).

Strictly speaking, any member of a culture with whom an anthropologist speaks or interacts can be considered an informant. But most fieldworkers soon discover that some informants seem more interested in the anthropologist's work and are better able to understand what he or she is trying to accomplish than others. According to Rabinow, these "key informants" not only are patient and intelligent, but also have "an imaginative ability to objectify [their] own culture for a foreigner, so as to present it in a number of ways" (1977, 95).

Key informants tend to be somewhat marginal to their own communities. They are likely to be as curi-

FIGURE 3.5 Paul Rabinow's reflections on his fieldwork experiences in a Moroccan village much like this one led him to reconceptualize the nature of anthropological fieldwork.

ous about the anthropologist's way of life as he or she is about their way of life. This should not be surprising since our informants are persons and, as Malcolm Crick reminds us, "to be a person requires the exercise of considerable anthropological skills. It requires self-understanding, communicative ability, and other-understanding. Thus it is that in all the social sciences those being investigated possess exactly the same powers as those doing the investigating" (1976, 104).

Fieldwork changes both the anthropologist and the informants. What kinds of effects can the fieldwork experience have on informants? Anthropologists have not always been able to report on this. In some cases, the effects of fieldwork on informants cannot be assessed until long after the anthropologist has returned home. In other cases, it becomes clear in the course of fieldwork that the anthropologist's presence and questions have made the informants aware of their own cultural selves in new ways that are both surprising and uncomfortable.

As he reflected on his own fieldwork in Morocco, Rabinow recalled some cases in which his informants' new reflexivity led to unanticipated consequences (Figure 3.5). One key informant, Malik, agreed to help Rabinow compile a list of landholdings and other possessions of the villagers of Sidi Lahcen Lyussi. (See EthnoProfile 3.7: Sidi Lahcen Lyussi.) As a first step in tracing the economic status of the middle stratum in society, Rabinow suggested that Malik list his own pos-

sessions. Malik appeared to be neither rich nor poor; in fact, he considered himself "not well off." "As we began to make a detailed list of his possessions, he became touchy and defensive. . . . It was clear that he was not as impoverished as he had portrayed himself. . . . This was confusing and troubling for him. . . . Malik began to see that there was a disparity between his self-image and my classification system. The emergence of this 'hard' data before his eyes and through his own efforts was highly disconcerting for him" (1977, 117–18).

Malik's easy understanding of himself and his world had been disrupted, and he could not ignore the disruption. He would either have to change his self-image or find some way to assimilate this new information about himself into the old self-image. In the end Malik managed to reaffirm his conclusion that he was not well-off by arguing that wealth lay not in material possessions alone. Although he might be rich in material goods, his son's health was bad, his own father was dead, he was responsible for his mother and unmarried brothers, and he had to be constantly vigilant in order to prevent his uncle from stealing his land (117–19).

Bettylou Valentine was determined from the outset to acknowledge the point of view of her informants in Blackston. Yet before the publication of her ethnography, she discovered that some informants were not pleased with what she had said about them. One woman read in the manuscript about her own illegal

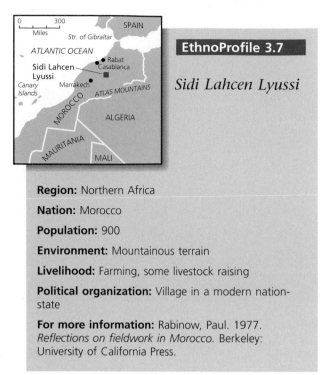

EthnoProfile 3.7

Sidi Lahcen Lyussi

Region: Northern Africa

Nation: Morocco

Population: 900

Environment: Mountainous terrain

Livelihood: Farming, some livestock raising

Political organization: Village in a modern nation-state

For more information: Rabinow, Paul. 1977. *Reflections on fieldwork in Morocco.* Berkeley: University of California Press.

attempts to combine work and welfare to better her family's standard of living. Angry, she denied to Valentine that she had ever done such a thing. Valentine talked to her informant at some length about this matter, which was well documented in field notes. It gradually became clear that the woman was concerned that if the data about her illegal activities were published, her friends and neighbors on the block would learn about it. In particular, she was afraid that the book would be sold on corner newsstands. Once Valentine explained how unlikely this was, her informant relaxed considerably: "The exchange made clear how different interests affect one's view. From my point of view, corner newsstand distribution would be excellent because it would mean the possibility of reaching the audience I feel needs to read and ponder the implications of the book. Yet Bernice and Velma [the informant and her friend] specified that they wouldn't mind where else it was distributed, even in Blackston more generally, if it could be kept from people on Paul Street and the surrounding blocks" (B. Valentine 1978, 122).

The Effect of Fieldwork on the Researcher

What does it feel like to be in the field, trying to figure out the workings of an unfamiliar way of life? What

are the consequences of this experience for the fieldworker? Graduate students in anthropology who have not yet been in the field often develop an idealized image of field experience: At first, the fieldworker is a bit disoriented and potential informants suspicious, but uncertainty soon gives way to understanding and trust as the anthropologist's good intentions are made known and accepted. The fieldworker succeeds in establishing rapport. In fact, the fieldworker becomes so well loved and trusted, so thoroughly accepted, that he or she is adopted into their family, treated as one of them, and allowed access to the culture's secrets. Presumably, all this happens as a result of the personal attributes of the fieldworker. If you have what it takes, you will be taken in and treated like one of the family. If this doesn't happen, you are obviously cut out for some other kind of work.

But much more than the anthropologist's personality is responsible for successful fieldwork. Establishing rapport with the people being studied is an achievement of anthropologist and informants together. Acceptance is problematic, rather than ensured, even for the most gifted fieldworkers. After all, fieldworkers are usually outsiders with no personal ties to the community in which they will do their research. According to Karp and Kendall (1982), it is therefore not just naive to think that the locals will accept you as one of them without any difficulty, it is also bad science. It is remarkable that anthropologists can still be seduced by such an idealized image in that they are trained by experienced fieldworkers and should know better.

Rabinow recalled the relationship he formed with his first Moroccan informant, a man called Ibrahim, whom he hired to teach him Arabic. Rabinow and Ibrahim seemed to get along well together, and, because of the language lessons, they saw each other a great deal, leading Rabinow to think of Ibrahim as a friend. When Rabinow planned a trip to another city, Ibrahim offered to go along as a guide and stay with relatives. This only confirmed Ibrahim's friendliness in Rabinow's eyes. But things changed once they arrived at their destination. Ibrahim told Rabinow that the relatives with whom he was to stay did not exist, that he had no money, and that he expected Rabinow to pay for his hotel room. When Rabinow was unable to do so, however, Ibrahim paid for it himself. Rabinow was shocked and hurt by this experience, and his relationship with Ibrahim was forever altered. Rabinow remarks: "Basically I had been conceiving of him as a friend because of the seeming personal relationship we had established. But Ibrahim, a lot less confusedly, had basically conceptualized me as a resource. He was not unjustly situating me with the other Europeans with whom he had dealings" (1977, 29).

Rabinow's experience illustrates what he calls the "shock of otherness." Fieldwork institutionalizes this shock. Having to anticipate **culture shock** at any and every turn, anthropologists sometimes find that fieldwork takes on a tone that is anything but pleasant and sunny. For many anthropologists, what characterizes fieldwork, at least in its early stages, is anxiety—the anxiety of an isolated individual with nothing familiar to turn to, no common sense on which to rely, and no relationships that can be taken for granted. There is a reason anthropologists have reported holing up for weeks at a time reading paperback novels and eating peanut-butter sandwiches. I (Emily Schultz) recall how difficult it was every morning to leave my compound in Guider, Cameroon. Despite the accomplishments of the previous day, I was always convinced that no one would want to talk to me *today*. (See EthnoProfile 8.1: Guider.)

Seeing one's informants as fully human requires anthropologists to allow their own humanity to express itself. But expressing their humanity is exceedingly difficult, for most anthropologists do not wish to offend their informants. The situation is complicated, particularly at the beginning, by the fieldworker's imperfect awareness of the sorts of behavior that are likely to offend informants. As a result, the fieldworkers have frequently felt that their motto ought to be, "The informant is always right." Many fieldworkers therefore forbid themselves to express anger or disgust or disagreement. But this behavior is likely to cause problems for both them and their informants. After all, what sort of person is always smiling, never angry, without opinions? Anthropologists who refuse to challenge or be challenged by their informants dehumanize both themselves and their informants. Clearly, it takes a good deal of diplomatic skill to walk a fine line between ethnocentrism and depersonalization. Sometimes this may not be possible, and the fieldwork itself may be put in jeopardy.

Rabinow came face to face with the consequences of the fieldworkers' motto in his relations with his informant Ali, who had agreed to take Rabinow to a wedding at some distance from town; they were to go in Rabinow's car. Unfortunately, Rabinow was ill the day

of the wedding. He did not want to break his promise and perhaps offend Ali and ruin any future chances to attend weddings, but he felt terrible. Ali agreed to stay only a short time at the wedding and then leave. Once they arrived, however, Ali disappeared for long stretches, returning to announce that they would definitely be leaving soon only to wander off again. Rabinow found himself feeling worse, trying to smile at members of the wedding party, and growing angrier and angrier with Ali. At last, many hours after their arrival, Rabinow managed to get Ali into the car and they headed for home. Things did not improve. Rabinow was certain that his annoyance must be obvious to Ali as they drove along, yet Ali kept asking him if he was happy, which was the sign of a pleased guest and a good host. When Rabinow steadfastly refused to answer him, Ali then declared that if Rabinow was unhappy, he, Ali, was insulted and would get out of the car and walk back to town. Rabinow had had enough. He stopped the car to let his companion out and drove on without him.

Rabinow was sure he had sabotaged his fieldwork completely. In retrospect, he acknowledges that this event led him to question seriously whether or not the informant is always right. He says, "If the informant was always right, then by implication the anthropologist had to become a sort of non-person. . . . He had to be willing to enter into any situation as a smiling observer. . . . One had to completely subordinate one's own code of ethics, conduct, and world view, to 'suspend disbelief' . . . and sympathetically and accurately record events" (1977, 46). The quarrel with Ali forced him to drop the anthropologist's all-accepting persona and allow the full force of his personality through. Rabinow chose to be true to himself on this occasion, regardless of the consequences for his fieldwork.

The results could have been disastrous, but Rabinow was lucky. This rupture of communication with Ali was the prelude to Rabinow's experiencing one of his most significant insights into Moroccan culture. After his anger had cooled, he attempted to make up with Ali. To his great surprise, after only a few hours of warm apologies, his relationship with Ali was not only restored but even closer than before! How was this possible? Rabinow had unwittingly behaved toward Ali

---

culture shock The feeling, akin to panic, that develops in people living in an unfamiliar society when they cannot understand what is happening around them.

The Relationship between Anthropologists and Informants

Many anthropologists have developed warm, lasting relationships with their informants. However, as Allyn Stearman points out, the nature of the anthropologist-informant relationship is not always unproblematic.

While doing fieldwork among the Ik (pronounced "eek") of Uganda, Africa, anthropologist Colin Turnbull challenged the old anthropological myth that the researcher will like and admire the people he or she is studying. A corollary of this assumption is that to the uninformed outsider who does not "understand" the culture, a group may seem hostile, unresponsive, or stoic, or may have any number of less admirable characteristics; but to the trained observer who truly knows "his or her" people, these attributes are only a façade presented to outsiders. What Turnbull finally had to concede, however, was that overall the Ik were not a very likable people. His portrait of the Ik as selfish, uncaring, and uninterested even in the survival of their own children is understandable when he describes their history of displacement, social disruption, and the constant threat of starvation. Nonetheless, an intellectual understanding of the factors contributing to Ik personality and behavior did not make it any easier for Turnbull to deal emotionally with the day-to-day interactions of fieldwork.

For me, knowing of Turnbull's situation alleviated some of my own anxieties in dealing with the Yuquí. As was Turnbull's, my previous field experiences among other peoples had been very positive. In the anthropologist's terms, this meant that I was accepted quite rapidly as a friend and that my informants were open and cooperative. The Yuquí did not fit any of these patterns. But like Turnbull, I understood something of the Yuquí past and thus on an intellectual level could comprehend that since they were a hunted, beleaguered people being threatened with extinction I could not expect them to be warm, friendly, and welcoming. Still, on an emotional level it was very difficult to cope with my frequent feelings of anger and resentment at having to put up with their teasing, taunting, and testing on an almost daily basis. My only consolation was that while I was often the brunt of this activity, so were they themselves. I am uncertain whether I finally came to understand the Yuquí, or simply became hardened to their particular way of dealing with the world. By doing favors for people, I incurred their indebtedness, and these debts could be translated into favors owed. How I chose to collect was up to me. As favors mounted, I found that relationships with individual Yuquí were better. Then came the challenges. Could I be easily duped or taken advantage of? At first, I extended kindnesses gratuitously and was mocked. I learned to show my anger and stubbornness, to demand something in return for a tool lent or a service provided. Rather than alienate the Yuquí, this behavior (which I found difficult and distasteful throughout my stay) conferred prestige. The more I provided and then demanded in return, the more the Yuquí were willing to accept me. In the Yuquí world, as in any other, respect must be earned. But unlike many other peoples, for the Yuquí, kindness alone is not enough. In the end it is strength that is valued and that earns respect.

Source: Stearman 1989, 7–10.

in the only manner that would impress him, in Moroccan terms. Rabinow learned that Moroccan men test each other all the time to see how far they can assert dominance before their assertions are challenged. In this world, anyone who is all-accepting, such as an anthropologist, is not respected or admired but viewed as weak. "There was a fortuitous congruence between my breaking point and Moroccan cultural style. Perhaps in another situation my behavior might have proved irreparable. . . . By standing up to Ali I had communicated to him" (1977, 49).

Jean Briggs's experience among the Utku illustrates how the same behavior in different cultural circumstances can be interpreted differently. Briggs understood from her informants that anger was dangerous and must never be shown. She also became aware of the various ways her informants diverted or diffused angry feelings. Nevertheless, she remained ignorant of the full power of this value in Utku culture until she found herself having seriously violated it.

Beginning a few years before her fieldwork, Briggs relates, sportsmen from the United States and Canada had begun to fly into the inlet where her informants lived during July and August. Once there, they borrowed canoes belonging to the Utku. Although there had at one time been several usable canoes in the community, only two remained when Briggs arrived. That summer some sportsmen borrowed one canoe, but ran it onto a rock. They then asked the Utkus if they could borrow the one remaining canoe, which happened to belong to Briggs's "father," Inuttiaq.

Briggs became the translator for the sportsmen. She was annoyed that their carelessness had led to the ruin of one of the last two good canoes. Because canoes are used for getting food and are not pleasure craft, the loss had serious economic consequences for her informants. When the outsiders asked to use the last canoe afloat, Briggs says, "I exploded." She lectured the sportsmen about their carelessness and insensitivity and explained how important canoes were to the Utku. Then, remembering Inuttiaq's often-repeated admonition never to lend his canoe, she told the sportsmen that the owner of the one remaining canoe did not want to lend it. You may imagine her shock and surprise, then, when Inuttiaq insisted that the canoe be lent.

But this was only the beginning. Briggs discovered that, following her outburst, her informants seemed to turn against her rather than against the sportsmen. "I had spoken unbidden and in anger. . . . Punishment was a subtle form of ostracism. . . . I was isolated. It was as though I were not there. . . . But . . . I was still treated with the most impeccable semblance of solicitude" (1980, 56–57). Unlike Rabinow, Briggs discovered just how much at odds her breaking point was with Utku cultural style. This breach might well have ended her fieldwork if a Westernized Utku friend, Ikayuqtuq, had not come to her rescue. "I had written my version of the story to Ikayuqtuq, had told her about my attempt to protect the Utku from the impositions of the kaplunas [white men] and asked her if she could help to explain my behavior to the Eskimos" (1980, 58). Ikayuqtuq did write to Allaq and Inuttiaq, although the letter did not arrive until three months later. During that time, Briggs seemed to be frozen out of Utku society.

Once the letter arrived, everything changed. Briggs's friend had found a way to translate her intentions into terms that Allaq and Inuttiaq could understand. As Briggs recalls, "the effect was magical." Inuttiaq began to tell the others what a dangerous task Briggs had taken on to defend the Utkus against the white men. The ice melted. And Briggs knew that relationships had been restored (and perhaps deepened) when Inuttiaq called her "daughter" once again.

Ruptures of communication between anthropolo- gists and their informants can ultimately lead to a deepening of insight and a broadening of mutual understanding. This is what all fieldworkers hope for—and dread, because negotiating the rupture can be dangerous, and no positive outcome is ensured. The risks may seem greater when the informants' culture is very different from the anthropologist's, and consequently, it might seem that the resulting insights must also be more startling. Yet Bettylou Valentine discovered that fieldwork in the United States, among African Americans like herself, also held surprises: "At the start of fieldwork I assumed at a subconscious level that my college education . . . would enable me, unlike many ghetto residents, to handle successfully any problem resulting from the impact of the larger society on my family, myself, or any less-skilled ghetto resident I chose to help. This assumption was proved totally wrong many, many times" (1978, 132).

The Humanizing Effect of Fieldwork

Anthropological knowledge is the fruit of reflexivity produced by the mutual attempts of anthropologist and informant to understand each other. As a result, anthropological knowledge ought to be able to provide answers to questions about human nature, human society, and human history. Somehow, good ethnography should not only persuade its readers, on intellectual grounds, that the ethnographer's informants were human beings. It should also allow readers to *experience* the informants' humanity.

Charles Valentine explicitly states this as the ultimate aim of his wife's ethnography about life in Blackston: "This book . . . reports how those who are both Black and poor persist in being human despite inhumane conditions" (1978, 2). One important element in retaining their humanity was institutionalized celebrating. By middle-class standards, Blackstonians had little money to spend. Bettylou Valentine was initially surprised at how much of their cash was used on food, drink, and such items as stereos, all used in entertaining friends and relatives: "Some people might characterize such lavish entertainment in the face of limited resources as improvident and likely to keep people from saving enough to escape from the slum. Yet the amounts of money spent could not really make a difference in the basic circumstances of inadequate housing, racial discrimination, limited job opportunities, poor city services, and all the other things that Blackstonians escape from, at least temporarily, through dancing and partying. The social life of Blackston, willingness to share, free and easy access to whatever liquor and food there was among friends, neighbors, and kin are the features that those who moved away commented on most often and said they missed" (B. Valentine 1978, 122). Indeed, in the best ethnographic writing, we can grasp the humanity—the pain, suffering, and ambiguities as well as the joys and pleasures—of the people who have granted the anthropologist the privilege of living with them for an extended period of time.

This privileged position, the extraordinary opportunity to experience "the other" as human beings while learning about their lives, is an experience that comes neither easily nor automatically. It must be cultivated, and it requires cooperation between and effort from one's informants and oneself. Those who have achieved a measure of cross-cultural understanding find themselves—or should find themselves—less willing to talk about "us" and "them." Indeed, the appropriate language should be "not 'they,' not 'we,' not 'you,' but 'some of us' are thus and so" (W. Smith 1982, 70). Perhaps one of the most powerful lessons fieldwork teaches is the realization in the mind and in the gut, that "there is no primitive. There are other [people] living other lives" (Rabinow 1977, 151).

COMING UP WITH THE FACTS OF ANTHROPOLOGY

If anthropological knowledge is the intersubjective creation of fieldworker and informant together, so too are the facts that anthropologists collect. The **facts** of anthropology are not ready-made, only waiting for someone to come along and pick them up. The facts of anthropology are created and recreated (1) in the field; (2) when the fieldworker, back home, reexamines field notes and is transported back into the field experience; and (3) when the fieldworker discusses his or her experiences with other anthropologists.

Facts do not speak for themselves. They speak only when they are interpreted and placed in a context of meaning that makes them intelligible. What constitutes a cultural fact is ambiguous. Anthropologists and informants can disagree; anthropologists can disagree

among themselves; informants can disagree among themselves. The facts of anthropology exist neither in the culture of the anthropologist nor in the culture of the informant. "Anthropological facts are cross-cultural, because they are made across cultural boundaries" (Rabinow 1977, 152).

ANTHROPOLOGICAL KNOWLEDGE AS OPEN-ENDED

We have suggested that there is no such thing as purely objective knowledge and that when human beings are both the subject and object of study, we must speak in terms of reflexivity rather than objectivity. Cultivating reflexivity allows us to produce less-distorted views of human nature and the human condition, and yet we remain human beings interpreting the lives of other human beings. We can never escape from our humanity to some point of view that would allow us to see human existence and human experience from the outside. Instead, we must rely on our common humanity and our interpretive powers to show us the parts of our nature that can be made visible.

If there truly is "no primitive," no subsection of humanity that is radically different in nature or in capacity from the anthropologists who study it, then the ethnographic record of anthropological knowledge is perhaps best understood as a vast commentary on human possibility. As with all commentaries, it depends on an original text—in this case, human experience. But that experience is ambiguous, speaking with many voices, capable of supporting more than one interpretation. Growth of anthropological knowledge is no different, then, from the growth of human self-understanding in general. It ought to contribute to the domain of human wisdom that concerns who we are as a species, where we have come from, and where we may be going.

Like all commentaries, the ethnographic record is and must be unfinished: Human beings are open systems; human history continues; and problems and their possible solutions change. There is no one, true version of human life. For anthropologists, the true version of human life consists of all versions of human life.

This is a sobering possibility. It makes it appear that "the anthropologist is condemned to a greater or lesser

IN THEIR OWN WORDS

The Skills of the Anthropologist

Anthropologists cannot avoid taking their own cultural and theoretical frameworks into the field. However, as Stephen Gudeman observes, fieldwork draws their attention in unanticipated directions, making them aware of new phenomena that constantly challenge those frameworks.

According to the accepted wisdom, poets should be especially facile with language and stretch our vision with freshly cut images. Historians, with their knowledge of past events, offer a wise and sweeping view of human change and continuities. Physical scientists, who have analytical yet creative minds, bring us discoveries and insights about the natural world.

What about anthropologists? Have we any finely honed talents and gifts for the world?

Because anthropology is the study of human life, the anthropologist needs to know a little something about everything—from psychology to legal history to ecology. Our field equipment is primitive, for we rely mainly on the eye, the ear, and the tongue. Because ethnographers carry few tools to the field and the tools they have can hardly capture the totality of the situation, the background and talents of the researcher strongly determine what is "seen" and how it is understood. But the field experience itself has a special impact, too. I studied economic practices in Panama because I was trained to do so, but the field research forced me to alter all the notions I had been taught. Most of them were useless! Anthropologists try to open themselves up to every facet of their field situation and to allow its richness to envelop them. In this, the tasks of the anthropologist are very unlike

those of the normal laboratory scientist: the anthropologist can have no predefined hypothesis and testing procedures. The best equipment an ethnographer can possess is a "good ear" and patience to let the "data talk."

This is not all. In the field, anthropologists carry out intense and internal conversations with themselves. Every observation, whether clearly seen or dimly realized, must be brought to consciousness, shuffled about, and questioned. Only by recognizing and acknowledging their own incomprehension can anthropologists generate new questions and lines of inquiry. In the solitude of the field, the anthropologist must try to understand the limits of her or his knowledge, have the courage to live with uncertainty, and retain the ambition to seize on openings to insight.

But field studies constitute only a part of the total research process. Once home, the field notes have to be read and reread, put aside, and then rearranged. The anthropologist is a pattern seeker, believing that within the data human designs are to be found. The task is like solving a puzzle, except that there is no fixed solution and the puzzle's pieces keep changing their shapes! With work and insight, however, a picture—an understanding or an explanation—begins to emerge.

Eventually, the results of all these efforts are conveyed to others, and so anthropologists also need to have expository skills and persuasive powers, for they have to convince others of their picture and their viewpoint about how cultures and social lives are put together.

Source: Gudeman 1990, 458–59.

---

degree of failure" in even trying to understand another culture (Basham 1978, 299). Informants would equally be condemned to never know fully even their own way of life. And the scientific attitude cultivated in the Western world resists any admission that the understanding of anything is impossible. But total pessimism does not seem warranted. We may never know everything, but it does not follow that our efforts can teach us nothing. "Two of the fundamental qualities of humanity are the capacity to understand one another and the capacity to be understood. Not fully certainly. Yet not negligibly, certainly. . . . There is no person on

earth that I can fully understand. There is and has been no person on earth that I cannot understand at all" (W. Smith 1982, 68–69).

Moreover, as our contact with the other is prolonged and as our efforts to communicate are rewarded by the construction of intersubjective understanding,

---

facts In anthropology, facts are created and recreated (1) in the field; (2) when the fieldworker, back home, reexamines field notes and is transported back into the field experience; and (3) when the fieldworker discusses his or her experiences with other anthropologists.

we can always learn more. Human beings are open organisms, and we have a vast ability to learn new things. This is significant, for even if we can never know everything, it does not seem that our capacities for understanding ourselves and others is likely to be exhausted soon. This is not only because we are open to change, but also because our culture and our wider environment can change, and all will continue to do so as long as human history continues. The ethnographic enterprise will never be finished, even if all nonindustrial ways of life disappeared forever, all people moved into cities, and everyone ended up speaking English. Such a superficial homogeneity would mask a vast heterogeneity beneath its bland surface. In any case, given the dynamics of human existence, nothing in human affairs can remain homogeneous for long.

Key Terms

fieldwork
participant-observation
positivism
objective knowledge
informants
intersubjective meanings

reflexivity
interpretation
translation
culture shock
facts

Chapter Summary

1. Anthropological fieldwork traditionally involves extended periods of close contact with members of another society. This form of research is called *participant-observation*.
2. The nineteenth century saw the birth of positivistic science in Western thought. Positivism is based on the assumption that reality can be known through the five senses. Positivists believe that a single scientific method can be used to investigate any domain of reality, and they expect that all scientific knowledge will eventually be unified. They argue that facts have nothing to do with values. Positivists' aim is to produce knowledge about reality that is true for all people in all times and places.
3. Early anthropologists who wanted to be scientific attempted to adapt positivism to their needs. They adopted a view of controlled laboratory research as the prototype of scientific investigation and attempted to apply the prototype to the field situation. In this way, highly accurate data were systematically collected in many parts of the world.
4. Anthropologists with a positivistic outlook have been charged with insensitivity to the humanity of their research subjects. The positivist program in anthropology attempts, metaphorically, to turn human beings into objects, similar to the rocks and molecules that physical scientists study. This attempt has dehumanized both the informants (who are reduced to objects) and the fieldworkers (who are reduced to intelligent recording machines).
5. When human beings study other human beings, research is inevitably colored by the context and cultural presuppositions of both the anthropologists and the people they study. If the objects of anthropology are human beings, scientific accuracy requires that we relate to them as human beings.
6. The positivist concern with objectivity should be replaced with a concern for reflexivity: Anthropologists must think about the way they think about other cultures. Successful fieldwork involves informants who also must think about the way they and others in their society think and try to convey their insights to the anthropologist.
7. The dialectic of fieldwork is a reflexive interchange between anthropologist and informant. It is a collaborative undertaking involving dialogue about the meaning of experience in the informant's culture. The outcome of this dialogue is an intersubjective understanding (an understanding between two subjects, anthropologist and informant) of the informant's culture.
8. Fieldwork is human experience. Knowledge of informants and their culture is gained in the same way that human beings gain knowledge about other human beings in any circumstances, even in their own cultures. Meaning must always be negotiated. There is no such thing as a final set of meanings or a final interpretation that cannot be renegotiated at some future date.
9. Fieldworkers must face the shock of the unfa-

miliar and their own vulnerability. As a result, fieldwork can be a profoundly alienating experience. The only remedy for this alienation is to construct, with the aid of one's informants, an intersubjective world of meaning.

10. Learning about another culture is often greatest following a rupture of communication between anthropologist and informant. Ruptures occur when current intersubjective understandings prove themselves inadequate to account for experience. A rupture always carries the possibility of bringing research to an end. But when the reasons for the rupture are explored and explanations for it are constructed, great insights are possible.

11. Fieldwork has the potential to change both fieldworkers and informants by expanding their experience of human possibility. This growth in self-awareness is not always comfortable. Nevertheless, the deepening of insight that it makes possible—the opportunity to experience the humanity of one's informants (or one's interviewer!)—can be immensely satisfying.

12. Because cultural meanings are intersubjectively constructed during fieldwork, cultural facts do not speak for themselves. The facts of anthropology are made and remade every time they are subjected to a fresh analysis and interpretation.

13. The ethnographic record of anthropological

knowledge is perhaps best understood as a vast commentary on human possibility. Like all commentaries, it is—and must be—unfinished. We may never learn all there is to know, but we can always learn more.

Suggested Readings

Briggs, Jean. 1970. *Never in anger: Portrait of an Eskimo family.* Cambridge, MA: Harvard University Press. *A moving, insightful study of fieldwork and of an Utku family.*

Kumar, Nita. 1992. *Friends, brothers, and informants: Fieldwork memories of Banaras.* Berkeley: University of California Press. *A moving and thought-provoking reflection on the experience of fieldwork in the author's own country but in a culture quite different from her own.*

Lévi-Strauss, Claude. 1974. *Tristes Tropiques.* New York: Pocket Books. *Originally published in French in 1955, this book (with an untranslatable title) is considered by some to be the greatest book ever written by an anthropologist (although not necessarily a great anthropology book). This is a multifaceted work about voyaging, fieldwork, self-knowledge, philosophy, and much more. It is a challenging read in some places but highly rewarding overall.*

Rabinow, Paul. 1977. *Reflection on fieldwork in Morocco.* Berkeley: University of California Press. *An important, brief, powerfully written reflection on the nature of fieldwork. Very accessible and highly recommended.*

Valentine, Bettylou. 1978. *Hustling and other hard work.* New York: Free Press. *An innovative, provocative study of African American inner-city life. Reads like a good novel.*

4

History, Anthropology, and the Explanation of Cultural Diversity

he five-element theory, which dates to the third century B.C.E., was one of the bases of all Chinese scientific thought. The five elements that make up the world were said to be water, fire, wood, metal, and earth. These elements were understood not as substances but as processes, differentiated by the kinds of changes they underwent. Water was associated with soaking, dripping, and descending. Fire was allied with heating, burning, and ascending. Wood was connected with that which accepted form by submitting to cutting and carving instruments. Metal was affiliated with that which accepted form by molding when in the liquid state and had the capacity to change form by remelting and remolding. Earth was associated with the production of edible vegetation.

In Han times (about 200 B.C.E. to 200 C.E.), the theory achieved a final form, which has been passed down through the ages. According to Colin Ronan and Joseph Needham in their *Shorter Science and Civilisation in China,* one aspect of the theory, the mutual conquest order,

> described the series in which each element was supposed to conquer its predecessor. It was based on a logical sequence of ideas that had their basis in everyday scientific facts: for instance that Wood conquers Earth because, presumably, when in the form of a spade, it can dig up earth. Again, Metal conquers Wood since it can cut and carve it; Fire conquers Metal for it can melt or even vaporise it; Water conquers Fire because it can extinguish it; and, finally, Earth conquers Water because it can dam it and contain it—a very natural metaphor for people to whom irrigation and hydraulic engineering were so important. This order was also considered significant from the political point of view; it was put forward as an explanation for the course of history, with the implication that it would continue to apply in the future and was, therefore, useful for prediction. . . . The Five Elements gradually came to be associated with every conceivable category of things in the universe that it was possible to classify in fives (1978, 142ff.).

This included the seasons, the points of the compass, tastes, smells, numbers, kinds of musical notes, heavenly bodies, planets, weather, colors, body parts, sense organs, affective states, and human psychological functions. It also included the periods of dynastic history, the ministries of government, and styles of government, which included relaxed, enlightened, careful, en-

ergetic, and quiet, corresponding respectively to wood, fire, earth, metal, and water.

"As we might imagine," Ronan and Needham conclude, "these correlations met with criticism, sometimes severe, because they led to many absurdities. . . . Yet in spite of such criticisms, it seems that in the beginning these correlations were helpful to scientific thought in China. They were certainly no worse than the Greek theory of the elements that dominated European medieval thinking, and it was only when they became overelaborate and fanciful, too far removed from the observation of Nature, that they were positively harmful" (1978, 156–57).

These observations are relevant to any apt metaphor or good scientific theory. They apply to anthropology as well. Like the Chinese sages, anthropologists' first step was to sort human cultures into different categories based on their similarities and differences. Over time, the purposes and the categories have been modified in ways that reflect changes in the wider world and changing research interests among anthropologists. This chapter considers some of the influential classifications, placing them in the context of the historical development of anthropology as a discipline.

HUMAN IMAGINATION AND THE MATERIAL WORLD

We argued in Chapter 2 that culture is an aspect of human nature that is as much a source of freedom as it is a requirement for our survival. Human imagination can suggest which aspects of the material world to pay attention to, and these suggestions can become part of a cultural tradition. At the same time, once a group commits itself to paying attention to some parts of the material world, it locks itself into a set of relationships that it may not be able to abandon freely. These relationships can and do exert a determinant pressure on future choices. This is the paradox of the human condition.

What parts of the material world do human beings pay attention to, and what parts do they ignore? To answer this question, we can begin by considering how the need to make a living in different natural environments has led to the development of a range of different forms of human social organization. At the same

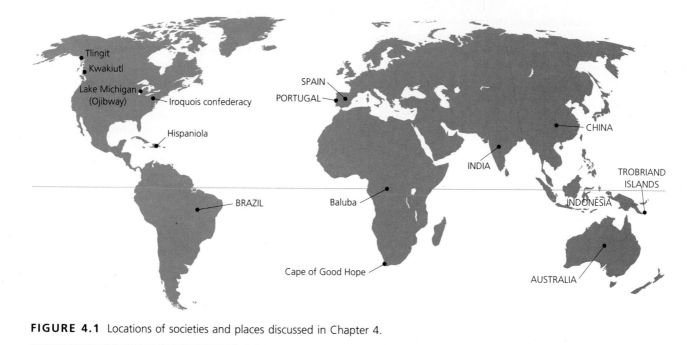

FIGURE 4.1 Locations of societies and places discussed in Chapter 4.

time, because people can make a living in different ways in the same environment, or in much the same way in different environments, we must also pay attention to those cultural and social factors that cannot be predicted on the basis of natural environment alone. Some of these factors arise out of the internal traditions of the group itself; others depend on external and unpredictable historical encounters with other human groups. By looking at both sets of factors, we will understand better why anthropologists classify forms of human society as they do and what these classifications suggest about the forces shaping human society and human history.

CROSS-CULTURAL CONTACTS BETWEEN THE WEST AND THE REST OF THE WORLD

The wider social environment cannot be forgotten when we consider the history of contact by anthropologists with cultures in the non-Western world. If we look carefully, we see that the arrival of anthropologists was only the most recent phase of centuries-long contact by Western cultures with other cultures. This contact dates from the so-called *Age of Exploration*, when Western explorers such as Christopher Columbus ventured beyond the boundaries of the world known to Europe and first encountered the inhabitants of America and parts of Africa and Asia (Figure 4.2).

These early explorers, and the traders and settlers who followed them, were not motivated to travel such distances and take great risks merely for exotic experience. They were in the pay of European monarchs or companies whose interest in new worlds was political and economic. Nearly every contact made between the West and the outside world sooner or later turned into conquest, leading to the establishment of far-flung colonial empires centered in Europe. Thus, contact between western Europe and the rest of the world neither began nor continued in neutral terms.

By the time anthropologists appeared on the scene in the late nineteenth century, contact between their world and the world of the peoples whose lives they wanted to study had long since been established. The anthropologists and the societies from which they came were in a superior economic and political position.

FIGURE 4.2 In the late fifteenth and sixteenth centuries, Western explorers such as Columbus ventured beyond the boundaries of the world known to Europe. This sixteenth-century engraving depicts Columbus meeting the inhabitants of Hispaniola, the first territory colonized by Spain in the New World.

They were not, for the most part, paying visits to independent, autonomous, thriving cultures. They came as representatives of a conquering society to observe remnants of a population that had been conquered.

Members of the conquered societies did recall and describe their past. Most had rallied in the aftermath of conquest to reconstitute their cultures under changed circumstances. Such is the strength and resilience of human beings in adversity. But we would be naive to believe, as many early anthropologists and other observers did, that these societies and cultures were "living fossils," intact representatives of ancient ways of life as yet untouched by history. Anthropologist Eric Wolf (1982) discusses this tendency of Western observers to

assume that people in the non-Western world are "people without history." Many of the "tribes" or "peoples" whom anthropologists later would study are relatively recent creations, forged in the contact between indigenous populations and Europeans. Before Europeans arrived in North America and Africa, the North American Ojibway or the African Baluba, for example, had no separate identity and did not exist as autonomous societies. They were a product of the historical contact— and clash—between aggressive Europeans and local populations. In response to the European presence, these populations had to regroup and reshape their cultures.

Our survey of the forms of human society will therefore also involve an ethnography of ethnography. That is, anthropologists now pay a lot of attention to the social, cultural, and political circumstances that shape their relationships with informants. Anthropologists realize that no societies have ever been totally isolated in time and space, unaffected by the world around them, and cut off from history. They are increasingly aware, moreover, that attempts by Europeans to define their own uniqueness led them to exaggerate the cultural and historical gulf that separated them from everyone else (Herzfeld 1987, Savigliano 1995).

THE EFFECTS OF WESTERN EXPANSION

To understand these changes among non-Western peoples, we must look at European history, too. Beginning in the fifteenth century, various European rulers attempted to gain independent access to sources of wealth outside their own territories. The earliest explorations were undertaken by Portugal. Castile and Aragon, the two kingdoms that formed the core of what later would be called Spain, followed soon thereafter. At the time, these kingdoms on the Iberian peninsula were among the weakest and poorest territories in Europe.

Until the end of the fifteenth century, most Iberian Christian leaders were engaged in protracted warfare, both among themselves and against the Muslim overlords who had controlled Iberia for the previous 800 years. Portugal freed itself from Muslim control in 1249, and by the late 1300s tried to expand. Checked to the north and east by continuing conflicts between their neighbors, the Portuguese moved south. Their aim was to discover an ocean passage to the mythical Christian kingdom of Prester John, which was placed in various locations in Africa and Asia. If the Portuguese found this kingdom, they might have direct access to the gold and other riches coming into Europe from Asia and Africa under the control of Muslim traders. Portuguese explorers never did find Prester John. During the fifteenth century, however, they "discovered" the southern Atlantic coast of Africa. Establishing trading posts as they went, explorers rounded the Cape of Good Hope at Africa's southern tip in 1488.

In the last half of the fifteenth century, Castile and Aragon, united by the marriage of their rulers Isabella and Ferdinand, were actively involved in the "reconquest" of the remaining Muslim-ruled areas of Iberia. As victory neared, they too began to support voyages of exploration. One, that of Columbus, led to the European discovery of the New World. This occurred in 1492, the same year that the Muslims were decisively expelled from Spain. By this time, the Portuguese had already explored the eastern coast of Africa and were about to establish direct trade with India. Competition between Spain and Portugal led to the Treaty of Tordesillas, in 1494, in which the pope divided the non-Christian world between them. The dividing line was intended to leave the Western Hemisphere to the Spanish and the Eastern Hemisphere to the Portuguese. Later exploration revealed that part of the coast of what is now Brazil fell on the Portuguese side of the line, giving Portugal a foothold in the New World too.

Iberians were the first Europeans in the New World, but they were soon challenged by Holland, England, and France. Holland and England were at the forefront of the mercantile development that fueled the growth and expansion of capitalism. Although the Portuguese were the first to sail around Africa to India, they were soon ousted by the Dutch, who had better fleets and stronger commerce. The Dutch also established colonies in North America and vied with the Portuguese and other Europeans for control of the Brazilian coast. However, the Dutch eventually withdrew from North America in favor of the English, devoting themselves to their holdings in what is now Indonesia. The English also assumed control of trade with India. The French—not to be left behind—moved into North America and India as well, competing intensely with the English for access to territory and to trade goods.

Expansion in Africa and the Americas

In western Africa, first the Portuguese and later the Dutch, British, and French found themselves confined for more than 400 years to trading posts built on the coast or on offshore islands. During this period, local peoples living along the coast procured the goods sought by their European trading partners. This long-lasting arrangement shows that western African societies were resilient enough to adapt to the European presence and strong enough to keep Europeans and their commercial interests at arm's length for several centuries. The European presence also reshaped coastal western African societies, stimulating the growth of hierarchical social forms in some areas where there had been none before. These changes had repercussions farther inland, as the new coastal kingdoms sought trade goods from the people of the African hinterland. Only in the second half of the nineteenth century did this relationship between Europe and western Africans change.

The situation in southern Africa was different. The Dutch community on the Cape of Good Hope was founded to service Dutch ships on the route to India, but soon attracted settlers who had moved inland by the late seventeenth century. Their arrival led to the subjugation and destruction of indigenous peoples, both by warfare and by disease. In western Africa, the situation was often just the reverse; Europeans succumbed to tropical maladies such as malaria to which coastal African populations had greater resistance.

In America, the complex civilizations of Mexico and Peru had been conquered within thirty years of the arrival of Columbus. Indigenous American populations, like those of southern Africa, were laid waste more by European-borne diseases such as measles and smallpox than by armed conflict. They suffered further dislocation after Spanish colonial administration was established. Spain was determined to keep control of the colonies in its own hands, and it checked the attempts of colonists to set themselves up as feudal lords commanding local indigenous groups as their peasants. These efforts, however, were far from successful. Conquered indigenous people were put to work in mines and on plantations. Hard labor further reduced their numbers and fractured their traditional forms of social organization. By the time the worst of these abuses were finally curtailed, in the early seventeenth century, indigenous life in New Spain had been drastically reshaped. Indeed, in the areas of greatest Spanish penetration and control, indigenous groups were reduced to but one component in the complex hierarchy of colonial society.

The Fur Trade in North America

The fur trade had important consequences for indigenous society in North America. When the Dutch first began to trade with indigenous Americans for furs, they already had trading links to Russia, where fur collecting and fur processing had been established for centuries (Wolf 1982, 158ff.). The fur trade was thus an international phenomenon, and the strong stimulus that indigenous American populations felt to seek fur was shaped by the demand of the fur-processing industry in eastern Europe. The most eagerly sought fur was beaver, used to make felt for cloth and especially hats. Indigenous American populations found their fortunes waxing as long as beaver flourished in their lands; once the beaver were gone, however, their fortunes waned, often suddenly, as their European trading partners moved on.

Involvement in the fur trade significantly modified the traditional ways that indigenous North American groups made a living. While the beaver supply lasted, they could obtain many of the material items they needed by exchanging pelts for them at the trading post. This gave them a strong incentive to neglect or even abandon the activities that previously had supplied those items and to devote themselves to fur trapping. Once the beaver were gone, however, people discovered that their highly successful new adaptation had become obsolete. They also discovered that a return to the old ways was impossible, either because those ways had been forgotten or because the new circumstances of life made them impossible to carry out. The result often was severe social dislocation.

Regrouping and Reworking Traditions

Indigenous North American societies were not all alike, and they experienced the European challenge in different ways. In all cases, however, they responded actively, struggling to rework their traditional understandings and practices to minimize the negative impact of European pressures.

The Iroquois confederacy was the outcome of one such struggle. Wolf argues that the indigenous members of the confederacy tried to create a form of society that could effectively counter the power of the European trading companies with which they dealt. In forming the confederacy, however, the groups did not simply borrow the social organization of the European traders. Rather, they drew on traditional kinship forms and reworked these into new and broader-reaching structures that, for a time at least, kept the Europeans at bay. The Iroquois confederacy was not an unchanging, timeless structure, predating the coming of Europeans to America. Quite the contrary; like the coastal trading kingdoms in Africa, it was new. Both were responses to the opportunities and challenges initiated by European contact.

As the fur trade moved westward, competition between France and England for fur increased. This, in turn, led to rivalries in which some indigenous groups, such as the Huron, were wiped out. Other groups actively reworked tradition to create new groups such as the Ojibway and Salteaux, and new ritual forms like the Midewiwin, which grew up among the Ojibway and their neighbors toward the end of the seventeenth century. The Midewiwin replaced older status ranking within local kinship groups with a new hierarchical association in which individuals were ranked in terms of wealth acquired in war or trade. The Midewiwin accepted the existence of European traders and missionaries, and its leaders were empowered to represent the members in dealings with them. The Midewiwin illustrates a creative response on the part of some indigenous North Americans to cope with a new and potentially threatening social experience.

The Slave and Commodities Trades

The fur trade was followed by the slave trade and the trade in commodities such as sugar and cotton, both of which accompanied the rise of capitalist industry. These ventures continued to reshape social life throughout the world even as they drew parts of that world ever closer together into an interdependent economic network shaped by the growing power and influence of capitalist markets centered in Europe.

The slave trade dominated commerce between Europeans and coastal Africans by the eighteenth century. The nature of the merchandise sought for this trade—people—had a devastating effect on the societies of the African hinterland whose members were captured and sold to meet European demand. The survivors actively sought refuge beyond the slavers' reach, regrouping themselves into new societies with new names and re-working their collective traditions into new forms. The slave trade did not alter social relations in Africa alone. The presence of slaves in the New World profoundly reshaped the lives of both local indigenous peoples and European colonists. The growth of plantation econo-mies in areas that had been used by hunters or gath-erers or small-scale farmers altered the local ecology as well as local society. And the wealth produced in these economies transformed both the local gentry and the European nations who claimed sovereignty over them. As a result, Africa, America, and Europe became inex-tricably intertwined in one another's fate.

TOWARD CLASSIFYING FORMS OF HUMAN SOCIETY

We can draw three general conclusions at this point. First, there are on this planet a variety of human soci-eties whose natures were radically affected by their "discovery" by Europeans. Thus, although life in the non-Western world today is undoubtedly culturally patterned, this patterning does not necessarily repre-sent a timeless, unchanged way of life, unaffected by history or the presence of others. Extant non-Western societies have not escaped the historical forces that have shaped everyone else.

Second, evidence of precontact cultural patterns can be discerned in the practices of surviving societies, but the task is a difficult one. Many groups shaped new identities and devised new social forms to deal with the effects of contact and conquest. In some cases, these new social forms drew on very ancient traditions, re-worked to meet the demands of new experiences. In other cases, a contemporary ethnographer can glimpse ways of life that were invented long ago and continue to prove their worth by being reproduced today. Some-times, modes of living that have endured successfully for centuries are at last falling before the advance of Western technology and the rigors of market capital-ism (see, for example, Lee 1992). Far from being static survivors of a timeless past, however, the members of these societies are people coping actively with con-temporary problems and opportunities, people whose history is also our history (Figure 4.3).

Finally, in spite of everything, human society re-tains an impressive variety of forms. Anthropologists

FIGURE 4.3 Far from being static survivors of a timeless past, Australian Aboriginal people—such as this dancer at a Gulf War peace rally in Sydney in January 1991—are very much involved with contemporary issues.

have been able to document this variety by recording the memories of old people and through fieldwork. Many similarities that people seem increasingly to show throughout the world turn out to be far less im-portant than the continuing differences in worldview and social organization that lie below the surface.

Making sense of the variety of forms of human so-ciety across space and over time is an ongoing task for anthropologists. One way they do this is by devising a **typology** to identify those societies that are most dis-tinct from one another based on certain criteria and then to sort known societies by their resemblance to these exemplars. This effort has much in common with the procedures used by paleoanthropologists sorting fossils. As in paleontology, such procedures are useful not only when they seem successful but also when they fail. The sections that follow examine some common typologies. They point out both the commonalities those classifications help us to see and the differences they help to obscure.

IN THEIR OWN WORDS

The Ecologically Noble Savage?

Part of the stereotype of the "primitive," as Paul Rabinow pointed out, includes the belief that "primitives" live in total harmony with their environment. Kent Redford explores how this stereotype has been recycled in recent years into the image of an idealized "ecologically noble savage."

To live and die with the land is to know its rules. When there is no hospital at the other end of the telephone and no grocery store at the end of the street, when there is no biweekly paycheck nor microwave oven, when there is nothing to fall back on but nature itself, then a society must discover the secrets of the plants and animals. Thus indigenous peoples possess extensive and intensive knowledge of the natural world. In every place where humans have existed, people have received this knowledge from their elders and taught it to their children, along with what has been newly acquired. . . . Writings of several scientists and indigenous rights advocates echo the early chroniclers' assumption that indigenous people lived in "balance" with their environment. Prominent conservationists have stated that in the past, indigenous people "lived in close harmony with their local environment." The rhetoric of Indian spokespersons is even stronger: "In the world of today there are two systems, two different irreconcilable 'ways of life.' The Indian world—collective, communal, human, respectful of nature, and wise—and the western world—greedy, destructive, individualist, and enemy of nature" (from a report to the International NGO Conference on Indigenous Peoples and the Land, 1981). The idealized figure of centuries past had been reborn, as the *ecologically noble savage.*

The recently accumulated evidence, however, refutes this concept of ecological nobility. Precontact Indians were not "ecosystem men"; they were not just another species of animal, largely incapable of altering the environment, who therefore lived within the "ecological limitations of their home area." Paleobiologists, archaeologists, and botanists are coming to believe that most tropical forests have been severely altered by human activities before European contact. Evidence of vast fires in the northern Amazonian forests and of the apparently anthropogenic origins of large areas of forest in eastern Amazonia suggests that before 1500, humans had tremendously affected the virgin forest, with ensuing impacts on plant and animal species. These people behaved as humans do now: they did whatever they had to to feed themselves and their families.

"Whatever they had to" is the key phrase in understanding the problem of the noble savage myth in its contemporary version. Countless examples make it clear that indigenous people can be either forced, seduced, or tempted into accepting new methods, new crops, and new technologies. No better example exists than the near-universal adoption of firearms for hunting by Indians in the Neotropics. Shotguns or rifles often combined with the use of flashlights and outboard motors, change completely the interaction between human hunters and their prey.

There is no cultural barrier to the Indians' adoption of means to "improve" their lives (i.e., make them more like Western lives), even if the long-term sustainability of the resource base is threatened. These means can include the sale of timber and mining rights to indigenous lands, commercial exploitation of flora and fauna, and invitations to tourists to observe "traditional lifestyles." Indians should not be blamed for engaging in these activities. They can hardly be faulted for failing to live up to Western expectations of the noble savage. They have the same capacities, desires, and perhaps, needs to overexploit their environment as did our European ancestors. Why shouldn't Indians have the same right to dispose of the timber on their land as the international timber companies have to sell theirs? An indigenous group responded to the siren call of the market economy in just this spirit in Brazil in 1989, when Guajajara Indians took prisoners in order to force the government Indian agency, FUNAI, to grant them permission to sell lumber from their lands.

Source: Redford 1993, 11–13.

Evolutionary Typologies: The Nineteenth Century

A system of classification reflects the features that its creator believes to be most significant. As a result, different assessments of what is significant can lead to different classifications. In the early years of anthropology, most Westerners who compared non-Western societies with their own were struck by certain features that set apart Europeans from the various peoples they

typology A classification system based on, in this case, forms of human society.

conquered. Westerners identified these differences between themselves and others as *deficiencies:* lack of a state, lack of sophisticated technology, lack of organized religion, and so forth. Perhaps without realizing it, observers took Western industrial capitalist society as the universal standard against which to measure all other human societies. Having done this, they often assumed that the alleged defects of non-Western societies were too obvious to require comment.

This approach to cultural differences was persuasive to nineteenth-century Westerners. It spoke directly to the cross-cultural experience that Western nations were having with the non-Western peoples they had colonized or with whom they traded. A colonial ruler eager to establish a smoothly working administration in New Spain or the operator of a trading post anxious to maximize profits in the fur trade would be most aware of the facets of a people's life that kept him from reaching his goals. How do you successfully collect taxes in a colony that has poor roads, lacks government officials who can read and write, and is populated by subjects who do not speak your language? How do you "pay" for beaver pelts when the "sellers" are not interested in money? Europeans faced with such practical problems were bound to see life outside Europe in terms of a series of deficiencies compared with what they could count on in the home country.

Observers of a more philosophical nature, too, were bound to wonder why there should be such deficiencies in societies outside western Europe (or in the more provincial areas of Europe outside the capital cities). Although their research usually never took them outside their libraries, they studied the reports of travelers and missionaries as well as history. They learned that many of the social and technological patterns they took for granted had not always existed, even in Europe. They became aware of the "advances" that had occurred and were continuing in all areas of European social life since the Middle Ages. It seemed clear that their ancestors too had once lacked the tools and ideas and social forms that made them powerful today. If they went back far enough, perhaps they would discover that their more distant ancestors had lived much as many peoples of America or Africa were living at that time. Indeed, ancient writers such as Julius Caesar had painted a picture of indigenous life in early Europe that resembled the contemporary customs of indigsenous Americans and Africans. As archaeology developed, particularly in

the nineteenth century, researchers could supplement written records with ancient artifacts presumably made by the primitive ancestors of modern Europeans.

UNILINEAL CULTURAL EVOLUTIONISM   For many nineteenth-century thinkers, the experience of social change, together with historical and archaeological evidence of past social change, was suggestive. Perhaps the ways of life of the non-Western peoples they were reading about were similar to, and even repeats of, the ways of life of European generations long past. That is, perhaps the West had already moved through periods of history in which ways of life had been the same as those of contemporary non-Western societies. According to these scholars, if non-Western societies were left to themselves and given enough time, they would make the same discoveries and change socially the same way that western Europe had.

This way of thinking about social and cultural change has been called **unilineal cultural evolutionism.** It reached its most elaborate development in the nineteenth century, when evolutionary ideas were popular in all areas of Western thought. Unilineal cultural evolutionism was one way to explain the widespread cultural diversity that Europeans had been finding since the Age of Exploration. It proposed to account for this diversity by arguing that different kinds of society represented different stages of societal evolution through which every human society either had passed or would pass, if it survived. Unilineal cultural evolutionists viewed their own late-nineteenth-century European capitalist industrial society as the most advanced stage of cultural evolution yet. Living societies that had not already reached this level were seen as relics of more primitive stages that the West had already left behind.

Today, anthropologists find this approach to the classification of forms of human society to be inadequate—if not totally misleading. Nevertheless, it is a powerful scheme, and its continuing popularity among ordinary members of Western societies is not difficult to understand: It offers a coherent framework for classifying all societies.

Unilineal cultural evolutionism gave scholars the tools to organize different types of living societies into a sequence based on the discoveries of history and archaeology. For example, contemporary groups who made a living by gathering, hunting, and fishing were assumed to represent the way of life that had once existed universally, before farming and herding were invented. By the nineteenth century, however, it was clear that agriculture and animal husbandry had been invented only a few thousand years ago, whereas human beings had been around far longer than that. Researchers concluded that contemporary foragers had somehow gotten stuck in the earliest stage of human cultural development, while other societies had managed to move upward by domesticating plants and animals. Many of the non-Western groups with which nineteenth-century Europeans and Americans were familiar did farm or herd for a living, however. Their societies were usually larger than those of the foragers and technologically more complex. Farmers usually also built permanent structures and made pottery and woven cloth, goods that were unknown among foragers. Their social patterns too were often more elaborate. These peoples clearly seemed to be a rung above the foragers. But they were also very different from Europeans. Most did not have writing, and their societies were not organized in anything resembling a European nation-state. For such reasons, this group of societies, midway between the foragers and modern Europeans, were given their own category. They seemed to typify the stage through which gatherers and hunters had to pass—through which Europe's ancestral populations had already passed—before attaining modern civilization.

In this manner, the first important anthropological typology of human social forms emerged. It had three basic categories, corresponding to the preceding distinctions. But the labels given these categories indicated more than objective differences; they also carried moral implications. The foragers—peoples who neither farmed nor herded—were called *savages*. Groups that had domesticated plants and animals but had not yet invented writing or the state were called *barbarians*. *Civilization* was limited to the early states of the Mediterranean basin and southwestern Asia (such as Mesopotamia and Egypt), their successors (such as Greece and Rome), and certain non-Western societies boasting a similar level of achievement (such as India and China). However, the advances that Europe had experienced since antiquity were seen to be unique, unmatched by social changes in other civilizations, which were understood to be declining. That decline seemed proven when representatives of Western civilization found they could conquer the rulers of such civiliza-

tions, as the English had done in India.

Unilineal cultural evolutionism was sweeping and powerful. An early American anthropologist, Lewis Henry Morgan, devoted himself to organizing the sequence and assigning known societies to various categories. His modifications had great and far-reaching implications.

MORGAN'S ETHNICAL PERIODS In his book *Ancient Society*, published in 1877, Morgan summarized the basic orientation of unilineal evolutionism: "The latest investigations respecting the early condition of the human race are tending to the conclusion that mankind commenced their career at the bottom of the scale and worked their way up from savagery to civilization through the slow accumulations of experimental knowledge" ([1877] 1963, 3). Morgan described this evolutionary career in terms of a series of stages, or *ethnical periods*, "connected with each other in a natural as well as necessary sequence of progress" (3). The major categories in this sequence were savagery, barbarism, and civilization. But Morgan felt the need to distinguish additional levels within savagery and barbarism in order better to classify the variety of social forms known in his day. He was fully aware that some human groups might not easily fit into these categories. Hoping that future research would help resolve such ambiguities, however, he concluded that for his purposes "it will be sufficient if the principal tribes of mankind can be classified, according to the degree of their relative progress, into conditions which can be recognized as distinct" (9).

Table 4.1 shows the sequence of ethnical periods suggested by Morgan. Note that, almost without exception, the criteria used to separate one period from another have to do with changes in the "arts of subsistence"—that is, in techniques for getting food. In some cases, however, the transformation from one stage to the next is not clearly marked by changes in the food-getting techniques. Morgan sought other criteria in these cases, such as the invention of pottery or writing, to mark the transition. Later scholars criticized him for these inconsistencies, but he himself was aware of the difficulty. For example, in discussing his choice of the invention of pottery to divide savagery from

---

unilineal cultural evolutionism A nineteenth-century theory that proposed a series of stages through which all societies must go (or had gone) in order to reach civilization.

TABLE 4.1   MORGAN'S ETHNICAL PERIODS

Period	Begins with
Savagery	
Lower	Origins of human race
Middle	Fishing, knowledge of use of fire
Upper	Invention of bow and arrow
Barbarism	
Lower	Invention of pottery
Middle	Domestication of animals and plants, invention of irrigation, use of adobe brick and stone
Upper	Smelting of iron ore, use of iron tools
Civilization	Invention of phonetic alphabet, use of writing

barbarism, Morgan wrote: "The invention or practice of the art of pottery, all things considered, is probably the most effective and conclusive test that can be selected to fix a boundary line, necessarily arbitrary, between savagery and barbarism. The distinctness of the two conditions has long been recognized, but no criterion of progress out of the former into the latter has hitherto been brought forward. All such tribes, then, as never attained to the art of pottery will be classed as savages, and those possessing this art but who never attained a phonetic alphabet and the use of writing will be classed as barbarians" ([1877] 1963, 10).

Morgan could find no consistent, unambiguous cultural feature to indicate progress from one stage to another, but he continued to believe that classifying forms of human society by evolutionary stage was a valid undertaking. From his perspective, the unilineal scheme made such good sense of cultural variation that exceptions or inconsistencies could only be due to inadequate data. Surely better research in the future would eliminate them! This hope is shared by scientists of all kinds who are committed to persuasive theories that cannot resolve every anomaly. It is, indeed, a widespread human hope. Worldviews, like scientific theories in general, cannot explain everything we experience in a totally consistent manner. Yet we usually do not abandon them for that reason. As long as they continue to make sense of our experience, we remain willing to hope that—if only we knew more—the contradictions or inconsistencies would disappear.

Social Structural Typologies: The British Emphasis

As time passed, better and more detailed information on more societies led anthropologists to become dissatisfied with grand generalizations about cultural diversity and cultural change. This change in perspective was the outcome of improved scholarship and better scientific reasoning, but it was also a consequence of the changes taking place in the world itself.

ORIGINS IN THE COLONIAL SETTING   The last quarter of the nineteenth century ushered in the final phase of Western colonialism. Most of Africa and much of Asia, which until then had remained nominally independent, were divided up among European powers. At the same time, the United States assumed a similarly powerful and dominating role in its relationships with the indigenous peoples in its territory and with the former colonies of Spain. Unilineal cultural evolutionism may have justified the global ambitions of Europe and made colonial rule appear inevitable and just. However, it was inadequate for meeting the practical needs of the rulers once they were in power.

Effective administration of subject peoples required accurate information about them. For example, one goal of a colonial administrator in Africa was to keep peace among the various groups over which he ruled. To do so, he needed to know how those people were accustomed to handling disputes. Most colonies included several societies with various customs for dispute resolution. Administrators had to be aware of the similarities and differences among their subjects in order to develop successful government policies. At the same time, colonial officials planned to introduce certain elements of European law uniformly throughout the colony. Common examples were commercial laws permitting the buying and selling of land on the open market. They also tried to eliminate practices like witchcraft accusations or local punishment for capital crimes. Reaching these goals without totally disrupting life in the colony required firsthand understanding of local practices. The earlier "armchair anthropology" was wholly incapable of providing that understanding.

These changes in the relationships between the West and the rest of the world encouraged the development of a new kind of anthropological research. Under the colonial "peace," anthropologists found that

FIGURE 4.4 Colonial officers often relied on traditional rulers to keep the peace among their subjects through traditional means. This 1895 photograph shows the British governor of the Gold Coast (seated on the right) together with a contingent of native police.

they could carry out long-term fieldwork. Unsettled conditions had made such work difficult in earlier times. Anthropologists also found that colonial governments would support their research when persuaded that it was scientific and could contribute to effective colonial rule. This did not mean that anthropologists who carried out fieldwork under colonial conditions supported colonialism. To the contrary, their sympathies often lay with the colonized peoples with whom they worked. For example, Sir E. E. Evans-Pritchard, who worked in central Africa for the British government in the 1920s and 1930s, saw himself as an educator of colonial administrators. He tried to convey to them the humanity and rationality of Africans. His goal was to combat the racism and oppression that seemed an inevitable consequence of colonial rule. For these reasons, colonial officials were often wary of anthropologists and distrustful of their motives. It was all too likely that the results of anthropological research might make colonial programs look self-serving and exploitative.

Colonial officials quickly learned that the task of administering their rule would be easier if they could rely on traditional rulers to keep the peace among their traditional subjects through traditional means (Figure 4.4). Thus developed the British policy of *indirect rule*. Colonial officials were at the top of the hierarchy. Under them, the traditional rulers (elders, chiefs, and so on) served as intermediaries with the common people. How could anthropologists contribute to the effectiveness of indirect rule? Perhaps the information they gathered about the traditional political structures of different groups might offer insights into the best way to adapt indirect rule to each group. As a result, anthropologists—especially British ones—developed a new way of classifying forms of human society. Their focus was on the **social structure**, especially the political structure, of groups under colonial rule. That British anthropologists came to call themselves *social anthropologists* reflects these developments.

In 1940, in a classic work on African political systems, Meyer Fortes and E. E. Evans-Pritchard distinguished between state and stateless societies. This distinction is similar to Morgan's unilineal evolutionary classifications in terms of ethnical periods. However, there is a significant difference in the terminology used

social structure The enduring aspects of the social forms in a society, including its political and kinship systems.

by Evans-Pritchard and Fortes: It makes no mention of "progress" from "lower" to "higher" forms of society. To be sure, the labels "savagery," "barbarism," and "civilization" were still part of the vocabulary of anthropology. Bronislaw Malinowski, for example, was quite comfortable referring to the inhabitants of the Trobriand Islands as *savages*. But the emphasis on contemporary social structures was bringing rich new insights to anthropology. Questions of evolution and social change took a back seat as social anthropologists concerned themselves with figuring out the enduring traditional structures of the societies in which they worked. A detailed knowledge of social structures was supposed to allow the anthropologist to identify the social type of any particular society. These types were treated as unchanging. They were compared for similarities and differences, and out of this comparison emerged a new classification of social forms.

THE CLASSIFICATION OF POLITICAL STRUCTURES

A contemporary example of a typical social structural classification of forms of human society is shown in Figure 4.5. Here, the major distinction is between *centralized* and *uncentralized,* or *egalitarian,* political systems. This distinction is similar to the one Evans-Pritchard and Fortes made between state societies and stateless societies; only the labels have been changed, perhaps so that societies without states can be identified in a positive fashion rather than in terms of what they lack. Uncentralized systems have no distinct, permanent institution exclusively concerned with public decision making. This is another way of saying that groups (and perhaps even individuals) within egalitarian systems enjoy relative autonomy and equal status and are not answerable to any higher authority.

In this scheme, egalitarian political systems can be further subdivided into two types. A **band** is a small social group whose members, like Morgan's savages, neither farm nor herd but depend on wild food sources. A **tribe** is a group that, like Morgan's barbarians, lies somewhere between a band and a centralized political system. A tribe is generally larger than a band and has domesticated plants and animals, but its political organization remains largely egalitarian and uncentralized. Ted Lewellen refers to three subtypes of band, including the *family band,* which are cases that do not fit into the other two subtypes. He also identifies five subtypes of tribe but comments that they hardly exhaust the variety of social arrangements that tribes display (Lewellen 1983, 26).

Centralized political systems differ from egalitarian systems because they have a central, institutionalized focus of authority such as a chief or a king. These systems also involve hierarchy; that is, some members of centralized societies have greater prestige, power, or wealth than do other members. Centralized systems are divided into two types. In a **chiefdom**, usually only the chief and the chief's family are set above the rest of society, which remains fairly egalitarian. In a **state**, different groups suffer permanent inequality of access to wealth, power, and prestige, which signals the presence of social stratification.

Lewellen's typology does not attempt to make any hypotheses about evolutionary relationships. Tracing change over time is not its purpose. Instead, the focus is on structural differences and similarities observed at one point in time: now. This is not accidental. Remember that classifications of this kind were made in response to practical needs in European colonies. Colonial rulers assumed that they were civilized and that their colonial subjects were primitive, but they cared little about such matters as the origin of the state. The pressing questions for them were more likely, "How do African states work today?" and "What do we need to know about them to make them work for us?"

Nevertheless, a typology that ignores change over time can be converted into an evolutionary typology with little difficulty. If you compare Table 4.2 with Table 4.1 (Morgan's ethnical periods), you will notice a rough correlation between bands and savagery; between tribes and lower and middle barbarism; between chiefdoms and upper barbarism; and between states and civilization. However, Lewellen's classification in Table 4.2 includes additional detail that was unknown in Morgan's day.

STRUCTURAL-FUNCTIONAL THEORY The theories of British social anthropologists dealt increasingly with how particular social forms function from day to day in order to reproduce their traditional structures. Such **structural-functional theory** was perhaps most highly developed by A. R. Radcliffe-Brown, whose major theoretical work was done in the 1930s and 1940s. Social anthropologists began to ask why things stayed the same rather than why they changed. Why do some social structures last for centuries (the Roman Catho-

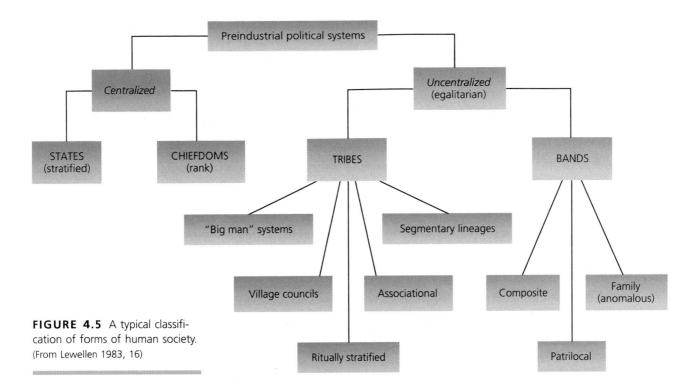

FIGURE 4.5 A typical classification of forms of human society. (From Lewellen 1983, 16)

lic church) and others disappear quickly (the utopian communities of nineteenth-century America)? Why did some societies abandon foraging for agriculture thousands of years ago, while others are still gathering and hunting in the twentieth century? Both kinds of questions are equally puzzling. However, an emphasis on social stability tends to downplay or ignore questions of change, just as an emphasis on social change tends to downplay or ignore questions of stability.

This new focus in British social anthropology, still with us today, has produced a succession of nonevolutionary classifications of human social forms. As data on more and more varieties of social structure grow, however, these typologies seem to overflow with more and more subtypes. It is not surprising that some anthropologists have begun to question the point of it all.

Doing without Typologies: Culture Area Studies in America

Anthropologists in the United States became dissatisfied with unilineal evolutionism at about the same time as their British colleagues, and for similar reasons.

The most important figure in this movement was Franz Boas, the man usually referred to as the father of American anthropology. Boas and his students worked primarily among the indigenous peoples of North America. They began to collect more and better data about these societies, especially data relating to the histories of individual groups. Change over time had not progressed

band The characteristic form of social organization found among foragers; a small group of people usually with 50 or fewer members. Labor is divided according to age and sex, and social relations are highly egalitarian.

tribe A form of social organization generally larger than a band; members usually farm or herd for a living. Social relations in a tribe are relatively egalitarian, although there may be a chief who speaks for the group or organizes group activities.

chiefdom A form of social organization in which the leader (a chief) and the chief's close relatives are set apart from the rest of the society and allowed privileged access to wealth, power, and prestige.

state A stratified society that possesses a territory that is defended from outside enemies with an army and from internal disorder with police. A state, which has a separate set of governmental institutions designed to enforce laws and collect taxes and tribute, is run by an elite that possesses a monopoly on the use of force.

structural-functional theory A position that explores how particular social forms function from day to day in order to reproduce the traditional structure of the society.

TABLE 4.2   PREINDUSTRIAL POLITICAL SYSTEMS: A STRUCTURAL-FUNCTIONAL TYPOLOGY

	Uncentralized		Centralized	
	Band	**Tribe**	**Chiefdom**	**State**
Type of subsistence	Hunting-gathering; little or no domestication	Extensive agriculture (horticulture) and pastoralism	Extensive agriculture; intensive fishing	Intensive agriculture
Type of leadership	Informal and situational leaders; may have a headman who acts as arbiter in group decision making	Charismatic headman with no "power" but some authority in group decision making	Charismatic chief with limited power based on bestowal of benefits on followers	Sovereign leader supported by an aristocratic bureaucracy
Type and importance of kinship	Bilateral kinship, with kin relations used differentially in changing size and composition of bands	Unilineal kinship (patrilineal or matrilineal) may form the basic structure of society	Unilineal, with some bilateral; descent groups are ranked in status	State demands suprakinship loyalties; access to power is based on ranked kin groups, either unilateral or bilateral
Major means of social integration	Marriage alliances unite larger groups; bands united by kinship and family; economic interdependence based on reciprocity	Pantribal sodalities based on kinship, voluntary associations, and/or age grades	Integration through loyalty to chief, ranked lineages, and voluntary associations	State loyalties supersede all lower-level loyalties; integration through commerce and specialization of function
Political succession	May be hereditary headman, but actual leadership falls to those with special knowledge or abilities	No formal means of political succession	Chief's position not directly inherited, but chief must come from a high-ranking lineage	Direct hereditary succession of sovereign; increasing appointment of bureaucratic functionaries
Major types of economic exchange	Reciprocity (sharing)	Reciprocity; trade may be more developed than in bands	Redistribution through chief; reciprocity at lower levels	Redistribution based on formal tribute and/or taxation; markets and trade

through uniform stages for all these societies. For example, two societies with similar forms of social organization might have arrived at that status through different historical routes: one through a process of simplification, the other through a process of elaboration.

Boas also emphasized that new cultural forms were more often borrowed from neighboring societies than invented independently. He and his followers were quick to note that if cultural borrowing, rather than in-

dependent invention, played an important role in culture change, then any unilineal evolutionary scheme was doomed. However, a focus on cultural borrowing also emphasized the porous boundaries around different societies that made such borrowing possible.

The view of society that developed in the United States was therefore quite different from the one that developed in Great Britain. Boas and his followers rejected the cultural evolutionists' view of societies as

| | Uncentralized | | Centralized | |
	Band	Tribe	Chiefdom	State
Social stratification	Egalitarian	Egalitarian	Rank (individual and lineage)	Classes (minimally of rulers and ruled)
Ownership of property	Little or no sense of personal ownership	Communal (lineage or clan) ownership of agricultural lands and cattle	Land communally owned by lineage, but strong sense of personal ownership of titles, names, privileges, ritual artifacts, and so on	Private and state ownership increases at the expense of communal ownership
Law and legitimate control of force	No formal laws or punishments; right to use force is communal	No formal laws or punishments; right to use force belongs to lineage, clan, or association	May be informal laws and specified punishments for breaking taboos; chief has limited access to physical coercion	Formal laws and punishments; state holds all legitimate access to use of physical force
Religion	No religious priesthood or full-time specialists; shamanistic	Shamanistic; strong emphasis on initiation rites and other rites of passage that unite lineages	Inchoate formal priesthood, hierarchical, ancestor-based religion	Full-time priesthood provides sacral legitimization of state
Recent and contemporary examples	!Kung* Bushmen (Africa), Pygmies (Africa), Eskimo (Canada, Alaska), and Shoshone (U.S.)	Kpelle (W. Africa), Yanomamo (Venezuela), Nuer (Sudan), and Cheyenne (U.S.)	Precolonial Hawaii, Kwakiutl (Canada), Tikopia (Polynesia), and Dagurs (Mongolia)	Ankole (Uganda), Jimma (Ethiopia), Kachari (India), and Volta (Africa)
Historic and prehistoric examples	Virtually all Paleolithic societies	Iroquois (U.S.) and Oaxaca Valley (Mexico), 1500–1000 B.C.E.	Precolonial Ashanti, Benin, Dahomy (Africa), and Scottish Highlanders	Precolonial Zulu (Africa), Aztec (Mexico), Inca (Peru), and Sumeria (Iraq)

Source: From Lewellen 1983, 20–21.
*Ju/'hoansi

isolated representatives of universal stages, closed to outside influences, responsible on their own for progressing or failing to progress. But they were also critical of the structural-functional view of societies as bounded, atemporal social types. Instead, they saw social groups as fundamentally open to the outside world; change over time was considered more a result of idiosyncratic borrowing from neighbors than of inevitable, law-governed progress. Consequently, the Boasians fo-

cused their attention on patterns of cultural borrowing over time, a form of research called *cultural area studies*. They developed lists of **culture traits**, or features characteristic of a particular group: a particular ritual, for example, or a musical style. They then

---

culture traits Particular features or parts of a cultural tradition, such as a dance, a ritual, or a style of pottery.

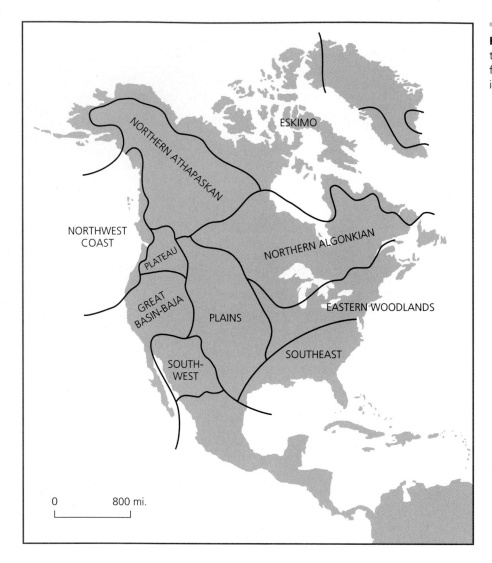

FIGURE 4.6 This map shows the native American culture areas for North America north of Mexico. (After Oswalt 1972)

determined how widely those cultural traits had spread into neighboring societies. A **culture area** was defined by the limits of borrowing, or the diffusion, of a particular trait or set of traits (Figure 4.6).

This emphasis in anthropological research had consequences for typologies of social forms. If borrowing allowed societies to skip evolutionary stages entirely, then any classification of universal stages was meaningless. Furthermore, even timeless classificatory schemes, like those of the social anthropologists, were of limited value. They depended on the assumption that societies were clear-cut entities with internally consistent social structures. But if societies are perpet-

ually open to cultural borrowing, it may be impossible to describe their structures in clear-cut terms. Area studies created cultural classifications that were either broader than an individual society (culture areas) or narrower than an individual society (culture traits). The end product was a list of traits and a map of cultural areas in which the traits are found. Boundaries around particular societies were ignored.

Postwar Realities

Then the world changed again. World War II was closely followed by the breakup of European colonial

FIGURE 4.7 By the end of the twentieth century, increasing numbers of anthropologists are coming from regions of the world outside the West: Sri Lankan anthropologist Arjun Guneratne converses with some of his informants in Nepal.

empires in Africa and Asia and by the civil rights movement in the United States. Former colonies were now independent states. Their citizens rejected the traditional Western view of them as savages or barbarians, asserting that they could govern their countries in a manner as civilized as that of Western nations.

Political realities thus created for Westerners new experiences of the non-Western other. These experiences made the pretensions of unilineal evolutionism even less plausible. As well, the leaders of the new states set out to consolidate national consciousness among the supposedly structurally separate societies within their borders. This effort made the structural focus of preindependence social anthropologists seem increasingly misguided, leading many Western anthropologists to recognize that the traditional societies they had been studying had not, in fact, been structurally separate even under colonialism. Decolonization allowed anthropologists to pay direct attention to colonialism as a form of political domination that eliminated the autonomy of indigenous social groups and forcibly restructured them into subordinate positions within a larger entity.

At the same time, anthropologists with roots in the non-Western world began to add their voices to those of Western anthropologists (Figure 4.7). They were and continue to be highly critical of the cultural stereotypes institutionalized by unilineal evolutionism and structural-functionalism. But this does not mean that typologies have disappeared altogether in contemporary cultural and social anthropology.

Studying Forms of Human Society Today

Opinions about the importance of classifying forms of human society vary greatly among contemporary anthropologists. Some anthropologists, especially those interested in political and economic issues, continue to find typologies useful. Still, most anthropologists would agree that an emphasis on similarities or differences in different types of society is closely related to the questions anthropologists are investigating and the theo-

culture area The limits of borrowing, or the diffusion, of a particular cultural trait or set of traits.

retical assumptions they bring to their research.

For example, let us turn again to Lewellen's classification of social types. How meaningful is it? What does it reflect? Lewellen argues that it is designed to reflect structural, organizational similarities and differences. To defend such criteria, he employs a house metaphor: "Two houses built of different materials but to the same floor plan will obviously be much more alike than two houses of the same materials but very different designs (say, a town house and a ranch house). . . . In short, a house is defined in terms of its organization, not its components, and that organization will be influenced by its physical environment and the level of technology of the people who designed it" (1983, 17).

Because he assumes that structural similarities and differences are both supremely significant and objectively obvious, Lewellen seems to be affiliated with the tradition of British social anthropology. Similarities and differences concerning the materials out of which the houses are made can safely be ignored. For certain purposes, and for certain observers, this may be true. But is a house's organization manifested in its floor plan or in the way the various rooms are *used* regardless of floor plan? Is a bedroom still a bedroom, whether in a town house or a ranch house, when the people living in that house use it to cook in? Does a family's ideas about how living space should properly be used change when the family moves from a thatched hut to an apartment with wooden floors and plaster walls?

Structural similarities and differences that seem obvious to many political anthropologists in the British tradition lead those anthropologists to set off states and chiefdoms sharply from tribes and bands. Would these similarities and differences seem so sharp to an anthropologist interested in classifying the ways different societies make a living? As we shall see, anthropologists interested in making such a classification employ concepts like *subsistence strategy* or *mode of production* to order their typologies, focusing on the strategies and technologies for organizing the production, distribution, and consumption of food, clothing, housing, tools, and other material goods. They therefore define a domain of relevance that may be quite different from that of political anthropologists—and these domains yield different typologies.

It is possible to preserve the fourfold distinction among states, chiefdoms, tribes, and bands and yet to group them differently. Consider, for example, the subsistence strategies that each category of society typically employs: Bands depend on foraging (gathering, fishing, hunting) whereas tribes, chiefdoms, and states depend on plant cultivation and herding. On this basis, bands can be set off from tribes, chiefdoms, and states. Now consider these social organizations in terms of their political organization: Tribes and bands are both egalitarian although they differ substantially in their subsistence strategies (see Table 4.2). Neither the similarities (political organization) nor the differences (subsistence strategies) are objectively more obvious than the other. Both depend on the topic of research as well as prior assumptions made by the researchers concerning what is worth paying attention to and what can be safely downplayed or ignored.

The situation gets even more complicated. Many typologists are confident about separating bands from tribes, chiefdoms, and states because, in an overwhelming number of ethnographic cases, a foraging subsistence strategy is not found together with developed lineages or social ranking or settled villages. But there are troublesome exceptions to this pattern, notably among the various societies of the northwest coast of North America: Such groups as the Tlingit and Kwakiutl fished, hunted, and gathered, but they created complex, settled societies with developed lineages and social ranking. Moreover, archaeological evidence from the Andes and elsewhere suggests that foraging societies were responsible for some of the earliest monumental architecture, the construction of which seems to imply a fair degree of social complexity (Keatinge 1988b). Lewellen acknowledges the problems these societies pose for any political typology: "Indian societies of the Northwest Coast of North America are usually categorized as chiefdoms . . . but the fit is far from perfect. . . . Perhaps all the cultures of the Northwest Coast would seem to represent a blending of elements of both tribes and chiefdoms" (1983, 33–34).

It is also possible that such societies reveal the limits of a particular typology. They might represent an authentic social form in their own right, one that the prototypes of traditional classification systems are unable to characterize unambiguously. Such societies fall between the categories of a classification and may only be recognized when new evidence, in this case from archaeology, supports their validity. This should remind us that typologies are human constructions, not pure reflections of objective reality, and that we may change them as our understanding changes.

Although it is sometimes easy to emphasize the shortcomings of past classificatory schemes in anthropology, it is important not to overlook the lasting contributions they have made. Despite its excesses, unilineal cultural evolutionism highlights the fact that cultures change over time and that our species has experienced a broad sequence of cultural developments. Structural-functionalist typologies may seem overly rigid and static, but the structural-functionalist ethnographies show just how intricate the social institutions and practices of so-called simple societies can be. The culture area studies of Boas and his students deemphasize boundaries between separate societies, but the attention they pay to diffusion makes clear that indigenous people have never been unthinking slaves to tradition. On the contrary, they have been alert to their surroundings, aware of cultural alternatives, and ready to adopt new ways from other people when it has suited them. It is indeed the cultural creativity of all human beings, in all societies, that keeps anthropologists busy.

Key Terms

typology	chiefdom
unilineal cultural	state
evolutionism	structural-functional
social structure	theory
band	culture traits
tribe	culture area

Chapter Summary

1. Cultural traditions take shape as a result of the dialectic between human imagination and the material world. Forms of human society are shaped by both the nonhuman natural environment and the human social environment.
2. The imperialist expansion of Europe, which coincided with the rise of industrial capitalism, was the central force leading to cross-cultural contact between the West and the rest of the world. Many of the groups anthropologists would later study were relatively recent creations, forged in the contact between indigenous populations and Europeans. An anthropological survey of the forms of human society needs to investigate the historical circumstances surrounding the contact between anthropologists and their informants.
3. Non-Western societies have not escaped the historical forces that have influenced everyone else, yet the societies that survive today show that conquered peoples can actively cope with contemporary problems and opportunities to reshape their own social identities. An impressive variety of forms of human society remains.
4. Anthropologists have created typologies of the forms of human society. They first identify those societies that are most distinct from one another based on certain criteria and then sort known societies by their resemblance to these exemplars. Depending upon an anthropologist's analytical purposes, the same social forms can be classified in different ways.
5. The earliest important anthropological typology of forms of human society was proposed by unilineal cultural evolutionists. They tried to explain contemporary cultural diversity by arguing that different kinds of society existing in the nineteenth century represented different stages of societal evolution. Every human society either had passed or would pass through the same stages. Societies in stages lower in the typology than Europe were viewed as living relics of Europe's past. This typology contained three basic categories: savagery, barbarism, and civilization.
6. Anthropologists doing research in a colonial setting in the first half of the twentieth century collected a vast amount of detailed, accurate information about aspects of indigenous life, which colonial administrators needed to understand in order to administer colonial rule. Their research led them to set aside questions about cultural evolution and to focus on social structural differences and similarities observed at a single point in time.
7. In American anthropology, the classification of forms of human society was ignored almost totally in the early part of the twentieth century.

Following Boas, American anthropologists rejected unilineal cultural evolutionism on the grounds that societies could easily borrow cultural forms from one another, thus skipping stages. Consequently, the aim of research shifted to making lists of culture traits and mapping the culture areas in which they were found.

8. Classifying forms of human society is not an ultimate goal for most anthropologists today, although some anthropologists find typologies useful. Classifications differ, depending upon the problems to be solved. Thus, societies grouped together because of similarities in political organization may be separated from one another because of differences in subsistence strategies. The fuzziness of category boundaries reminds us that taxonomies are human constructions, not pure reflections of objective reality.

Suggested Readings

Lewellen, Ted. 1983. *Political anthropology.* South Hadley, MA: Bergin and Garvey. *Contains much useful information about the different kinds of societies that different scholars have identified.*

Weatherford, Jack. 1988. *Indian givers: How the Indians of the Americas transformed the world.* New York: Fawcett Columbine.

———. 1991. *Native roots: How the Indians enriched America.* New York: Fawcett Columbine.

———. 1994. *Savages and civilization.* New York: Random House. *All three of these books are engaging accounts of the consequences of contact between the Old World and New World in the past and in the present.*

Wolf, Eric. 1982. *Europe and the people without history.* Berkeley: University of California Press. *A classic text about the connection of European expansion to the rest of the world. This work also discusses the effect of European contact on indigenous societies.*

PART II

The Resources of Culture

These four chapters focus on a range of human capacities that lie at the center of human cultural creativity, flexibility, and diversity. Human beings survive in a material world by means of open, flexible symbolic patterns that assign meanings to various aspects of that world. As a result, human beings never confront the material world directly, but always through a web of meanings of their own creation. Cultural meaning is perhaps most directly encountered in language, but it is also revealed in habitual patterns of thought and action and is at its most elaborate in those creations that Westerners traditionally call art, myth, ritual, and worldview. Since the dependence of the human species on culture for our survival is total, a proper awareness of the depth, breadth, and complexity of human culture is, from the anthropological perspective, indispensable for an adequate understanding of the human condition.

5

Language

The system of arbitrary vocal symbols human beings use to encode and communicate about their experience of the world and of one another is called **language**. It is a unique faculty that sets human beings apart from other living species. It provides basic tools for human creativity, making possible the cultural achievements that we view as monuments to our species' genius. And yet, despite all that language makes possible, its tools are double edged. Language allows people to communicate with one another, but it also creates barriers to communication. One major barrier is linguistic diversity (Figure 5.1). There are some 3,000 mutually unintelligible languages spoken in the world today. Why should there be such barriers to communication? This chapter will explore the ambiguity, limitations, and power of human language.

LANGUAGE AND CULTURE

Human language is a biocultural phenomenon. The human brain and the anatomy of our mouth and throat make language a biological possibility for us. At the same time, every human language is clearly a cultural product. It is shared by a group of speakers, encoded in symbols, and historically transmitted through teaching and learning; it tends to be coherent, thus making communication possible.

Anthropological Interest in Language

Language is of primary interest to anthropologists for at least three reasons. First, anthropologists often do fieldwork among people whose language is different from theirs. In the past these languages were often unwritten and had to be learned without formal instruction. Second, anthropologists can transcribe or tape-record speech and thus lift it out of its cultural context to be analyzed on its own. The grammatical intricacies revealed by such analysis suggested to many that what was true about language was true about the rest of culture. Indeed, some schools of anthropological theory have based their theories of culture explicitly on ideas taken from **linguistics**, the scientific study of language. Third, and most important, all people use language to encode their experience and to structure their understanding of the world and of themselves. By learning another society's language, we learn something about their culture as well. In fact, learning another language inevitably provides unsuspected insights into the nature of our own language and culture, often making it impossible to take language of any kind for granted ever again.

It is useful to distinguish *Language* from *languages*.

FIGURE 5.1

Reprinted with special permission of King Features Syndicate.

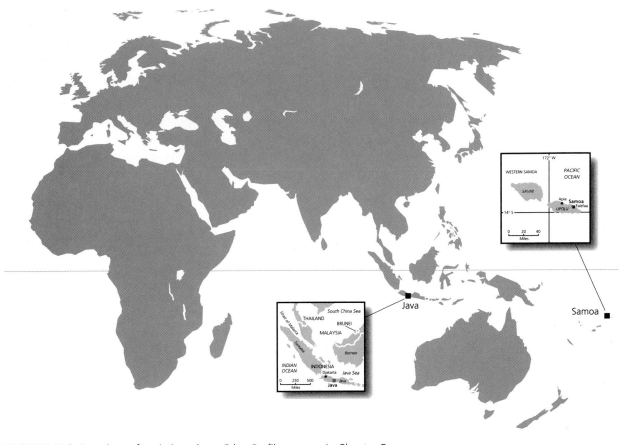

FIGURE 5.2 Locations of societies whose EthnoProfiles appear in Chapter 5.

Language with a capital *L* (like *Culture* with a capital *C*) is an abstract property belonging to the human species as a whole. Anthropologists deduced this when they realized that all human groups had their own particular *languages*. It is also useful to distinguish *Language* (or *languages*) from *speech* and *communication*. We usually think of spoken language (speech) when we use the term *language,* but English can be communicated in writing, Morse code, or American Sign Language, to name just three nonspoken media. *Human communication* can be defined as the transfer of information from one person to another, which can take place without the use of words, spoken or otherwise. People communicate with one another nonverbally all the time, sending messages with the clothes they wear, the way

they walk, or how long they keep other people waiting for them.

In fact, even linguistic communication depends on more than words alone. Native speakers of one language share not just vocabulary and grammar but also a number of assumptions about how to speak that may not be shared by speakers of a different language. Students learning a new language discover early on that word-for-word translation from one language to another does not work. Sometimes there are no equivalent words in the second language; but even when

---

language The system of arbitrary vocal symbols we use to encode our experience of the world.
linguistics The scientific study of language.

there appear to be such words, a word-for-word translation may not mean in language B what it meant in
language A. For example, when English speakers have
eaten enough, they say, "I'm full." This may be translated directly into French as *Je suis plein*. To a native
speaker of French, this sentence (especially when uttered at the end of a meal) has the nonsensical meaning "I am a pregnant [male] animal." Alternatively, if
uttered by a man who has just consumed a lot of wine,
it means "I'm drunk."

Speaking a second language is often frustrating and
even unsettling; someone who once found the world
simple to talk about suddenly turns into a babbling
fool. Studying a second language, then, is less a matter of learning new labels for old objects than it is of
learning how to identify new objects that go with new
labels. The student must also learn the appropriate contexts in which different linguistic forms may be used:
A person can be "full" after eating in English, but not
in French. Knowledge about context is cultural knowledge. The linguistic system abstracted from its cultural
context must be returned to that context if a holistic
understanding of language is to be achieved.

Talking about Experience

Language, like the rest of culture, is a product of human attempts to come to terms with experience. Each
natural human language is adequate for its speakers'
needs, given their particular way of life. Speakers of a
particular language tend to develop larger vocabular-
ies to discuss those aspects of life that are of importance to them. The Aymara, who live in the Andes of
South America, have invented hundreds of different
words for the many varieties of potato they grow (see
EthnoProfile 5.1: Aymara.) By contrast, speakers of English have created an elaborate vocabulary for discussing computers. However, despite differences in
vocabulary and grammar, all natural human languages
ever studied by linguists prove to be equally complex.
Just as there is no such thing as a "primitive" human
culture, there is no such thing as a "primitive" human
language.

Traditionally, languages are associated with concrete groups of people called *speech communities*. Nevertheless, because all languages possess alternative
ways of speaking, members of particular speech communities do not all possess identical knowledge about
the language they share, nor do they all speak the same

way. Individuals and subgroups within a speech community make use of linguistic resources in different
ways. Consequently, there is a tension in language
between diversity and commonality. Individuals and
subgroups attempt to use the varied resources of a language to create unique, personal voices. These efforts
are countered by the pressure to negotiate a common
code for communication within the larger social group.
In this way, language is produced and reproduced
through the activity of its speakers. Any particular language that we may identify at a given moment is a
snapshot of a continuing process.

There are many ways to communicate our experiences, and there is no absolute standard favoring one
way over another. Some things that are easy to say in
language A may be difficult to say in language B, yet
other aspects of language B may appear much simpler
than equivalent aspects of language A. For example,
English ordinarily requires the use of determiners (*a,
an, the*) before nouns, but this rule is not found in all
languages. Likewise, the verb *to be*, called the *copula* by
linguists, is not found in all languages, although the
relationships we convey when we use *to be* in English
may still be communicated. In English, we might say
"There *are* many people in the market." Translating
this sentence into Fulfulde, the language of the Fulbe
of northern Cameroon, we get *Him'be boi 'don nder
luumo*, which, word-for-word, reads something like
"people-many-there-in-market" (Figure 5.3). No single
Fulfulde word corresponds to the English *are* or *the*.

Differences across languages are not absolute. In
Chinese, for example, verbs never change to indicate
tense; instead, separate expressions referring to time
are used. English speakers may conclude that Chinese
speakers cannot distinguish between past, present, and
future. This structure seems completely different from
English structure. But consider such English sentences
as "Have a hard day at the office today?" and "Your in-
terview go well?" These abbreviated questions, used in
informal English, are very similar to the formal patterns of Chinese and other languages of southeastern
Asia (Akmajian, Demers, and Harnish 1984, 194–95).

This kind of overlap between two very different languages demonstrates at least four things. First, it shows
the kind of cross-linguistic commonality that forms the
foundation both for learning new languages and for
translation. Second, it highlights the variety of expres-
sive resources to be found in any single language. We
learn that English allows us to use either tense mark-

FIGURE 5.3 *Him'be boi 'don nder luumo.*

ers on verbs (*-s, -ed*) or unmarked verbs with adverbs of time (*have + today*). Third, we learn that the former grammatical pattern is associated with formal usage, whereas the latter is associated with informal usage. Finally, it shows that the same structures can have different functions in different languages. As anthropological linguist Elinor Ochs observes, most cross-cultural differences in language use "turn out to be differences in *context* and/or *frequency of occurrence*" (1986, 10).

DESIGN FEATURES OF HUMAN LANGUAGE

In 1966, anthropological linguist Charles Hockett listed sixteen different **design features** of human language that, in his estimation, set it apart from other forms of animal communication. Six of these design features seem especially helpful in defining what makes human language distinctive: openness, displacement, arbitrariness, duality of patterning, semanticity, and prevarication.

Openness, probably the most important feature, emphasizes the same point that the linguist Noam Chomsky emphasized (1965, 6): Human language is creative. Speakers of any given language not only can create new

messages but also can understand new messages created by other speakers. Someone may have never said to you, "Put this Babel fish in your ear," but knowing English, you can understand the message. Openness might also be defined as "the ability to understand the same thing from different points of view" (Ortony 1979, 14). In language, this means being able to talk about the same experiences from different perspectives, to paraphrase using different words and various grammatical constructions. Indeed, it means that the experiences themselves can be differently conceived, labeled, and discussed. In this view, no single perspective would necessarily emerge as more correct in every respect than all others.

The importance of openness for human verbal communication is striking when we compare, for example, spoken human language to the vocal communication systems (or *call systems*) of monkeys and apes. Nonhuman primates can communicate in rather subtle ways using channels of transmission other than voice. However, these channels are far less sophisticated than, say, American Sign Language, and their call systems are very different from spoken human

design features Those characteristics of language that, when taken together, differentiate it from other known animal communication systems.

language. The number of calls are few and are produced only when the animal finds itself in a situation including such features as the presence of food or danger; friendly interest and the desire for company; or the desire to mark the animal's location or to signal pain, sexual interest, or the need for maternal care. If the animal is not in the appropriate situation, it does not produce the call. At most, it may refrain from uttering a call in a situation that would normally trigger it. In addition, nonhuman primates cannot emit a signal that has some features of one call and some of another. For example, if the animal encounters food and danger at the same time, one of the calls takes precedence. For these reasons, the call systems of nonhuman primates are said to be *closed* when compared to open human languages.

Closed call systems also lack *displacement,* our human ability to talk about absent or nonexistent objects and past or future events as easily as we discuss our immediate situations. Although nonhuman primates clearly have good memories, and some species, such as chimpanzees, seem to be able to plan social action in advance (such as when hunting for meat), they cannot use their call systems to discuss such events.

Closed call systems also lack *arbitrariness,* the absence of any link between sound and meaning in language. For example, the sound sequence /boi/ refers to a "young male human being" in English, but means "more" or "many" in Fulfulde. One aspect of linguistic creativity is the free, creative production of new links between sounds and meanings. Thus, arbitrariness is the flip side of openness: If all links between sound and meaning are open, then the particular link between particular sounds and particular meanings in a particular language must be arbitrary. In primate call systems, by contrast, links between the sounds of calls and their meanings appear to be fixed and under considerable direct biological control.

Arbitrariness is evident in the design feature of language that Hockett called *duality of patterning.* Human language, Hockett claimed, is patterned on two different levels: sound and meaning. On the first level, the small set of significant sounds (or *phonemes*) that characterize any particular language are not random but are systematically patterned. On the second level of patterning, however, grammar puts the sound units together according to an entirely different set of rules: The resulting sound clusters are the smallest meaning-bearing units of the language, called *morphemes.*

Since Hockett first wrote, many linguists have suggested that there are more than just two levels of patterning in language. (We will discuss some additional levels later in the chapter.) In all cases, the principle relating levels to each other is the same: Units at one level, patterned in one way (sounds), can be used to create units at a different level, patterned in a different way (morphemes, or units of meaning). The rules governing morphemes, in turn, are different from the rules by which morphemes are combined into sentences, which are different from the rules combining sentences into discourse. Today, linguists recognize many levels of patterning in human language, and the patterns that characterize one level cannot be reduced to the patterns of any other level. By contrast, ape call systems lack multilevel patterning (Wallman 1992).

Arbitrariness shows up again in the design feature of *semanticity*—the association of linguistic signals with aspects of the social, cultural, and physical world of a speech community. People use language to refer to and make sense of objects and processes in the world. Nevertheless, any linguistic description of reality is always somewhat arbitrary because all linguistic descriptions are selective, highlighting some features of the world and downplaying others.

Perhaps the most striking consequence of linguistic openness is the design feature *prevarication.* Hockett's remarks about this design feature deserve particular attention: "Linguistic messages can be false, and they can be meaningless in the logician's sense." In other words, not only can people use language to lie, but utterances that seem perfectly well formed grammatically may yield semantic nonsense. As an example, Chomsky offered the following sentence: "Colorless green ideas sleep furiously" (1957, 15). This is a grammatical sentence on one level—the right kinds of words are used in the right places—but on another level it contains multiple contradictions. The ability of language users to prevaricate—to make statements or ask questions that violate convention—is a major consequence of open symbolic systems. Apes using their closed call systems can neither lie nor formulate theories.

Opening Closed Call Systems

Charles Hockett and Robert Ascher (1964) hypothesize that the major switch in human evolution occurred when the closed call systems of our apelike ancestors opened up. When this happened, different sounds

Cultural Translation

Linguistic translation is complicated and beset with pitfalls, as we have seen. Cultural translation, as David Parkin describes, requires not just knowledge of different grammars but also of the various different cultural contexts in which grammatical forms are put to use.

Cultural translation, like translation from one language to another, never produces a rendering that is semantically and stylistically an exact replica of the original. That much we accept. What is not often recognized, perhaps not even by the translators themselves, is that the very act of having to decide how to phrase an event, sentiment, or human character engages the translator in an act of creation. The translator does not simply represent a picture made by an author. He or she creates a new version, and perhaps in some respects a new picture—a matter that is often of some great value.

So it is with anthropologists. But while this act of creation in reporting on "the other" may reasonably be regarded as a self-sustaining pleasure, it is also an entry into the pitfalls and traps of language use itself. One of the most interesting new fields in anthropology is the study of the relationship between language and human knowledge, both among ourselves as professional anthropologists and laypeople, and among peoples of other cultures. The study is at once both reflexive and critical.

The hidden influences at work in language use attract the most interest. For example, systems of greetings have many built-in elaborations that differentiate subtly between those who are old and young, male and female, rich and poor, and powerful and powerless. When physicians discuss a patient in his or her presence and refer to the patient in the third-person singular, they are in effect defining the patient as a passive object unable to enter into the discussion. When anthropologists present elegant accounts of "their" people that fit the demands of a convincing theory admirably, do they not also leave out [of] the description any consideration of the informants' own fears and feelings? Or do we go too far in making such claims, and is it often the anthropologist who is indulged by the people, who give him or her the data they think is sought, either in exchange for something they want or simply because it pleases them to do so? If the latter, how did the anthropologist's account miss this critical part of the dialogue?

Source: Parkin 1990, 290–91.

could be freely associated with the same meaning or the same meaning with different sounds. Multilevel patterning became possible. As a result, semanticity widened and became more complex and ambiguous. Eventually, sounds and meanings became further detached, and detachable, from the immediate context in which they were being used, giving birth to displacement.

LANGUAGE AND CONTEXT

Anthropologists are powerfully aware of the influence of context on what people choose to say. Years ago, for example, studies of child language amounted to a list of errors that children make when attempting to gain what Chomsky calls **linguistic competence**, or mastery of adult grammar. Today, however, linguists study children's verbal interactions in social and cultural context and draw attention to what children can do

very well. "From an early age they appear to communicate very fluently, producing utterances which are not just remarkably well-formed according to the linguist's standards but also appropriate to the social context in which the speakers find themselves. Children are thus learning far more about language than rules of grammar. [They are] acquiring communicative competence" (Elliot 1981, 13).

Communicative competence, or mastery of adult rules for socially and culturally appropriate speech, is a term coined by American anthropological linguist Dell Hymes (1972). As an anthropologist, Hymes objected to Chomsky's notion that linguistic competence consisted only of being able to make correct judgments

linguistic competence A term coined by linguist Noam Chomsky to refer to the mastery of adult grammar.
communicative competence A term coined by anthropological linguist Dell Hymes to refer to the mastery of adult rules for socially and culturally appropriate speech.

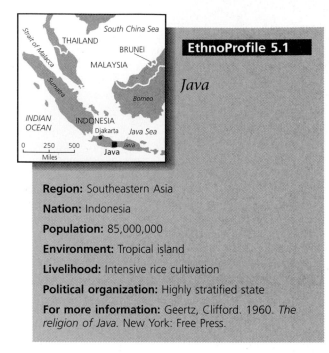

EthnoProfile 5.1

Java

Region: Southeastern Asia

Nation: Indonesia

Population: 85,000,000

Environment: Tropical island

Livelihood: Intensive rice cultivation

Political organization: Highly stratified state

For more information: Geertz, Clifford. 1960. *The religion of Java.* New York: Free Press.

ate use of *tu* and *vous* seem to have nothing to do with grammar, yet the choice between one form and the other indicates whether the speaker is someone who does or does not know how to speak French.

But French seems quite straightforward when compared with Javanese, in which all the words in a sentence must be carefully selected to reflect the social relationship between the speaker and the person addressed. (See EthnoProfile 5.1: Java.) It is impossible to say anything in Javanese without also communicating your social position relative to the person to whom you are speaking. Even a simple request like, "Are you going to eat rice and cassava now?" requires that speakers know at least five different varieties of the language in order to communicate socially as well as to make the request (Figure 5.4). This example illustrates the range of diversity present in a single language and how different varieties of a language are related to different subgroups within the speech community.

of sentence grammaticality (Chomsky 1965, 4). Hymes observed that competent adult speakers do more than follow grammatical rules when they speak. They are also able to choose words and topics of conversation appropriate to their social position, the social position of the person they are addressing, and the social context of interaction.

For example, consider the issue of using personal pronouns appropriately when talking to others. For native speakers of English, the problem almost never arises with regard to pronoun choice because we address all people as "you." But any English speaker who has ever tried to learn French has worried about when to address an individual using the second-person plural (*vous*) and when to use the first-person singular (*tu*). To be safe, most students use *vous* for all individuals because it is the more formal term and they want to avoid appearing too familiar with native speakers whom they do not know well. But if you are dating a French person, at which point in the relationship does the change from *vous* to *tu* occur, and who decides? Moreover, sometimes—for example, among university students— the normal term of address is *tu* (even among strangers); it is used to indicate social solidarity. Native speakers of English who are learning French wrestle with these and other linguistic dilemmas. Rules for the appropri-

THE SAPIR-WHORF HYPOTHESIS

During the first half of the twentieth century, two American anthropological linguists noted that the grammars of different languages often described the same situation in different ways. Edward Sapir and Benjamin Whorf were impressed enough to conclude that language has the power to shape the way people see the world. This claim has been called the *linguistic relativity principle,* or the **Sapir-Whorf hypothesis.** This hypothesis has been highly controversial because it is difficult to test and the results of testing have been ambiguous.

The so-called strong version of the Sapir-Whorf hypothesis is also known as *linguistic determinism.* It reduces patterns of thought and culture to the patterns of the grammar of the language we speak. If a grammar classifies nouns in male and female gender categories, for example, linguistic determinism concludes that speakers of that language are forced to think of males and females as radically different kinds of beings. By contrast, a language that makes no grammatical distinctions on the basis of gender presumably trains its speakers to think of males and females as exactly the same. If linguistic determinism is correct, then a change in grammar should change thought patterns:

Speaking to persons of:	Level	"Are	you	going	to eat	rice	and	cassava	now?"	Complete sentence
Very high position	3a	menapa	pandjenengan	badé	ḍahar		kalijan		samenika	Menapa pandjenengan badé ḍahar sekul kalijan kaspé samenika?
High position	3					sekul				Menapa sampéjan badé neḍa sekul kalijan kaspé samenika?
Same position, not close	2	napa	sampéjan	adjéng	neḍa			kaspé	saniki	Napa sampéjan adjéng neḍa sekul lan kaspé saniki?
Same position, casual acquaintance	1a						lan			Apa sampéjan arep neḍa sega lan kaspé saiki?
Close friends of any rank; also to lower status (basic language)	1	apa	kowé	arep	mangan	sega			saiki	Apa kowé arep mangan sega lan kaspé saiki?

FIGURE 5.4 The dialect of nonnoble, urbanized, somewhat educated people in central Java. (From Geertz 1960).

If English speakers replaced *he* and *she* with a new, gender-neutral, third-person singular pronoun, such as *te*, then, linguistic determinists predict, English speakers would begin to treat men and women as equals.

There are a number of problems with linguistic determinism. In the first place, there are languages such as Fulfulde in which only one third-person pronoun is used for males and females (*o*); however, male-dominant social patterns are quite evident among Fulfulde speakers. In the second place, if language determined thought in this way, it would be impossible to translate from one language to another or even to learn another language with a different grammatical structure. Because human beings do learn foreign languages and translate from one language to another, the strong version of the Sapir-Whorf hypothesis cannot be correct. Third, even if it were possible to draw firm boundaries around speech communities (which it isn't), every language provides its native speakers with alternative ways of describing the world. Finally, in most of the world's societies, monolingualism is the exception rather than the rule yet people who grow up bilingual do not also grow up schizophrenic, as if trying to reconcile two contradictory views of reality. Indeed, bilingual children ordinarily benefit from knowing two languages, do not confuse them, can switch readily from one to another, and even appear to demonstrate greater cognitive flexibility on psychological tests than

Sapir-Whorf hypothesis A position, associated with Edward Sapir and Benjamin Whorf, that asserts that language has the power to shape the way people see the world.

IN THEIR OWN WORDS

Eskimo Words for Snow

Word-for-word translation from one language to another is often difficult because the vocabulary referring to a given topic may be well developed in one language and poorly developed in another. However, as Laura Martin shows, we may draw erroneous conclusions from these differences without a deeper knowledge of the grammars of the languages concerned.

The earliest reference to Eskimos and snow was apparently made by Franz Boas. Among many examples of cross-linguistic variation in the patterns of form/meaning association, Boas presents a brief citation of four lexically unrelated words for snow in Eskimo: *aput* 'snow on the ground,' *qana* 'falling snow,' *piqsirpoq* 'drifting snow,' and *qimuqsuq* 'a snow drift.' In this casual example, Boas makes little distinction among "roots," "words," and "independent terms." He intends to illustrate the noncomparability of language structures, not to examine their cultural or cognitive implications.

The example became inextricably identified with Benjamin Whorf through the popularity of "Science and Linguistics," his 1940 article (see Carroll 1956: 207–219) exploring the same ideas that interested Boas, lexical elaboration not chief among them. Although for Boas the example illustrated a similarity between English and "Eskimo," Whorf reorients it to contrast them (1956: 216). It is a minor diversion in a discussion of pervasive semantic categories such as time and

space, and he develops it no further, here or elsewhere in his writings.

Of particular significance is Whorf's failure to cite specific data, numbers, or sources. His English glosses suggest as many as five words, but not the same set given by Boas. Although Whorf's source is uncertain, if he did rely on Boas, his apparently casual revisions of numbers and glosses are but the first mistreatments to which the original data have been subjected.

Anthropological fascination with the example is traceable to two influential textbooks, written in the late 1950s by members of the large group of language scientists familiar with "Science and Linguistics," and adopted in a variety of disciplines well into the 1970s. One or both of these were probably read by most anthropologists trained between 1960 and 1970, and by countless other students as well during that heyday of anthropology's popularity.

In the first, *The Silent Language,* Edward Hall mentions the example only three times, but his treatment of it suggests that he considered it already familiar to many potential readers. Hall credits Boas, but misrepresents both the intent and extent of the original citation. Even the data are misplaced. Hall inexplicably describes the Eskimo data as "nouns" and, although his argument implies quite a large inventory, specific numbers are not provided. Hall introduces still another context for the example, using it in the analysis of cultural categories.

monolinguals (Elliot 1981, 56).

In the face of these objections, other researchers offer a "weak" version of the Sapir-Whorf hypothesis that rejects linguistic determinism but continues to claim that language shapes thought and culture. Thus, grammatical gender might not determine a male-dominant social order, but it might facilitate the acceptance of such a social order because the grammatical distinction between *he* and *she* might make separate and unequal gender roles seem "natural." Since many native speakers of English turn out to be strong promoters of gender equality, however, the shaping power of grammar would seem far too weak to merit any scientific attention.

Neither Sapir nor Whorf favored linguistic determinism. Sapir argued that language's importance lies

in the way it directs attention to some aspects of experience rather than to others. He was impressed by the fact that "it is generally difficult to make a complete divorce between objective reality and our linguistic symbols of reference to it" (E. Sapir [1933] 1966, 9, 15). Whorf's views have been more sharply criticized by later scholars. His discussions of the linguistic relativity principle are complex and ambiguous. At least part of the problem arises from Whorf's attempt to view grammar as the linguistic pattern that shapes culture and thought. Whorf's contemporaries understood grammar to refer to rules for combining sounds into words and words into sentences. Whorf believed that grammar needed to be thought of in broader terms (Schultz 1990), but he died before working out the theoretical language to describe such a level.

At approximately the same time, Roger Brown's *Words and Things* (1958) appeared, intended as a textbook in the "psychology of language." Here the example is associated with Whorf and thoroughly recast. Brown claims precisely "three Eskimo words for snow," an assertion apparently based solely on a drawing in Whorf's paper. Psychological and cognitive issues provide still another context in Brown's discussion of a theory about the effects of lexical categorization on perception.

Brown's discussion illustrates a creeping carelessness about the actual linguistic facts of the example; this carelessness is no less shocking because it has become so commonplace. Consider Brown's application of Zipf's Law to buttress arguments about the relationship between lexicon and perception. Since Zipf's Law concerns word length, Brown's hypothesis must assume something about the length of his "three" "Eskimo" "snow" words; his argument stands or falls on the assumption that they must be both short and frequent. Eskimo words, however, are the products of an extremely synthetic morphology in which all word building is accomplished by multiple suffixation. Their length is well beyond the limits of Zipf's calculations. Furthermore, precisely identical whole "words" are unlikely to recur because the particular combination of suffixes used with a "snow" root, or any other, varies by speaker and situation as well as by syntactic role.

A minimal knowledge of Eskimo grammar would have confirmed the relevance of these facts to the central hypotheses, and would, moreover, have established the even more relevant fact that there is nothing at all peculiar about the behavior or distribution of "snow words" in these languages. The structure of Eskimo grammar means that the number of "words" for snow is literally incalculable, a conclusion that is inescapable for any other root as well.

Any sensible case for perceptual variation based on lexical inventory should, therefore, require reference to distinct "roots" rather than to "words," but this subtlety has escaped most authors. Brown, for example, repeatedly refers to linguistic units such as "verbal expression," "phrase," and "word" in a way that underscores the inadequacy of his understanding of Eskimo grammar. His assumption that English and "Eskimo" are directly comparable, together with his acceptance of pseudo-facts about lexical elaboration in an unfamiliar language, cause him to construct a complex psychocultural argument based on cross-linguistic "evidence" related to the example with not a single item of Eskimo data in support. This complete absence of data (and of accurate references) sets a dangerous precedent because it not only prevents direct evaluation of Brown's claims but suggests that such evaluation is unnecessary.

Source: Laura Martin 1986, 418–19.

COMPONENTS OF LANGUAGE

Linguistic study involves a search for patterns in the way speakers use language; linguists aim to describe these patterns by reducing them to a set of rules called a **grammar.** As Edward Sapir once commented, however, "all grammars leak" (1921, 38). Over time linguists came to recognize a growing number of language components; each new component was an attempt to plug the "leaks" in an earlier grammar, to explain what had previously resisted explanation. The following discussion pinpoints the various leaks linguists have recognized (as well as their attempts to plug the leaks) and demonstrates how culture and language influence each other.

Phonology: Sounds

The study of the sounds of language is called **phonology.** The sounds of human language are special because they are produced by a set of organs, the speech organs, that belong only to the human species (Figure 5.5). The actual sounds that come out of our mouths are called *phones,* and they vary continuously in acoustic properties. However, we hear all the phones within a particular range of variation as functionally equivalent *allophones* of the same *phoneme,* or characteristic speech

---

grammar A set of rules that aim to describe fully the patterns of linguistic usage observed by members of a particular speech community.
phonology The study of the sounds of language.

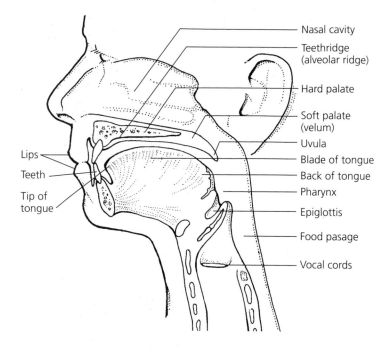

FIGURE 5.5 The speech organs.

Nasal cavity

Teethridge
(alveolar ridge)

Hard palate

Soft palate
(velum)

Uvula

Blade of tongue

Back of tongue

Pharynx

Epiglottis

Food pasage

Vocal cords

Lips

Teeth

Tip of
tongue

sound in the language. Part of the phonologist's job is to map out possible arrangements of speech organs that human beings may use to create the sounds of language. Another part is to examine individual languages to discover the particular sound combinations they contain and the patterns into which those sound combinations are organized. No language makes use of all the many sounds the human speech organs can produce, and no two languages use exactly the same set. American English uses only 38 sounds. Most work in phonology has been done from the perspective of the speaker, who produces, or articulates, the sounds of language using the speech organs.

Although all languages rely on only a handful of phonemes, no two languages use exactly the same set. Furthermore, different speakers of the same language often differ from one another in the way their phonemes are patterned, producing "accents," which constitute one kind of variety within a language. This variety is not random; the speech sounds characteristic of any particular accent follow a pattern. Speakers with different accents are usually able to understand one another in most circumstances, but their distinctive articulation is a clue to their ethnic, regional, or social-class origins. The sound changes that occur over

time within any particular phonemic system (accent) are equally orderly.

Morphology: Word Structure

Morphology, the study of how words are put together, developed as a subfield of linguistics as soon as linguists realized that the rules they had devised to explain sound patterns in language could not explain the structure of words.

What is a word? English speakers tend to think of words as the building blocks of sentences and of sentences as strings of words. But words are not all alike: Some words (*book*), cannot be broken down into smaller elements; others (*bookworm*) can. The puzzle deepens when we try to translate words from one language into another. Sometimes expressions that require only one word in one language (*préciser* in French) require more than one word in another (*to make precise* in English). Other times, we must deal with languages whose utterances cannot easily be broken down into words at all. Consider the utterance *nikookitepeena* from Shawnee (an indigenous North American language), which translates into English as "I dipped his head in the water" (Whorf 1956, 172). Although the Shawnee utterance

TABLE 5.1   MORPHEMES OF SHAWNEE UTTERANCE AND THEIR GLOSSES

ni	*kooki*	*tepe*	*en*	*a*
I	immersed in water	point of action at head	by hand action	cause to him

is composed of parts, the parts do not possess the characteristics we attribute to words in, say, English or French (Table 5.1).

To make sense of the structure of languages such as Shawnee, anthropological linguists needed a concept that could refer to both words (like those in the English sentence above) and the parts of an utterance that could not be broken down into words. This led to the development of the concept of *morphemes,* traditionally defined as "the minimal units of meaning in a language." The various parts of a Shawnee utterance can be identified as morphemes, and so can many English words. Describing minimal units of meaning as morphemes, and not as words, allows us to compare the morphology of different languages.

Morphemic patterning in languages like Shawnee may seem hopelessly complicated to native English speakers, yet the patterning of morphemes in English is equally complex. Why is it that some morphemes can stand alone as words (*sing, red*) and others cannot (*-ing, -ed*)? What determines a word boundary in the first place? Words, or the morphemes they contain, are the minimal units of meaning. Thus, they represent the fundamental point at which the arbitrary pairing of sound and meaning occurs.

Syntax: Sentence Structure

A third component of language is **syntax,** or sentence structure. Linguists began to study syntax when they discovered that morphological rules alone could not account for certain patterns of morpheme use. In languages like English, for example, rules governing word order cannot explain what is puzzling about the following English sentence: "Smoking grass means trouble." For many native speakers of American English, this sentence exhibits what linguists call *structural ambiguity.* That is, we must ask ourselves what *trouble* means: the act of smoking grass (marijuana) or observing grass (the grass that grows on the prairie) that

is giving off smoke. In the first reading, smoking is a gerund working as a noun; in the second, it is a gerund working as an adjective.

We can explain the existence of structurally ambiguous sentences if we assume that the role a word plays in a sentence depends on the overall structure of the sentence in which the word is found and not on the structure of the word itself. Thus, sentences can be defined as ordered strings of words, and those words can be classified as parts of speech in terms of the function they fulfill in a sentence. But these two assumptions cannot account for the ambiguity in a sentence like: "The father of the girl and the boy fell into the lake." How many people fell into the lake? Just the father, or the father and the boy? Each reading of the sentence depends on how the words of the sentence are grouped together.

This sort of grouping, called *structural grouping,* separates the various parts of speech into categories that represent the actual building blocks of the sentence itself. In this case, we had to decide which noun phrase was the *subject* of the sentence because there were two noun phrases that might have filled that role.

But even these three features cannot account for the structure of all well-formed English sentences. Chomsky (1965) noted that native speakers of English understand that sentences such as (1) "The boy watered the garden" and (2) "The garden was watered by the boy" are related to one another. He argued that this perceived connection could be explained if we could show that these two sentences have something in common even though they appear to be structured differently. Chomsky called the visible (or audible) appearance of a sentence its *surface structure.* But he argued that all sentences also possess a *deep structure,* which cannot be seen (or heard). He claimed that native speakers sense

---

morphology In linguistics, the study of the minimal units of meaning in a language.

syntax The study of sentence structure.

that two sentences are related because the sentences share the same deep structure. In the preceding example, the surface structure of the first sentence accurately reflects its deep structure. The second sentence, however, has been derived from the first by applying a grammatical rule called the *passive transformation*. That is, it transforms an active sentence ("The boy watered the garden") into a passive one ("The garden was watered by the boy"). Chomsky's transformational linguistics has inspired many years of active research into the structure of sentences in English and other languages.

Semantics: Meaning

Semantics, the study of meaning, was avoided by linguists for many years because *meaning* is a highly ambiguous term. What do we mean when we say that a sentence means something? We may be talking about what each individual word in the sentence means, or what the sentence as a whole means, or what I mean when I utter the sentence, which may differ from what someone else would mean even if uttering the same sentence.

In the 1960s, formal semantics took off when Chomsky argued that grammars needed to represent all of the linguistic knowledge in a speaker's head, and word meanings were part of that knowledge. Formal semanticists focused attention on how words are linked to each other within a language, exploring such relations as *synonymy,* or "same meaning" (*old* and *aged*); *homophony,* or "same sound, different meaning" (*would* and *wood*); and *antonymy,* or "opposite meaning" (*tall* and *short*). They also defined words in terms of *denotation,* or what they referred to in the "real world."

The denotations of words like *table* or *monkey,* seems fairly straightforward, but this is not the case with words like *truth* or *and.* Moreover, even if we believe a word can be linked to a concrete object in the world, it may still be difficult to decide exactly what the term refers to. Suppose we decide to find out what *monkey* refers to by visiting the zoo. In one cage we see small animals with grasping hands feeding on fruit. In a second cage are much larger animals that resemble the ones in the first cage in many ways, except that they have no tails. And in a third cage are yet other animals who resemble those in the first two cages except that they are far smaller and use their long tails

to swing from the branches of a tree. Which of these animals are monkeys?

To answer this question, the observer must decide which features of similarity or difference are important and which are not. Having made this decision, it is easier to decide if the animals in the first cage are monkeys and whether the animals in the other cages are monkeys as well. But such decisions are not easy to come by. Biologists have spent the last 300 years or so attempting to classify all living things on the planet into mutually exclusive categories. To do so, they have had to decide, of all the traits that living things exhibit, which ones matter.

This suggests that meaning must be constructed in the face of ambiguity. Formal linguistics, however, tries to deal with ambiguity by eliminating it, by "disambiguating" ambiguous utterances. To find a word's "unambiguous" denotation, we might consult a dictionary. According to the *American Heritage Dictionary,* for example, a pig is "any of several mammals of the family Suidae, having short legs, cloven hoofs, bristly hair, and a cartilaginous snout used for digging." A formal definition of this sort does indeed relate the word *pig* to other words in English, such as *cow* and *chicken,* and these meaning relations would hold even if all real pigs, cows, and chickens were wiped off the face of the earth. But words also have *connotations,* additional meanings that derive from the typical contexts in which they are used in everyday speech. In the context of antiwar demonstrations in the 1960s, for example, a pig was a police officer.

From a denotative point of view, to call police officers *pigs* is to create ambiguity deliberately, to muddle rather than to clarify. It is an example of **metaphor,** a form of figurative or nonliteral language that violates the formal rules of denotation by linking expressions from unrelated semantic domains. Metaphors are used all the time in everyday speech, however. Does this mean, therefore, that people who use metaphors are talking nonsense? What can it possibly mean to call police officers *pigs?*

We cannot know until we place the statement into some kind of context. If we know, for example, that protesters in the 1960s viewed the police as the paid enforcers of racist elites responsible for violence against the poor, and that pigs are domesticated animals, not humans, who are often viewed as fat, greedy, and dirty, then the metaphor "police are pigs" begins to make sense. This interpretation, however, does not reveal the "true meaning" of the metaphor for all time. In a different context, the same phrase might be used, for example, to distinguish the costumes worn by police officers to a charity function from the costumes of other groups of government functionaries. Our ability to use the same words in different ways (and different words in the same way) is the hallmark of openness, and formal semantics is powerless to contain it. This suggests that much of the referential meaning of language escapes us if we neglect the context of language use.

Pragmatics: Language in Contexts of Use

Pragmatics can be defined as the study of language in the context of its use. Each context offers limitations and opportunities concerning what we may say and how we may say it. Everyday language use is thus often characterized by a struggle between speakers and listeners over definitions of context and appropriate word use.

Formal linguistic pragmatics developed during the 1970s and 1980s; it has recently been described as the "last stand" of formal linguists who wanted to explain speech entirely in terms of invariant grammatical rules (Hanks 1996, 94). Indeed, both language use and context are narrowly defined in formal pragmatics, bearing only on those uses and contexts that are presumably common to all speakers of all languages.

Linguistic anthropologist Michael Silverstein (1976, 1985) was one of the first to argue that the referential meaning of certain expressions in language cannot be determined unless we go beyond the boundaries of a sentence and place the expressions in a wider context of use. Two kinds of context must be considered. *Linguistic context* refers to the other words, expressions, and sentences that surround the expression whose meaning we are trying to determine. The meaning of *it* in the sentence "I really enjoyed it" cannot be determined if the sentence is considered on its own. However, if we know that the previous sentence was "My aunt gave me this book for my birthday," we have a linguistic context that allows us to deduce that it refers to this book. *Nonlinguistic context* consists of objects and activities that are present in the situation of speech at the same time we are speaking. Consider the sentence, "Who is that standing by the door?" We need to inspect the actual physical context at the moment

this sentence is uttered to find the door and the person standing by the door and thus give a referential meaning to the words who and that. Furthermore, even if we know what a door is in a formal sense, we need the nonlinguistic context to clarify what counts as a door in this instance (for example, it could be a rough opening in the wall).

By forcing analysts to go beyond syntax and semantics, pragmatics directs our attention to *discourse,* which is formally defined as a stretch of speech longer than a sentence united by a common theme. Discourse may be a series of sentences uttered by a single individual or a series of rejoinders in a conversation among two or more speakers. Many linguistic anthropologists accept the arguments of M. M. Bakhtin and V. N. Voloshinov (see, for example, Voloshinov [1929] 1986), that the series of rejoinders in conversation are the primary form of discourse. In this view, the speech of any single individual, whether a simple *yes* or a book-length dissertation, is only one rejoinder in an ongoing dialogue.

Ethnopragmatics

Linguistic anthropologists analyze the way discourse is produced when people talk to one another. But they go far beyond formal pragmatics, paying attention not only to the immediate context of speech, linguistic and nonlinguistic, but also to broader contexts that are shaped by unequal social relationships and rooted in history (Brenneis and Macauley 1996; Hill and Irvine 1992). Alessandro Duranti calls this **ethnopragmatics**, "a study of language use which relies on ethnography to illuminate the ways in which speech is both constituted by and constitutive of social interaction" (Duranti 1994, 11). Such a study focuses on *practice,* human activity in which the rules of grammar, cultural values, and physical action are all conjoined (Hanks 1996, 11). Such a perspective locates the source of meaning in everyday routine social activity, or habitus, rather than in grammar. As a result, phonemes,

---

semantics The study of meaning.
metaphor A form of thought and language that asserts a meaningful link between two expressions from different semantic domains.
pragmatics The study of language in the context of its use.
ethnopragmatics A study of language use which relies on ethnography to illuminate the ways in which speech is both constituted by and constitutive of social interaction.

morphemes, syntax, and semantics are viewed as linguistic resources people can make use of, rather than rigid forms that determine what people can and cannot think or say.

If mutual understanding is shaped by shared routine activity and not by grammar, then communication is possible even if the people interacting with one another speak mutually unintelligible languages. All they need is a shared sense of "what is going on here" and the ability to negotiate successfully who will do what (Hanks 1996, 234). Such mutually coengaged people shape *communicative practices* that involve spoken language but also include values and shared habitual knowledge that may never be put into words. Since most people in most societies regularly engage in a wide range of practical activities with different subgroups, each one will also end up knowledgeable about a variety of different communicative practices and the linguistic habits that go with them. For example, a college student might know the linguistic habits appropriate to dinner with her parents, to the classroom, to worship services, to conversations in the dorm with friends, and to her part-time job as a waitress. Each set of linguistic habits she knows is called a **discourse genre.** Since our student simultaneously knows a multiplicity of different discourse genres she can use in speech, she embodies what Bakhtin called *heteroglossia* (Bakhtin 1981).

For Bakhtin, heteroglossia is the normal condition of linguistic knowledge in any society with internal divisions. Heteroglossia describes a coexisting multiplicity of linguistic norms and forms, many of which are anchored in more than one social subgroup. Because we all participate in more than one of these subgroups, we inevitably become multilingual, even if the only language we know is English! Our capacity for heteroglossia is an example of linguistic openness: It means that our thought and speech are not imprisoned in a single set of grammatical forms, as linguistic determinists argued. Indeed, if our college student reflects on the overlap as well as the contrasts between the language habits used in the dorm with those used in the restaurant, she might well find herself raising questions about what words really mean. To the extent, however, that her habitual ways of speaking are deeply rooted in everyday routine activity, they may guide the way she typically thinks, perceives, and acts. And to that extent, the linguistic relativity hypothesis may be correct—

not on the level of grammatical categories, but on the level of discourse (Hanks 1996, 176, 246; Schultz 1990).

A practice approach to language use aims to show how grammar, human action, and human values are all inextricably intertwined. But this does not mean that formal grammar can be ignored. As William Hanks puts it, "The system of language does have unique properties, and we do better to recognize this than to try to pretend it isn't so" (1996, 232). Each language, as a system, has a particular set of formal possibilities that can be mobilized as resources when people talk to one another. At the same time, "context saturates linguistic forms, right down to the semantic bones" (142). Meaning is the outcome, thus, both of the formal properties of language uttered and the contextual situation in which it is uttered. And context always includes understandings about social relationships and previous history that may never be put into words.

How all this works is best illustrated with an example. One of the most obvious ways that context influences speech is when speakers tailor their words for a particular audience. Advertising agencies, for example, are notorious for slanting their messages to appeal to the people they want to buy their clients' products or services. Alessandro Duranti learned that a sense of audience is highly cultivated among the professional orators who argue cases before the titled people, called *matai,* who meet regularly in the Samoan village council, or *fono* (Figure 5.6). (See EthnoProfile 5.2: Samoa.) Orators make use of a discourse genre midway in formality between everyday speech and ceremonial speech. Because the fono renders judgments that assign praise and blame, the main struggle between orators for different sides is "often centered on the ability to frame the reason for the meeting as involving or not involving certain key social actors" (Duranti 1994, 3). Of all the grammatical resources used by orators, one particular form, called the *ergative Agent,* most attracted Duranti's attention.

In semantic terms, an ergative Agent can be understood as a "willful initiator of an event that may be depicted as having consequences" for either an object or a passive recipient of the event (125). In Samoan, ergative Agents are marked by the preposition *e,* to distinguish them grammatically. Other forms of agency are marked by different prepositions: For example, *i* or *ia* frames the human agent as the source of the transaction, rather than as its willful initiator; and the pos-

FIGURE 5.6 Although nominal power rests with Samoan chiefs, when village elders meet in the *fono,* titled orators like this man from the island of Tutuila, tend to direct its proceedings.

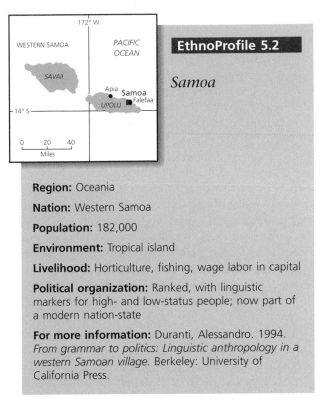

EthnoProfile 5.2

Samoa

Region: Oceania

Nation: Western Samoa

Population: 182,000

Environment: Tropical island

Livelihood: Horticulture, fishing, wage labor in capital

Political organization: Ranked, with linguistic markers for high- and low-status people; now part of a modern nation-state

For more information: Duranti, Alessandro. 1994. *From grammar to politics: Linguistic anthropology in a western Samoan village.* Berkeley: University of California Press.

sessive marker *o* or *a* attached to an agent focuses attention not on the possessor, but on the object possessed, that is, on John's *food* rather than on *John's* food. These ways of framing agency in grammatical terms are common in the fono, as disputants argue over who should be held accountable for some act. Possible agents include God, particular individuals, or groups. It is perhaps not surprising that the speaker who produced the highest number of ergative Agents in his speech was the senior orator, who ran the meetings and often served as prosecutor. "Powerful actors are more likely to define others as ergative Agents when they want to accuse them of something. Less powerful actors can try to resist such accusations by suggesting alternative linguistic definitions of events and people's roles in them" (133). In all cases, final judgments are the outcome of talk, but of talk saturated with sociopolitical awareness and deeply rooted in local historical context.

PIDGIN LANGUAGES: NEGOTIATED MEANING

The Samoan village fono is a setting in which speakers and listeners are able, for the most part, to draw upon knowledge of overlapping language habits in order to struggle verbally over moral and political issues. In some instances, however, potential parties to a verbal exchange find themselves sharing little more than physical proximity to one another. Such situations arise when members of communities with radically different language traditions and no history of previous contact with one another come face to face and are forced to communicate. There is no way to predict the outcome of such enforced contact on either speech community, yet from these new shared experiences, new

discourse genre A set of distinctive linguistic habits rooted in shared routine activity.

forms of practice including a new form of language—**pidgin**—may develop.

"When the chips are down, meaning is negotiated" (Lakoff and Johnson 1980, 231). The study of pidgin languages is the study of the radical negotiation of new meaning, the dialectical production of a new whole (the pidgin language) that is different from and reducible to neither of the languages that gave birth to it. The shape of a pidgin reflects the context in which it arises—generally one of colonial conquest or commercial domination. Vocabulary is usually taken from the language of the dominant group, making it easy for that group to learn. Syntax and phonology may be similar to the subordinate language (or languages), however, making it easier for subordinated speakers to learn. Morphemes that mark the gender or number of nouns or the tenses of verbs tend to disappear (Holm 1988).

Pidgins are traditionally defined as reduced languages that have no native speakers. They develop, in a single generation, between groups of speakers that possess distinct native languages. When speakers of a pidgin language pass that language on to a new generation, linguists traditionally referred to the language as a *creole*. The creolization of pidgins was said to involve growing complexity in phonology, morphology, syntax, semantics, and pragmatics, such that the pidgin came to resemble a conventional language.

This traditional view suggested to Derek Bickerton (1981) that the way in which pidgins form could shed light on the universal biological bases of human language. He found that Hawaiian Pidgin English differed in many ways from Hawaiian Creole, which descended from it. Since, in his view, none of these differences could be connected to any of the languages available to those who invented Hawaiian Creole, he concluded that they were produced by the innate linguistic "bioprogram" of the creole creators, and he claimed that these same forms could be found in other unrelated creoles as well.

Other students of pidgins and creoles tried to test his hypotheses. While their work did not confirm his views, it did reveal other important data. One discovery was that the old distinction between pidgins and creoles did not seem to hold up. In the Pacific, for example, linguists have discovered pidgin dialects, pidgin languages used as main languages of permanently settled groups, and pidgins that have become native languages. Moreover, creolization can take place at any time after a pidgin forms, creoles can exist without

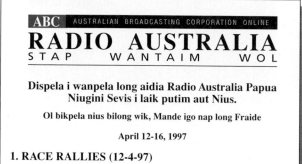

FIGURE 5.7 Tok Pisin, a pidgin language that developed in New Guinea following colonization by English-speakers, has become a major medium of communication in New Guinea. The news in Tok Pisin is available now on the World Wide Web (http://www.abc.net.au/ra/png/pnghome.htm).

having been preceded by pidgins, pidgins can remain pidgins for long periods and undergo linguistic change without acquiring native speakers, and pidgin and creole varieties of the same language can coexist in the same society (Jourdan 1991, 192ff.). In fact, it looks as if heteroglossia is as widespread among speakers of pidgins and creoles as among speakers of other languages.

More information has been gathered about the historical and sociocultural contexts within which pidgins first formed. Here as elsewhere in linguistic anthropology, the focus has turned to practice. Awareness of heteroglossia in pidgin/creole speech communities has led to redefinition of a pidgin as a secondary language in a speech community that uses some other main language, and a creole as a main language in a speech community, whether or not it has native speakers. According to the new view, creolization is likely when pidgin speakers find themselves in new social contexts requiring a new language for *all* the practical activities of everyday life; without such a context, it is unlikely that creoles will emerge (Jourdan 1991, 196).

Viewing pidgin creation as a form of communicative practice means that attention must be paid to the role of pidgin creators as agents in the process (Figure 5.7). As we negotiate meaning across language barriers, it appears that all humans have intuitions about which parts of our speech carry the most meaning and which parts can be safely dropped. Neither party to the negotiation, moreover, may be trying to learn the other's language; rather, "speakers in the course of negotiating communication use whatever linguistic and sociolinguistic resources they have at their disposal, until the shared meaning is established and conventionalized" (Jourdan 1991, 200).

LINGUISTIC INEQUALITY

Pidgins and creoles turn out to be far more complex and the result of far more active human input than we used to think, which is why they are so attractive to linguists and linguistic anthropologists as objects of study. Where they coexist, however, alongside the language of the dominant group (e.g., Hawaiian Pidgin English and English), they are ordinarily viewed as defective and inferior languages. Such views can be seen as an outgrowth of the situation that led to the formation of most of the pidgins we know about: European colonial domination. In a colonial or postcolonial setting, the language of the colonizer is often viewed as better than pidgin or creole languages, which are frequently thought to be broken, imperfect versions of the colonizer's language. The situation only worsens when formal education, the key to participation in the European-dominated society, is carried out in the colonial language. Speakers of pidgin who remain illiterate may never be able to master the colonial tongue and may find themselves effectively barred from equal participation in the civic life of their societies.

To take one language variety as the standard against which all other varieties are measured might be described as linguistic ethnocentrism, and such a standard may be applied to any language, not just pidgins and creoles. This is one kind of linguistic inequality: making value judgments about other people's speech in a context of dominance and subordination. A powerful example of the effects of linguistic inequality is found in the history and controversies surrounding African American English in the United States.

Language Habits of African Americans

In the 1960s, some psychologists claimed that African American children living in urban areas of the northern United States suffered from linguistic deprivation.

They argued that these children started school with a limited vocabulary and no grammar and thus could not perform as well as European American children in the classroom—that their language was unequal to the challenges of communication. Sociolinguist William Labov and his colleagues found such claims incredible and undertook research of their own (Labov 1972), which demonstrated two things. First, they proved that the form of English spoken in the inner city was not defective pseudolanguage. Second, they showed how a change in research context permitted inner-city African American children to display a level of linguistic sophistication that the psychologists had never dreamed they possessed.

When African American children were in the classroom (a European American–dominated context) being interrogated by European American adults about topics of no interest to them, they said little. This did not necessarily mean, Labov argued, that they had no language. Rather, their minimal responses were better understood as defensive attempts to keep threatening European American questioners from learning anything about them. For the African American children, the classroom was only one part of a broader racist culture. The psychologists, due to their ethnocentrism, had been oblivious to the effect this context might have on their research.

Reasoning that reliable samples of African American speech had to be collected in contexts where the racist threat was lessened, Labov and his colleagues conducted fieldwork in the homes and on the streets of the inner city. They recorded enormous amounts of speech in African American English (AAE) produced by the same children who had had nothing to say when questioned in the classroom. Labov's analysis demonstrated that AAE was a variety of English that had certain rules not found in Standard English. This is a strictly linguistic difference: Most middle-class speakers of Standard English would not use these rules but most African American speakers of AAE would. However, neither variety of English should be seen as "defective" as a result of this difference. This kind of linguistic difference, apparent when speakers of two varieties converse, marks the speaker's membership in a particular speech community. Such differences can exist in

pidgin A language with no native speakers that develops in a single generation between members of communities that possess distinct native languages.

IN THEIR OWN WORDS

Varieties of African American English

The school board of Oakland, California, gained national attention in December of 1996 when its members voted to recognize Ebonics as an official second language. What they called Ebonics is also known as Black English Vernacular (BEV), Black English (BE), African American English Vernacular (AAEV), and African American English (AAE). The school board decision generated controversy both within and outside the African American community because it seemed to be equating Ebonics with other "official second languages," such as Spanish and Chinese. This implied that Standard English was as much a "foreign language" to native speakers of Ebonics as it was to native speakers of Spanish and Chinese, and that Oakland school students who were native speakers of Ebonics should be entitled not only to the respect accorded native Spanish- or Chinese-speaking students, but also, perhaps, to the same kind of funding for bilingual education. The uproar produced by this dispute caused the school board to amend the resolution a month later. African American linguistic anthropologist Marcyliena Morgan's commentary highlights one issue that many disputants ignored: namely, that the African American community is not monoglot in Ebonics, but is in fact characterized by heteroglossia.

After sitting through a string of tasteless jokes about the Oakland school district's approval of a language education policy for African American students, I realize that linguists and educators have failed to inform Americans about varieties of English used throughout the country and the link between these dialects and culture, social class, geographic region and identity. After all, linguists have been a part of language and education debates around AAE and the furor that surrounds them since the late 1970s. Then the Ann Arbor school district received a court order to train teachers on aspects of AAE to properly assess and teach children in their care.

Like any language and dialect, African American varieties of English—ranging from that spoken by children and some adults with limited education to those spoken by adults with advanced degrees—are based on the cultural, social, historical and political experiences shared by many US people of African descent. This experience is one of family, community and love as well as racism, poverty and discrimination. Every African American does not speak AAE. Moreover, some argue that children who speak the vernacular, typically grow up to speak both AAE as well as mainstream varieties of English. It is therefore not surprising that the community separates its views of AAE, ranging from loyalty to abhorrence, from issues surrounding the literacy education of their children. Unfortunately, society's ambivalent attitudes toward African American students' cognitive abilities, like Jensen's 1970s deficit models and the 1990s' *The Bell Curve,* suggest that when it comes to African American kids, intelligence and competence in school can be considered genetic.

African American children who speak the vernacular form of AAE may be the only English-speaking children in this country who attend community schools in which teachers not only are ignorant of their dialect but refuse to accept its existence. This attitude leads to children being marginalized and designated as learning disabled. The educational failure of African American children can, at best, be only partially addressed through teacher training on AAE. When children go to school, they bring not only their homework and textbooks but also their language, culture and identity. Sooner rather than later, the educational system must address its exclusion of cultural and dialect difference in teacher training and school curriculum.

Source: Morgan 1997, 8.

phonology, morphology, syntax, semantics, or pragmatics (Figure 5.8). Indeed, similar linguistic differences distinguish the language habits of most social subgroups in a society, like that of the United States, that is characterized by heteroglossia.

What is distinctive about African American English from a practice perspective, however, are the historical

and sociocultural circumstances that led to its creation. For some time, linguists have viewed AAE as one of many creole languages that developed in the New World after Africans were brought there to work as slaves on plantations owned by Europeans. Dominant English-speaking elites have regarded AAE with the same disdain that European colonial elites have accorded creole languages elsewhere. Because African Americans have always lived in socially and politically charged contexts that questioned their full citizenship, statements about their language habits are inevitably thought to imply something about their intelligence and culture. Those psychologists who claimed that inner-city African American children suffered from linguistic deprivation, for example, seemed to be suggesting either that these children were too stupid to speak or that their cultural surroundings were too meager to allow normal language development. The work of Labov and his colleagues showed that the children were not linguistically deprived, were not stupid, and participated in a rich linguistic culture. But this work itself became controversial in later decades when it became clear that the rich African American language and culture described was primarily that of adolescent males. These young men saw themselves as bearers of authentic African American language habits, and dismissed African Americans who did not speak the way they did as "lames." This implied that everyone else in the African American community was somehow not genuinely African American, a challenge which those excluded could not ignore. Linguists like Labov's team, who thought their work undermined racism, were thus bewildered when middle-class African Americans, who spoke Standard English, refused to accept AAE as representative of "true" African American culture (Morgan 1995, 337).

From the perspective of linguistic anthropology, this debate shows that the African American community is not homogeneous, linguistically or culturally, but is instead characterized by heteroglossia. At a minimum, language habits are shaped by social class, age cohort, and gender. Moreover, members of all of these subgroups use both Standard English and AAE in their speech. Morgan reports, for example, that upper-middle-class African American students at elite colleges who did not grow up speaking AAE regularly adopt many of its features and that hip-hop artists combine the grammar of Standard English with the phonology and morphology of AAE (1995, 338). This situation is not so paradoxical if we recall, once again, the politically charged context of African American life in the United States. African Americans both affirm and deny the significance of AAE for their identity, perhaps because AAE symbolizes both the oppression of slavery and resistance to that oppression (339). A quarter of a

FIGURE 5.8 The language habits of African Americans are not homogeneous, but vary according to social class, gender, region, and situation.

century ago, Claudia Mitchell Kernan described African Americans as "bicultural" and struggling to develop language habits that could reconcile "good" English and AAE (1972, 209). That struggle continues at the end of the twentieth century.

Language Habits of Women and Men

Differences in language habits not only distinguish ethnic groups from one another; they also distinguish the speech habits of women and men. Indeed, one of the early objections to early work on African American English was that it focused on the discourse genres of men only. Since the 1970s, the language habits of African American women and girls have figured in numerous studies (see Morgan 1995, 336ff.). One interesting counterpoint to the early focus on the speech of adolescent males is Goodwin's study of "he-said-she-said" disputes among African American girls. These girls regularly passed on gossip about one another, and a girl who was gossiped about would make extraordinary efforts to find out who had started the rumors about her. Often enough, the source of the rumors turned out to be someone who was deliberately trying to make trouble (Goodwin 1990).

Sociolinguist Deborah Tannen (1990) gained much popular attention in the media with her study of speech patterns of men and women in the United States. Tannen focuses on typical male and female styles of discourse, arguing that men and women use language for different reasons: Men tend to use language as a competitive weapon in public settings, whereas women tend to use language as a way of building closeness in private settings. Tannen shows what happens when men and women each assume that their rules are the only rules without realizing that the other gender may be defining appropriate language use from a different perspective. For example, when a husband and wife get home from work at the end of the day, she may be eager to talk while he is just as eager to remain silent. She may interpret his silence as a sign of distance or coldness and be hurt. He, by contrast, may be weary of the day's verbal combat and resent his wife's attempts at conversation, not because he is rejecting her personally, but because he believes he has a right to remain silent.

LANGUAGE AND TRUTH

For Thomas Kuhn, a philosopher of science, metaphor lies at the heart of science, and changes in scientific theories are "accompanied by a change in some of the relevant metaphors and in corresponding parts of the network of similarities through which terms attach to nature" (1979, 416). Kuhn argues that these changes in the way scientific terms link to nature are not reducible to logic or grammar. "They come about in response to pressures generated by observation or experiment"—that is, by experience and context. And there is no neutral language into which rival theories can be translated and subsequently evaluated as unambiguously right or wrong (416). Kuhn asks the question, "Is what we refer to as 'the world' perhaps a product of mutual accommodation between experience and language?"

If our understanding of reality is the product of a dialectic between experience and language (or, more broadly, culture), then ambiguity will never be perma-

nently removed from any of the symbolic systems that human beings invent. Reflexive consciousness makes humans aware of alternatives. The experience of doubt, of not being sure what to believe, is never far behind.

This is not merely the experience of people in Western societies. E. E. Evans-Pritchard (1963) describes the same sort of disorientation among the Azande of central Africa. (See EthnoProfile 8.3: Azande.) The Azande people are well aware of the ambiguity inherent in language, and they exploit it by using metaphor (what they call *sanza*) to disguise speech that might be received badly if uttered directly. For example, "A man says in the presence of his wife to his friend, 'Friend, those swallows, how they flit about in there.' He is speaking about the flightiness of his wife and in case she should understand the allusion, he covers himself by looking up at the swallows as he makes his seemingly innocent remark" (Evans-Pritchard 1963, 211). Evans-Pritchard later observes that *sanza* "adds greatly to the difficulties of anthropological inquiry. Eventually the anthropologist's sense of security is undermined and his confidence shaken. He learns the language, can say what he wants to say in it, and can understand what he hears, but then he begins to wonder whether he has really understood . . . he cannot be sure, and even they [the Azande] cannot be sure, whether the words do have a nuance or someone imagines that they do" (228).

However much we learn about language, we will never be able to exhaust its meanings or circumscribe its rules once and for all. Human language is an open system, and as long as human history continues, new forms will be created and old forms will continue to be put to new uses.

Key Terms

language	morphology
linguistics	syntax
design features	semantics
linguistic competence	metaphor
communicative	pragmatics
competence	ethnopragmatics
Sapir-Whorf hypothesis	discourse genre
grammar	metaphor
phonology	pidgin

Chapter Summary

1. Language is a uniquely human faculty that both permits us to communicate and sets up barriers to communication. It is a part of culture that people use to encode their experience and structure their understanding of the world and of themselves. The study of different languages reveals the shared nature of language and culture and the contextual assumptions that speakers make and share.

2. There are many ways to communicate our experiences, and there is no absolute standard favoring one way over another. Individual efforts to create a unique voice are countered by pressures to negotiate a common code within the larger social group.

3. Of the sixteen design features of language, six are particularly important: openness, arbitrariness, duality of patterning, displacement, semanticity, and prevarication.

4. The Sapir-Whorf hypothesis suggests that language has the power to shape the way people see the world. The strong version of this hypothesis amounts to linguistic determinism; the weak version makes the shaping force of language too weak to be of interest. Neither Sapir nor Whorf favored linguistic determinism.

5. Today the study of language is usually subdivided into five specialties: phonology, the study of the sounds of language; morphology, the study of minimal units of meaning in language; syntax, the study of sentence structure; semantics, the study of meaning patterns; and pragmatics, the study of language in context of use.

6. Ethnopragmatics pays attention both to the immediate context of speech and to broader contexts that are shaped by unequal social relationships and rooted in history. It locates meaning in routine practical activities, which turn grammatical features of language into resources people can make use of in their interactions with others.

7. Because linguistic meaning is rooted in practical activity, which carries the burden of meaning, the activity and the linguistic usage together shape communicative practices. Different social groups generate different communicative practices. The linguistic habits that are part of each set of communicative practices constitute discourse genres. People normally command a range of discourse genres, which means that each person's linguistic knowledge is best understood as an example of heteroglossia.

8. The study of pidgin languages is the study of the radical negotiation of new meaning. In pidgins, two groups of language speakers who come in contact (often as a result of colonization or commercial domination) invent a new language different from either parent language. Pidgins may not reveal the innate bioprogram for human language, but pidgin languages do exhibit many of the same linguistic features as nonpidgin languages, including heteroglossia. Pidgin and creole languages are no longer rigidly distinguished from each other. Studies of African American English illustrate the historical circumstances that can give rise to creoles and illuminate the basis of some forms of linguistic inequality.

9. Linguists and anthropologists have described differences in the linguistic habits of women and men, relating them to gender-based communicative practices.

Suggested Readings

Akmajian, A., R. Demers, A. Farmer, and R. Harnish. 1991. *Linguistics*. 3d ed. Cambridge, MA: MIT Press. *A fine introduction to the study of language as a formal system.*

Brenncis, Donald, and Ronald K. S. Macauley, eds. 1996. *The matrix of language*. Boulder, CO: Westview. *A wide-ranging collection of essays by anthropologists studying linguistic habits in their sociocultural contexts.*

Lakoff, George, and Mark Johnson. 1980. *Metaphors we live by*. Berkeley: University of California Press. *An important, clear, and very accessible book that presents a radical and persuasive view of metaphor.*

Salzmann, Zdenek. 1993. *Language, culture, and society: An introduction to linguistic anthropology*. Boulder, CO: Westview. *An up-to-date and thorough text on linguistic anthropology.*

Smitherman, Geneva. 1977. *Talking and testifying: The language of Black America*. Detroit: Wayne State University Press. *An engaging introduction to Black English Vernacular, for native and nonnative speakers alike, with exercises to test your mastery of BEV grammar.*

6

Cognition

I f you examine Figure 6.1, you will see that marks on a piece of paper can be ambiguous. The signals we receive from the outside world tend to be open to more than one interpretation, be they patterns of light and dark striking the retinas of our eyes, smells, tastes, shapes or words.

THE DIALECTIC BETWEEN COGNITION AND CULTURE

In any human society, experience itself tends to be patterned. We repeatedly witness the change of seasons or the transformation of water into ice and ice into water. From day to day, we watch the people around us perform the same routine activities, and we watch them grow from childhood to adulthood to old age.

Chunks of experience that appear to hang together as wholes, exhibiting the same properties in the same configuration whenever they recur, are called **schemas.** As human beings grow up, they gradually become aware of the schemas that their culture (or subculture) recognizes. Such schemas are often embedded in practical activities and labeled linguistically, and they may serve as a focus for discourse.

People living in the United States, for example, cannot avoid a schema called *Christmas,* a chunk of experience that recurs once every year. The Christmas schema can include features like cold and snowy weather and activities like baking cookies, singing carols, going to church, putting up a Christmas tree, and buying and wrapping gifts. In the experience of a child, all these elements may appear to be equally relevant parts of a seamless whole. It may take time and conditioning for Christian parents to persuade children what the "true meaning of Christmas" really is. Some adults who celebrate Christmas disagree about its true meaning. Non-Christians living in the United States must also come to terms with this schema and may struggle to explain to their children why the activities associated with it are not appropriate for them.

People take for granted most of the schemas that their culture recognizes, using them as simplified interpretive frameworks for judging new experiences as typical or not, human or not (D'Andrade 1992, 48).

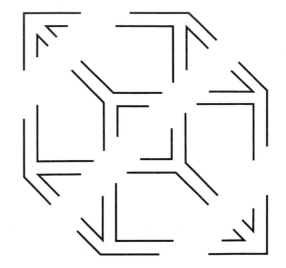

FIGURE 6.1 Ambiguous marks.

That is, they learn to use schemas as **prototypes.** Prototypes of various sorts appear to be central to the way meaning is organized in human language. The words we use refer to typical instances, typical elements or relations, and are embedded, as we saw in Chapter 5, in genres of discourse associated with routine cultural practices.

When we organize experience and assign meaning on the basis of prototypes, however, the categories we use have fuzzy boundaries. And because our experiences do not always neatly fit our prototypes, we are often not sure which prototype applies. Is a tossed salad a prototypical tossed salad if in addition to lettuce and tomatoes and onions it also contains raisins and apple slices? Is a library a prototypical library when it contains fewer books than microfilms and videotapes and electronic databases? In cases like this, suggests linguist R. A. Hudson (1980), a speaker must simply recognize the openness of language and apply linguistic labels creatively.

schemas Patterned, repetitive experiences.
prototypes Examples of a typical instance, element, relation, or experience within a culturally relevant semantic domain.

FIGURE 6.2 Locations of societies whose EthnoProfiles appear in Chapter 6.

COGNITION AS AN OPEN SYSTEM

LIKE language, cognition is an open system. Human beings not only talk about the world in a variety of ways, they also think about it in a variety of ways; and if no one way of thinking is obligatory, then any particular way of thinking must be arbitrary. Human cognition develops in the context of routine cultural activities that draw our attention to some parts of the world while ignoring others. What we think about depends greatly on what we have learned to pay attention to in the past. As a result, different groups in a society—with different histories and experiences—are likely to develop unique points of view and pay attention to

different things. When we learn from this culturally shaped experience, we can use preexisting categories to help us interpret new experiences. This is a version of displacement. All our senses can play tricks on us, moreover, and if they are artful enough, people can trick other people into perceiving something that "does not exist." Prevarication is thus a built-in feature of cognition, just as it is of language.

Cognition is also a symbolic process. Language and visual perception, for example, both require human beings to construct symbolic representations of their experiences in order to make sense of them. As a result, the meaning of what we see, touch, smell, taste, or hear depends on context. As with language, two contexts are normally invoked: the immediate context of the

perception itself and the displaced context stored in memory and shaped by culture. As with sentences, so too with the objects of perception. The "same" object can mean different things in different contexts. Consider what seeing a butcher knife means (1) lying on a cutting board in your kitchen next to a pile of mushrooms or (2) wielded by a burglar who has cornered you in your kitchen at midnight.

Cognition is often thought to have three aspects: perceptual, intellectual, and emotional. Perception as a cognitive process has been thought to link people to the world around them or within them: We perceive size, shape, color, pain, and so on. Intellect and emotion have referred to the two principal ways in which perceptions might be dealt with: rationally and logically on the one hand, passionately and intuitively on the other. Anthropologists and some psychologists suggest, however, that this approach to cognition is highly problematic. Particularly troubling is the traditional split between reason and emotion, which has often been accompanied by the overvaluing of reason and neglect of other cognitive capacities.

Cognitive Capacities and Intelligence

What makes it possible for human beings to receive signals from the outside world (or from within our own bodies) and then interpret those signals in a way that makes appropriate action possible? One traditional answer has been that every person either possesses at birth or develops over time certain basic cognitive capacities. At one time, these hypothetical capacities were thought of as substances or properties, and the goal of psychological testing was to measure how much of each cognitive capacity an individual had. Consequently, intelligence has traditionally been "measured" using an "instrument" called the *intelligence test;* the "amount" of intelligence measured is assigned a number called the *Intelligence Quotient,* or *IQ.* In the past, some researchers were quick to equate differences in performance on intelligence tests with differences in intelligence. Today, such a reductionist approach is subjected to intense scrutiny.

If it is difficult to identify and measure cognitive capacities in individuals, it may be impossible to do so for entire groups. Michael Cole and Sylvia Scribner are two psychological anthropologists who developed extensive experience in cross-cultural psychological testing. In their fieldwork, they repeatedly encountered situations in which the same psychological test produced results that differed between Western and non-Western subjects. They rejected the idea that non-Western subjects were just less intelligent, because, outside the laboratory setting, in the routine contexts of everyday life, their informants' intelligence and full humanity were obvious.

So why do intelligent informants often perform poorly on psychological tests? In the work of the Russian psychologist Lev Vygotsky, Cole and Scribner (1974) found an approach that pointed toward an answer. Vygotsky distinguished between **elementary cognitive processes** and the higher systems into which these processes are organized. Elementary cognitive processes include the ability to make abstractions, to categorize, to reason inferentially, and so forth. All normal humans everywhere are equipped with these abilities. Different cultures, however, organize these elementary processes into different **functional cognitive systems.** Culture also assigns different functional systems to different tasks in different contexts.

Consider once again the African American children whose "speech capacity" was measured by European American psychologists (see Chapter 5). When testing both African American and European American children, the same test, instructions, and controlled testing situation were used. The European American children responded easily and fluently, whereas the African American children responded in monosyllables or not

at all. Following Vygotsky, we have no reason to doubt that both groups of children possessed the same range of elementary cognitive processes. The difference in group performance was related to how the members of each group combined these elementary cognitive processes to interpret the testing situation and to function within it. The European American children interpreted the test and the testing situation as a nonthreatening opportunity to display their verbal ability, which they did. The African American children interpreted the same test and situation as a threatening personal and social attack, and they responded by refusing to respond. When interviewed in a nonthreatening context, however, these same children displayed considerable verbal ability.

In other words, there are different ways of defining tasks; once tasks are defined, there are different strategies for carrying them out; and routine strategies for carrying out (or refusing to carry out) tasks cannot be separated from the broader cultural and political contexts in which people live. As a result, administering an adequate psychological test starts to look as difficult as doing good anthropological fieldwork, with the same rewards and pitfalls.

PERCEPTION

Perception can be defined as the "processes by which people organize and experience information that is primarily of sensory origin" (Cole and Scribner 1974, 61). Identifying the nature of perception has long been central to understanding human cognition. As we saw in Chapter 3, the only evidence recognized by traditional positivist science is the evidence of our five senses. In this view, a suitably objective observer should be able to see and describe the world as it truly is. If other people describe the world differently, then their perceptions must in some way be distorted. Either they are not being objective, or their ability to discriminate among sensations is impaired, or they are attempting to trick and mislead.

Most modern researchers are far less certain about what perception entails. True, our perception is sometimes impaired, either for physical reasons (we are not wearing our glasses) or because our observations aren't disinterested (our child's forehead feels cool because we

FIGURE 6.3 Pictures used for the study of depth perception in Africa.

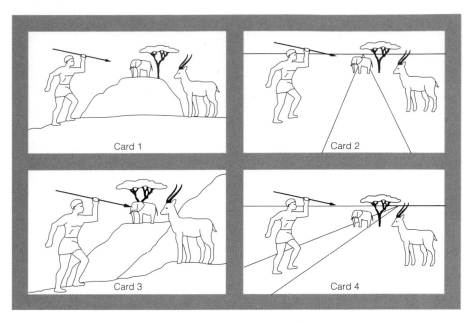

are afraid he or she might have a fever). And people do sometimes play jokes on one another, insisting that they have seen things they really have not seen. But what about people whose physiological equipment is functioning properly, who have no stake in the outcome, and who are not trying to deceive and yet who perceive things differently?

Today, many investigators ask questions that attempt to relate people's descriptions of their experiences, or their performances on psychological tests, to their understandings of context. For example, nonliterate South African mine workers were tested using two-dimensional line drawings of three-dimensional objects (Figure 6.3). The test results indicated that the mine workers consistently interpreted the drawings in two dimensions. When asked at which animal the man was pointing his spear on Card 1, subjects would usually respond, "the elephant." The elephant is, in fact, directly in line with and closest to the spear point in the drawing. However, the elephant ought to be seen as standing on top of the distant hill if the subjects interpret the drawings three-dimensionally. Did their responses mean that these Africans could not perceive in three dimensions?

J. B. Deregowski devised the following test. He presented different African subjects with the same drawings, asked them to describe what they saw, and got

two-dimensional verbal reports. Next, he presented the same subjects with the line drawings in Figure 6.4. This time, he asked his subjects to construct models based on the drawings using materials he provided. His subjects had no difficulty producing three-dimensional models.

In these tests, the "correct" solution depended on the subject's mastery of a Western convention for interpreting two-dimensional drawings and photographs. For the drawings in Figure 6.3, the Western convention includes assumptions about perspective that relate the size of objects to their distance from the observer. Without such a convention in mind, it is not obvious that the size of a drawn object has any connection with distance. Far from providing us with new insights about the African perceptual abilities, perhaps the most interesting result of such tests is what they teach us about Western perceptual conventions. That is, drawings do not necessarily speak for themselves. They can

elementary cognitive processes The ability to make abstractions, reason inferentially, categorize, and perform other mental tasks common to all normal humans.
functional cognitive systems Culturally linked sets of cognitive processes that guide perception, conception, reason, and emotion.
perception The processes by which people organize and experience information that is primarily of sensory origin.

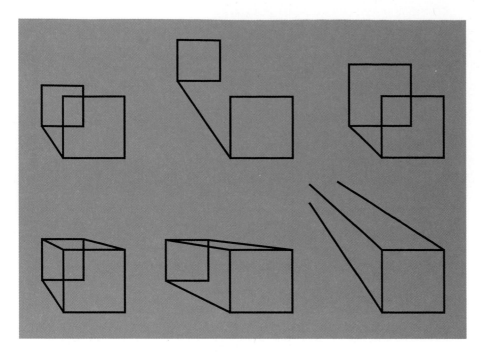

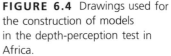

FIGURE 6.4 Drawings used for the construction of models in the depth-perception test in Africa.

make sense to us only once we accept certain rules for interpreting them (Cole and Scribner 1974).

Illusion

Just as studies of metaphor provide insight into the nature of literal language, so studies of visual illusions provide insight into the nature of visual perception. Indeed, the contrast between literal and metaphorical language is not unlike the contrast between reality and illusion as it relates to perception. In both cases, knowledge of context permits us to distinguish between the literal and the metaphorical, the real and the illusory.

Richard Gregory is a cognitive psychologist who has spent most of his career studying visual illusions. In his view, illusions are produced by *misplaced procedures:* perfectly normal, ordinary cognitive processes that have somehow been inappropriately selected and applied to a particular set of visual signals. For him, perceptions are symbolic representations of reality, not direct samples of reality. Perceivers must often work very hard to make sense of the visual signals they receive. When they are wrong, they are subject to illusion.

Gregory (1983) describes four types of visual illusion. The first is *distortion:* What you see appears larger or smaller, longer or shorter, and so on, than it really

is. Consider the Ponzo illusion in Figure 6.5. Typically, the upper parallel line appears to be longer than the lower one when, in fact, they are equal. The standard explanation of this illusion is that we are looking at a two-dimensional drawing but interpreting it as if it were in three dimensions. In other words, the Ponzo illusion plays on our ability to see three-dimensional space in a two-dimensional drawing.

This explanation helps us understand the responses of the African mine workers to the drawings reproduced in Figure 6.3. Western observers interpret that drawing as a two-dimensional representation of three-dimensional reality. In the Ponzo illusion, the shapes trick us because they are very similar to what we perceive when we stand on a railroad track and look toward its vanishing point on the horizon. Africans are also familiar with railroad tracks, but they did not attempt to interpret the Ponzo-like lines on Card 2 of Figure 6.3 as representations of three-dimensional reality. On the contrary, they seemed to work very hard to keep the relationships between objects in two dimensions, even if this meant that the sizes of the objects themselves appeared distorted. When we compare the Western interpretation of the Ponzo illusion with the African interpretation of the pictures in Figure 6.3, we discover something important: Both sets of draw-

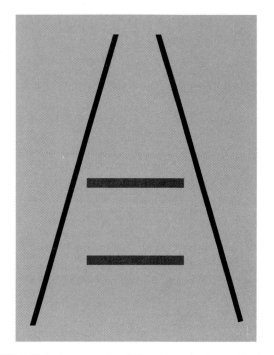

FIGURE 6.5 An example of distortion: the Ponzo illusion.

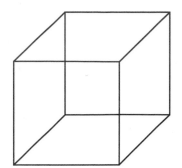

FIGURE 6.6 An example of ambiguity: the Necker cube.

ings are ambiguous, and both are potentially open to distortion. How people interpret them depends on pre-existing cultural conventions.

The second type of visual illusion, *ambiguity,* occurs when a set of visual signals is constant but the perceiver's awareness of it flips from one image to another. Consider the Necker cube in Figure 6.6. As you stare at this pattern, it seems to move. First one face of the Necker cube is in front; a second later it pops to the back. Experiments demonstrate that this flipping back and forth of the image has nothing to do with the visual signals themselves; the pattern of lines on the retina remains fixed. What seems to be happening is that the mind is confronting a pattern that can be interpreted in at least two equally probable ways. It keeps hopping between each probable interpretation, testing various interpretive hypotheses in an attempt to resolve the ambiguity. But because the signals are so perfectly ambiguous, no resolution is possible. The image appears to flip endlessly from one possibility to the other.

Gregory's third type of illusion is *paradox:* an image that appears to be visually contradictory. Consider Fig-

ure 6.7. Here we are tripped up again and again as we apply a given set of cognitive procedures to make sense of the visual signals we are receiving. We seem to make sense of the image only to encounter some other part of it that upsets our previous theory.

Gregory's fourth type of illusion is *fiction:* seeing things that are not there. Consider the Kanizsa illusion in Figure 6.8. A white triangle's sides appear to curve inward and its points to block out portions of three black circles beneath them. This image is fiction because nothing—no change in brightness across the edges of the "overlapping triangles," for example—signals to us that there are overlapping triangles rather than six separate black shapes arranged in a ring on a white background. Gregory argues that we respond as we do to illusions of this kind because experience has made us familiar with certain patterns we come to expect. For example, when we encounter surprising gaps where we would normally expect to encounter continuous edges, we tend to assume that something is getting in the way of those continuous edges.

Perceptions are shaped by our habitual experience, then, by the schemas and practices we use to order our lives. We all encounter visual illusions from time to time in the everyday world. Unlike the drawings used for psychological tests, the sources of these illusions are not often abstract patterns devoid of context. And unlike subjects in a laboratory, we usually are free to use our other senses, to move our bodies in space, to manipulate the source of the puzzling signals until we resolve the ambiguity to our satisfaction. As with figurative language, however, we resolve the ambiguity only with respect to that particular context. Technically,

FIGURE 6.8 An example of fiction: a Kanizsa illusion.

according to Gregory, we are making hypotheses about what those visual signals most probably represent in the world we know, a world that is culturally shaped.

Cognitive Style

Cognitive style refers to a recurring pattern of perceptual and intellectual activity. Cultures provide people with a range of cognitive styles that are appropriate for different cognitive tasks in different contexts. Psychological anthropologists have attempted to compare cognitive styles cross-culturally. Some have argued that the styles of individuals and of groups can be located on a continuum between a global style and an articulated style. People who use a **global style** tend to view the world holistically; they see first a bundle of relationships and only later the bits and pieces that are related. They are said to be *field dependent.* By contrast, people who use an **articulated style** tend to break up the world into smaller and smaller pieces, which can then be organized into larger chunks. They also tend to see a sharp boundary between their own bodies and the outside world. People using an articulated style are able to consider whatever they happen to be paying attention to apart from its context and so are said to be *field independent* (Cole and Scribner 1974, 82).

Originally, most people in Western societies were thought to be field independent, whereas most people in most non-Western cultures were thought to be field dependent. However, more detailed research shows that these generalizations are misleading. For instance, the preferred cognitive style of an individual often varies from task to task and from context to context. People who use articulated styles for some tasks also use global styles for other tasks. In fact, they may bring a range of different styles to bear on a single task.

Research by Jean Lave and her colleagues (1988) demonstrated that middle-class North Americans are not field independent in all contexts, even when the task involves mathematics, which would seem to be the most field independent of all cognitive activities. Lave and her associates wanted to test the widespread assumption that cognitive style does not vary across contexts. In particular, they wanted to find out whether ordinary people use the same mathematical skills in the supermarket and the kitchen that they use in the classroom. As part of the research, subjects were given a pencil-and-paper math test to determine how well they could solve certain problems in a schoollike context. Researchers also observed how the same subjects used mathematics while making buying decisions at the grocery store. Finally, the subjects were presented with paired grocery items and asked to calculate the best buy.

The results of this research were surprising. First, the subjects averaged only 59 percent correct on the pencil-and-paper test but achieved averages of 98 percent on the supermarket experiment and 93 percent on the best-buy experiment. Second, the researchers found that the high scores on the last two experiments were achieved with very little reliance on mathematics taught in school. Many observers would have expected subjects trained in formal mathematics to rely on its infallible methods to help them make wise economic decisions. On the contrary, the test results suggest that shoppers were better able to make wise economic decisions using informal calculation strategies. The three most common informal strategies were *inspection* (recognizing that one item was both lower in price and larger in volume), *best-buy calculations* (comparing two quantities and two prices first and choosing the better

value), and a *difference strategy* (deciding whether a marginal difference in quantity was worth the marginal difference in price; Lave 1988, 107ff.).

Lave notes that some psychologists would conclude from these results that there was something primitive or illogical about the informal strategies—and, by extension, about the people who used them (see, for example, Lave 1988, 79ff., 107ff.). In the terms we used earlier, these strategies are all closer to the global, field-dependent end of the cognitive-style continuum. Should we conclude, therefore, that ordinary middle-class North Americans fail to think rationally when they shop for groceries? This conclusion is contradicted by the experimental evidence showing that the shoppers' informal strategies were exceptionally accurate. In addition, shoppers did occasionally use formal mathematics as an alternative to the other informal strategies, but they did so only when the numbers for quantity and price were easy to transform into unit-price ratios. This did not happen very often, however, because units and prices in supermarkets are often given in prime numbers, making rapid mental calculation tedious and complicated. Rather than waste time dividing $5.27 by 13 ounces to obtain the price per ounce, the shoppers preferred to rely on other calculation strategies.

This last observation points to a major difference between "school" math and "grocery store" math. In school, the only purpose of a mathematical exercise is to obtain a single correct answer. "The puzzles or problems are assumed to be objective and factual. . . . Problem solvers have no choice but to try to solve problems, and if they choose not to, or do not find the correct answer, they 'fail'" (Lave 1988, 35). Matters are otherwise outside the classroom. Shoppers do not visit supermarkets as an excuse to practice formal mathematics; they go to buy food for their families.

---

cognitive style Recurring patterns of cognitive activity that characterize an individual's perceptual and intellectual activities.

global style A way of viewing the world that is holistic. People who use such a style first see a bundle of relationships and only later see the bits and pieces that are related. They are said to be *field dependent*.

articulated style A way of viewing the world that breaks it up into smaller and smaller pieces, which can then be organized into larger chunks. People who use such a style consider whatever they happen to be paying attention to apart from its context. They are said to be *field independent*.

Consequently, the choices they make are influenced not merely by unit-price ratios but by the food preferences of the other family members, the amount of storage space at home, the amount of time they can spend shopping, and so on. In the supermarket, as Lave puts it, " 'problems' are dilemmas to be resolved, rarely problems to be solved" (20). Formal mathematical calculations and knowledge of what costs less per unit may help resolve some dilemmas, but in other cases they may be too troublesome to bother with, or even irrelevant. Shoppers, unlike students in the classroom, are free to abandon calculation, to use means other than formal mathematics to resolve a dilemma (58).

One feature all Lave's subjects shared was the knowledge that pencil-and-paper tests in schoollike settings required an articulated, field-independent style. In non-Western societies, attending a European- or American-style school seems to impart the same knowledge to non-Western people. But even Western subjects may reserve that cognitive style for the classroom, preferring a variety of more global strategies to resolve the dilemmas of everyday life. We have seen how some of these dilemmas can be generated by a lack of fit between the background information we take for granted and sensory signals that are ambiguous. This lack of fit may be between, say, our family's food preferences and confusing price ratio information on two products we are comparing. It may be between our expectation that straight edges are normally continuous and surprising gaps in our visual field. In any case, our awareness of the cognitive dilemmas we face should make us more sympathetic to cognitive "errors" we see being made by people from different cultures who may be employing different cognitive styles.

Colin Turnbull was an anthropologist who worked for many years among the Mbuti of northeastern Democratic Republic of the Congo (Zaire). (See EthnoProfile 6.1: Mbuti.) He discovered that people who live all their lives in a dense forest have no experience of distance greater than a few feet and are therefore not accustomed to taking distance into consideration when estimating the size of an object in the visual field. Turnbull took one of his informants, Kenge, on a trip that brought them out of the forest and into a game park. For the first time in his life, Kenge faced vast, rolling grasslands nearly empty of trees. Kenge's response to this experience was dramatic: "When Kenge topped the

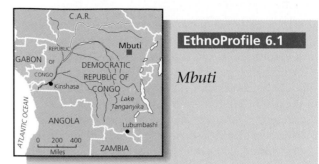

EthnoProfile 6.1

Mbuti

Region: Central Africa

Nation: Democratic Republic of the Congo (Zaire)

Population: 40,000

Environment: Dense tropical forest

Livelihood: Nomadic hunting and gathering

Political organization: Traditionally, communal bands of 7 to 30 families (average 17 families); today, part of a modern nation-state

For more information: Turnbull, Colin. 1961. *The forest people*. New York: Simon and Schuster.

rise, he stopped dead. Every smallest sign of mirth suddenly left his face. He opened his mouth but could say nothing. He moved his head and eyes slowly and unbelievingly" (1961, 251). When Kenge finally saw the far-off animals grazing on the plain, he asked Turnbull what insects they were. When told that they were buffalo, Kenge laughed and accused Turnbull of lying. Then he strained to see better and inquired what kind of buffalo could be so small. Later, when Turnbull pointed out a fishing boat on the lake, Kenge scoffed at him and insisted it was a floating piece of wood (252).

Cole and Scribner had a similar experience with one of their informants, a young Liberian who had lived his entire life inland. He had never seen the ocean until they took him to Monrovia, the Liberian capital, which is also a large port city. On seeing specks in the distance that the anthropologists insisted were boats, he observed that men who put out to sea in such small boats must be very brave (1974, 97).

When people in another culture fail to see similarities between people or objects that we think ought to be obvious to any observer, we are apt to become impatient. Yet in the United States, where racist stereotypes influence perceptions of mixed peoples, many of us are subject to similar blindness. Puerto Ricans, for example, experience racial distinctions in Puerto Rico in terms of a continuum of phenotypes and skin shades. When they move to the United States, however, they often find that their cultural identity as Puerto Ricans is ignored and they are classified as either "white" or "black" (Rodriguez 1994).

The study of illusion thus demonstrates that there can be a gulf between what we see and what we know, what we perceive and what we conceive. Nevertheless, in the ordinary contexts of everyday life, these discrepancies seem to be manageable: There is coherence between perceptions and conceptions. Moreover, because our link with the world is a dialectical one, there is no sharp boundary between what we perceive and what we conceive. Not only can new perceptions lead us to modify our conceptions (that is, we learn), but new conceptions can also lead us to perceive aspects of the world around us that we didn't pay attention to before. As a result, **cognition** is perhaps best understood as "a nexus of relations between the mind at work and the world in which it works" (Lave 1988, 1).

CONCEPTION

One way to illustrate the link between perception and conception, between what we see and what we know, is to compare the way different societies classify various phenomena. Patricia Greenfield carried out a study among the Wolof of Senegal using sets of pictures mounted on cards (Figure 6.9). (See EthnoProfile 6.2: Wolof.) Each subject was asked to select the two pictures in a set that were most alike and then to explain why they were most alike. This test was administered to three different groups: rural Wolof people who had never been to school, ranging from six years of age to adulthood; schoolchildren from the same rural town from which the first group was taken; and schoolchildren from Dakar, the capital of Senegal.

The most striking correlation existed between the amount of Western-style schooling a subject had received and the kinds of classifications made. All the schoolchildren, whether urban or rural, performed much the same way American schoolchildren did. That is, the greater the number of years in school, the greater the children's preference to classify by form

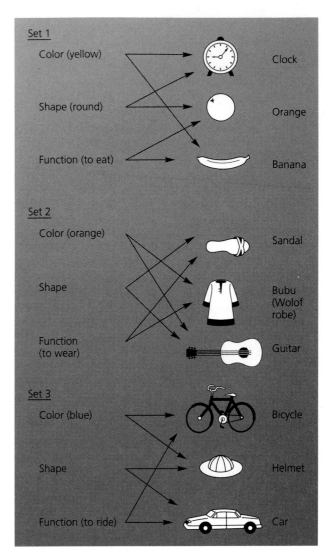

FIGURE 6.9 Three picture displays used in the Wolof classification study, with their attributes.

(shape and size) or function and the lesser their preference to classify by color. In addition, children with more schooling tended to explain their classifications in terms of conceptual categories ("round ones"). Those who had never been to school, regardless of age,

cognition (1) The mental process by which human beings gain knowledge; (2) the nexus of relations between the mind at work and the world in which it works.

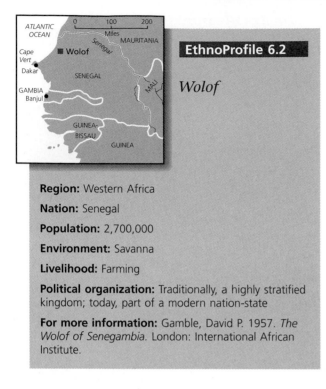

EthnoProfile 6.2

Wolof

Region: Western Africa

Nation: Senegal

Population: 2,700,000

Environment: Savanna

Livelihood: Farming

Political organization: Traditionally, a highly stratified kingdom; today, part of a modern nation-state

For more information: Gamble, David P. 1957. *The Wolof of Senegambia.* London: International African Institute.

preferred to classify by color. Greenfield concluded that this difference could be attributed to the experience of Western schooling, in which people with normal perceptual abilities were trained in "European habits of perceptual *analysis.*" Presumably Wolof who do not receive such training have little need or motivation (at least in the testing situation, as they understood it) to pay attention to features other than color to create a classification (Cole and Scribner 1974, 103–5).

The probable influence of Western-style education on ways of classifying appeared in another study by D. W. Sharp and Michael Cole in Yucatán, Mexico. (See EthnoProfile 6.3: Yucatecan Maya.) Using the cards pictured in Figure 6.10, they tested four groups of rural children and young adults: first graders, third graders, sixth graders, and teenagers who had attended no more than three years of school during their lives. They discovered that not all subjects were able to sort all the cards successfully according to a single rule (color, shape, or number). However, the third graders were more successful than the first graders, and the sixth graders were more successful than the third graders. Given these data alone, it might seem that age is the important variable. But the teenagers with three years of school or less performed at a level between that of

the first graders and the third graders. Sharp and Cole concluded: "It seems quite possible that one consequence of educational experience is to instill the notion that any set of objects can be treated (classified) in a variety of ways—there is no 'one correct way,' regardless of the task at hand." That would explain the teenagers' level of performance (quoted in Cole and Scribner 1974, 106–8).

Douglas Price-Williams (cited in Cole and Scribner 1974, 116–17) suspected that the performance of African children on classification tests had been negatively affected because the children had been asked to sort unfamiliar abstract shapes. In his research among the Tiv of Nigeria, he decided to choose as test items ten different kinds of animals (represented mostly by plastic toys) and ten different kinds of plants familiar to Tiv children. (See EthnoProfile 6.4: Tiv.) With each set of objects, he asked the children to pick out the ones that belonged together and to tell him why they had chosen as they did. Each child was then asked to regroup the objects again and again until the child found no other groupings possible. The results were impressive. The youngest children (six years old) could classify and reclassify all the objects three or four different ways, whereas the oldest children (eleven years old) found five or six ways to do so, and it made no difference whether they had attended school or not. Price-Williams also observed how the children had gone about constructing their classifications. Although they grouped the animals primarily in terms of concrete attributes, such as size, color, or place where they are found, they grouped the plants primarily in terms of an abstract attribute, edibility.

These studies, taken together, reinforce the conclusion that competent members of all societies employ a range of cognitive styles. We cannot speak of abstract thinking and concrete thinking as mutually exclusive. Anthropologists have found that many non-Western peoples are not used to thinking about things without relating them to some kind of context. Members of those societies can learn to use a context-free cognitive style if they attend school, but, as the Tiv research illustrates, this does not mean that they never use abstract categories outside the classroom. Paradoxically, the Tiv children were able to display sophisticated classifying skills when the experimental task was made more, rather than less, context dependent: when they sorted the animals and plants on the

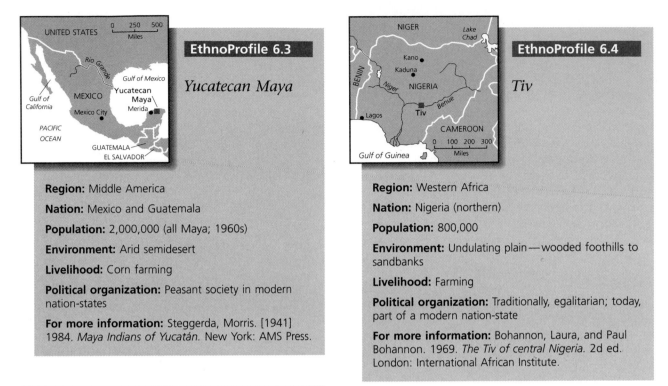

EthnoProfile 6.3

Yucatecan Maya

Region: Middle America

Nation: Mexico and Guatemala

Population: 2,000,000 (all Maya; 1960s)

Environment: Arid semidesert

Livelihood: Corn farming

Political organization: Peasant society in modern nation-states

For more information: Steggerda, Morris. [1941] 1984. *Maya Indians of Yucatán.* New York: AMS Press.

EthnoProfile 6.4

Tiv

Region: Western Africa

Nation: Nigeria (northern)

Population: 800,000

Environment: Undulating plain—wooded foothills to sandbanks

Livelihood: Farming

Political organization: Traditionally, egalitarian; today, part of a modern nation-state

For more information: Bohannon, Laura, and Paul Bohannon. 1969. *The Tiv of central Nigeria.* 2d ed. London: International African Institute.

FIGURE 6.10 Cards used in the Mexican reclassification study.

basis of which could be eaten and which could not. But perhaps the paradox is not so great after all. In Lave's research, the full range of her shoppers' calculating skills were displayed only when she studied mathematics in the supermarket rather than in the classroom and became aware of the range of factors in addition to price that influenced buying decisions.

Cross-cultural research in cognition is a delicate business. For the researcher, the trick is first to devise a test that will give people who use different cognitive styles an opportunity to show what they know and what they can do. The researcher must also discover whether different groups of subjects share the same understanding of tasks they are being asked to perform. In recent years, a number of researchers have worked to develop methods to assess cognition that are not bound to the traditional psychological testing laboratory or to the classroom.

Reason and the Reasoning Process

As we have just seen, one great example of Western dualism is between what we see and what we know. Another, at least equally great, is between what we think and what we feel. From the earliest days of the West's discovery of other societies, there has been a debate about the extent to which nonliterate non-Western peoples might be said to possess reason. Rooted in the context of Western colonialism, this debate was rarely disinterested, for domination by Europeans was often justified on the grounds that those dominated were irrational. Faced with this problematic history, how might anthropologists study rational thinking?

Most cognitive psychologists have adopted Jerome Bruner's famous definition of **thinking** as "going beyond the information given." This means that thinking is different from remembering (which refers to information already given) and also from learning (which involves acquiring information that was not given beforehand). Going beyond the information given thus implies a dialectic between some information already at hand and the cognitive processes of the person who is attempting to cope with that information. This definition highlights the "nexus of relations between the mind at work and the world in which it works." Thinking is open and active, and it has no predetermined outcome.

Many psychologists and anthropologists have tried to assess the levels of rational thinking in non-Western populations. One frequently used measure is the test of *conservation.* Swiss psychologist Jean Piaget devised this test as a way of measuring children's cognitive development. Children who conserve are able to recognize that the quantity of some substance remains constant even when its shape changes. According to Piaget, attaining this ability is an important step toward mature rational thought.

A classic conservation experiment proceeds in the following way. Children are shown a short, squat beaker of water. The experimenter pours the water from this beaker into a tall, thin beaker. Naturally the water level rises much higher in the tall, thin beaker. The experimenter then asks each child whether the amount of water has changed. Not until Western children reach the age of six or seven do they become aware that the amount of water remains the same, or is "conserved"; before this time, they tend to argue that the tall, thin beaker holds more water. This experiment—used to demonstrate concept formation (that is, the concept of volume)—has often been used to demonstrate the presence or absence of rational thought. This is presumably because to conclude that the same volume

changes in amount as it is poured from one beaker into another is "irrational" in any normal adult (Cole and Scribner 1974, 146ff.). Conservation tests have been tried in several different societies, always with ambiguous results. Some people pass the test while others do not, and there is no clear way to predict who will be successful and who will not be. "Until we have some better idea of what induces some members of traditional societies to solve conservation problems while their neighbors do not, we cannot be certain about the significance of conservation tests as a tool for understanding the relation between culture and cognitive development" (Cole and Scribner 1974, 156).

Culture and Logic

Another set of cognitive tests has to do with verbal reasoning ability. These tests present subjects with three statements in the form of a syllogism—for example, "All men are mortal, Socrates is a man, therefore Socrates is mortal." The first two propositions are called the *premises,* and the third statement is the *conclusion.* For a syllogism to be sound, the conclusion must follow from the premises.

Syllogistic reasoning is enshrined in Western culture as the quintessence of rational thought. Researchers thus suggested that the rational capacities of non-Western peoples could be tested using logical problems in syllogistic form. Presumably their rationality would be confirmed if they could deduce correctly when the conclusion followed logically from the premises and when it did not.

Cole and Scribner presented logical problems involving syllogistic reasoning to their Kpelle subjects. (See EthnoProfile 6.5: Kpelle.) Typically, the logical problem was embedded in a folktalelike story. The experimenter read the story to the subjects and then asked them a series of follow-up questions designed to reveal whether the subjects could draw a correct conclusion from the premises given.

Here is one story Cole and Scribner prepared: "At one time Spider went to a feast. He was told to answer this question before he could eat any of the food. The question is: Spider and Black Deer always eat together. Spider is eating. Is Black Deer eating?" (1974, 162). Given the two premises, the conclusion should be that Black Deer is eating. Now consider a typical Kpelle response to hearing this story:

Subject: Were they in the bush?

Experimenter: Yes.

Subject: Were they eating together?

Experimenter: Spider and Black Deer always eat together. Spider is eating. Is Black Deer eating?

Subject: But I was not there. How can I answer such a question?

Experimenter: Can't you answer it? Even if you were not there, you can answer it. (Repeats the question.)

Subject: Oh, oh, Black Deer is eating.

Experimenter: What is your reason for saying that Black Deer was eating?

Subject: The reason is that Black Deer always walks about all day eating green leaves in the bush. Then he rests for a while and gets up again to eat. (Cole and Scribner 1974, 162)

The subject's answer to the question and subsequent justification for that answer seem to have nothing whatever to do with the logical problem the subject is being asked to solve.

The experimenters devised this story the same way schoolteachers devise mathematical word problems. That is, the contextual material is nothing more than a kind of window dressing. Schoolchildren quickly learn to disregard the window dressing and seek out the mathematical problem it hides. In the same way, the Kpelle subjects hearing the story about Spider and Black Deer are supposed to demonstrate logic by disregarding the contextual material about the feast and seeking out the syllogism embedded within it. However, Kpelle subjects did not understand that they were being read this story in a testing situation for which considerations of context or meaningfulness were irrelevant. In the preceding example, the subject seemed to have difficulty separating the logical problem both from the introductory material about the feast and from the rest of his experiential knowledge.

Cole and Scribner interpreted their subject's response to this problem as being due not to irrationality but to a "failure to accept the logical task" (Cole and Scribner 1974, 162). In a follow up study, Cole and Scribner discovered that Kpelle high school children responded "correctly" to the logical problems 90 percent of the time. This suggests a strong correlation between Western-style schooling and a willingness to accept context-free analytic tasks in testing situations (164).

But this is not all. David Lancy, one of Cole and Scribner's colleagues, discovered that Western-style syl-

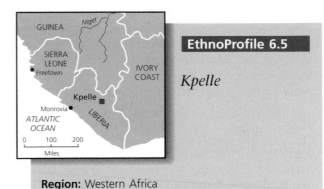

EthnoProfile 6.5

Kpelle

Region: Western Africa

Nation: Liberia (central and western)

Population: 86,000

Environment: Tropical forest

Livelihood: Rice farming

Political organization: Traditionally, chiefdoms; today, part of a modern nation-state

For more information: Bellman, Beryl. 1975. *Village of curers and assassins: On the production of Fala Kpelle cosmological categories.* The Hague: Mouton.

logisms are very similar to certain forms of Kpelle riddles. Unlike syllogisms, however, those riddles have no single, "logically correct" answer. "Rather, as the riddle is posed to a group, the right answer is the one among many offered that seems most illuminating, resourceful, and convincing as determined by consensus and circumstance. This emphasis on edification as a criterion for 'rightness' is found in Kpelle jurisprudence as well" (Lancy cited in Fernandez 1980, 47–48). In other words, the "right" answer cannot be extracted from the form of the riddle by logical operations. Rather, it is the answer that seems most enlightening and informative to the particular audience in the particular setting where the riddle is posed.

Enlightening answers, moreover, appear to be rooted in shared cultural schemas. Roy D'Andrade has shown that college undergraduates at the University of Cali-

---

thinking An active cognitive process that involves going beyond the information given.

syllogistic reasoning A form of reasoning based on the syllogism, a series of three statements in which the first two statements are the premises and the last is the conclusion, which must follow from the premises.

fornia, San Diego, are unable to complete syllogisms similar to the Spider–Black Deer story when the content is arbitrary. Only 53 percent of UCSD undergraduates (a result only slightly above chance) selected the correct answer to the following syllogism:

1. *Given:* If Tom is drinking a Pepsi then Peter is sitting down.
2. *Suppose:* Peter is not sitting down.
3. Then:
   a. It must be the case that Tom is drinking a Pepsi.
   b. Maybe Tom is drinking a Pepsi or maybe he isn't.
   c. It must be the case that Tom is not drinking a Pepsi.

The correct answer (c) exactly parallels the correct answer to the Spider–Black Deer story. And, indeed, the reasoning processes of the undergraduates bear a striking similarity to those of Cole and Scribner's Kpelle informants: "When arbitrary relations are presented, the typical respondent does not seem to integrate the state of affairs described by the first. Respondents say . . . 'So what if *Peter* is not sitting down. That doesn't have anything to do with *Tom's* drinking a Pepsi'" (D'Andrade 1992, 49). By contrast, 86 percent of UCSD undergraduates chose the correct answer to the same kind of syllogism that involved a well-formed North American cultural schema (that cities are located within states). There is no reason to doubt that Liberians, North Americans, and other humans come equipped with the same elementary cognitive processes: the ability to make abstractions, to create conceptual categories, and to reason inferentially. The difficulty is to understand how these elementary cognitive processes are put to work within culturally shared schemas to produce different, functional cognitive systems known as **reasoning styles.**

If "riddle interpretation" is a reasoning style characteristic of Kpelle culture, then formal Western **logic** is perhaps best understood as a reasoning style characteristic of Western culture. Given D'Andrade's evidence, it would seem that formal logic is different from both informal Western reasoning styles and many non-Western reasoning styles, and for the same reason. That is, formal logic requires thinkers to draw conclusions in the absence of context without the aid of helpful cultural schemas. Indeed, it denies that ambiguity is genuine, views contextual information as the source of ambiguity, and assumes that clear understanding will emerge once all contextual contamination is removed. Non-Western reasoning and informal Western reasoning, however, are rooted in cultural schemas and therefore depend upon cultural context. If this were not the case, there would be no need to take college courses in logic. Traditionally, logicians have scorned the illogical, irrational thought processes used in everyday life. But everyday reasoning clearly has its own order, as Lave's grocery shoppers and D'Andrade's undergraduates illustrate.

Logical systems represent objects and relationships between objects in the world. But the objects and relationships we experience in our lives can always be represented in more than one way. As Barry Barnes and David Bloor put it, "Just as our experience of a shared material world does not itself guarantee shared verbal descriptions of it, so our shared rationality does not guarantee a unique logical system" (1982, 44). Barnes and Bloor prefer to view traditional Western logic as "a learned body of scholarly lore, growing and varying over time" (45). This is not to claim that the rules of formal Western logic are useless. On the contrary, because they are in part engendered by careful attention to human experience of the world, they can be very useful in some contexts. But other logics, rooted in different cultural schemas, may be equally useful in different cultural contexts. Formal Western logic, like literal language, does not offer us the only plausible, meaningful, or useful perspective on the human condition.

EMOTION

Psychological anthropologists who try to define **emotion** in cross-cultural terms run into a familiar problem: They discover not just that different cultures talk about emotion in different languages but that not all languages even possess a term that might be translated as *emotion.* To get out of this tangle, they have tried to develop a theory of cognitive functioning that accounts for the experiences that some cultures recognize as emotional.

In traditional Western dualism, reason and thought are associated with the mind and emotion with the body. Any attempt to explain emotion must deal with

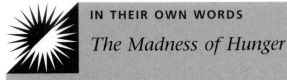

IN THEIR OWN WORDS

The Madness of Hunger

Medical anthropologist Nancy Scheper-Hughes describes how symptoms of a rural Brazilian folk ailment can be understood as a form of protest against physical exploitation and abuse.

Among the agricultural wage laborers living in the hillside shantytown of Alto do Cruzeiro, on the margins of a large, interior market town in the plantation zone of Pernambuco, Brazil, and who sell their labor for as little as a dollar a day, socioeconomic and political contradictions often take shape in the "natural" contradictions of angry, sick, and afflicted bodies. In addition to the wholly expectable epidemics of parasitic infections and communicable fevers, there are the more unexpected outbreaks and explosions of unruly and subversive symptoms that will not readily materialize under the health station's microscope. Among these are the fluid symptoms of *nervos* (angry, frenzied nervousness): trembling, fainting, seizures, hysterical weeping, angry recriminations, blackouts, and paralysis of face and limbs.

These nervous attacks are in part coded metaphors through which the workers express their dangerous and unacceptable condition of chronic hunger and need (see Scheper-Hughes, 1988) and in part acts of defiance and dissent that graphically register the refusal to endure what is, in fact, unendurable and their protest against their availability for physical exploitation and abuse. And so, rural workers who have cut sugarcane since the age of seven or eight years will sometimes collapse, their legs giving way under an *ataque de nervos,* a nervous attack. They cannot walk, they cannot stand upright; they are left, like Oliver Sacks (1984), without a leg to stand on.

In the exchange of meanings between the body personal and the body social, the nervous-hungry, nervous-angry body of the cane cutter offers itself as metaphor and metonym of the nervous sociopolitical system and for the paralyzed position of the rural worker in the current economic and political dis-order. In "lying down" on the job, in refusing to return to the work that has overly determined their entire lives, the cane cutters' body language signifies both surrender and defeat. But one also notes a drama of mockery and refusal. For if the folk ailment *nervos* attacks the legs and the face, it leaves the arms and hands intact and free for less physically ruinous work. Consequently, otherwise healthy young men suffering from nervous attacks press their claims as sick men on their various political bosses and patrons to find them alternative work, explicitly "sitting down" work, arm work (but not clerical work for these men are illiterate).

The analysis of *nervos* does not end here, for nervous attack is an expansive and polysemic form of disease. Shantytown women, too, suffer from *nervos*—both the *nervos de trabalhar muito,* "overwork" nerves from which male cane cutters suffer, and also the more gender-specific *nervos de sofrir muito,* the nerves of those who have endured and suffered much. "Sufferers' nerves" attacks those who have endured a recent, especially a violent, tragedy. Widows of husbands and mothers of sons who have been abducted and violently "disappeared" are prone to the mute, enraged, white-knuckled shaking of "sufferers' nerves."

Source: Scheper-Hughes 1994, 236–37.

---

the nature of the bodily arousal we associate with it. But there is more to emotion, as commonly understood, than mere bodily arousal. Recall the butcher knife referred to earlier in this chapter. What do we feel when we see a butcher knife sitting beside mushrooms on a cutting board in our kitchen? What do we feel when we see that same knife in the hands of a burglar bent on attacking us? The knife alone does not trigger our feeling. The situation, or context, in which we encounter the knife is equally important. The context itself is often ambiguous, and our emotional experience changes as our interpretation of the context changes.

Thus, emotion can be understood as the product of a dialectic between bodily arousal and cognitive interpretation. Cognitive psychologist George Mandler

reasoning styles How we understand a cognitive task, how we encode the information presented to us, and what transformations the information undergoes as we think. Reasoning styles differ from culture to culture and from context to context within the same culture.

logic A symbolic system used to represent objects and relationships between objects in the world.

emotion The product of a dialectic between bodily arousal and cognitive interpretation, emotion comprises states, values, and arousals.

suggests that bodily arousal can trigger an emotional experience by attracting our attention and prompting us to seek the source of arousal (1975, 97). Conversely, a particular interpretation of our experience can trigger bodily arousal. Arousal may heighten or diminish, depending on how we interpret what is happening around us.

Mandler's discussion of emotion, like Cole and Scribner's discussion of cognition, describes emotions as *functional systems*. Each links elementary processes that involve the body's arousal system to other elementary processes that play a role in the construction of perception, conception, and reasoning. "Emotions are not something that people 'have,' they are constituted of people's states, values and arousals" (Mandler 1983, 151). Approaching emotion from this perspective accomplishes three things: (1) It integrates mind and body in a holistic fashion; (2) it acknowledges ambiguity as a central feature of emotional experience, just as we have argued it is central to linguistic, perceptual, and conceptual experience; and (3) it suggests how different cultural interpretive frameworks might shape not only what we think but also what we feel.

Why should we experience emotion at all? The role of emotion in human life may be rooted in the evolutionary history of a highly intelligent species that is capable of thinking before acting. Bodily arousal alerts us to something new and unexpected in our environment, something that does not easily fit into any conventional schema. Once our attention is caught in this way, the rest of our cognitive processes focus on the interrupting phenomenon. From this perspective, a person would be foolish to ignore his or her guts when trying to sort out a confusing experience. Indeed, the guts are usually what alert us to confusion in the first place. The need of "whole-body" experience for understanding also becomes more comprehensible. Mandler reminds us, "Just telling people what a situation is going to be like isn't enough, and it isn't good enough training when you encounter the real situation" (1983, 152). Generations of new spouses, new parents, and anthropological fieldworkers can testify to the overwhelming truth of this statement.

In sum, we experience bodily arousal when our familiar world is somehow interrupted. That arousal may either fade away or develop into an emotional experience depending on the meaning we assign to it. Possible meanings arise out of cultural interpretations of

recurring experiential schemas. We should not be surprised to find some overlap in the categories of feeling recognized by different cultures. After all, certain experiential schemas that interrupt the familiar world—birth and death, for example—are human universals. At the same time, we should expect that the wider cultural context will in each case modify the angle from which such experiences are understood and, thus, the categories of feeling associated with them.

Emotion in an Eastern African Culture

David Parkin (1984) has studied the cultural construction of emotion among the Giriama of coastal Kenya. (See EthnoProfile 6.6: Giriama.) We must explain several features of Giriama thinking before considering their understanding of what we call emotion. First, the Giriama theory of human nature does not recognize a mind-body dualism of the Western sort. Indeed, the Giriama are unwilling to set up sharp, mutually exclusive oppositions of any kind when discussing human nature. Parkin tells us that such behavior as spirit possession, madness, hysteria, witchcraft, persistent violence, drunkenness, and thieving are explained "as the result of what we might call imbalances in human nature. . . . I call them imbalances because the Giriama do not believe that a person can be intrinsically or irredeemably evil: At some stage, usually remarkably quickly, he will be brought back into the fold, even if he subsequently leaves it again. A large number of terms, roughly translatable as greed, lust, envy, jealousy, malice, resentment, anger, are used to refer to these imbalances of character and the accompanying behavior" (14).

As with us, the Giriama associate different feelings with different parts of the body. In the West, we conventionally connect the brain with reason and the heart with emotion. For the Giriama, however, the heart, liver, kidneys, and eyes are the seat of reason and emotion. Although the Giriama may distinguish thinking from feeling in discussing the actual behavior of real people, they nevertheless presume a common origin for both (Parkin 1984, 17). Indeed, the Giriama framework for understanding human cognition has much in common with the anthropological perspective described throughout this chapter.

What about particular emotions? Although the categories of feeling recognized by Giriama overlap in

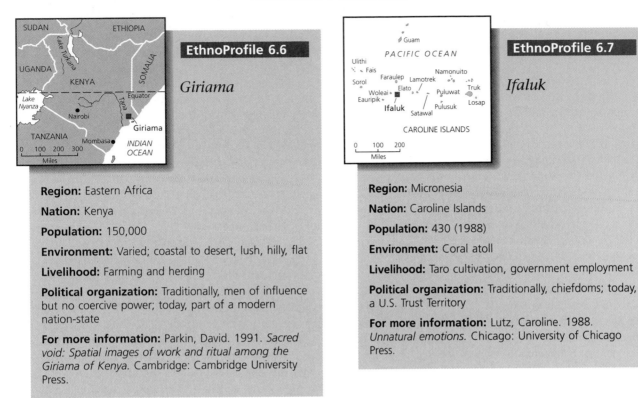

EthnoProfile 6.6

Giriama

Region: Eastern Africa

Nation: Kenya

Population: 150,000

Environment: Varied; coastal to desert, lush, hilly, flat

Livelihood: Farming and herding

Political organization: Traditionally, men of influence but no coercive power; today, part of a modern nation-state

For more information: Parkin, David. 1991. *Sacred void: Spatial images of work and ritual among the Giriama of Kenya.* Cambridge: Cambridge University Press.

EthnoProfile 6.7

Ifaluk

Region: Micronesia

Nation: Caroline Islands

Population: 430 (1988)

Environment: Coral atoll

Livelihood: Taro cultivation, government employment

Political organization: Traditionally, chiefdoms; today, a U.S. Trust Territory

For more information: Lutz, Caroline. 1988. *Unnatural emotions.* Chicago: University of Chicago Press.

some respects with the experiences labeled by English terms for emotions, Parkin suggests that there are important differences that stem from the nature of the schemas that Giriama culture conventionally recognizes and from the prototypical thoughts and feelings that are appropriate to those schemas. Consider what the term *utsungu* means as a label for a category of feeling: "Utsungu means poison, bitterness, resentment, and anger, on the one hand, but also grief on the other. It is the feeling experienced at a funeral of a loved or respected relative or friend. A man or woman is grieved at the loss but also bitter that it has happened at all, and angry with the witch who caused the death. Since the witch will be made to pay, the sentiment carried with it both the consequences of the loss of a dear one and the intention to avenge his or her death" (118).

We too feel "grief" at the death of a loved one. But the prototypical Western experience of grief does not contain the additional meaning involving anger at witchcraft and the desire for vengeance. Perhaps one would have to be a Giriama—or have lived in another culture in which witchcraft was understood as the usual cause of death and in which such wrongful death

could be avenged—to experience the emotional configuration that Parkin describes for the Giriama.

Emotion in Oceania

Catherine Lutz (1988) is concerned with situating the way people understand emotion more fully within the social structures and social behaviors that drive it. Lutz did fieldwork among the Ifaluk of the Caroline Islands in the Pacific. (See EthnoProfile 6.7: Ifaluk.) While not denying the links of emotion to the body, she emphasizes how emotions can be understood as a form of social discourse. That is, people's use of the language of emotion can be understood as a way of talking about social relationships. Like the Giriama, the Ifaluk do not distinguish sharply between thought and emotion; They understand events in a way that is simultaneously cognitive and affective. Saying that they are experiencing *song* (justifiable anger) is not just the description of an internal bodily state, it is also a comment about someone else's failure to observe appropriate social behavior. That is, inappropriate social behavior interrupts the world of social expectations, producing an emotional response. The Ifaluk expect that the person who provoked *song* in another will naturally experience *metagu* (fear/anxiety) once he or she finds out. Indeed the Ifaluk often link categories of thought/feeling in pairs: *song* and *metagu, gafago* (neediness) and *fago* (compassion/love/sadness).

Lutz writes, "the mental state of *any* mature individual is seen as having fundamentally social roots. Others can then be held responsible for the social conditions that produce the state" (1988, 101). Consequently, claiming to be justifiably angry is the first step in a process of negotiating the meaning of other people's actions in relation to oneself. Claims of *song* made by people of higher status or greater power (such as lineage heads and chiefs) tend to be accepted publicly, and the responsible party is expected to experience *metagu* as a result. Claims concerning others of similar status or power, however, may involve more negotiation over whether or not they have the right to apply *song* in a particular situation. Extended negotiation is also common when Ifaluk are unsure of what to feel/think about a newly introduced cultural item like cash, which does not fit into traditional schemas about proper social behavior and yet must be dealt with.

Lutz relates the Ifaluk's particular configuration of emotion/thought to the natural and political conditions of everyday life on a small coral atoll with a high rate of infant mortality and the ever-present threat of sudden devastation and death from typhoons. *Fago,* for example, motivates people to share food, adopt one another's children, and provide close personal care to those who are ill or in some other way *gafago* (needy).

THE PROCESS OF SOCIALIZATION AND ENCULTURATION

Children use their own bodies and brains to explore their world. But from their earliest days, other people are actively working to steer their activity and attention in particular directions. Consequently, their exploration of the world is not merely trial and error: The path is cleared for them by others who shape their experiences—and their interpretations of their experiences—for them.

Two terms in the social sciences refer to this process of culturally and socially shaped cognitive development.

The first, **socialization**, focuses on the organizational problems facing human beings as material organisms who must live with each other and cope with the behavioral rules established by their respective societies. The second term, **enculturation**, focuses on the cognitive challenges facing human beings who live together and must come to terms with the ways of thinking and feeling that are considered appropriate in their respective cultures. Becoming human involves both these processes, for children learn how to act, think, feel, and speak at the same time, as they participate in the joint activities carried out by social groups to which they belong. We will use the term *socialization/enculturation* to represent this holistic experience.

Socialization/enculturation produces a socially and culturally constructed **self** capable of functioning successfully in society. Anthropologists need a theory of cognitive development that is holistic; therefore, many psychologists and anthropologists have been attracted to the ideas of George Herbert Mead (1863–1931) and, more recently, to the work of Soviet psychologist Lev Vygotsky (1896–1934). Although both men were contemporaries, Vygotsky's work has become influential in the West only recently. Before his early death, Vygotsky had helped to found a major school of Soviet psychology that continues to thrive. The writings of this *sociohistorical school* have inspired some of the most interesting recent research in cognitive anthropology.

For Mead and Vygotsky alike, human life is social from the outset. As Vygotsky wrote, "The social dimension of consciousness is primary in time and in fact. The individual dimension of consciousness is derivative and secondary" (1978, 30). Like Vygotsky, Mead (1934) believed that human nature is completed and enhanced, not curtailed or damaged, by socialization and enculturation. Indeed, the successful humanization of human beings lies in people's mastery of symbols, which begins when children start to learn language. As children come to control the symbolic systems of their cultures, they gain the ability to distinguish objects and relationships in the world. Most important, they come to see themselves as objects as well as subjects.

For Mead, this ability is acquired through the process of *role playing*. Very young children are at first unaware that they and the world around them are not continuous with one another. Gradually, however, they come to recognize, for example, that their parent's point of view is different from their own, entering a stage of development in which they imitate the roles of those few people—or *particular others*—with whom they are well acquainted.

Older children move into the *game stage,* in which they become able to enter into complex interactions with others because they can keep in mind not only their own role but also the roles of other participants. As their experience of other people widens beyond the immediate family, they learn to distinguish self and particularly others from the *generalized other,* or society at large. Being able to play games and take the role of the generalized other successfully requires a mastery of symbolism, because the games' rules and society's point of view are both highly abstract and mediated by language.

Mead's analysis focused primarily on face-to-face interactions, but anthropologists need a theoretical framework that goes beyond such interactions. Here Vygotsky's work is important because Vygotsky's understanding of context goes beyond Mead's. Vygotsky wanted to create a psychology that was compatible with a marxian analysis of society. His ideas are far from doctrinaire; indeed, during the Stalin years in Russia, his work was censored. At the same time, his marxian orientation directed attention to the social, cultural, and historical context in which face-to-face interaction is embedded.

At the beginning of the chapter, we introduced one of Vygotsky's theoretical contributions: the distinction between elementary cognitive processes and functional cognitive systems. This distinction is useful in anthropology because it provides a way of describing the similarities and differences observed when we compare how people from different cultures think and feel. These differences have implications for cognitive development as well. The functional systems employed by adult members of society must be acquired during childhood. For Vygotsky, acquisition takes place in a context of face-to-face interactions between, typically, a child and an adult. When children learn about the world in such a context, they are not working on their own; on the contrary, they are learning about the world as they learn the symbolic forms (usually language) that others use to represent the world.

This learning process creates in the child a new plane of consciousness based on the dialogue-based, question-and-answer format of social interaction. From

this, Vygotsky inferred that our internal thought processes would also take the format of a dialogue. Mead suggested something similar when he spoke of every person as being able to carry on internal conversations between the *I* (the unsocialized self) and the *me* (the socially conditioned self). Only on this basis can an individual's sense of identity develop as the self comes to distinguish itself from the conversational other.

One interesting Vygotskian concept is the *zone of proximal development,* which is the distance between a child's "actual development level as determined by independent problem solving" and the level of "potential development as determined through problem solving under adult guidance or in collaboration with more capable peers" (Vygotsky 1978, 86). Psychologists everywhere have long been aware that children can often achieve more when they are coached than when they work alone. Western psychologists, with their individualist bias, have viewed this difference in achievement as contamination of the testing situation or as the result of cheating. Vygotsky and his followers see it as an indispensable measure of potential growth that simultaneously demonstrates how growth is rooted in social interaction, especially in educational settings (Moll 1990).

The concept of the zone of proximal development enables us to describe the inadequacies of traditional IQ tests. It also enables anthropologists and comparative psychologists to link cognitive development to society, culture, and history. This conclusion is based on Vygotsky's explicit association of coaching or formal instruction with, as he put it, the "historical characteristics of humans" (Wertsch 1985, 71). That is, the size of the zone of proximal development is shaped by social, cultural, and historical factors. To the extent that these factors vary from society to society, we can expect cognitive development to vary as well.

---

socialization The process by which human beings as material organisms, living together with other similar organisms, cope with the behavioral rules established by their respective societies.
enculturation The process by which human beings living with one another must learn to come to terms with the ways of thinking and feeling that are considered appropriate in their respective cultures.
self The result of the process of socialization/enculturation for an individual.

American Premenstrual Syndrome

Anthropologist Alma Gottlieb explores some of the contradictions surrounding the North American biocultural construction known as PMS.

To what extent might PMS be seen as an "escape valve," a means whereby American women "let off steam" from the enervating machine of the daily domestic grind? To some extent this explanation is valid, but it tells only part of the story. It ignores the specific contours of PMS and its predictable trajectory; moreover it puts PMS in a place that is peripheral to the American vision of womanhood, whereas my contention is that the current understanding of PMS (and, before its creation, of the menstrual period itself) is integral to how we view femininity. Even if it occupies a small portion of women's lives (although some women may see the paramenstruum as occupying half the month), and even if not all women suffer from it, I contend that the contemporary vision of PMS is so much a part of general cultural consciousness that it constitutes, qualitatively, half the female story. It combines with the other part of the month to produce a bifurcated vision of femininity whose two halves are asymmetrically valued.

Married women who suffer from PMS report that during the "normal" phase of the month they allow their husbands' myriad irritating acts to go uncriticized. But while premenstrual they are hyper-critical of such acts, sometimes "ranting and raving" for hours over trivial annoyances. Unable to act "nice" continually, women break down and are regularly "irritable" and even "hostile." Their protest is recurrent but futile, for they are made to feel guilty about it, or, worse, they are treated condescendingly. "We both know you're going to have your period tomorrow so why don't we just go to bed?" one husband regularly tells his wife at the first sign of an argument, thereby dismissing any claim to legitimate disagreement. Without legitimacy, as Weber taught us long ago, protests are doomed to failure; and so it is with PMS.

I suggest that these women in effect choose, however unconsciously, to voice their complaints at a time that they know those complaints will be rejected as illegitimate. If complaints were made during the non-premenstrual portion of the month, they would have to be taken seriously. But many American women have not found a voice with which to speak such complaints and at the same time retain their feminine allure. They save their complaints for that "time of the month" when they are in effect permitted to voice them yet by means of hormones do not have to claim responsibility for such negative feelings. In knowing when their complaints will not be taken seriously yet voicing them precisely during such a time, perhaps women are punishing themselves for their critical thoughts. In this way, and despite the surface-level aggression they display premenstrually, women continue to enact a model of behavior doomed to failure, as is consistent with what some feminists have argued is a pervasive tendency among American women in other arenas (Horner 1972).

So long as American society recreates its unrealistic expectations of the female personality, it is inevitable that there will be a PMS, or something playing its role: a regular rejection of the stringent expectations of female behavior. But PMS masks the protest even as it embodies it: for, cast in a biological idiom, PMS is made to seem an autonomous force that is often uncontrollable (see Martin 1987, 132–3); or if it can be controlled, it is only by drugs not acts of personal volition. Thus women's authorship of their own states of mind is denied them. As women in contemporary America struggle to find their voices, it is to be hoped that they will be able to reclaim their bodies as vehicles for the creation of their own metaphors, rather than autonomous forces causing them to suffer and needing to be drugged.

Source: Gottlieb 1993, 57–58.

IS COGNITIVE DEVELOPMENT THE SAME FOR EVERYONE?

Most theories, including Mead's, portray cognitive development as a progression through a series of stages. With the exception of Vygotsky's theory, these theories ordinarily assume that the stages are the same for all human beings, or at least all human beings in a particular society. A Vygotskian perspective helps us explain not only cross-cultural differences in development, but also differences in the cognitive development of different subgroups in a single society.

For example, since their birth in 1973 through the

late 1980s, a sample of 4,299 children were followed by a team of Cuban researchers who periodically collected information on their cognitive, social, economic, physical, and academic development (Gutierrez Muñiz, López Hurtado, and Arias Beatón n.d.). The researchers identified a series of correlations between levels of education, wage employment, living standards, and health of mothers and levels of development and achievement of the children. Put in Vygotskian terms, the data show that the zone of proximal development is greater for children of mothers with higher levels of education and participation in the paid work force than it is for children of mothers with lower educational levels who do not work outside the home. These findings contradicted popular beliefs that the children of educated working mothers would suffer as a result of their mothers' activities (Arias Beatón, personal communication).

Carol Gilligan (1982) carried out a comparative study on the moral development of women and men in North American society. She argues that middle-class boys and girls in the United States begin their moral development in different sociocultural contexts. Boys are encouraged from an early age to break away from their mothers and families and make it on their own. In this context, they learn that independence is good, that dependency is weakness, and that their first duty is to themselves and what they stand for. By contrast, girls mature in a sociocultural context in which their bond to their mothers and families is never sharply ruptured. They learn that connection to others is good, that the destruction of relationships is damaging, and that their first responsibility in any difficult situation is to ensure that nobody gets hurt.

Gilligan did not adopt a Vygotskian perspective in this study, although she was influenced by Mead. But the Vygotskian concept of the zone of proximal development provides a useful tool for describing how the differential moral development of boys and girls is accomplished. In Vygotskian terms, the moral development of boys and girls proceeds in different directions because boys and girls are coached differently by more mature members of society. That is, when faced with the same dilemmas but unsure of how to act, boys are encouraged to make one set of choices, girls another. In this way, each gender category builds up a different set of schemas as to what constitutes the "good." As a result, American men and women consistently see one

another acting immorally. For example, when men and boys try to be true to themselves and strike out on their own, women and girls may condemn such action as being highly destructive to personal relationships. When women and girls try to encourage intimacy and closeness, men and boys may view such ties as confining and repressive.

Like Vygotsky, Gilligan situates the development of moral reasoning in sociocultural and historical context. She argues that men are able to present their moral perspective as universally correct because men as a group hold power over women as a group in American society. As American women gain power, however, their "different voice" may acquire more legitimacy, and the culturally embedded paths of moral development may themselves be altered.

COGNITION AND CONTEXT

Human cognition is a holistic phenomenon: What we perceive triggers thoughts and feelings and suggests possible actions; yet how we think and feel and act shapes our perceptions. This is so, it appears, because "any fact, or small set of facts, is open to a wide variety of interpretations" (Cole and Scribner 1974, 172). The question then becomes one of trying to explain the different interpretations.

There are no clear-cut answers to this question. However, cross-cultural studies of cognition make us increasingly aware of the importance of context—not just the immediate context of the laboratory situation but also the displaced context of culture and history that may be invisible in the lab but is present in people's minds. When administering a psychological test on visual illusions to the Fang, for example, James Fernandez (1980) discovered that many questioned his explanation of the "real" reason behind such a bizarre activity as psychological testing. (See EthnoProfile 7.4: Fang.) Years of colonial domination and exploitation at the hands of outsiders made their suspicions of the anthropologist's motives far from irrational.

If human understanding of the world is holistic, moreover, then so is the anthropologist's understanding of another culture. An excellent description of just this kind of holistic experience is given by anthropologist Michael Gilsenan (1982), who worked for a time

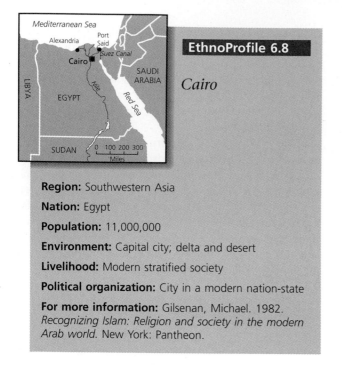

EthnoProfile 6.8

Cairo

Region: Southwestern Asia

Nation: Egypt

Population: 11,000,000

Environment: Capital city; delta and desert

Livelihood: Modern stratified society

Political organization: City in a modern nation-state

For more information: Gilsenan, Michael. 1982. *Recognizing Islam: Religion and society in the modern Arab world.* New York: Pantheon.

among urban Muslims in Cairo, Egypt. (See Ethno-Profile 6.8: Cairo.) Gilsenan spent many hours with his informants observing their prayers in the local mosque. Along the inside wall of the mosque were verses from the Qur'an shaped out of bright green neon tubing. Green is the color of the prophet Muhammad, so finding that color used prominently in mosque decoration is not surprising. However, Gilsenan's experiences in Western culture did not include schemas in which neon light and serious worship went together, and for several months the neon interfered with his attempts to assume a properly reverential attitude. Then one day, Gilsenan reports, "I turned unthinkingly away from the swaying bodies and the rhythms of the remembrance of God and saw, not neon, but simply greenness. . . . No gaps existed between color, shape, light, and form. From that unreflecting and unsuspecting moment I ceased to see neon at all" (1982, 266).

Nothing had happened to Gilsenan's eyes or his other senses, which continued to receive the same signals they had always received, but the meaning of the signals had been altered. Gilsenan's experience in the mosque situated neon light within a new schema, and his growing familiarity with that schema made the neon seem more and more natural. Eventually, Gilsenan was

noticing only the color green. He was still able to report, of course, that the green light was produced by green neon tubing; however, that fact seemed irrelevant given the new schema he used to interpret his experience.

These transformations of perception and understanding remain mysterious, but they seem to occur whenever we have an insight of any kind. Insights, like apt metaphors, reshape the world for us, throwing new aspects into sharp focus and casting other aspects into the background. Our ability to achieve insights, like our ability to create apt metaphors, remains the most central and most mysterious aspect of human cognition.

Key Terms

schemas	cognition
prototypes	thinking
elementary cognitive processes	syllogistic reasoning
	reasoning styles
functional cognitive systems	logic
	emotion
perception	socialization
cognitive style	enculturation
global style	self
articulated style	

Chapter Summary

1. The capacities we possess for making sense of our world—cognitive capacities—share many of the design features of language. The evidence of our senses depends upon context: both immediate context and cultural context. As human beings grow up, we gradually become aware of the schemas that our culture recognizes. We learn to use these schemas as prototypes for interpreting new experiences. When our prototypes do not seem to apply, we exercise cognitive openness and organize experiences creatively.

2. Researchers have often pictured human intelligence metaphorically as a substance that could be measured by intelligence tests. Today, however, it is unclear exactly what the results of intelligence

tests represent. Consequently, research has shifted its focus to cognitive processes and the way these are organized into culturally shaped functional systems.

3. Psychological anthropologists have tried to explain why intelligent informants perform poorly on Western intelligence tests that require subjects to interpret drawings and photographs. Western subjects are able to separate an object from a particular context, but the elimination of context is a Western perceptual convention that may not be shared by non-Western people. Drawings and photographs do not speak for themselves and can only make sense once we have mastered a particular group's conventions for interpreting them.

4. Illusions may be understood as the result of normal cognitive processes that have somehow been inappropriately selected and applied to a particular set of visual signals. Four important types of visual illusion are distortion, ambiguity, paradox, and fiction.

5. Some anthropologists argue that people in different cultures have different cognitive styles that can be located on a continuum ranging from global style at one end to articulated style at the other. Research suggests that an individual may use a global style for some tasks and an articulated style for others. Indeed, one culture may use an articulated style for a task that another culture would approach with a global style. Jean Lave has shown that cognitive activity outside the laboratory often involves the use of a variety of cognitive strategies. In these everyday situations, the goal of cognition is not to solve a problem by finding the single correct answer. Instead, people try to resolve dilemmas in a way that allows them to get on with life. Cognition is thus best understood as the relations that link the mind at work to the world in which it works.

6. We may become impatient with people from a different culture if they fail to see similarities or differences that we think ought to be obvious to any observer. Yet the obviousness of particular features depends upon what any given culture chooses to emphasize and what it chooses to ignore. People may be perfectly aware of certain features if asked about them and simply ignore those features in ordinary circumstances because they carry no cultural relevance. Western schooling trains people to pay attention to a wider variety of perceptual features than are ordinarily culturally relevant.

7. Several attempts have been made to measure the levels of rational thinking in non-Western populations. The results are mixed. There seems to be no way to predict who will perform well or poorly on Piaget's conservation test, and tests of syllogistic reasoning require background knowledge that subjects may not have. In addition, informants may have a hard time interpreting syllogisms with arbitrary content.

8. Rational thinking is not the same as logic. Formal Western logic is better understood as a learned reasoning style characteristic of Western culture. Rules of Western logic can be very useful, but other logics may be equally valid in other societies—or on other occasions in Western societies—when considering contextual factors is vital.

9. Our emotions, like our thoughts, are not just something we have; they are culturally constructed of our state of mind, our cultural interpretations, and our levels of bodily arousal. Different cultures recognize different domains of experience and different categories of feeling as being appropriate to these domains. For this reason, it is difficult to translate what emotions mean from one culture to another.

10. Humans must learn to pattern and adapt behavior and ways of thinking and feeling to the standards considered appropriate in their respective cultures. The result of this process is the formation of a socially and culturally constructed self. Mead and Vygotsky argued that society and culture enhance and complete the development of the self, which occurs as language is mastered. Vygotsky's concept of the zone of proximal development stresses that cognitive development results from a dialogue. Children progress through that process at different rates and in different directions, depending on the amount and kind of coaching they receive by others. This concept makes it possible to explain why people in different cultural subgroups are socialized and enculturated in different ways.

Suggested Readings

Barnouw, Victor. 1985. *Culture and personality.* 4th ed. Homewood, IL: Dorsey. *An enduring classic, this book is an encyclopedia of psychological anthropology prior to the rise of the cognitive science approach.*

Cole, Michael, and Sylvia Scribner. 1974. *Culture and thought: A psychological introduction.* New York: Wiley. *A clear, readable survey of the literature and case studies on the cultural shaping of cognition.*

Miller, Jonathan. 1983. *States of mind.* New York: Pantheon. *A series of interviews in which Jonathan Miller (English actor, writer, physician, director) talks to several of the most interesting scholars on the mind, including George Mandler, Richard Gregory, and Clifford Geertz. This book is witty and enjoyable.*

Schwartz, Theodore, Geoffrey M. White, and Catherine A. Lutz, eds. 1992. *New directions in psychological anthropology.* Cambridge: Cambridge University Press. *An up-to-date survey of psychological anthropology with articles by experts in the fields of cognition, human development, biopsychological studies, and psychiatric and psychoanalytic anthropology.*

Play, Art, Myth, and Ritual

ne of the authors of this book, Robert Lavenda, was carrying out fieldwork in Caracas, Venezuela, toward the end of October 1974, when excitement about the heavyweight boxing championship featuring George Foreman and Muhammad Ali began to build. Boxing is extremely popular in Venezuela, and the Caracas newspapers devoted a great deal of attention to this bout. They gave Ali little chance of winning. It was late in his career, and he had already lost once to Foreman. Too old, they said, too out of shape, too big a mouth, too strong an opponent.

I (Lavenda) managed to resist interest in the fight until the last moment. I had other work to do and didn't care for boxing. Besides, I didn't have a television in my apartment. On the night the fight was to be telecast on the national network, I went out to dinner alone. On my way home, I was surprised to see the city almost deserted. Then I remembered that the fight was about to start. I was feeling lonely, and my curiosity got the better of me. I passed a bar that had a television, so I stopped in. The preliminaries, native dancing from Congo, were just ending. The bar gradually filled up. A couple of people seemed to know each other, but the rest were strangers.

As the fight began, I became aware that we were all Ali fans. As he did better and better, we became increasingly excited, and communication among the

FIGURE 7.1 Locations of societies whose EthnoProfiles appear in Chapter 7.

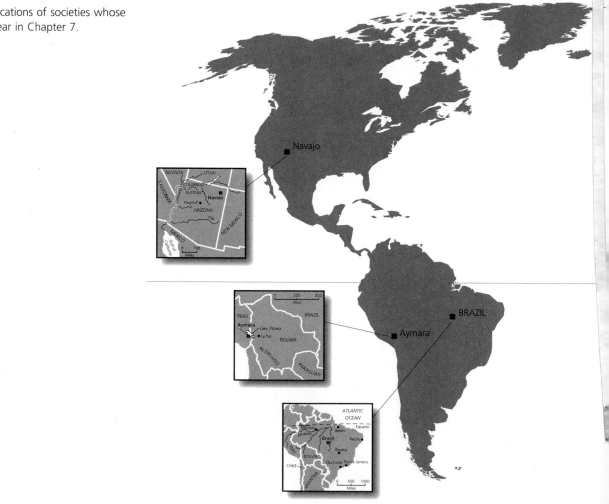

A DIALECTIC BETWEEN THE MEANINGFUL AND THE MATERIAL

Material goods carry culturally defined meanings, and what is viewed as meaningful (as stipulated by culture) can have material consequences. It is out of this dialectic between the meaningful and the material that the modes of livelihood followed by human beings everywhere emerge.

Key Terms

scarcity	formalists
institutions	substantivists
economy	modes of exchange
subsistence strategies	reciprocity
food collectors	redistribution
food producers	market exchange
extensive agriculture	labor
intensive agriculture	mode of production
mechanized industrial	means of production
agriculture	relations of
production	production
distribution	ideology
consumption	ecology
neoclassical economic	ecozone
theory	affluence

Chapter Summary

1. Survival requires that people make use of the natural resources in the wider world, and yet our culture tells us which resources to use and in what way. Human beings have devised a variety of subsistence strategies to satisfy their material survival needs. The basic division is between food collectors and food producers. Farmers may practice extensive or intensive agriculture, and in industrialized societies, food production may become mechanized.

2. Human economic activity is usefully divided into three phases: production, distribution, and consumption. In capitalist societies, market exchange is the dominant mode of distribution, yet many non-Western societies have traditionally carried out distribution without money or markets. Some economic anthropologists claim that exchange determines the nature of production and consumption. Others argue that production determines the nature of exchange and consumption. Still others are persuaded that culturally shaped consumption standards determine patterns of production and exchange. And there are those who believe that storage practices affect production, distribution, and consumption.

3. Formal neoclassical economic theory developed in an attempt to explain how capitalism works. After World War II, formalist economic anthropologists applied the market model to local activities in non-Western societies that bore a family resemblance to markets in Western societies. Formalists assumed that non-Western actors were rational maximizers of their individual self-interest.

4. During the 1960s and 1970s, substantivists criticized formalists and emphasized that economic activities were embedded in cultural institutions. They distinguished three major modes of exchange in human societies: reciprocity, redistribution, and market exchange. Substantivists viewed market exchange, and the maximizing rationality that goes with it, as a recent invention of capitalist societies.

5. Marxian economic anthropologists view production as more important than exchange in determining the patterns of economic life in a society. They argue that societies can be classified in terms of their modes of production. Each mode of production contains within it the potential for conflict between classes of people who receive differential benefits and losses from the productive process.

6. The internal explanation for consumption patterns argues that people produce material goods to satisfy basic human needs. The external explanation argues that consumption patterns depend not on the hunger drive, which is the same for everyone, but on the particular external resources available within the ecozone to which a particular society must adapt. Ethnographic evidence demonstrates that both internal and external explanations for consumption patterns are inadequate because they

ignore how culture defines our needs and provides for their satisfaction according to its own logic—a logic that is reducible neither to biology nor to psychology nor to ecological pressure.

7. Particular consumption preferences that may seem irrational make sense when considered in the context of other consumption preferences and prohibitions in the same culture. The Jewish prohibition against pork consumption makes sense when considered together with other Jewish dietary rules. The accumulation of banana leaves in the Trobriand Islands makes sense in the context of Trobriand kinship and economic arrangements. Institutionalized sharing among the Plains Cree makes sense in the context of Cree history and traditional social arrangements.

8. Even middle-class North Americans and Europeans, who are committed to economic rationality and efficiency, exhibit irrational—that is, culturally motivated—consumption patterns, as illustrated by the central role of meat in our diets.

Suggested Readings

Douglas, Mary, and Baron Isherwood. 1979. *The world of goods: Towards an anthropology of consumption.* New York: Norton. *A discussion of consumption, economic theories about consumption, and what anthropologists can contribute to the study of consumption.*

Lee, Richard. 1992. *The Dobe Ju/'hoansi.* 2d ed. New York: Holt, Rinehart and Winston. *This highly readable ethnography contains important discussions about foraging as a way of making a living.*

Plattner, Stuart, ed. 1989. *Economic anthropology.* Palo Alto, CA: Stanford University Press. *A readable, up-to-date collection of articles by economic anthropologists. Displaying the achievements of formalist-inspired research, it also reconciles with substantivism and recognizes the contribution of marxian analyses.*

Sahlins, Marshall. 1972. *Stone Age economics.* Chicago: Aldine. *A series of classic essays on economic life, written from a substantivist position. Includes "The original affluent society."*

Wilk, Richard. 1996. *Economies and cultures.* Boulder, CO: Westview. *A current, accessible "theoretical guidebook" to the conflicting views of human nature that underlie disputes in economic anthropology.*

PART IV

Systems of Relationships

Human life is group life, and in this part, we examine some of the principles that human beings have used to organize themselves into groups. Variation in social relations is due in part to cultural creativity, but it is always shaped by the political and economic circumstances that people must contend with. At the same time, inventive human beings draw on the cultural resources available to them to struggle against the material conditions they encounter. The following three chapters explore how people can bind themselves to one another by creating cultural relationships of kinship, marriage, and family as well as other forms of community that reach beyond the bounds of these institutions to create larger and more complex groupings.

11 ☀

Kinship

artha Macintyre, an Australian anthropologist, did field research on the small island of Tubetube in Papua New Guinea from 1979 to 1983. She writes:

Like many anthropologists, I was initially taken in as "fictive kin." The explanations given to me for this were several. First, as I was going to stay on the island for a long time, I had to live in an appropriate place. I therefore needed to belong to the totemic "clan" that would enable me to live near to the main hamlet. This was a pragmatic decision. Secondly, as the only person who could translate for me was a young married man, I must become his "elder sister" in order to avoid scandal. Later a *post hoc* explanation emerged which drew on a long tradition of incorporating migrants and exiles into the community. My reddish hair, my habit of running my fingers through my hair when nervous, and the way that I hold my head at a slight angle when I listen to people intently, were indicators of my natural connection to Magisubu, the sea eagle clan. This view gained currency as I was "naturalised," and was proved to everybody's satisfaction when an elderly woman from another island pronounced that the lines on my hand proclaimed me as Magisubu.

An equally pressing reason for incorporating me was the need to minimize the disruption I caused by having no rightful place. People found it difficult to use my first name, as first names are used exclusively by spouses, or in intimate contexts. This left them with the honorific "sinabada," a form of address for senior women that was used in the colonial context for white women. It is now redolent of subservience and I hated being addressed in this way. In making me a part of the Magisubu clan, Tubetube leaders lessened my anomalous status and gave everyone on the island a way of speaking to me. Set in a large lineage with two older sisters, a mother and three powerful men as my mother's brothers, as well as numerous younger siblings, I could be managed, instructed, and guided in ways that did not threaten their dignity or mine. Although I was unaware of it at the time, there was a meeting of people who decided my fate in these terms within days of my arrival.

The adoption by Magisubu people carried with it numerous obligations, most of which were unknown to me until I was instructed as to their nature. In retrospect, they were advantageous to my research in the sense that I was given a role in various events affecting my adoptive family and so learned within a defined context. Usually, before any occasion where I

might be expected to behave in some role appropriate to my (fictive) status, some senior person would explain to me what I should do. So, for example, I was told that I must on no account step over people's belongings nor stand so that I looked down on the head of a senior man or woman, nor sit close to any affines [in-laws]. . . . On neighbouring islands I was treated as an honoured guest, unless I was accompanied by a group of Magisubu people, in which case the hosts would treat me in accordance with my fictive status within that clan. (1993, 51–52)

In many societies, kinship is so fundamental a way of defining who people are and how they connect with others that outsiders, even anthropologists, are made part of the system. Kinship enmeshes people in a web of relatives. Each person in the web is aware of his or her responsibilities and rights; the position of each in relation to all others is made clear. Life together becomes organized.

KINSHIP SYSTEMS: WAYS OF ORGANIZING HUMAN INTERDEPENDENCE

Human life is group life. A human infant is brought into the world able to do little more than grasp, suck, and cry. To survive, it depends on other human beings. Even after childhood, however, human survival is immeasurably enhanced when people organize in groups. How we choose to organize ourselves is open to creative variation, as we have seen. But each of us was born into a society whose political, economic, and cultural practices were already well-established when we arrived. These traditional practices make survival possible, but also constrain the forms it may take. As a result, much can be predicted about a child's probable career just by knowing the kind of social group he or she is born into.

In previous chapters, we have outlined some of the broader political and economic forces that impinge on people's lives in society. This chapter addresses cultural factors that further specify the child's social identity and the practical activities he or she will one day be expected to perform. Indeed, this chapter and the one that follows focus specifically on how such human experiences as sexuality, conception, birth, and nurturance are selectively interpreted and culturally shaped

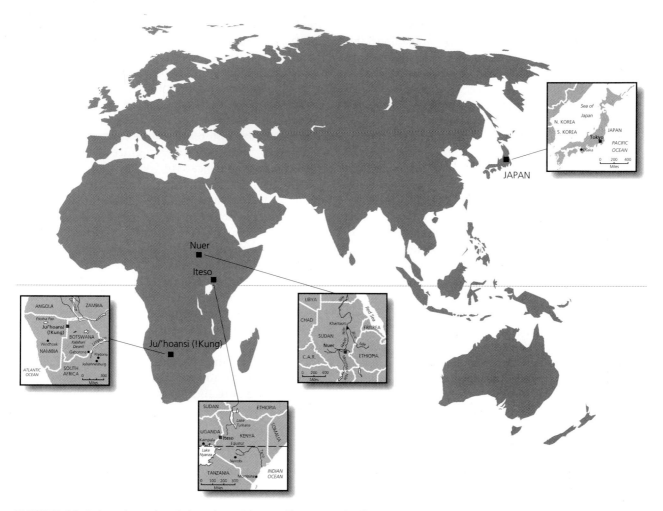

FIGURE 11.1 Locations of societies whose EthnoProfiles appear in Chapter 11.

into the deeply layered practices that anthropologists call *kinship, gender, marriage,* and *family.* Although relationships between kin reveal complexities that require special study, it is important to remember that these relationships are always embedded in, and shaped by, politics, economics, and worldviews.

Determining Group Membership and Relationships

A venerable way of organizing human society is on the basis of **kinship**—that is, on relationships derived from the universal human experiences of mating,

birth, and nurturance. Anthropologists call relationships based on mating **marriage** (discussed in Chapter 12) and those based on birth **descent.** Although

---

kinship Social relationships that are prototypically derived from the universal human experiences of mating, birth, and nurturance.

marriage An institution that prototypically involves a man and a woman, transforms the status of the participants, carries implications about sexual access, gives offspring a position in the society, and establishes connections between the kin of the husband and the kin of the wife.

descent The principle based on culturally recognized parent-child connections that define the social categories to which people belong.

nurturance is ordinarily seen to be closely connected with mating and birth, it need not be, and all societies have ways of acknowledging a relationship based on nurturance alone. In the United States, we call this relationship **adoption.**

Although marriage is based on mating, descent on birth, and adoption on nurturance, marriage is not the same thing as mating, descent is not the same thing as birth, and adoption is not the same thing as nurturance. The human experiences of mating, birth, and nurturance are ambiguous. The fascinating thing about kinship systems is that different societies choose to highlight some features of those experiences while downplaying or even ignoring others. Europeans and North Americans know that in their societies, mating is not the same as marriage, although a valid marriage encourages mating between the married partners. Similarly, all births do not constitute valid links of descent: Children whose parents have not been married according to accepted legal or religious specifications do not fit the cultural logic of descent, and many societies offer no positions that they can properly fill. Finally, not all acts of nurturance are recognized as adoption: Consider, for example, foster parents in the United States, whose custody of foster children is officially temporary. Put another way, through kinship, a culture emphasizes certain aspects of human experience, constructs its own theory of human nature, and specifies "the processes by which an individual comes into being and develops into a complete (i.e., mature) social person" (Kelly 1993, 521).

Marriage, descent, and adoption are thus selective. One society may emphasize women as the bearers of children and base its kinship system on this fact, paying little formal attention to the male's role in conception. Another society may trace connections through men, emphasizing the paternal role in conception and reducing the maternal role. A third society may encourage its members to adopt not only children but adult siblings, blurring the link between biological reproduction and family creation. Even though they contradict one another, all three understandings can be justified with reference to the panhuman experiences of mating, birth, and nurturance.

Consider the North American kinship term *aunt.* This term seems to refer to a woman who occupies a unique biological position. In fact, an aunt may be related to a person in one of four different ways: as father's sister, mother's sister, father's brother's wife, or mother's brother's wife. From the perspective of North American kinship, all those women have something in common, and they are all placed into a kinship category. Prototypically, a person's aunts are women one generation older than he or she is and are sisters or sisters-in-law of a person's parents. However, North Americans may also refer to their mother's best friend as *aunt.* By doing so, they recognize the strengths of this system of classification.

Thus, kinship is an idiom. It is a selective interpretation of the common human experiences of mating, birth, and nurturance. The result is a set of coherent principles that allow people to assign one another group membership. These principles normally cover several significant issues: how to carry out the reproduction of legitimate group members (marriage or adoption); where group members should live after marriage (residence rules); how to establish links between generations (descent); and how to pass on positions in society (succession) or material goods (inheritance). Taken together, kinship principles define social groups, locate people within those groups, and position the people and groups in relation to one another both in space and over time.

Sex, Gender, and Kinship

Kinship is based on but is not reducible to biology. It is a cultural interpretation of the culturally recognized "facts" of human reproduction. One of the most basic of these "facts," recognized in some form in all societies, is that two different kinds of human beings must cooperate sexually to produce offspring. Anthropologists use the term **sex** to refer to the observable physical characteristics that distinguish the two kinds of human beings, females and males, needed for reproduction. People everywhere pay attention to *morphological sex* (the appearance of external genitalia and observable secondary sex characteristics such as enlarged breasts in females). Scientists further distinguish females from males on the basis of *gonadal sex* (presence of ovaries in females, testes in males) and *chromosomal sex* (two X chromosomes in females, one X chromosome and one Y chromosome in males).

At the same time, cross-cultural research repeatedly demonstrates that physical sex differences do not allow us to predict the roles that females or males will play

FIGURE 11.2 Cross-cultural research repeatedly demonstrates that physical indicators of sex difference do not allow us to predict the roles that females or males will play in any particular society. In Hopi society, men were responsible for the weaving, whereas this woman of the Libinza people in the Democratic Republic of Congo is responsible for hunting.

in any particular society. Consequently, anthropologists distinguish sex from **gender**—the cultural construction of beliefs and behaviors considered appropriate for each sex. As Barbara Miller puts it, "In some societies, people with XX chromosomes do the cooking, in others it is the XY people who cook, in others both XX and XY people cook. The same goes for sewing, transplanting rice seedlings, worshipping deities, and speaking in public. Even the exclusion of women from hunting and warfare has been reduced by recent studies from the level of a universal to a generality. While it is generally true that men hunt and women do not, and that men fight in wars and women do not, important counter cases exist" (1993, 5; Figure 11.2).

In fact, the outward physical features used to distinguish females from males may not be obvious either. Sometimes genetic or hormonal factors produce ambiguous external genitalia, a phenomenon called *hermaphroditism.* Steroid 5-alpha reductase deficiency, for example, is a rare hormonal defect that causes males who are otherwise biologically normal to be born with ambiguous genitals, leading some to be categorized as male and others as female. At puberty, however, increased testosterone levels cause these individuals to experience changes typical of males: a deepening voice, muscle development, growth of the penis, and descent of the testicles. Gilbert Herdt (1994b) investigated cases of individuals with steroid 5-alpha reductase deficiency in the Dominican Republic and in New Guinea. In both places, the sexually anomalous individuals had been assigned to a locally recognized third sex, called *guevedoche* ("testicles at twelve") in the Dominican Republic and *kwolu-aatmwol* ("changing into a male thing") among the Sambia of New Guinea.

In other cases, however, anthropologists have documented the existence of *supernumerary* (that is, more

---

adoption Kinship relationships based on nurturance, often in the absence of other connections based on mating or birth.
sex Observable physical characteristics that distinguish two kinds of humans, females and males, needed for biological reproduction.
gender The cultural construction of beliefs and behaviors considered appropriate for each sex.

than the standard two) sexes in cultures where the presence of ambiguous genitalia at birth seem to play no obvious role. In the Byzantine civilization of late antiquity, phenotypic differences were deliberately created in the case of eunuchs, whose testicles were removed or destroyed, often before puberty (Ringrose 1994). In the case of the hijras of Gujarat, India, adult males deliberately cut off both penis and testicles in order to become ritual performers dedicated to the Mother Goddess Bahuchara Mata (Nanda 1994). In both these cases, third gender roles distinct from traditional feminine and masculine gender roles are believed appropriate for third-sexed individuals.

Elsewhere, supernumerary gender roles developed that apparently had nothing to do with morphological sex anomalies. Perhaps the most famous case is that of the *berdache*. Male berdaches have been described in almost 150 indigenous North American societies and female berdaches in perhaps half that number. Will Roscoe points out that "the key features of male and female berdache roles were, in order of importance, *productive specialization* (crafts and domestic work for male berdaches and warfare, hunting, and leadership roles in the case of female berdaches), *supernatural sanction* (in the form of an authorization and/or bestowal of powers from extrasocietal sources) and *gender variation* (in relation to normative cultural expectations for male and female genders)," commonly but not always marked by cross-dressing (1994, 332). Some berdaches may have engaged in sexual practices that Westerners consider homosexual or bisexual. Berdaches were accepted and respected members of their communities, and their economic and religious pursuits seem to have been culturally more significant than their sexual practices.

For many people, the "natural" existence of only two sexes, each with its own gender role, seems too obvious to question. Nevertheless, Thomas Laqueur (1990) has shown that the "two-sex model," which most contemporary Westerners accept as transparently obvious, only took root after the Renaissance. Prior to that, the bodies of all human beings were evaluated in terms of a "one-sex model" based on the Platonic notion that there was one ideal human form, which all actual human beings embodied to greater or lesser degrees. Moreover, as Roscoe points out, "the presence of multiple genders does not require belief in the existence of three or more physical sexes but, minimally, a view of physical differences as unfixed, or insufficient

on their own to establish gender, or simply less important than individual and social factors" (1994, 342). These observations sustain the key assertion of Sylvia Yanagisako and Jane Collier: "there are no 'facts,' biological or material, that have social consequences and cultural meanings in and of themselves" (1987, 39).

Herdt's survey of ethnographic literature leads him to conclude that it is difficult for societies to maintain supernumerary sexes or genders. Still, anthropologists can argue convincingly that societies have such statuses when a culture defines for each "a symbolic niche and a social pathway of development into later adult life distinctly different from the cultural life plan set out by a model based on male/female duality" (1994a, 68).

Interestingly, supernumerary sexes and genders can coexist alongside strongly marked male-female duality, as among the Sambia, perhaps serving to temper the absolutism of that duality. That male-female duality should be an issue for the Sambia reminds us that no human society is unconcerned about biological and social reproduction. However, kinship institutions, which build on gender duality, do more than provide for reproduction. Kinship not only classifies people, it also establishes and enforces the conventions by which different classes of people interact with one another. In this way, societies are able to maintain social order without central government.

Understanding Different Kinship Systems

Kinship practices, rather than written statutes, clarify for people what rights and obligations they owe one another. But the first Westerners who encountered different kinship practices found some of them highly unusual. Western explorers discovered, for example, that some non-Western people distinguished among their relatives only on the basis of age and sex. To refer to people one generation older than the speaker required only two terms: one applying to men and one applying to women. The explorers mistakenly concluded that these people were unable to tell the difference between their fathers and their uncles because they used the same kin term for both. They did not understand that *father* and *uncle* are not universally recognized kinship categories. For the people whom the explorers met, the man who was married to their mother, although known to them and personally important to them, was socially no more or less significant than that man's brothers or their mother's brothers. By referring to all these men by the same kin term, they were no more deluded than English speakers are when they assert that their father's sister and mother's brother's wife are equally their *aunts.*

Beyond that, the categories of feeling these people associated with different kin were as real as, but different from, the emotions Westerners associate with kin. "Just as the word *father* in English means a great deal more than lineal male ancestor of the first ascending generation, *aita* in Basque has many local connotations not reducible to *father,* as we understand the term" (Greenwood and Stini 1977, 333). Because the world of kin is a world of expectations and obligations, it is fundamentally a moral world charged with feeling. In some societies, a man's principal authority figure is his mother's brother, and his father is a figure of affection and unwavering support. "God the Father" would not mean the same thing in those societies as it does in a society in which the father has life-and-death control over his children and a mother's brothers are without significant authority.

PATTERNS OF DESCENT IN KINSHIP

An important part of kinship is descent—the cultural principle that defines social categories through culturally recognized parent-child connections. Descent groups are defined by ancestry and so have a time depth. Descent involves transmission and incorporation: the transmission of membership through parent-child links and the incorporation of these people into groups. In some societies, descent group membership controls how people mobilize for social action.

Two major strategies are employed in establishing patterns of descent. In the first strategy, the descent group is formed by people who believe they are related to each other by connections made through their mothers and fathers *equally.* That is, they believe themselves to be just as related to their father's side of the family as to their mother's. Anthropologists call this **bilateral descent** (or *cognatic descent*). Two kinds of bilateral kinship groups have been identified by anthropologists. One is made up of people who claim to be related to one another through ties either from the mother's or father's side to a common ancestor. This

bilateral descent group is rare. The other kind, called a *bilateral kindred,* is much more common and consists of the relatives of one person or group of siblings.

The second major strategy, **unilineal descent**, is based on the assumption that the most significant kin relationships must be traced through *either* the mother *or* the father. Such descent groups are the most common kind of descent group in the world today. Unilineal descent groups that are made up of links traced through a father are called *patrilineal;* those traced through a mother are called *matrilineal.*

Bilateral Kindreds

The **bilateral kindred** is the kinship group that most Europeans and North Americans know. This group forms around a particular individual and includes all the people linked to that individual through kin of both sexes—people conventionally called *relatives* in English (Figure 11.3). These people form a group only because of their connection to the central person or persons, known in the terminology of kinship as *Ego.* In North American society, bilateral kindreds assemble when Ego is baptized, confirmed, bar or bat mitzvahed, married, or buried. Each person within Ego's bilateral kindred has his or her own separate kindred. For example, Ego's father's sister's daughter has a kindred that includes people related to her through her father and his siblings—people to whom Ego is not related. This is simultaneously the major strength and major weakness of bilateral kindreds. That is, they have overlapping memberships and they do not endure beyond the lifetime of an individual Ego. But they are widely extended and can form broad networks of people who are somehow related to one another.

A classic bilateral kindred is found among the Ju/'hoansi (!Kung) of the Kalahari Desert in southern Africa. (See EthnoProfile 11.1: Ju/'hoansi [!Kung].) Anthropologist Richard Lee points out that for the

---

bilateral descent The principle that a descent group is formed by people who believe they are related to each other by connections made through their mothers and fathers equally (sometimes called *cognatic descent*).
unilineal descent The principle that a descent group is formed by people who believe they are related to each other by links made through a father or mother only.
bilateral kindred A kinship group that consists of the relatives of one person or group of siblings.

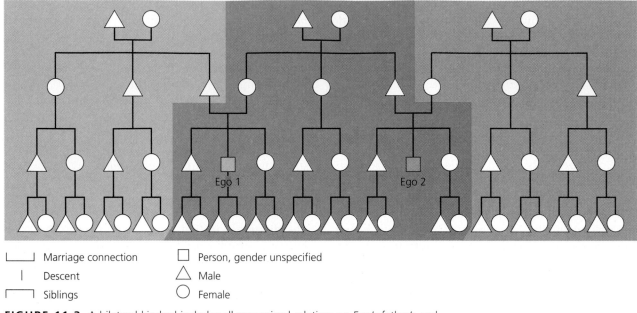

⊏__⊐ Marriage connection	☐	Person, gender unspecified
| Descent	△	Male
⊏‾⊐ Siblings	◯	Female

FIGURE 11.3 A bilateral kindred includes all recognized relatives on Ego's father's and mother's sides. The dark area in the center indicates where the kindreds of Ego 1 and Ego 2 overlap.

Ju/'hoansi, every individual in the society can be linked to every other individual by a kinship term, either through males or through females. As a result, a person can expect to find a relative everywhere there are Ju/'hoansi. When they were full-time foragers, the Ju/'hoansi lived in groups that were relatively small (10 to 30 people) but made up of a constantly changing set of individuals. "In essence, a Ju/'hoan camp consists of relatives, friends, and in-laws who have found that they can live and work well together. Under this flexible principle, brothers may be united or divided; fathers and sons may live together or apart. Further, during his or her lifetime a Ju/'hoan may live at many waterholes with many different groups" (1992b, 62). A wide range of kinspeople makes this flexibility possible. When someone wanted to move, he or she had kin at many different waterholes and could choose to activate any of several appropriate kin ties.

For the Ju/'hoansi, the bilateral kindred provides social flexibility. However, flexible group boundaries become problematic in at least four kinds of social circumstances: (1) where clear-cut membership in a particular social group must be determined, (2) where social action requires the formation of groups that are larger than individual families, (3) where conflicting claims to land and labor must be resolved, and (4) where people are concerned to perpetuate a particular social order over time. In societies that face these dilemmas, unilineal descent groups are usually formed.

Unilineal Descent Groups

Unilineal descent groups are found all over the world. They are all based on the principle that certain kinds of parent-child relationships are more important than others. Membership in a unilineal descent group is based on the membership of the appropriate parent in the group. In patrilineal systems, an individual belongs to a group formed through male sex links, the lineage of his or her father. In matrilineal systems, an individual belongs to a group formed by links through women, the lineage of his or her mother. *Patrilineal* and *matrilineal* do not mean that only men belong to one and women to the other; rather, the terms refer to the prin-

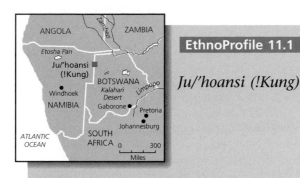

EthnoProfile 11.1

Ju/'hoansi (!Kung)

Region: Southern Africa

Nations: Botswana and Namibia

Population: 45,000

Environment: Desert

Livelihood: Hunting and gathering

Political organization: Traditionally, egalitarian bands; today, part of modern nation-states

For more information: Lee, Richard B. 1992. *The Dobe Ju/'hoansi.* 2d ed. New York: Holt, Rinehart and Winston.

ciple by which membership is conferred. In a patrilineal society, women and men belong to a **patrilineage** formed by father-child links (Figure 11.4); similarly, in a matrilineal society, men and women belong to a **matrilineage** formed by mother-child connections (Figure 11.5). In other words, membership in the group is, on the face of it, unambiguous. An individual belongs to only one lineage. This is in contrast to a bilateral kindred, in which an individual belongs to overlapping groups. Nevertheless, as Martine Segalen observes, a pattern of unilineal descent itself is "no more than a kind of external framework," which can support a wide range of cultural variations (1986, 51–52).

LINEAGES

The *lineal* in patrilineal and matrilineal refers to the nature of the social group formed. These **lineages** are composed of people who believe they can specify the parent-child links that unite them. Although the abstract kinship diagrams that anthropologists draw in-

clude just a few people, lineages in the world vary in size, ranging from 20 or 30 members to several hundred. Before 1949, some Chinese lineages were composed of more than 1,000 members.

Lineage Membership

The most important feature of lineages is that they are *corporate* in organization—that is, a lineage has a single legal personality. As the Ashanti put it, a lineage is "one person" (Fortes 1953). To outsiders, all members of a lineage are equal *in law* to all others. For example, in the case of a blood feud, the death of any opposing lineage member avenges the death of the person who started the feud. Lineages are also corporate in that they control property, specifically land, as a unit. Such groups are found only in societies where rights to use land are crucial and must be monitored over time.

Lineages are also the main political associations in the societies that have them. Individuals have no political or legal status in such societies except through lineage membership. They have relatives outside the lineage, but their own political and legal status comes through the lineage.

Because membership in a lineage comes through a direct line from father or mother to child, lineages can endure over time and in a sense have an independent existence. As long as people can remember from whom they are descended, lineages can endure. Most lineages have a time depth of about five generations: grandparents, parents, Ego, children, and grandchildren. When members of a group believe that they can no longer accurately specify the genealogical links that connect them but believe that they are "in some way" connected, we find what anthropologists call *clans*. A **clan** is usually made up of lineages that the society's members believe to be related to each other through links that go back into mythic times. Sometimes the common ancestor of each clan is said to be an animal that

---

patrilineage A social group formed by people connected by father-child links.

matrilineage A social group formed by people connected by mother-child links.

lineages The consanguineal members of descent groups who believe they can trace their descent from known ancestors.

clan A descent group formed by members who believe they have a common (sometimes mythical) ancestor, even if they cannot specify the genealogical links.

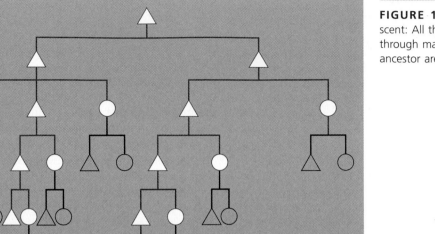

FIGURE 11.4 Patrilineal descent: All those who trace descent through males to a common male ancestor are indicated in white.

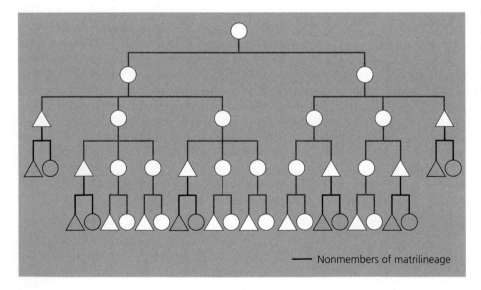

FIGURE 11.5 Matrilineal descent: All those who trace descent through females to a common female ancestor are indicated in white.

lived at the beginning of time. The important point is that lineage members can specify all the generational links back to their common ancestor, whereas clan members ordinarily cannot. The clan is thus larger than any lineage and also more diffuse in both membership and the hold it has over individuals.

The Logic of Lineage Relationships

Lineages endure over time in societies in which no other form of organization lasts. Hence, they provide for the "perpetual exercise of defined rights, duties, office and social tasks vested in the lineage" (Fortes 1953,

165). In other words, the system of lineages becomes the foundation of social life in the society.

While lineages might look solid and unchanging, they are often more flexible than they appear. The memories people have of their ancestry are often transmitted in the form of myth or legend. Rather than accurate historical records, they are better understood, in Malinowskian terms, as mythical charters, justifications from the invisible world for the visible arrangements of the society. In showing how this relationship works, Fortes (1953, 165) quotes anthropologists Paul and Laura Bohannan, whose research was among the Tiv of Nigeria. (See EthnoProfile 6.4: Tiv.) The Bohannans observed that Tiv who had not previously viewed one another as kin sometimes renegotiated their lineage relationships, announcing publicly that they shared some of the same ancestors. Such changes were plausible to the Tiv because they assumed that traditional lineage relationships determined current social arrangements. If current social arrangements and tradition conflicted, therefore, the Tiv concluded that errors had crept into the tradition. Such renegotiation enabled the Tiv to keep their lineage relationships in line with changing legal and political relationships.

Patrilineages

By far the most common form of lineage organization is the patrilineage, which consists of all the people (male and female) who believe themselves related to each other because they are related to a common male ancestor by links through men. The prototypical kernel of a patrilineage is the father-son pair. Women members of patrilineages normally leave the lineages when they marry, but they do not relinquish their interest in their own lineages. In a number of societies, they play an active role in the affairs of their own patrilineages for many years.

An assumption of hierarchy exists in patrilineal societies: Men believe they are superior to women, and many women seem to agree. However, there is a puzzle at the heart of these societies. Women with little power, who are strangers to the lineage, nevertheless marry its members and produce the children who perpetuate the lineage. Ironically, the future of the patrilineage depends on people who do not belong to it! A second irony is that women must leave their own lineages to reproduce the next generation of somebody

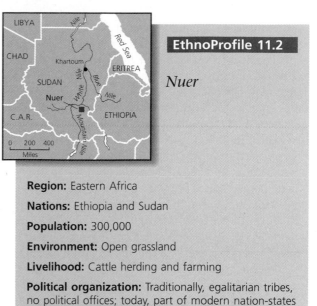

EthnoProfile 11.2

Nuer

Region: Eastern Africa

Nations: Ethiopia and Sudan

Population: 300,000

Environment: Open grassland

Livelihood: Cattle herding and farming

Political organization: Traditionally, egalitarian tribes, no political offices; today, part of modern nation-states

For more information: Evans-Pritchard, E. E. 1940. *The Nuer.* Oxford: Oxford University Press, and Hutchinson, Sharon. 1996. *Nuer Dilemmas.* Berkeley: University of California Press.

else's lineage. Women in patrilineal societies are often torn between conflicting interests and loyalties (see Karp 1986). Should they support their own children or their fathers and brothers?

A classic patrilineal system is found among the Nuer of the Sudan and Ethiopia. (See EthnoProfile 11.2: Nuer.) At the time of his fieldwork in the 1930s, English anthropologist E. E. Evans-Pritchard noted that the Nuer were divided into at least 20 clans. Evans-Pritchard defined *clan* as the largest group of people who (1) trace their descent patrilineally from a common ancestor, (2) cannot marry each other, and (3) consider sexual relations within the group to be incestuous. The clan is divided, or segmented, into lineages that are themselves linked to each other by presumed ties of patrilineal descent. The most basic stage of lineage segmentation is the *minimal lineage,* which has a time depth of three to five generations.

Evans-Pritchard observed that the Nuer kinship system worked in the following way: Members of lineages A and B might consider themselves related because they believed that the founder of lineage A had been the older brother of the founder of lineage B. These two minimal lineages together formed a *minor lineage*—all those descended from a common father. Minor lineages connect to other minor lineages by yet another presumed common ancestor, forming *major lineages*. These major lineages are also believed to share a common ancestor and thus form a *maximal lineage*. The members of two maximal lineages believe their founders had been the sons of the clan ancestor; thus, all members of the clan are believed to be patrilineally related.

According to Evans-Pritchard, disputes among the Nuer emerged along the lines created by lineages. Suppose a quarrel erupted between two men whose minimal lineages were in different minor lineages. Each would be joined by men who belonged to his minor lineage, even if they were not in his minimal lineage. The dispute would be resolved when the quarreling minor lineages recognized that they were all part of the same major lineage. Similarly, the minor lineages to one major lineage would ally if a dispute with an opposed major lineage broke out. This process of groups coming together and opposing one another, called **segmentary opposition**, is expressed in kinship terms but represents a very common social process.

Evans-Pritchard noted that lineages were important to the Nuer for political purposes. Members of the same lineage in the same village were conscious of being in a social group with common ancestors and symbols, corporate rights in territory, and common interests in cattle. When a son in the lineage married, these people helped provide the **bridewealth** cattle. If the son were killed, they—indeed, all members of his patrilineage, regardless of where they lived—would avenge him and would hold the funeral ceremony for him. Nevertheless, relationships among the members of a patrilineage were not necessarily harmonious: "A Nuer is bound to his paternal kin from whom he derives aid, security, and status, but in return for these benefits he has many obligations and commitments. Their often indefinite character may be both evidence of, and a reason for, their force, but it also gives ample scope for disagreement. Duties and rights easily conflict. Moreover, the privileges of [patrilineal] kinship cannot be divorced from authority, discipline, and a strong sense of moral obligation, all of which are irksome to Nuer. They do not deny them, but they kick against them when their personal interests run counter to them" (1951, 162).

Although the Nuer were patrilineal, they recognized as kin people who were not members of their lineage. In the Nuer language, the word *mar* referred to "kin": all the people to whom a person could trace a relationship of any kind, including people on the mother's side as well as those on the father's side. In fact, at such important ceremonial occasions as a bridewealth distribution after a woman in the lineage had been married, special attention was paid to kin on the mother's side. Certain important relatives, such as the mother's brother and the mother's sister, were given cattle. A man's mother's brother was his great supporter when he was in trouble. The mother's brother was kind to him as a boy and even provided a second home after he reached manhood. If he liked his sister's son, a mother's brother would even be willing to help pay the bridewealth so that he could marry. "Nuer say of the maternal uncle that he is both father and mother, but most frequently that 'he is your mother'" (Evans-Pritchard 1951, 162).

Matrilineages

In matrilineages, descent is traced through women rather than through men. Recall that in a patrilineage a woman's children are not in her lineage. In a matrilineage, a man's children are not in his. However, certain features of matrilineages make them more than just mirror images of patrilineages.

First, the prototypical kernel of a matrilineage is the sister-brother pair; a matrilineage may be thought of as a group of brothers and sisters connected through links made by women. Brothers marry out and often live with the family of their wives, but they maintain an active interest in the affairs of their lineage. Second, the most important man in a boy's life is not his father (who is not in his lineage) but his mother's brother, from whom he will receive his lineage inheritance. Third, the amount of power women exercise in matrilineages is still being hotly debated in anthropology. A matrilineage is not the same thing as a *matriarchy* (a society in which women rule); brothers often

---

segmentary opposition A mode of hierarchical social organization in which groups beyond the most basic emerge only in opposition to other groups on the same hierarchical level.

bridewealth The transfer of certain symbolically important goods from the family of the groom to the family of the bride on the occasion of their marriage. It represents compensation to the wife's lineage for the loss of her labor and childbearing capacities.

IN THEIR OWN WORDS

What Do Men Want?

Women and men in societies with patriarchal traditions, such as those of western Europe and the United States, are familiar with the attempts women have made to challenge social and legal rules that favor men's access to wealth, power, and prestige. Syed Zubair Ahmed writes here about the struggle of some Khasi men in northeastern India against the rules of a matrilineal system that they believe places them at a disadvantage.

Shillong, India

The matrilineal Khasi society in northeastern India, one of the few surviving female bastions in the world, is making a fervent effort to keep men in their place.

Though an all-male organization that is battling the centuries-old matrilineal system has yet to make any significant dent, the rebels claim to have enlisted the support of some prominent Khasi women. Their struggle to break free, they say, has resulted in small victories; some have begun to have a say in family affairs and are even inheriting property. But they constitute an insignificant minority in the 800,000-member Khasi society.

The men say the Khasi women are overbearing and dominating. "We are sick of playing the roles of breeding bulls and baby sitters," complains Mr. A. Swer, who heads the organization of maverick males. Another member laments: "We have no lines of succession. We have no land, no business. Our generation ends with us."

The demand for restructuring Khasi society in the patriarchal mold is a fallout from the growing number of women who are marrying outsiders. That, according to male opinion, has resulted in the bastardization of Khasi society. Following custom, the youngest daughter inherits the property and after marriage her husband moves into the family house. Outsiders are said to marry the Khasi women for their property, while the women say they prefer to marry outsiders because their own tribesmen tend to be irresponsible in family matters.

In rebuttal, many Khasi men say the outsiders take advantage of the immaturity, youth and vulnerability of the youngest daughters and devour all their property and business. As a result, many Khasi men become paupers. And if the young men are often lazy and have no sense of a family, the rebels argue, it's the matrilineal system that is to blame.

Another problem caused by these marriages is the disintegration of families. About 27,000 Khasi women were divorced by their non-Khasi husbands in recent years, the highest number among India's northeastern tribes.

The identity crisis has led the Khasi Student Union to issue a stern warning to young Khasi women against marrying "non-tribals," saying they may be ostracized if they do. The Student Union is against switching over to the patrilineal system, however. So is a prominent Khasi scholar, H. W. Sten, who cautions that a patrilineal shift "would result in cross-marriages between clans, which is taboo in Khasi society," and adds, "Ultimately, it would lead to genetic defects in the offspring."

He points out that a Khasi son or daughter takes the surname of the mother. Therefore, if two sisters marry two men of different clans, in a patriarchal system the surnames of their children would be different and the marriages between cousins would be valid. "This goes against the basic principle of Khasi custom," he said.

At the same time, Mr. Sten condemns those who are opposed to Khasi women's marrying outside the tribe. "Khasi culture is very flexible," he said. "No problem if a non-tribal wants to marry a Khasi girl as long as he is prepared to live with her and follow the Khasi custom. It will only add to the variety in Khasi society."

But Mr. Swer, president of the male group of social reformers, says such liberalism is the root cause of bastardization of his tribe. "Today, we have over 2,000 clans, but very few of them are pure Khasis," he observed. His demand for change, he adds, would stop outsiders from chasing Khasi young women, since under the patrilineal system their wives could not inherit property. But what about men marrying outside their tribe? "The girls will be taken into the Khasi fold," he replied. "The children from the wedlock will automatically be Khasis."

While some men would like to end female domination, they do not support Mr. Swer's movement to abandon the deeply held tradition. "We Khasis underestimate the contributions of our fathers to the family," said Mr. H. T. Wells, a cousin of Mr. Sten. "Our fathers do a lot, but the credit goes to the mothers. I would love to have the patriarchal system but for the respect of our custom."

Mr. Swer admits that the Khasi men's demand for a patrilineal society is still a distant hope. But people like Mr. Wells, half converts to his idea, sustain his dream.

Source: Ahmed 1994.

FIGURE 11.6 The head mother of a Navajo subsistence residence unit is identified with the land, the herd, and the agricultural fields.

retain what appears to be a controlling interest in the lineage. Some anthropologists claim that the male members of a matrilineage are supposed to run the lineage even though there is more autonomy for women in matrilineal societies than in patrilineal ones; that the day-to-day exercise of power tends to be carried out by the brothers or sometimes the husbands. A number of studies, however, have questioned the validity of these generalizations. Trying to say something about matrilineal societies in general is difficult. The ethnographic evidence suggests that matrilineages must be examined on a case-by-case basis.

The Navajo are a matrilineal people. (See Ethno-Profile 7.2: Navajo.) The basic unit of Navajo social organization is the subsistence residential unit composed of a head mother, her husband, and some of their children with their spouses and children (Witherspoon 1975, 82; Figure 11.6). The leader of the unit is normally a man, usually the husband of the head mother. He directs livestock and agricultural operations and is the one who deals with the outside world: "He speaks for the unit at community meetings, negotiates with the traders and car salesmen, arranges marriages and ceremonies, talks to visiting strangers, and so on." He

seems to be in charge. But it is the head mother around whom the unit is organized:

> [The head mother] is identified with the land, the herd, and the agricultural fields. All residence rights can be traced back to her, and her opinions and wishes are always given the greatest consideration and usually prevail. In a sense, however, she delegates much of her role and prestige to the leader of the unit. If we think of the unit as a corporation, and the leader as its president, the head mother will be the chairman of the board. She usually has more sheep than the leader does. Because the power and importance of the head mother offer a deceptive appearance to the observer, many students of the Navajo have failed to see the importance of her role. But if one has lived a long time in one of these units, one soon becomes aware of who ultimately has the cards and directs the game. When there is a divorce between the leader and the head, it is always the leader who leaves and the head mother who returns, even if the land originally belonged to the mother of the leader. (Witherspoon, 1975, 82–83)

Overall, evidence from matrilineal societies reveals some domains of experience in which men and women are equal, some in which men are in control, and some in which women are in control. Observers and participants may disagree about which of these domains of experience is more or less central to Navajo life.

In discussing patrilineages, we referred to a patrilineal puzzle. Matrilineal societies also have a paradox, sometimes called the *matrilineal puzzle*—the contradiction between the rule of residence and the rule of inheritance. The contradiction is especially clear in societies that are strongly matrilineal and encourage residence with the wife's matrilineage. Among the Bemba of Zambia, for example, a man is a stranger in his wife's house, where he goes when he marries. A man may feel great affection for his father, but he will not be his father's heir. He will inherit from his mother's brother, who lives elsewhere. And although a father may wish to have his son inherit from him, he must give to his sister's son (Richards 1954).

The classic case of the matrilineal puzzle comes from the Trobriand Islands, and Malinowski interpreted it in the way just described. (See EthnoProfile 3.4: Trobriand Islanders.) But research on the Trobriand Islanders by anthropologist Annette Weiner calls Malinowski's interpretation into question. Weiner argues that to understand matrilineal kinship in the Trobriand Islanders, one must begin by seeing the sister-brother pair as an integral unit: "[The sister-brother pair] makes complementary contributions both to a woman's brother's children and to a woman's own children. . . . In the former instance, a man and his sister (father and father's sister to a child) contribute their own [lineage] resources to the man's children, thus building up these children with resources that they may use, but may not subsequently pass on to their own children. . . . In the latter case, a woman and her brother (mother and mother's brother) contribute to the regeneration of [the matrilineage]—the woman through the process of conception and the man through the control and transmission of [matrilineage] property such as land and palm trees" (1980, 286–87). The result is that both a man and his sister "give" to the man's children, and his children return things to them later in life.

KINSHIP TERMINOLOGIES

People everywhere use special terms to refer to people they recognize as kin. Despite the variety of kinship systems in the world, anthropologists have identified

six major patterns of kinship terminology based on how people categorize their cousins. The six patterns reflect common solutions to structural problems faced by societies organized in terms of kinship. They provide clues concerning how the vast and undifferentiated world of potential kin may be divided up. Kinship terminologies suggest both the external boundaries and internal divisions of the kinship groups, and they outline the structure of rights and obligations assigned to different members of the society.

Criteria for Distinctions

Kinship terminologies are built on certain widely recognized kinship criteria. From the most common to the least common, these criteria include the following:

◆ *Generation.* Kin terms distinguish relatives according to the generation to which the relatives belong. In English, the term *cousin* conventionally refers to someone of the same generation as Ego.

◆ *Sex.* The sex of an individual is used to differentiate kin. In Spanish, *primo* refers to a male cousin and *prima* to a female cousin. In English, cousins are not distinguished on the basis of sex, but *uncle* and *aunt* are distinguished on the basis of both generation and sex.

◆ *Affinity.* A distinction is made on the basis of connection through marriage, or **affinity**. This criterion is used in Spanish when *suegra* (Ego's spouse's mother) is distinguished from *madre* (Ego's mother). In matrilineal societies, Ego's mother's sister and father's sister are distinguished from one another on the basis of affinity. The mother's sister is a direct, lineal relative; the father's sister is an affine; and they are called by different terms.

◆ *Collaterality.* A distinction is made between kin who are believed to be in a direct line and those who are "off to one side," linked to Ego through a lineal relative. In English, the distinction of **collaterality** is exemplified by the distinction between *mother* and *aunt* or *father* and *uncle*.

affinity Connection through marriage.
collaterality A criterion employed in the analysis of kinship terminologies in which a distinction is made between kin who are believed to be in a direct line and those who are "off to one side," linked to the speaker by a lineal relative.

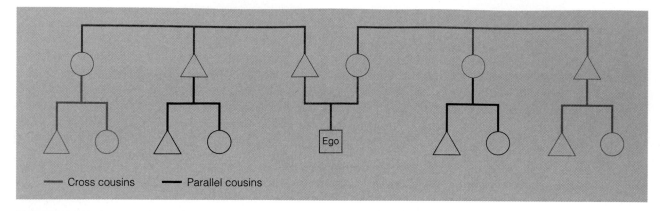

FIGURE 11.7 Cross cousins and parallel cousins: Ego's cross cousins are the children of Ego's father's sister and mother's brother. Ego's parallel cousins are the children of Ego's father's brother and mother's sister.

- ◆ *Bifurcation.* The distinction of **bifurcation** is employed when kinship terms referring to the mother's side of the family differ from those referring to the father's side.

- ◆ *Relative age.* Relatives of the same category may be distinguished on the basis of whether they are older or younger than Ego. Among the Ju/'hoansi, for example, speakers must separate "older brother" (*!ko*) from "younger brother" (*tsin*).

- ◆ *Sex of linking relative.* This criterion is related to collaterality. It distinguishes *cross relatives* (usually cousins) from *parallel relatives* (also usually cousins). Parallel relatives are linked through two brothers or two sisters. **Parallel cousins,** for example, are Ego's father's brother's children or mother's sister's children. Cross relatives are linked through a brother-sister pair. Thus, **cross cousins** are Ego's mother's brother's children or father's sister's children. The sex of either Ego or the cousins does not matter; rather the important factor is the sex of the linking relative (Figure 11.7).

Patterns of Kinship Terminology

The six major patterns of kinship terminology are based on how cousins are classified. These patterns were named after the societies that represent the prototypes. The first two patterns are found in association with bi-lateral descent systems; the remaining four are found in association with unilineal descent.

BILATERAL PATTERNS The *Hawaiian* pattern is based on the application of the first two criteria: generation and sex (Figure 11.8). The kin group is divided horizontally by generation, and within each generation there are only two kinship terms, one for males and one for females. In this system, Ego maintains a maximum degree of flexibility in choosing the descent group with which to affiliate. Ego is also forced to look for a spouse in another kin group because Ego may not marry anyone in the same terminological category as a genetic parent, sibling, or offspring.

The *Eskimo* pattern reflects the symmetry of bilateral kindreds (Figure 11.9). A lineal core—the nuclear family—is distinguished from collateral relatives, who are not identified with the father's or the mother's side. Once past the immediate collateral line (aunts and uncles, great-aunts and great-uncles, nephews and nieces), generation is ignored. The remaining relatives are all "cousins," sometimes distinguished by *number* (second or third) or by *removal* (generations away from Ego*).

---

*Ego's "first cousin once removed" can be one generation older or younger than Ego. Your cousin Phil's daughter is your first cousin once removed, but so is your father's cousin Marlys. Her son, Marvin, is your second cousin.

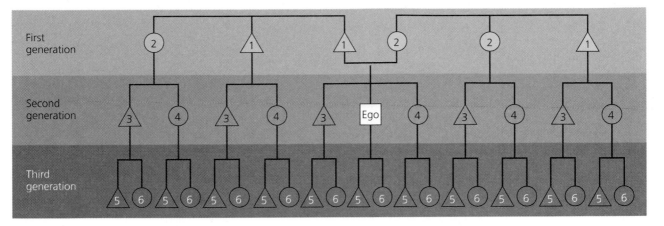

FIGURE 11.8 Hawaiian kinship terminology: Numbers represent kin terms. Ego uses the same kin term to refer to all those assigned the same number.

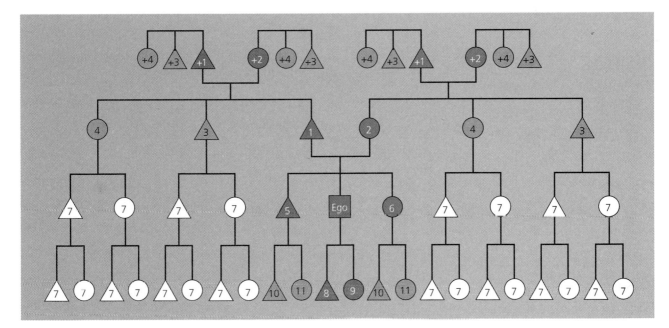

FIGURE 11.9 Eskimo kinship terminology: All those indicated in purple represent Ego's lineal relatives; those in gray represent Ego's collateral relatives; and those in white are cousins. The symbol + equals grand (for example, +1 = grandfather).

bifurcation A criterion employed in the analysis of kinship terminologies in which kinship terms referring to the mother's side of the family are distinguished from those referring to the father's side.

parallel cousins The children of a person's parents' same-sex siblings (a father's brother's children or a mother's sister's children).

cross cousins The children of a person's parents' opposite-sex siblings (a father's sister's children or a mother's brother's children).

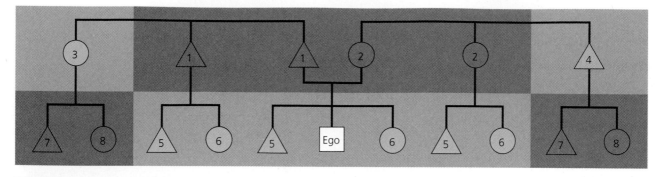

FIGURE 11.10 Iroquois kinship terminology.

This is the only terminological system that sets the nuclear family apart from all other kin. If the Hawaiian system is like a layer cake made up of horizontal layers of kin, this system is like an onion with layers of kin surrounding a core (Fox 1967, 259).

UNILINEAL PATTERNS   The *Iroquois* pattern is sometimes known as *bifurcate merging*, because it merges Ego's mother's and father's parallel siblings with Ego's parents (Figure 11.10). The sex of the linking relatives is important in this system: The parents' parallel siblings are grouped together with the parents, whereas cross siblings are set apart. This is repeated on the level of cousins. In a bilateral system, these distinctions would be meaningless, but in a unilineal system they mirror the lines of lineage membership. If Ego is a male, he will use one term to refer to all women of his matrilineage who are one generation older than he is. Their children are all referred to by another set of terms, one for males and one for females. Similarly, in his father's matrilineage, all men in the father's generation are referred to by one term. Their children are called by the same set of terms used for the cousins on the mother's side.

The pattern called *Crow* is a matrilineal system named after the Crow people of North America, but it is found in many other matrilineal societies, including the Trobriand Islands (Figure 11.11). The Crow system distinguishes the two matrilineages that are important to Ego: Ego's own and that of Ego's father. As in the Iroquois system, the sex of the linking relative is important, and both parents and their same-sex siblings are grouped together. Their children—Ego's parallel cousins—are in the same category as Ego's siblings.

The terms for cross cousins follow lineage membership, which is more important than generation. In Ego's own matrilineage, all the children of males are referred to by the same term regardless of their generation; their fathers are in Ego's matrilineage, but *they* are not. On the side of Ego's father's matrilineage, all male members are distinguished by one term and all female members by another, regardless of generational relationship to Ego.

The system known as *Omaha* (Figure 11.12), found among patrilineal peoples, represents the mirror image of the Crow system. All the members of Ego's mother's patrilineage are distinguished only by sex, and all the children of women in Ego's patrilineage are referred to by the same terms, one for males and one for females. Lineage membership again is more important than generation, a principle that is often hard for people living in bilateral kindreds to grasp.

Finally, in the *Sudanese* pattern, each related person is referred to by a separate term (Figure 11.13). This is a relatively rare terminological pattern. It is found in patrilineal societies, especially in northern Africa.

KINSHIP AND ALLIANCE THROUGH MARRIAGE

Any society divided into subgroups must devise a way to manage intergroup relations, and its members usually want to make sure that those relations are carried on from one generation to the next. Societies based on kinship attempt to resolve these difficulties by connecting kinship with marriage. By promoting or *pre-*

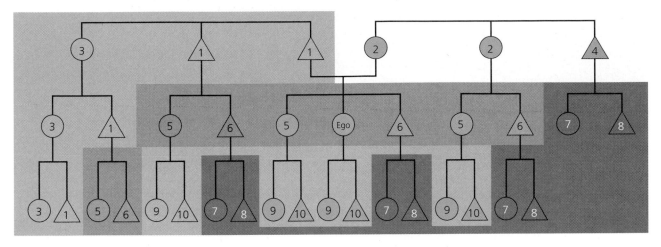

FIGURE 11.11 Crow kinship terminology: Members of Ego's matriline are represented in purple. Note the merging of generations and what follows as a result: All children of 3s are 1s and 3s; all children of 2s are 5s and 6s; all children of 5s are 9s and 10s; and all children of 4s and 6s are 7s and 8s—*regardless of generation.*

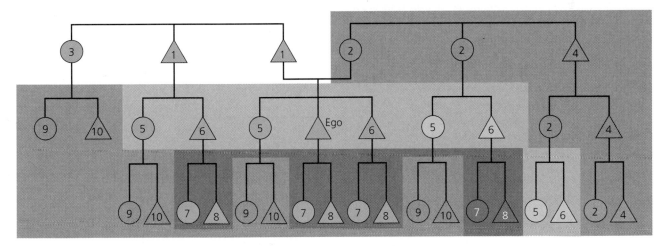

FIGURE 11.12 Omaha kinship terminology: Members of Ego's patriline are represented in purple. Note the merging of generations and what follows as a result: All children of 4s are 2s and 4s; all children of 1s are 5s and 6s; all children of 6s are 7s and 8s; and all children of 3s and 5s are 9s and 10s—*regardless of generation.*

scribing certain kinds of marriage, such societies both ensure the reproduction of their own memberships and establish long-term alliances with other groups.

Anthropologists find two major types of prescrip-tive marriage patterns in unilineal societies. One is a man's marriage with the father's sister's daughter. The more common is a man's marriage with the mother's brother's daughter.

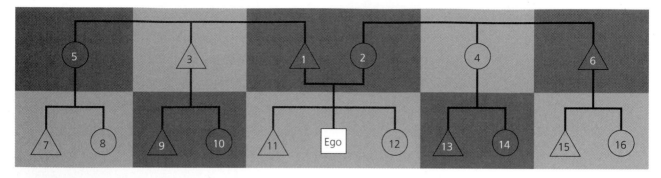

FIGURE 11.13 Sudanese kinship terminology: Each person related to Ego is referred to by a separate term.

In patrilineal societies, a "father's sister's daughter marriage" sets up a pattern of **direct exchange marriage.** In this pattern, a line that has received a wife from another line in one generation gives a wife back in the next generation. That is, if line A receives a wife for one of its members from line B in generation I, line A will provide a wife for a member of line B in generation II. But in generation I, the men of line B cannot marry women from line A. They must find wives from somewhere else, say line C. This pattern reverses itself in the next generation, when the obligation has been fulfilled and the original balance restored. This is called a *father's sister's daughter marriage system* because, from a man's point of view, that woman is the prototypical spouse. However, any woman of the appropriate line is an eligible marriage partner for him. Before the marriage occurs, the men and women of the groom's line negotiate with those of the bride's line to determine the appropriate match.

A *mother's brother's daughter marriage system* sets up a pattern of **asymmetrical exchange marriage.** Unlike direct exchange systems, this marriage pattern does not balance out after two generations. Instead, one line always gets wives from the same line and gives wives to a different line. Put another way, women always marry into the line their father's sisters married into, and men always find wives in the line their mothers came from. This pattern provides a permanent alliance among the lines involved. The prototypical wife for a man is his mother's brother's daughter. If a man in a matrilineal society actually does marry his mother's brother's daughter, he inherits both what his mother's brother

would give him and what his wife's father would give her husband.

Here, then, is the final piece in the lineage puzzle. People recognize certain classes of kin as potential marriage partners, and their kinship terminologies reflect this fact. Hence, if Ego's mother's brother doesn't have a daughter, all is not lost. Ego may not be looking for a literal mother's brother's daughter. Women whom anthropologists refer to as "mother's brother's daughters" are any women of Ego's generation who are members of his mother's patrilineage.

ADOPTION

Kinship systems may appear to be fairly rigid sets of rules that use the accident of birth to thrust people into social positions laden with rights and obligations they cannot escape. Social positions that people are assigned at birth are sometimes called **ascribed statuses,** and positions within a kinship system have long been viewed as the prototypical ascribed statuses in any society. Ascribed statuses are often contrasted with **achieved statuses,** those social positions that people may attain later in life, often as the result of their own (or other people's) effort, such as spouse or college graduate. All societies have ways of incorporating outsiders into their kinship groups, however, which they achieve by converting supposedly ascribed kinship statuses into achieved ones, thus undermining the distinction between them. We will use the term *adoption* to refer to these practices, which allow people to transform relationships based on nurturance into relations of kinship.

Adoption in Highland Ecuador

Mary Weismantel is an anthropologist who carried out fieldwork among indigenous farmers living outside the community of Zumbagua, in highland Ecuador (1995). The farmers' households were based on lifelong heterosexual relationships, but she discovered that Zumbaguans recognized kin ties that were very different from those found in European American cultures. Most striking was her discovery that every adult seemed to have several kinds of parents and several kinds of children.

In some societies, like that of ancient Rome, people distinguish between Ego's biological father (or *genitor*) and social father (or *pater*); they may also distinguish between Ego's biological mother (or *genetrix*) and social mother (or *mater*). Social parents are those who nurture a child, and they are often the child's biological parents as well. Zumbaguans use the Quichua term *tayta* for both genitor and pater and *mama* for both genetrix and mater. In their society, however, genitor, pater, genetrix, and mater are often entirely different people.

Weismantel learned that this use of kin terms was related to local forms of adoption, most of which occur within the family. In 1991, for example, a young girl named Nancy moved into the household of her father Alfonso's prosperous, unmarried older sister, Heloisa, whom Nancy called *tía* ("aunt"). By 1993, however, Nancy was calling Heloisa *mama*. Everyone concerned viewed this transition positively, a way of strengthening family solidarity in a difficult economic situation, and no one seemed worried about whether Heloisa was Nancy's "natural" mother or not.

People also often adopted children who were not kin. In both cases, however, the bond of adoption was created through nurturing, symbolized by the provision of food. Heloisa became Nancy's adoptive *mama* because she took care of her, fed her. Men in Zumbagua can also become the adoptive *tayta* of children by feeding them in front of witnesses who verbally proclaim what a "good father" the man is. However, the adoptive relationship does not gain recognition unless the adoptive parent continues feeding the child regularly for a long time. Weismantel discovered that the Zumbaguan family consists of those who eat together. The

kinship bond results, they believe, because people who regularly eat the same food together eventually come to share "the same flesh," no matter who gave birth to them. Weismantel points out that feeding children is every bit as biological as giving birth to them: It is simply a different aspect of biology.

Indeed, in Zumbagua, a woman's biological tie to her offspring is given no greater weight than a man's biological tie to his. Many Zumbaguans are closer to their adopted family than they are to their biological parents. If genitor and genetrix are young and poor, moreover, they run a very real risk that they will lose their children to adoption by older, wealthier individuals. In other words, enduring kin ties in Zumbagua are achieved, not merely ascribed, statuses.

KINSHIP EXTENDED

Negotiation of Kin Ties among the Ju/'hoansi

Michael Peletz observes that many contemporary kinship studies in anthropology "tend to devote considerable analytic attention to themes of contradiction, paradox and ambivalence" (1995, 343). This is true both of Weismangel's study in Zumbagua and Richard Lee's analysis of kinship among the Ju/'hoansi. Lee learned that for the Ju/'hoansi, "the principles of kinship constitute, not an invariant code of laws written in stone, but instead a whole series of codes, consistent enough to provide structure but open enough to be flexible." He adds: "I found the best way to look at [Ju/'hoansi] kinship is as a game, full of ambiguity and nuance" (1992b, 62).

The Ju/'hoansi have what seems to be a straightforward Eskimo system with alternating generations. Outside the nuclear core of the system, the same terms are used by Ego for kin of his or her generation, his or

---

direct exchange marriage A marriage system in which a line that receives a wife from a different line in one generation provides one back to that line in the next generation (sometimes called a *father's sister's daughter marriage*).

asymmetrical exchange marriage A marriage system in which a line always gets wives from the same line and gives wives to a different line (sometimes called a *mother's brother's daughter marriage*).

ascribed statuses Social positions people are assigned at birth.

achieved statuses Social positions people may attain later in life, often as the result of their own (or other people's) effort.

her grandparents' generation, and his or her grand-children's generation. Likewise, the same terms are used for Ego's parents' generation and children's generation. These terms have behavioral correlates, which Lee calls "joking" and "avoidance." Anyone in Ego's own generation (except opposite-sex siblings) and in the grandparents' generation or the grandchildren's generation is joking kin. Anyone in Ego's parents' generation or children's generation is avoidance kin, as are Ego's same-sex siblings. Relatives in a joking relationship can be relaxed and affectionate and can speak using familiar forms. In an avoidance relationship, however, respect and reserve are required, and formal language must be used. Many of these relationships may be warm and friendly if the proper respect is shown in public: However, people in an avoidance relationship may not marry one another.

The "game," as Lee puts it, in the Ju/'hoansi system begins when a child is named. The Ju/'hoansi have very few names: 36 for men and 32 for women. Every child must be named for someone: A first-born son should get his father's father's name and a first-born daughter her father's mother's name. Second-born children are supposed to be named after the mother's father and mother. Later children are named after the father's brothers and sisters and the mother's brothers and sisters. It is no wonder that the Ju/'hoansi invent a host of nicknames to distinguish among people who have the same name. Ju/'hoansi naming practices impinge upon the kinship system because all people with the same name will claim to be related. A man older than you with your name is called *!kun!a* ("old name") which is the same term used for *grandfather*. A man younger than you with your name is called *!kuna* ("young name"), the same term used for *grandson*. It does not matter how people are "really" related to others with the same name or even if they are related at all according to formal kinship terminology; the name relationship takes precedence.

But the complications do not end here. By metaphorical extension, anyone with your father's name you call *father*, anyone with your wife's name you call *wife*, and so on. Worse, "a woman may not marry a man with her father's or brother's name, and a man may not marry a woman with his mother's or sister's name" (Lee 1992b, 74). Sometimes a man can marry a woman but because his name is the same as her father's she can't marry him! Further, you may not marry anyone with the name of one of your avoidance kin. As a result, parents who do not want their children to marry can almost always find a kinship-related reason to block the marriage. Once again, it does not matter what the exact genealogical relationships are.

The name relationship ties Ju/'hoansi society closer together by making close relatives out of distant ones. At the same time, it makes nonsense of the formal kinship system. How is this dilemma resolved? The Ju/'hoansi have a third component to their kinship system, the principle of *wi*, which operates as follows: Relative age is one of the few ways the Ju/'hoansi have of marking distinctions. Thus, in any relationship that can be described by more than one kin relationship, the older party chooses the kin term to be used. For example, a man may get married only to discover that his wife's aunt's husband has the same name he has. What will he and his wife's aunt call each other? According to the principle of *wi*, the aunt decides because she is older. If she calls him *nephew* (rather than *husband*), he knows to call her *aunt*.

The principle of *wi* means that a person's involvement with the kinship system is continually changing over the course of his or her lifetime. For the first half of people's lives, they must accept the kin terms their elders choose, whether they understand why or not. After midlife, however, they begin to impose wi on their juniors. For the Ju/'hoansi, kinship connections are open to manipulation and negotiation rather than being rigidly imposed from the outside.

European American Kinship and New Reproductive Technologies

Western medicine has developed new reproductive technologies, such as *in vitro* fertilization, sperm banks, and surrogate motherhood, that are creating challenges not only for law and morality, but also for Western concepts of kinship (Figure 11.14). Marilyn Strathern (1992) observes that in the European American world, kinship is understood as the social construction of natural facts, a logic that both combines and separates the social and natural worlds. That is, European Americans recognize kin related by blood and kin related by marriage, but they also believe that the process—procreation—that brings kin into existence is part of nature. "The rooting of social relations in natural facts traditionally served to impart a certain quality to one significant dimension of kin relations. For all that one exercised choice, it was also the case that these rela-

FIGURE 11.14 In-vitro fertilization, one of the new reproductive technologies, is already having an effect on what it means to be a "natural" parent. All of these babies are the result of in-vitro fertilization.

tions were at base non-negotiable" (Strathern 1992, 28). Ties of kinship are supposed to stand for what is unalterable in a person's social world in contrast to what is open to change. Yet the new reproductive technologies make clear that nothing is unalterable: Even the world of natural facts is subject to social intervention.

As Janet Dolgin (1995) reports, contemporary ambiguities surrounding kinship in the United States have put pressure on the courts to decide what constitutes biological parenthood and how it is related to legal parenthood. She examines two sets of recent cases, the first involving the paternal rights of unwed putative fathers and the second focusing on the rights of parties involved in surrogate motherhood agreements. In two cases involving putative unwed fathers, courts reasoned that biological maternity automatically made a woman a social mother but biological paternity did not automatically make a man a social father. Because the men in these two cases had failed to participate in rearing their children, their paternity rights were not recognized. In another case, the biological father had lived

with his child and her mother for extended periods during the child's early years and had actively participated in her upbringing. However, the child's mother had been married to another man during this period, and the law proclaimed her legal husband to be the child's father. Although the genitor had established a supportive relationship with his daughter, the court labeled him "the adulterous natural father," arguing, in effect, that a genitor can never be a pater unless he is involved in an ongoing relationship with the child's mother, something that was clearly impossible, since she was already married to someone else.

The surrogacy cases demonstrate directly the complications that can result from new reproductive technologies. The "Baby M" situation was a traditional surrogacy arrangement in which the surrogate, Mary Beth Whitehead, was impregnated with the sperm of the husband in the couple who intended to become the legal parents of the child she bore. Whitehead was supposed to terminate all parental rights when the child was born, but she refused to do so. The court faced a dilemma. Existing law backed Whitehead's maternal rights, but the court was also concerned that the surrogacy agreement looked too much like babyselling or womb-rental. The court's opinion focused on Whitehead's attempt to break the surrogacy contract to justify terminating her legal rights, although she was awarded visitation rights.

More complicated than traditional surrogacy, *gestational surrogacy* deconstructs the role of genetrix into two roles that can be performed by two different women. In a key case, the Calverts, a childless married couple, provided egg and sperm that were used in the laboratory to create an embryo, which was then implanted in Anna Johnson's uterus. But when Johnson gave birth to the baby, she refused to give it up. As Dolgin points out, this case "provided a context in which to measure the generality of the assumption that the gestational role both produces and constitutes maternity" (1995, 58). As we have seen, several other court cases emphasized the role of gestation in forming an indissoluble bond between mother and child. In this case, however, the court referred to Anna Johnson "as a 'gestational carrier,' a 'genetic hereditary stranger' to the child, who acted like a 'foster parent'" (1995, 59). The court declared the Calverts and the child a family unit on genetic grounds and ruled that the Calverts were the baby's "natural" and legal parents.

Dolgin notes that in all of these cases, the courts awarded legal custody to those parties whose living arrangements most closely approximated the traditional middle-class, North American two-parent family. "Biological facts were called into judicial play only . . . when they justified the preservation of traditional families" (1995, 63). Biological facts that might have undermined such families were systematically overlooked. Perhaps the clearcut biological basis of North American kinship is not so clearcut after all.

Compadrazgo in Latin America

An important set of kinship practices in Roman Catholic Latin America is *compadrazgo,* or ritual coparenthood. The baptism of a child requires the presence of a godmother and a godfather as sponsors. By participating in this ritual, the sponsors become the ritual coparents of the child. In Latin America, godparents are expected to take an active interest in their godchildren and to help them wherever possible. However, the more important relationship is between the godparents and the parents. They become *compadres* ("coparents"),

and they are expected to behave toward each other in new ways.

Sometimes the godparents are already kin; in recent years, for example, Nicaraguans have been choosing relatives living in the United States as compadres (Lancaster 1992, 66). A couple often chooses godparents whose social standing is higher than their own: the owners of the land they farm, for example, or of the factory where they work. Participating together in the baptism changes these unequal strangers into ritual kin whose relationship, while still unequal, is now personalized, friendlier, more open. The parents will support the godparents when that support is needed (politically, for example) and the godparents will do favors for the parents. They even call each other *compadre* rather than, say, "Señor López" and "José."

Catherine Allen notes that the bonds of *compadrazgo,* in combination with marriage alliances and kinship, "form constellations of mutual obligation and dependence that shift with time as new *compadrazgo* relationships are formed, young relatives come of age, and old bonds fall into disuse through death or quarreling. Like kin ties, bonds of *compadrazgo* can become as much a burden as an asset, and like kin ties they can be ignored or honored in the breach" (1988, 90).

Ie in Contemporary Japan

In a study that focuses on a small family-owned factory in Japan, Dorinne Kondo (1990) discusses the *ie,* a kinshiplike organization. (See EthnoProfile 11.3: Japan.) *Ie* is sometimes translated as "household." It is not simply a kinship unit based on blood relationship; rather, it is a corporate group based on social and economic ties. The *ie* holds property (land, a reputation, the practice of an art, and so on), it can serve important religious functions, and it provides the primary form of social welfare in Japan, including care of the aged and infirm. The *ie* is better understood as a "task performance unit" in which the core of the group may be composed of people not necessarily related biologically.

Ie organization is based on a set of positions rather than on a set of kinship relations. In any given adult generation, there are only two people in permanent positions in the *ie*—a married couple. "They are, so to speak, the trustees of the corporation, who will take care of the family property and fortunes during the period of their tenure. They should do their best to ensure the survival and, ideally, the increasing prosperity

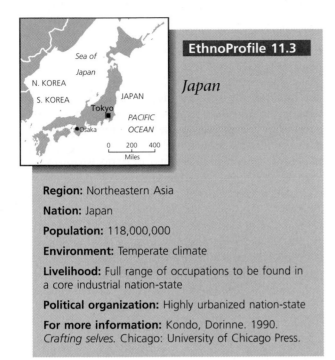

EthnoProfile 11.3

Japan

Region: Northeastern Asia

Nation: Japan

Population: 118,000,000

Environment: Temperate climate

Livelihood: Full range of occupations to be found in a core industrial nation-state

Political organization: Highly urbanized nation-state

For more information: Kondo, Dorinne. 1990. *Crafting selves.* Chicago: University of Chicago Press.

marriage, and so on" (1990, 125). Because the *ie* requires two permanent members, there are three strategies for recruitment by marriage: (1) the son of the married couple marries a woman from an out-group, the usual version of "marriage"; (2) the daughter of the married couple marries a man from an out-group, the so-called *adopted bridegroom;* (3) both the man and woman come from an out-group, the so-called *fufu yoshi,* or adoption of a married couple. The resort to an adopted bridegroom or an adopted couple emphasize the desire for *ie* continuity. Where the couple's sons cannot or will not take over the *ie,* the couple acts to ensure that the *ie* continues. Unlike in the United States, where adoption generally takes place at a young age, in Japan, adoption usually occurs in adulthood as a form of marriage. Indeed, the second most common form of marriage/succession is bringing in a man from the outside to marry into the family and take over the family name and, usually, the family business.

of their *ie,* which they can then hand over to their successors" (Kondo 1990, 122). But of the children of the married couple, only one, along with his or her spouse, can be the successors. Thus, the household of one's birth may not be the household a person joins as a permanent member.

The difference between *ie* and unilineal descent groups emerges more clearly when examining succession to the permanent positions in the *ie.* Because the *ie* is a corporate group, like the unilineages examined earlier in this chapter, the overriding concern is the continuity of the group over time. Thus, two permanent *ie* members must be recruited in each generation. Kinship, in the sense of blood relationship, is only one of the recruitment mechanisms. The person(s) who take over the *ie* may in fact be totally unrelated by blood. Ideally, people would prefer not to take this course, but they may choose to do so if the continuity of the *ie* is sufficiently critical to them.

People prefer *primogeniture,* succession by the eldest son, but Kondo notes that the system of succession is composed of ranked preferences that can be modified according to various factors: "the presence of appropriate successors; their competence; the relationships with other households one may want to create through

KINSHIP AND PRACTICE

Formal kinship systems are not straitjackets; as we have seen, they offer a flexible series of opportunities for people to choose how to deal with others. They also provide multiple social vectors along which relations of alliance, association, mutual support, opposition, and hatred may develop.

In his work on the Iteso of Kenya, Ivan Karp discusses the options for action that a kinship system can provide (principally Karp 1978). (See EthnoProfile 11.4: Iteso.) Karp notes that among the Iteso, affinal and **consanguineal** kin have very different and even contradictory rights and obligations to one another. Two people who share links both through marriage and patrilineal descent must choose which tie to emphasize; it is often the affinal tie rather than the consanguineal tie. However, they may be ambivalent about the choice. Close members of a patrilineage often quarrel and may be ritually dangerous to one another, but they

---

compadrazgo Ritual coparenthood in Latin America and Spain, established through the Roman Catholic practice of having godparents for children.

consanguineal Kinship connections based on descent.

EthnoProfile 11.4

Iteso

Region: Eastern Africa

Nations: Kenya and Uganda

Population: 150,000 in Kenya; 600,000 in Uganda (1970s)

Environment: High-rainfall savanna and hills

Livelihood: Agriculture, both subsistence and cash

Political organization: Traditionally, chiefs, subchiefs, headmen; today, part of modern nation-states

For more information: Karp, Ivan. 1978. *Fields of change among the Iteso of Kenya.* London: Routledge and Kegan Paul.

will—indeed, must—help one another in ritual and conflict situations. By contrast, affinal relatives are amiable and helpful but cannot be counted on in times of crisis.

Karp recounts a story that serves as an example. An Iteso man who was widowed and had remarried moved away from his lineage and was living with his maternal kin. His daughters by his first marriage were living with their mother's brother. One daughter was bitten by a snake and died. Karp was asked to help bring the body back to her father's house for burial. The father went to all his neighbors—his maternal kin—for help in burying her, but none would help. Only at the last moment did some members of his patrilineage arrive to help with the burial. This story illustrates the drawbacks associated with living apart from one's close lineage mates. The father had left himself open to a lack of support in a crisis by cutting himself off from his lineage and choosing to live with his maternal kin. Moreover, the Iteso kinship system provides no rule for resolving conflicting loyalties to maternal and paternal kin. Indeed, the system almost ensures the creation of overlapping loyalties that are difficult to resolve.

KINSHIP: A FRAMEWORK FOR INTERPRETING LIFE

Kinship may seem awesomely complete and utterly basic to the life of the societies just described; however, it varies in importance between societies and even between subgroups within the same society. In addition, the Nuer, the Ju/'hoansi, the Trobriand Islanders, and even North Americans demonstrate that formal kinship categories can also be used metaphorically. To use kinship in this way is to experience one kind of thing—the division of labor, religion, political struggle, social order—in terms of another phenomenon that is better understood. Kinship is built on an interpretation of mating, birth, and nurturance. But our understanding of these basic human experiences is shaped by the principles of our kinship system. Kinship is "a variety of social idiom, a way of talking about and understanding, and thus of shaping, some aspects of social life" (Geertz and Geertz 1975, 169). There is more to life than kinship, but kinship provides one holistic framework for interpreting life.

Key Terms

kinship	bridewealth
marriage	affinity
descent	collaterality
adoption	bifurcation
sex	parallel cousins
gender	cross cousins
bilateral descent	direct exchange marriage
unilineal descent	asymmetrical exchange
bilateral kindred	marriage
patrilineage	ascribed statuses
matrilineage	achieved statuses
lineages	*compadrazgo*
clan	consanguineal
segmentary opposition	

Chapter Summary

1. Human life is group life; we depend upon one another to survive. The idiom of kinship is one

way all societies organize this interdependence. Kinship relations are based on, but not reducible to, the universal experiences of mating, birth, and nurturance. Kinship principles construct a coherent cultural framework by defining groups, locating people within those groups, and positioning people and groups in relation to one another in space and time. Although female-male duality is basic to kinship, many societies have developed supernumerary sexes or genders. Kinship systems help societies maintain social order without central government.

2. Kinship systems are selective. Matrilineal societies emphasize that women bear children and trace descent through women. Patrilineal societies emphasize that men impregnate women and trace descent through men. Adoption pays attention to relationships based on nurturance, whether or not they are also based on mating and birth.

3. Descent links members of different generations with one another. Bilateral descent results in the formation of groups called *kindreds* that include all relatives from both parents' families. Unilineal descent results in the formation of groups called *lineages* that trace descent through either the mother or the father. Unlike kindreds, lineages are corporate groups. Lineages control important property, such as land, that collectively belongs to their members. The language of lineage is the idiom of political discussion, and lineage relationships are of political significance.

4. Kinship terminologies pay attention to certain attributes of people that are then used to define different classes of kin. The attributes most often recognized include, from most to least common, generation, sex, affinity, collaterality, bifurcation, relative age, and the sex of the linking relative.

5. Anthropologists recognize six basic terminological systems according to their patterns of classifying cousins. These systems are named after societies that represent the prototype of each pattern: Hawaiian, Eskimo, Iroquois, Crow, Omaha, and Sudanese. The first two are found in association with bilateral descent systems, and the remaining four are found in association with unilineal descent.

6. By prescribing certain kinds of marriage, lineages establish long-term alliances with one another. Two major types of prescriptive marriage patterns in unilineal societies are a father's sister's daughter marriage system (which sets up a pattern of direct exchange marriage) and a mother's brother's daughter marriage system (which sets up a pattern of asymmetrical exchange marriage).

7. Ascribed kinship statuses can be converted into achieved ones by means of adoption. In Zumbagua, Ecuador, most adults have several kinds of parents and several kinds of children, some adopted and some not. Zumbaguan adoptions are based on nurturance, in this case, the feeding by the adoptive parent of the adopted child. Many Zumbaguans are closer to their adoptive families than they are to the families into which they were born, but no one seems concerned about who are the "natural" parents of a child.

8. The complexities of Ju/'hoansi kinship negotiations and the dilemmas created in North America and Europe by new reproductive technologies, as well as the unique features of compadrazgo in Latin America and the *ie* in Japan, demonstrate some of the varied ways in which kinship is a cultural construction that cannot be reduced to biology.

Suggested Readings

Bohannan, Paul, and John Middleton. 1968. *Kinship and social organization.* New York: Natural History Press. *A collection of important, classic articles from a wide range of theoretical perspectives.*

Collier, Jane, and Sylvia Yanagisako. 1987. *Gender and kinship: Essays toward a unified analysis.* Stanford: Stanford University Press. *An important collection of work on the connections between gender and kinship.*

Ginsburg, Faye D. 1989. *Contested lives: The abortion debate in an American community.* Berkeley: University of California Press. *A study of gender and procreation in the context of the abortion debate in Fargo, North Dakota, in the 1980s.*

Ginsburg, Faye D., and Rayna Rapp, eds. 1995. *Conceiving the new world order: The global politics of reproduction.* Berkeley: University of California Press. *An important collection of articles by anthropologists who address the ways human reproduction is structured across social and cultural boundaries.*

Graburn, Nelson. 1971. *Readings in kinship and social structure.* New York: Harper and Row. *Another collection of classic essays, this volume covers a wider range of topics than, but overlaps little with, the Bohannan and Middleton volume.*

12

Marriage and the Family

he distinguished Indian novelist R. K. Narayan (b. 1908) writes in his autobiography about falling in love and getting married.

. . . In July 1933, I had gone to Coimbatore, escorting my elder sister, and then stayed on in her house. There was no reason why I should ever hurry away from one place to another. I was a free-lance writer and I could work wherever I might be at a particular time. One day, I saw a girl drawing water from the street-tap and immediately fell in love with her. Of course, I could not talk to her. I learned later that she had not even noticed me passing and repassing in front of her while she waited to fill the brass vessels. I craved to get a clear, fixed, mental impression of her features, but I was handicapped by the time factor, as she would be available for staring at only until her vessels filled, when she would carry them off, and not come out again until the next water-filling time. I could not really stand and stare; whatever impression I had of her would be through a side-glance while passing the tap. I suffered from a continually melting vision. The only thing I was certain of was that I loved her, and I suffered the agonies of restraint imposed by the social conditions in which I lived. The tall headmaster, her father, was a friend of the family and often dropped in for a chat with the elders at home while on his way to the school, which was at a corner of our street. The headmaster, headmaster's daughter, and the school were all within geographical reach and hailing distance, but the restraint imposed by the social code created barriers. I attempted to overcome them by befriending the headmaster. He was a booklover and interested in literary matters, and we found many common subjects for talk. We got into the habit of meeting at his school after the school-hours and discussing the world, seated comfortably on a cool granite *pyol* in front of a little shrine of Ganesha in the school compound. One memorable evening, when the stars had come out, I interrupted some talk we were having on political matters to make a bold, blunt announcement of my affection for his daughter. He was taken aback, but did not show it. In answer to my proposal, he just turned to the god in the shrine and shut his eyes in prayer. No one in our social condition could dare to proceed in the manner I had done. There were formalities to be observed, and any talk for a marriage proposal could proceed only between the elders of the families. What I had done was unheard of. But

the headmaster was sporting enough not to shut me up immediately. Our families were known to each other, and the class, community, and caste requirements were all right. He just said, "if God wills it," and left it at that. He also said, "Marriages are made in Heaven, and who are we to say Yes or No?" After this he explained the difficulties. His wife and womenfolk at home were to be consulted, and my parents had to approve, and so on and so forth, and then the matching of the horoscopes—this last became a great hurdle at the end. . . .

What really mattered was not my economic outlook, but my stars. My father-in-law, himself an adept at the study of horoscopes, had consultations with one or two other experts and came to the conclusion that my horoscope and the girl's were incompatible. My horoscope had the Seventh House occupied by Mars, the Seventh House being the one that indicated . . . nothing but disaster unless the partner's horoscope also contained the same flaw, a case in which two wrongs make one right. . . .

In spite of all these fluctuations and hurdles, my marriage came off in a few months, celebrated with all the pomp, show, festivity, exchange of gifts, and the overcrowding, that my parents desired and expected.

Soon after my marriage, my father became bedridden with a paralytic stroke, and most of my mother's time was spent at his side upstairs. The new entrant into the family, my wife Rajam, was her deputy downstairs, managing my three younger brothers, who were still at school, a cook in the kitchen, a general servant, and a gigantic black-and-white Great Dane acquired by my elder brother, who was a dog-lover. She kept an eye on the stores, replenishing the food-stuffs and guarding them from being squandered or stolen by the cook. Rajam was less than twenty, but managed the housekeeping expertly and earned my mother's praise. She got on excellently with my brothers. This was one advantage of a joint family system—one had plenty of company at home. (1974, 106–10)

Narayan had fallen in love, gotten married, and set up housekeeping with his wife. These are familiar phases in the relationship of a man and a woman, yet the details of his description seem extraordinary to a North American. Narayan's essay illustrates how the patterns of courtship, marriage, and housekeeping in India engage people in the wider patterns of Indian life. They channel emotion and economic activity. They also link previously unrelated people while binding

FIGURE 12.1 Locations of societies whose EthnoProfiles appear in Chapter 12.

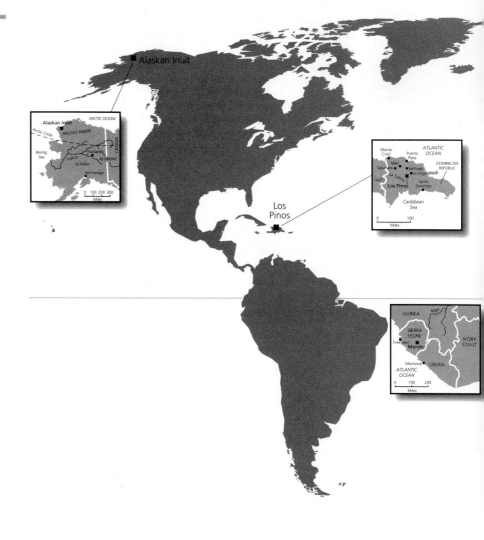

individuals firmly to groups. One individual, Narayan, fell in love with and married another, Rajam. But they could never have become a married couple without knowing how to maneuver within the cultural patterns that shaped their society. Neither could they have gotten married without the active intervention of the wider social groups to which they belonged—specifically, their families.

Marriage and *family* are two concepts anthropologists use to describe how mating and its consequences are understood and organized in different societies.

TOWARD A DEFINITION OF MARRIAGE?

Each culture has its own definition of marriage, yet nowhere is *marriage* synonymous with *mating*. Marriage involves a change in the social position of two people and affects the social position of their offspring.

Some criteria for defining marriage are common in most societies; we will concentrate on these in our own definition of marriage. A prototypical **marriage** (1) trans-

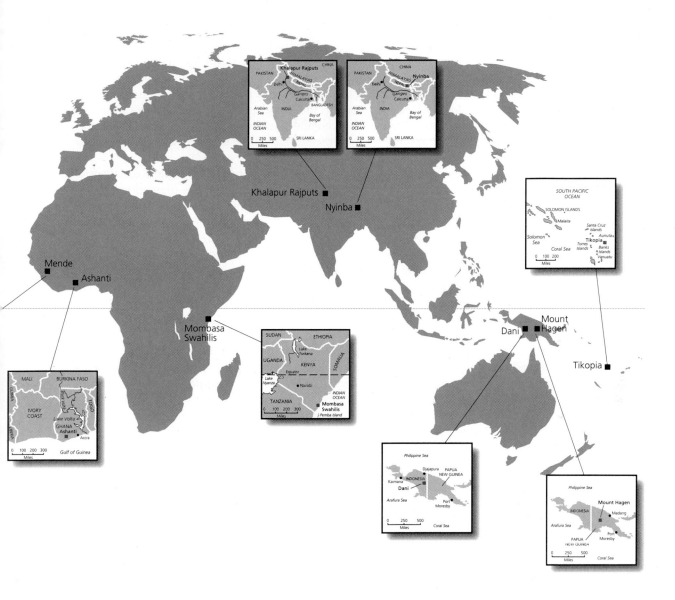

forms the status of a man and a woman and (2) stipulates the degree of sexual access the married partners may have to each other, ranging from exclusive to preferential. It also (3) establishes the legitimacy of children born to the wife, and (4) creates relationships between the kin of the wife and the kin of the husband.

If a prototypical marriage involves a man and a woman, however, what are we to make of the following cases? Each offers an alternative way of understanding the combination of features that define appropriate unions in a particular society.

Woman Marriage and Ghost Marriage among the Nuer

Among the Nuer, as E. E. Evans-Pritchard observed during his fieldwork in the 1930s, a woman could marry

---

marriage An institution that prototypically transforms the status of a man and a woman, carries implications about permitted sexual access, gives the offspring a position in society, and establishes connections between the kin of the husband and the kin of the wife.

another woman and become the "father" of the children the wife bore. (See EthnoProfile 11.2: Nuer.) This practice, which also appears in some other parts of Africa, involves a distinction between pater and genitor (see Chapter 11). The female husband (the pater) had to have some cattle of her own to use for bridewealth payments to the wife's lineage. Once the bridewealth had been paid, the marriage was established. The female husband then got a male kinsman, friend, or neighbor (the genitor) to impregnate the wife and to help with certain tasks around the homestead that the Nuer believed could be done only by men.

Generally, Evans-Pritchard (1951) noted, a female husband was unable to have children herself, "and for this reason counts in some respects as a man." In other words, the Nuer metaphorically labeled such a woman as a near-man. Indeed, she played the social role of a man. She could marry several wives if she was wealthy. She could demand damage payment if those wives engaged in sexual activity without her consent. She was the pater of her wives' children. On the marriage of her daughters, she received the portion of the bridewealth that traditionally went to the father, and her brothers and sisters received the portions appropriate to the father's side. Her children were named after her, as though she were a man, and they addressed her as *Father*. She administered her compound and her herds as a male head of household would, and she was treated by her wives and children with the same deference shown a male husband and father.

More common in Nuer social life was what Evans-Pritchard called the *ghost marriage*. The Nuer believed that a man who died without male heirs left an unhappy and angry spirit who might trouble his living kin. The spirit was angry because a basic obligation of Nuer kinship was for a man to be remembered through and by his sons: His name had to be continued in his lineage. To appease the angry spirit, a kinsman of the dead man—a brother or a brother's son—would often marry a woman "to his name." Bridewealth cattle were paid in the name of the dead man to the patrilineage of a woman. She was then married to the ghost but resided with his living kinsman. In the marriage ceremonies and afterwards, this kinsman acted as though he were the true husband. The children of the union were referred to as though they were the kinsman's—but officially they were not. That is, the ghost husband was their pater, and his kinsman their genitor. As the

children got older, the name of their ghost father became increasingly important to them. The ghost father's name, not his stand-in's name, would be remembered in the history of the lineage. The essential feature of the ghost marriage was the provision of children to the ghost husband's lineage. The social union between the ghost and the woman took precedence over the sexual union between the ghost's surrogate and the woman.

Ghost marriage serves to perpetuate social patterns. Although it was common for a man to marry a wife "to his kinsman's name" before he himself married, it became difficult, if not impossible, for him to marry later in his own right. His relatives would tell him he was "already married" and that he should allow his younger brothers to use cattle from the family herd so they could marry. Even if he eventually accumulated enough cattle to afford to marry, he would feel that those cattle should provide the bridewealth for the sons he had raised for his dead kinsman. When he died, he died childless because the children he had raised were legally the children of the ghost. He was then an angry spirit, and someone else (in fact, one of the sons he had raised for the ghost) had to marry a wife to *his* name. Thus the pattern continued.

MARRIAGE AS A SOCIAL PROCESS

Marriages set up new relationships between the kin of the husband and the kin of the wife. These are called **affinal** relationships (based on *affinity*—relationships created via marriage) and contrast with **consanguineal** (or "blood") relationships. Affinity and consanguinity are centrally associated with the definition of marriage and the formation of social groups. Mating alone does not create in-laws, nor does it set up a way of locating the offspring in space and time as members of a particular social group. Marriage does both.

Socially, marriage has four characteristics: (1) It transforms the status of the participants; (2) it alters the relationships among the kin of each party; (3) it perpetuates social patterns through the production of offspring, who also have certain kinds of rights and obligations (see Karp 1986); and (4) it is always symbolically marked in some way, from an elaborate wedding to simply the appearance of a husband and wife seated one morning outside her hut. Marriage marks a major transformation of social position: Two individuals become one married couple. In an important way, the third party to any wedding—the rest of the community—must acknowledge the legitimacy of the new union.

Every society has ways of matching the right groom with the right bride. Sometimes marriages must be contracted within a particular social group, a pattern called **endogamy.** In other cases, marriage partners must be found outside a particular group, a pattern called **exogamy.** In Nuer society, for example, a person had to marry outside his or her lineage. Even in North American society, we prefer people to marry within the bounds of certain groups. We are told to marry "our own kind," which usually means our own ethnic or racial group, religious group, or social class. In all societies, some close kin are off limits as spouses or as sexual partners. This exogamous pattern is known as the *incest taboo.*

Patterns of Residence after Marriage

Once married, a couple must live somewhere. There are four major patterns of postmarital residence. Most familiar to North Americans is **neolocal** residence, in which the new couple sets up an independent household at a place of their own choosing. Neolocal residence tends to be found in societies that are more or less individualistic in their social organization, especially those with Eskimo kinship systems.

When the married couple lives with (or near) the husband's father's family, it is called **patrilocal** residence, which is observed by more societies in the contemporary world than any other residence pattern. It produces a characteristic social grouping of related men: A man, his brothers, and their sons, along with in-marrying wives, all live and work together. This pattern is common in both herding and farming societies; some anthropologists argue that survival in such societies depends on activities that are best carried out by groups of men who have worked together all their lives.

When the married couple lives with (or near) the family in which the wife was raised, it is called **matrilocal** residence, which is usually found in association with matrilineal kinship systems. Here, the core of the social group consists of a woman, her sisters, and their daughters, together with in-marrying men. This

pattern is most common among horticultural groups.

Less common, but also found in matrilineal societies, is the pattern known as **avunculocal** residence. Here, the married couple lives with (or near) the husband's mother's brother. The most significant man in a boy's matrilineage is his mother's brother, from whom he will inherit. Avunculocal residence emphasizes this relationship.

There are other, even less common patterns of residence. In *ambilocal* residence, the couple shifts residence, living first with the family of one spouse and later with the family of the other. At some point, the couple usually has to choose which family they want to affiliate with permanently. *Duolocal* residence is found where lineage membership is so important that husbands and wives continue to live with their own lineages even after they are married. The Ashanti of Ghana observe duolocal residence. (See EthnoProfile 12.1: Ashanti.) We will see later how this residence pattern affects other aspects of Ashanti social and cultural life.

Single and Plural Spouses

The number of spouses a person may have varies cross-culturally. Anthropologists distinguish, first of all, between forms of marriage that allow a person only one spouse (**monogamy**) and allow several (**polygamy**). Within the category of polygamy are two subcategories: **polygyny,** or multiple wives, and **polyandry,** or

---

affinal Kinship connections through marriage, or affinity.

consanguineal Kinship connections based on descent.

endogamy Marriage within a defined social group.

exogamy Marriage outside a defined social group.

neolocal A postmarital residence pattern in which a married couple sets up an independent household at a place of their own choosing.

patrilocal A postmarital residence pattern in which a married couple lives with (or near) the husband's father.

matrilocal A postmarital residence pattern in which a married couple lives with (or near) the wife's mother.

avunculocal A postmarital residence pattern in which a married couple lives with (or near) the husband's mother's brother (from *avuncular,* "of uncles").

monogamy A marriage pattern in which a person may be married to only one spouse at a time.

polygamy A marriage pattern in which a person may be married to more than one spouse at a time.

polygyny A marriage pattern in which a man may be married to more than one wife at a time.

polyandry A marriage pattern in which a woman may be married to more than one husband at a time.

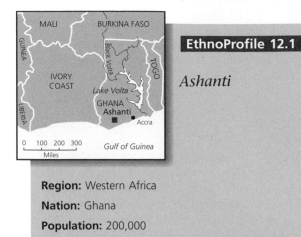

multiple husbands. Most societies in the world permit polygyny.

MONOGAMY   Monogamy is the only legal spousal pattern of the United States and most industrialized nations. (Indeed, in 1896, a condition of statehood for the territory of Utah was the abolition of polygyny, which had been practiced by Mormon settlers for nearly 50 years.) There are variations in the number of times a monogamous person can be married. Before the twentieth century, people in western European societies generally married only once unless death intervened. Today, some observers suggest that we practice *serial monogamy;* we may be married to several different people but only one at a time.

POLYGYNY   Polygynous societies vary in the number of wives a man may have. Islam permits a man to have as many as four wives but only on the condition that he can support them equally. Some Muslim authorities today argue, however, that equal support must be emotional and affective, not just financial. Convinced that

no man can feel the same toward each of his wives, they have concluded that monogamy must be the rule. Other polygynous societies have no limit on the number of wives a man may marry. Nevertheless, not every man can be polygynous. There is a clear demographic problem: For every man with two wives, there is one man without a wife. Men can wait until they are older to marry and women can marry very young, but this imbalance cannot be eliminated. Polygyny is also expensive, for a husband must support all his wives as well as their children (Figure 12.2).

POLYANDRY   Polyandry is the rarest of the three marriage forms. In some polyandrous societies, a woman may marry several brothers. In others, she may marry men who are not related to each other and who all will live together in a single household. Sometimes a woman is allowed to marry several men who are not related, but she will live only with the one she most recently married. Polyandry traditionally has gotten short shrift in anthropology and has sometimes been dismissed as an oddity; however recent studies have challenged our traditional understanding of polyandry and have shed new light on the dynamics of polygyny and monogamy.

Polyandry, Sexuality, and the Reproductive Capacity of Women

Different marriage patterns reflect significant variation in the social definition of male and female sexuality. Monogamy and polygyny are in some ways similar because both are concerned with controlling women's sexuality while giving men freer rein. Even in monogamous societies, men (but not women) are often expected to have extramarital sexual adventures. Polyandry is worth a closer look; it differs from polygyny or monogamy in instructive ways.

Polyandry is found in three major regions of the world: Tibet and Nepal, southern India and Sri Lanka, and northern Nigeria and northern Cameroon. The forms of polyandry in these areas are different, but all involve women with several husbands.

FRATERNAL POLYANDRY   The traditional anthropological prototype of polyandry has been found among some groups in Nepal and Tibet, where a group of brothers marry one woman. This is known as *fraternal*

FIGURE 12.2 The wives and children of a polygynous family.

polyandry. During one wedding, one brother, usually the oldest, serves as the groom. All brothers (including those yet to be born to the husbands' parents) are married by this wedding, which establishes public recognition of the marriage. The wife and her husbands live together, usually patrilocally. All brothers have equal sexual access to the wife, and all act as fathers to the children. In some cases—notably among the Nyinba of Nepal (Levine 1980, 1988)—each child is recognized as having one particular genitor, who may be a different brother than the genitor of his or her siblings. (See EthnoProfile 12.2: Nyinba.) In other cases, all the brothers are considered jointly as the father, without distinguishing the identity of the genitor.

There appears to be little sexual jealousy among the men, and the brothers have a strong sense of solidarity with one another. Levine (1988) emphasizes this point for the Nyinba. If the wife proves sterile, the brothers may marry another woman in hopes that she may be fertile. All brothers also have equal sexual access to the new wife and are treated as fathers by her children. In societies that practice fraternal polyandry, marrying sisters (or *sororal polygyny*) may be preferred or permitted. In this system, a group of brothers could marry a group of sisters.

According to Levine, Nyinba polyandry is reinforced by a variety of cultural beliefs and practices (1988, 158ff.). First, it has a special cultural value. Nyinba myth provides a social charter for the practice because Nyinba legendary ancestors are polyandrous, and they are praised for the harmony of their family life. Second, the solidarity of brothers is a central kinship ideal. Third, the corporate, landholding household, central to Nyinba life, presupposes polyandry. Fourth, the closed corporate structure of Nyinba villages is based on a limited number of households, and polyandry is highly effective in checking the proliferation of households. Finally, a household's political position and economic viability increase when its resources are concentrated.

ASSOCIATED POLYANDRY A second form of polyandry, known as *associated polyandry*, refers to any system in which polyandry is open to men who are not necessarily brothers (Levine and Sangree 1980). There is some evidence that associated polyandry was an acceptable marriage variant in parts of the Pacific and among some indigenous peoples of North and South America. The best-described form of associated polyandry, however, is from Sri Lanka. (See EthnoProfile 7.7:

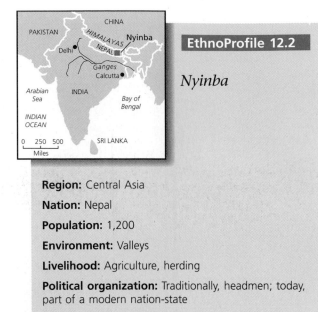

EthnoProfile 12.2

Nyinba

Region: Central Asia

Nation: Nepal

Population: 1,200

Environment: Valleys

Livelihood: Agriculture, herding

Political organization: Traditionally, headmen; today, part of a modern nation-state

For more information: Levine, Nancy. 1988. *The dynamics of polyandry: Kinship, domesticity, and population on the Tibetan border.* Chicago: University of Chicago Press.

Sinhalese.) Among the Sinhalese of Sri Lanka, a woman may marry two men, but rarely more than two. Unlike fraternal polyandry, which begins as a joint venture, Sinhalese associated polyandry begins monogamously. The second husband is brought into the union later. Also unlike fraternal polyandry, the first husband is the principal husband in terms of authority. A woman and her husbands live and work together, although economic resources are held independently. Both husbands are considered fathers to any children the wife bears.

This system allows many individual choices. For example, two husbands and their wife may decide to take another woman into the marriage—often the sister of the wife. Thus, their household becomes simultaneously polygynous and polyandrous, a marriage pattern called *polygynandry*. Thus, depending on relative wealth and the availability of economic opportunity, a Sinhalese household may be monogamous, polyandrous, or polygynandrous.

As we mentioned at the beginning of the chapter, one important aspect of marriage is the creation of ties between the bride's and the groom's families. The two forms of polyandry just discussed sharply curtail the potential network of ties created by marriage. This is particularly true where fraternal polyandry occurs with preferred or permitted sororal polygyny. For example, in a Tibetan household of four brothers married to one woman, the entire household is tied affinally only to the family of the wife. If these same brothers take another wife by marrying a sister of their first wife, they would be giving up the possibility of establishing ties with other households in favor of fortifying the relationship already established by the first marriage. Nancy Levine and Walter Sangree call this *alliance intensifying* (1980).

SECONDARY MARRIAGE   The final form of polyandry, sometimes referred to as *secondary marriage,* is found only in northern Nigeria and northern Cameroon. In secondary marriage, a woman marries one or more secondary husbands while staying married to all her previous husbands (Levine and Sangree 1980, 400). The woman lives with only one husband at a time, but she retains the right to return to a previous husband and to have legitimate children by him at a later date. No divorce is permitted in the societies that practice secondary marriage; marriage is for life.

In this system, men are polygynous and women polyandrous. A man marries a series of women and lives with one or more of them at his homestead. At the same time, the women independently pursue their own marital careers. Secondary marriage is really neither polyandry nor polygyny but rather a combination of the two, resulting from the overlap of men seeking several wives and women seeking several husbands. Secondary marriage is the opposite of Tibetan fraternal polyandry. It is *alliance proliferative,* serving to connect rather than to concentrate groups as people build extensive networks of marriage-based ties throughout a region.

THE DISTINCTION BETWEEN SEXUALITY AND REPRODUCTIVE CAPACITY   Polyandry demonstrates how a woman's sexuality can be distinguished from her reproductive capacity. This distinction is absent in monogamous or purely polygynous systems, in which polyandry is not permitted; such societies resist perceiving women's sexual and reproductive capacities as separable (except, perhaps, in prostitution), yet they usually accept such separation for men without question. "It may well be a fundamental feature of the [worldview] of polyandrous peoples that they recog-

FIGURE 12.3 This photograph illustrates a bridewealth ceremony in southern Africa. Bridewealth is usually understood as a way of compensating the bride's relatives for the loss of her labor and child-bearing capacities. Cash may also be used for bridewealth, as here among the Lese of the Democratic Republic of Congo.

nize such a distinction for *both* men and women" (Levine and Sangree 1980, 388). In the better-known polyandrous groups, a woman's sexuality can be shared among an unlimited number of men, but her childbearing capacities cannot be. Indeed, among the Nyinba (Levine 1980), a woman's childbearing capacities are carefully controlled and limited to one husband at a time. But she is free to engage in sexual activity outside her marriage to the brothers as long as she is not likely to get pregnant.

MARRIAGE AND ECONOMIC EXCHANGE

In many societies, marriage is accompanied by the transfer of certain symbolically important goods. Anthropologists have identified two major categories of marriage payments, usually called *bridewealth* and *dowry*.

Bridewealth is most common in patrilineal societies that combine agriculture, pastoralism, and patrilocal marriage, although it is found in other types of

societies as well (Figure 12.3). When it occurs among matrilineal peoples, a postmarital residence rule (avunculocal, for example) usually takes the woman away from her matrilineage.

The goods exchanged have significant symbolic value to the people concerned. They may include shell ornaments, ivory tusks, brass gongs, bird feathers, cotton cloth, and animals. Bridewealth in animals is prevalent in eastern and southern Africa, where cattle have the most profound symbolic and economic value. In these societies, a man's father, and often his entire patrilineage, give a specified number of cattle (often in installments) to the patrilineage of the man's bride. Anthropologists view bridewealth as a way of compensating the bride's relatives for the loss of her labor and childbearing capacities. When the bride leaves her home, she goes to live with her husband and his

---

bridewealth The transfer of certain symbolically important goods from the family of the groom to the family of the bride on the occasion of their marriage. It represents compensation to the wife's lineage for the loss of her labor and her childbearing capacities.

FIGURE 12.4 A large dowry display in Khalapur, India, from 1955.

lineage. She will be working and producing children for his people, not her own.

Bridewealth transactions create affinal relations between the relatives of the wife and those of the husband. The wife's relatives, in turn, use the bridewealth they receive for her to find a bride for her brother in yet another kinship group. In many societies in eastern and southern Africa, a woman gains power and influence over her brother because her marriage brings the cattle that allow him to marry and continue their lineage. This is why Jack Goody describes bridewealth as "a societal fund, a circulating pool of resources, the movement of which corresponds to the movement of rights over spouses, usually women" (1973, 17). Or, as the Southern Bantu put it, "cattle beget children" (Kuper 1982, 3).

Dowry, by contrast, is typically a transfer of family wealth, usually from parents to their daughter, at the time of her marriage (Figure 12.4). It is found primarily in the agricultural societies of Europe and Asia, but has been brought to some parts of Africa with the arrival of religions like Islam that support the practice. In societies where both women and men are seen as heirs to family wealth, dowry is sometimes regarded as the way women receive their inheritance. Dowries are often considered the wife's contribution to the establishment of a new household, to which the husband may bring other forms of wealth. In stratified societies, the size of a woman's dowry often ensures that when she marries, she will continue to enjoy her accustomed style of life. The goods included in dowries vary in different societies and may or may not include land (Goody and Tambiah 1973).

Leigh Minturn (1993), who worked among the Khalapur Rajputs of northern India, studied how dowries fit into their marriage system. (See EthnoProfile 12.3: Khalapur Rajputs.) To begin with, all land is held and inherited by men, who live together in a patrilocal *joint family* centering on a group of brothers with their wives and children. Rajput marriages are not only village exogamous but also *hypergamous:* That is, women normally marry into caste groups (see Chapter 13), or *jatis,* of higher status than the ones into which they were born. This means that women must leave their home villages to live as low-ranking outsiders in the households of their husbands. How well they marry and how well they are treated by their in-laws

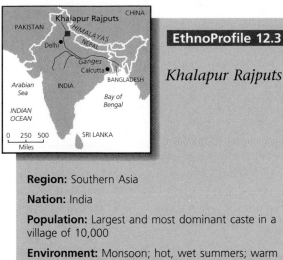

EthnoProfile 12.3

Khalapur Rajputs

Region: Southern Asia

Nation: India

Population: Largest and most dominant caste in a village of 10,000

Environment: Monsoon; hot, wet summers; warm winters; very hot springs

Livelihood: Formerly warriors, now farmers

Political organization: Village in modern nation-state

For more information: Minturn, Leigh. *Sita's daughters: Coming out of purdah. 1993.* Oxford: Oxford University Press.

depend on the size of their dowries. Rajputs told Minturn that "It is best to have two sons and one daughter, because then you will receive two dowries, but give only one" (1993, 130). Poor people whose sons cannot attract women with dowries often engage in a practice called "buying a wife," in which the husband's family gives money to the bride's family to purchase her dowry goods. Rajput dowries consisted exclusively of transportable items such as money, jewelry, clothing, and household decorations.

In the 1950s, when Minturn first visited Khalapur, new Rajput wives were under the strict control of their mothers-in-law, who assigned them tasks, limited their contact with their husbands, and controlled their dowries. Every time a wife visited her parents, moreover, she was expected to return with more gifts for her husband's family. In 1961, the government of India passed a law prohibiting dowries, but it has proven impossible to enforce. Nevertheless, by 1975, attitudes and practices regarding dowries had changed, especially among educated Rajputs. Many believed that dowries were a woman's rightful inheritance from her parents, and educated brides refused to relinquish con-

trol of theirs to their mothers-in-law. Indeed, following the passage of a law in 1956 that permitted daughters, widows, and mothers to inherit land, the size of dowries in Khalapur increased in order to discourage daughters from claiming family land. Much was at stake, and Minturn knew of wives who had been killed to keep them from withdrawing their husband's portion of the land from traditional joint holdings.

BROTHERS AND SISTERS IN CROSS-CULTURAL PERSPECTIVE

The brother-sister relationship and its link to marriage deserves special attention. In North American society, we tend to interpret all relationships between men and women in terms of the prototypical relationship between husbands and wives. Such an interpretation is unnecessarily limiting and overlooks significant variations in how people view relationships (see Sacks 1979). In some cultures, the most important relationships a man and a woman have are those with their opposite-sex siblings. This is perhaps clearest in matrilineal societies, where, for example, a man's closest ties to the next generation are with his sister's children.

Brothers and Sisters in a Matrilineal Society

A classic illustration comes from the Ashanti of Ghana. The central legal relationship in Ashanti society is the tie between brother and sister. A brother has power over his sister's children because he is their closest male relative and because Ashanti legal power is vested in males (Fortes 1950). A sister has claims on her brother because she is his closest female relative and represents the only source of the continuity of his lineage. In patrilineal societies like that of the Nuer, a man is centrally concerned with his own ability to produce children. Among the Ashanti, a man is centrally concerned with his *sister's* ability to produce children. "Men find it difficult to decide which is more important to them, to have children or for their sisters to have children. But after discussion most men conclude that sad as it may

---

dowry The transfer of wealth, usually from parents to their daughter, at the time of her marriage.

be to die childless, a good citizen's first anxiety is for his lineage to survive" (274–75).

More than this, the Ashanti brother and sister are supposed to be close confidants:

> Quoting their own experiences, men say that it is to his sister that a man entrusts weighty matters, never to his wife. He will discuss confidential matters, such as those that concern property, money, public office, legal suits, and even the future of his children or his matrimonial difficulties with his sister, secure in the knowledge that she will tell nobody else. He will give his valuables into her care, not his wife's. He will use her as go-between with a secret lover, knowing that she will never betray him to his wife. His sister is the appropriate person to fetch a man's bride home to him, and so a sister is the best watch-dog of a wife's fidelity. Women, again, agree that in a crisis they will side with their brothers against their husbands. There is often jealousy between a man's sister and his wife because each is thinking of what he can be made to do for her children. That is why they cannot easily live in the same house. Divorce after many years of marriage is common, and is said to be due very often to the conflict between loyalties towards spouse and towards sibling. (Fortes 1950, 275)

Because Ashanti women may be sisters and wives simultaneously, they often experience conflict between these two roles. In the United States, the relationship of husband and wife ordinarily takes precedence over the brother-sister relationship, which is attenuated at marriage. But for the Ashanti, the lineage comes first. In part, the closeness of brothers and sisters are reinforced by the Ashanti residence pattern: People live in their matrilineages' neighborhoods, and often husbands and wives do not live together.

Brothers and Sisters in a Patrilineal Society

The relationship of brother and sister is important in patrilineal societies too, and even in some contemporary urban nation-states. Thomas Belmonte notes that in the slums of Naples, Italy, a brother still maintains a moral control over his sister that her husband does not have (1978, 193). In patrilineal societies, the strength of the relationship depends on how the kinship group is organized. Where sisters do not move too far from home upon marriage and where they are not incorporated into their husbands' lineages, a group of brothers and sisters may control the lineage and its economic,

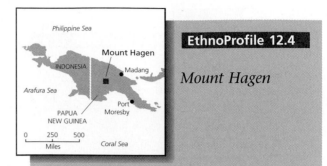

EthnoProfile 12.4

Mount Hagen

Region: Southeastern Asia

Nation: Papua New Guinea (western highlands)

Population: 75,000 (1960s)

Environment: Forested mountain slopes, grassy plains

Livelihood: Farming, pig raising

Political organization: Traditionally, some men of influence but no coercive power; today, part of a modern nation-state

For more information: Strathern, Marilyn. 1972. *Women in between.* London: Academic Press.

political, social, and religious aspects. The senior members of the lineage—males and females alike—exercise control over the junior members. Although the brothers generally have more control than the sisters (in part because they are the ones who stay in place while the sisters move when they marry), sisters still have influence.

In the Mount Hagen area of the New Guinea highlands, for example, women marry into many different subtribes, usually within a two-hour walk from home. (See EthnoProfile 12.4: Mount Hagen.) However, they retain rights to the wealth of their own lineages and to its disposal. A clan sister married outside the clan is believed to remain under the control of her clan ghosts. At her death, in association with them, she is able to influence the affairs of her own lineage. Nevertheless, over the course of time, a woman becomes more interested and involved in the affairs of her husband's clan. As this happens, it is believed that she comes increasingly under the control of her husband's clan ghosts. After her death, in addition to her influence on her own clan as a ghostly sister, she is believed to have influence on her husband's clan as a ghostly mother (Strathern 1972, 124).

FAMILY STRUCTURE

The process by which a woman becomes gradually involved in her husband's clan or lineage was recorded by Evans-Pritchard during his fieldwork among the Nuer. (See EthnoProfile 11.2: Nuer.) Affinal ties gradually become kinship ties: *Ruagh* (in-law relationship) became *mar* (kinship; Evans-Pritchard 1951, 96). The birth of a child gave the wife kinship with her husband's relatives, and it gave the husband kinship with the wife's relatives. In many patrilineal societies, a woman begins to identify with and become more interested in the affairs of her husband's lineage, partly because she has been living there for many years and comes to be more intimate with the details of her husband's lineage. More significantly, however, what had been her *husband's* lineage becomes her *children's* lineage. The children create a link to the lineage that is independent of her husband. This is one example of how family relationships inevitably transform over time. The transformations people experience vary from one society to the next according to how families are organized.

The Nuclear Family

The structure and dynamics of neolocal monogamous families are familiar to North Americans. They are called *nuclear families,* and it is often assumed that most North Americans live in them. For anthropologists, a **nuclear family** is made up of two generations: the parents and their unmarried children. Each member of a nuclear family has a series of evolving relationships with every other member: husband and wife, parents and children, and children with each other. These are the principal lines along which jealousy, controversy, and affection develop in neolocal monogamous families.

The Polygynous Family

Polygynous families are significantly different in their dynamics. Each wife has a relationship with her cowives as individuals and as a group (Figure 12.5). Cowives, in turn, individually and collectively, interact with the husband. These relationships change over time, as we (Emily Schultz and Robert Lavenda) were once informed during our fieldwork in Guider, north-ern Cameroon. (See EthnoProfile 8.1: Guider.) The nine-year-old daughter of our landlord announced one day that she was going to become Lavenda's second wife. "Madame [Schultz]," she said, "will be angry at first, because that's how first wives are when their husbands take a second wife. But after a while, she will stop being angry and will get to know me and we will become friends. That's what always happens."

The differences in internal dynamics in polygynous families are not confined to the relationships of husband and wives. An important distinction is made between children with the same mother and children with a different mother. In Guider, people ordinarily refer to all their siblings (half and full) as brothers or sisters. When they want to emphasize the close connection with a particular brother or sister, however, they say that he or she is "same father, same mother." This terminology conveys a relationship of special intimacy and significance. Children, logically, also have different kinds of relationships with their own mothers and their fathers' other wives—and with their fathers as well.

Where there is a significant inheritance, these relationships serve as the channels for jealousy and conflict. The children of the same mother, and especially the children of different mothers, compete with one another for their father's favor. Each mother tries to protect the interests of her own children, sometimes at the expense of her cowives' children.

COMPETITION IN THE POLYGYNOUS FAMILY Although the relationships among wives in a polygynous society may be very close, among the Mende of Sierra Leone, cowives eventually compete with each other. (See EthnoProfile 12.5: Mende.) Caroline Bledsoe (1993) explains that this competition is often focused on children: how many each wife has and how likely it is that each child will obtain things of value, especially education. Husbands in polygynous Mende households should avoid overt signs of favoritism, but wives differ from one another in status. First, wives are ranked by order of marriage. The senior wife is the first wife in the household, and she has authority over junior wives. Marriage-order ranking structures the household but

---

nuclear family A family pattern made up of two generations: the parents and their unmarried children.

also lays the groundwork for rivalries. Second, wives are also ranked in terms of the status of the families from which they came. Serious problems arise if the husband shows favoritism toward a wife from a high-status family by educating her children ahead of older children of other wives or children of wives higher in the marriage-order ranking.

The level of her children's education matters intensely to a Mende woman because her principal claim to her husband's land or cash, and her expectations of future support after he dies, comes through her children. She depends not only on the income that a child may earn to support her but also on the rights her children have to inherit property and positions of leadership.

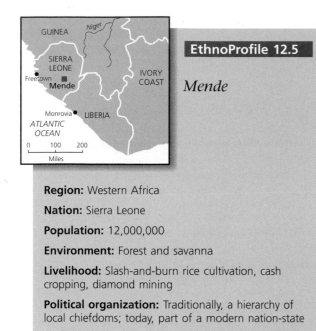

EthnoProfile 12.5

Mende

Region: Western Africa

Nation: Sierra Leone

Population: 12,000,000

Environment: Forest and savanna

Livelihood: Slash-and-burn rice cultivation, cash cropping, diamond mining

Political organization: Traditionally, a hierarchy of local chiefdoms; today, part of a modern nation-state

For more information: Little, Kenneth. 1967. *The Mende of Sierra Leone.* London: Routledge and Kegan Paul.

Nevertheless, education requires a significant cash outlay in school fees, uniforms, books, and so on. A man may be able to send only one child to school, or he may be able to send one child to a prestigious private school only if he sends another to a trade apprenticeship. These economic realities make sense to husbands but can lead to bitter feuds—and even divorce—among cowives who blame the husband for disparities in the accomplishments of their children. In extreme cases, cowives are said to use witchcraft to make their rivals' children fail their exams. To avoid these problems, children are frequently sent to live with relatives who will send them to school. Such competition is missing in monogamous households unless they include adopted children or spouses who already have children from a previous marriage.

Extended and Joint Families

Within any society, certain patterns of family organization are considered proper. In American nuclear families, two generations live together. In some societies, three generations—parents, married children, and grandchildren—are expected to live together in a vertical **extended family.** In still other societies, the extension is horizontal: Brothers and their wives (or sisters and their husbands) live together in a **joint family,** as we saw among the Khalapur Rajputs. These are ideal patterns, which all families may not be able or willing to emulate.

Individual families also change in their basic structures over time. In a polygynous society with extended families, consider a recently married husband and wife who set up housekeeping by themselves. They are monogamous. After a while, a child is born, and they become a monogamous nuclear family. Some time later, elderly parents come to live with them, and they become an extended family. Later the husband takes another wife, and the family becomes polygynous. Then the elderly parents die, and the family is no longer extended. After a time, the husband's younger brother and his wife and children move in, creating a joint household. One wife leaves, and the husband is monogamous again. His brother and his wife and children leave, the husband takes another wife, and the family is polygynous again. The eldest son marries and brings his wife to live in the household, and the household is once again an extended family. One wife dies, and the children all move away, and there is now a monogamous couple living in the household. Finally, with the death of the husband, there is a solitary family, made up of the widow, who is supported by her eldest son but lives alone.

In this example, each household structure is different in its dynamics. These are not several nuclear families that overlap. Extended and joint families are fundamentally different from a nuclear family with regard to the relationships they engender.

TRANSFORMATIONS IN FAMILIES OVER TIME

As we just saw, families change over time. They have a life cycle and a life span. The same family takes on different forms and provides different opportunities for the interaction of family members at different points

---

extended family A family pattern made up of three generations living together: parents, married children, and grandchildren.

joint family A family pattern made up of brothers and their wives or sisters and their husbands (along with their children) living together.

IN THEIR OWN WORDS

Law, Custom, and Crimes against Women

John van Willigen and V. C. Channa describe the social and cultural practices surrounding dowry payments that appear to be responsible for violence against women in some parts of India.

A 25-year-old woman was allegedly burnt to death by her husband and mother-in-law at their East Delhi home yesterday. The housewife, Mrs. Sunita, stated before her death at the Jaya Prakash Narayana Hospital that members of her husband's family had been harassing her for bringing inadequate dowry.

The woman told the Shahdara subdivisional magistrate that during a quarrel over dowry at their Pratap Park house yesterday, her husband gripped her from behind while the mother-in-law poured kerosene over her clothes.

Her clothes were then set ablaze. The police have registered a case against the victim's husband, Suraj Prakash, and his mother.

—Times of India,
February 19, 1988

This routinely reported news story describes what in India is termed a "bride-burning" or "dowry death." Such incidents are frequently reported in the newspapers of Delhi and other Indian cities. In addition, there are cases in which the evidence may be ambiguous, so that deaths of women by fire may be recorded as kitchen accidents, suicides, or murders. Dowry violence takes a characteristic form. Following marriage and the requisite giving of dowry, the family of the groom makes additional demands for the payment of more cash or the provision of more goods. These demands are expressed in unremitting harassment of the bride, who is living in the household of her husband's parents, culminating in the murder of the woman by members of her husband's family

or by her suicide. The woman is typically burned to death with kerosene, a fuel used in pressurized cook stoves, hence the use of the term "bride-burning" in public discourse.

Dowry death statistics appear frequently in the press and parliamentary debates. Parliamentary sources report the following figures for married women 16 to 30 years of age in Delhi: 452 deaths by burning for 1985; 478 for 1986 and 300 for the first six months of 1987. There were 1,319 cases reported nationally in 1986 (Times of India, January 10, 1988). Police records do not match hospital records for third degree burn cases among younger married women; far more violence occurs than the crime reports indicate.

There is other violence against women related both directly and indirectly to the institution of dowry. For example, there are unmarried women who commit suicide so as to relieve their families of the burden of providing a dowry. A recent case that received national attention in the Indian press involved the triple suicide of three sisters in the industrial city of Kanpur. A photograph was widely published showing the three young women hanging from ceiling fans by their scarves. Their father, who earned about 4000 Rs. [rupees] per month, was not able to negotiate marriage for his oldest daughter. The grooms were requesting approximately 100,000 Rs. Also linked to the dowry problem is selective female abortion made possible by amniocentesis. This issue was brought to national attention with a startling statistic reported out of a seminar held in Delhi in 1985. Of 3000 abortions carried out after sex determination through amniocentesis, only one involved a male fetus. As a result of these developments, the government of the state of Maharashtra banned sex determination tests except those carried out in government hospitals.

Source: van Willigen and Channa 1991, 369–70.

in its development. New households are formed and old households change through divorce, remarriage, the departure of children, and the breakup of extended families.

Divorce and Remarriage

Most human societies make it possible for married couples to separate. In some societies, the process is long, drawn out, and difficult, especially when bridewealth must be returned; a man who divorces a wife in such

societies, or whose wife leaves him, expects some of the bridewealth back. But for the wife's family to give the bridewealth back, a whole chain of marriages may have to be broken up. Brothers of the divorced wife may have to divorce to get back enough bridewealth from their in-laws. Sometimes a new husband will repay the bridewealth to the former husband's line, thus letting the bride's relatives off the hook.

DIVORCE IN GUIDER In other societies, divorce is easier. Marriages in Guider, for example, are easily bro-

ken up. (See EthnoProfile 8.1: Guider.) The Fulbe of
Guider prefer that a man marry his father's brother's
daughter. In many cases, such marriages are contracted
simply to oblige the families involved; after a few
months, the couple splits up. In other cases, a young
girl (12 or 13 years old) is married to a man considerably her senior, despite any interest she may have had
in men closer to her own age. Here too the marriage
may not last long. In general, there is enough dissatisfaction with marriage in Guider to make household
transformation through divorce quite common.

Among Muslims in Guider, divorce is controlled by
men; women are not allowed legally to initiate divorces. A man wanting a divorce need only follow the
simple procedure laid down in the Qur'an and sanc-
tioned by long practice in Guider: He appears before
two witnesses and pronounces the formula "I divorce
you" three times. He is then divorced, and his wife
must leave his household. She may take an infant with
her, but any children at the toddler stage or older stay
with the father. If she takes an infant, she must return
the child to the father's household by the time the
child is 6 to 8 years old. In case she was pregnant at
the time of the divorce, a woman must wait 3 months
after she is divorced before she can remarry. After this
time, the vast majority of women remarry.

Do women in Guider, then, have no power to escape from marriages that are unsatisfactory? Legally,
perhaps not. But several conventionally recognized
practices allow a woman to communicate her desire for
a divorce. She can ask her husband for a divorce, and
in some cases he will comply. If he does not or if she
is unwilling to confront him directly, she can neglect
household duties—burn his food or stop cooking for
him entirely or refuse to sleep with him. She can also
leave, going to live in the compound of her father or
brother.

GROUNDS FOR DIVORCE Depending on the society,
nagging, quarreling, cruelty, stinginess, or adultery
may be cited as causes for divorce. In almost all societies, childlessness is grounds for divorce as well. For
the Ju/'hoansi (!Kung), most divorces are initiated by
women, mainly because they do not like their husbands or do not want to be married (Lee 1992b; Shostak
1983). (See EthnoProfile 11.1: Ju/'hoansi [!Kung].) After
what is often considerable debate, a couple that decides
to break up merely separates. There is no bridewealth
to return, no legal contract to be renegotiated. Mutual

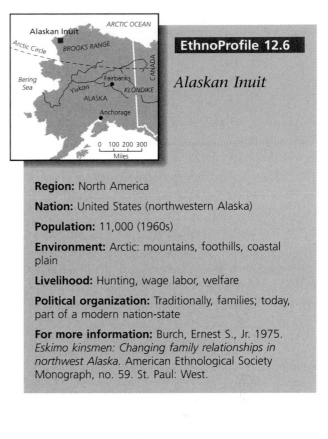

EthnoProfile 12.6

Alaskan Inuit

Region: North America

Nation: United States (northwestern Alaska)

Population: 11,000 (1960s)

Environment: Arctic: mountains, foothills, coastal
plain

Livelihood: Hunting, wage labor, welfare

Political organization: Traditionally, families; today,
part of a modern nation-state

For more information: Burch, Ernest S., Jr. 1975.
*Eskimo kinsmen: Changing family relationships in
northwest Alaska.* American Ethnological Society
Monograph, no. 59. St. Paul: West.

consent is all that is necessary. The children go with
the mother. Ju/'hoansi divorces are cordial, Richard Lee
(1992b) tells us, at least compared with the Western
norm. Ex-spouses may continue to joke with each
other and even live next to each other with their new
spouses.

There are very few societies in which divorce is not
recognized. In ancient Rome, for example, divorce was
impossible. This followed from legal consequences of
the marriage ritual. When she married, a woman was
cut off from the patrilineage into which she was born
and incorporated into her husband's patrilineage. Were
she to leave her husband, she would have no place to
go and no lineage to protect her.

SEPARATION AMONG THE INUIT Among the northwestern Inuit, the traditional view is that all kin relationships, including marital ones, are permanent (Burch
1970). (See EthnoProfile 12.6: Alaskan Inuit.) Thus, although it is possible to deactivate a marriage by separating, a marriage can never be permanently dissolved.
(Conversely, reestablishing the residence tie is all that's
needed to reactivate the relationship.) A husband and

wife who stop living together and having sexual relations with each other are considered to be separated and ready for another marriage. If each member of a separated couple remarried, the two husbands of the wife would become cohusbands; the two wives of the husband, cowives; and the children of the first and second marriages, cosiblings. In effect, a "divorce" among the Inuit results in more, not fewer, connections.

Breaking Up Complex Households

The formation of new households following the breakup of extended families is best illustrated in joint families. In a joint family, the pressures that build up among coresident brothers or sisters often increase dramatically on the death of the father. In theory, the eldest son inherits the position of head of the household from his father, but his younger brothers may not accept his authority as readily as they did their father's. Some younger brothers may decide to establish their own households, and gradually the joint family splits. Each brother whose household splits off from the joint stem usually hopes to start his own joint family; eventually, his sons will bring their wives into the household, and a new joint family emerges out of the ashes of an old one.

Something similar happens among the Nyinba, the polyandrous people of Nepal discussed earlier. (See EthnoProfile 12.2: Nyinba.) In a family with many brothers widely separated in age, the corporation of brothers may take a second wife. At first, all brothers have equal sexual access to her, but in time the brothers will tend to form groups around each wife, with some preferring the first and others preferring the second. At this point, the time is ripe for splitting the household in two. The Nyinba recognize that bringing a second fertile wife into the house sets in motion the transformation of the family into two polyandrous households and the division of land ownership. Hence, family systems contain within them the seeds of their own transformation.

International Migration and the Family

Migration to find work in another country has become increasingly common worldwide and has important effects on families. Anthropologist Eugenia Georges (1990) examined its effects on people who migrated to

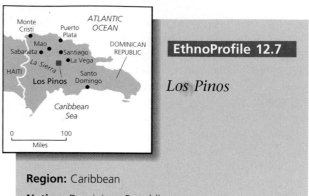

EthnoProfile 12.7

Los Pinos

Region: Caribbean

Nation: Dominican Republic

Population: 1,000

Environment: Rugged mountain region

Livelihood: Peasant agriculture (tobacco, coffee, cacao) and labor migration

Political organization: Part of a modern nation-state

For more information: Georges, Eugenia. 1990. *The making of a transnational community: Migration, development, and cultural change in the Dominican Republic.* New York: Columbia University Press.

the United States from Los Pinos, a small town in the Dominican Republic. (See EthnoProfile 12.7: Los Pinos.) Migration divided these families, with some members moving to New York and some remaining in Los Pinos. Some parents stayed in the Dominican Republic while their children went to the United States. A more common pattern was for spouses to separate, with the husband migrating and the wife staying home. Consequently, many households in Los Pinos were headed by women. In most cases, however, the spouse in the United States worked to bring the spouse and children in Los Pinos there.

This sometimes took several years because it involved completing paperwork for the visa and saving money beyond the amount regularly sent to Los Pinos. Children of the couple who were close to working age also came to the United States, frequently with their mother, and younger children were sent for as they approached working age. Finally, after several years in the United States, the couple who started the migration cycle would often take their savings and return home to the Dominican Republic. Their children stayed in the United States and continued to send money home. Return migrants tended not to give up their residence visas, and therefore had to return to the United States annually. Often they stayed for a month or more to work. This also provided them with the opportunity to buy clothing and household goods at a more reasonable cost, as well as other items—clothing, cosmetics, and the like—to sell to neighbors, friends, and kin in the Dominican Republic.

Georges observes that the absent family member maintained an active role in family life despite the heavy psychological burden of separation. Although he might be working in a hotel in New York, for example, the husband was still the breadwinner and the main decision maker in the household. He communicated by visits, letters, and occasional telephone calls. Despite the strains of migration, moreover, the divorce rate was actually slightly lower in migrant families. In part, this was because the exchange of information between Los Pinos and New York was both dense and frequent, but also because strong ties of affection connected many couples. Finally, "the goal of the overwhelming majority of the migrants [from Los Pinos] I spoke with was permanent return to the Dominican Republic. Achievement of this goal was hastened by sponsoring the migration of dependents, both wives and children, so that they could work and save as part of the reconstituted household in the United States" (1990, 201). This pressure also helped keep families together.

Families by Choice

In spite of the range of variation in family forms that we have surveyed, some readers may still be convinced that family ties depend on blood, and that blood is thicker than water. It is therefore instructive to consider the results of research carried out by Kath Weston (1991) on family forms among gays and lesbians in the San Francisco Bay Area during the 1980s. A lesbian herself, Weston knew that a turning point in the lives of most gays and lesbians was the decision to announce their sexual orientation to their parents and siblings. If blood truly were thicker than water, this announcement should not destroy family bonds, and many parents have indeed been supportive of their children after the announcement. Often enough, however, shocked parents have turned away, declaring that this person is

no longer their son or daughter. Living through—or even contemplating—such an experience has been enough to force gays and lesbians to think seriously about the sources of family ties.

By the 1980s, some North American gays and lesbians had reached two conclusions: (1) that blood ties *cannot* guarantee the "enduring diffuse solidarity" supposedly at the core of North American kinship (Schneider 1968); and (2) that new kin ties *can* be created over time as friends and lovers demonstrate their genuine commitment to one another by creating families of choice. "Like their heterosexual counterparts, most gay men and lesbians insisted that family members are people who are 'there for you,' people you can count on emotionally and materially" (1991, 113). Some gay kinship ideologies now argue that "whatever endures is real" as a way of claiming legitimacy for chosen families that were not the product of heterosexual marriages. Such a definition of family is compatible with understandings of kinship based on nurturance described in Chapter 11. Gay and lesbian activists have used this similarity as a resource in their struggles to obtain for longstanding families by choice some of the same legal rights enjoyed by traditional heterosexual families, such as hospital visiting privileges, joint adoption, and property rights (Weston 1995, 99).

THE FLEXIBILITY OF MARRIAGE

It is easy to get the impression that marriage rules compel people to do things they really do not want to do. Younger people, for example, seem forced by elders to marry complete strangers of a certain kin category belonging to particular social groups; or women appear to be pawns in men's games of prestige and power. Marriage rules, however, are always subject to some negotiation, as illustrated by the marriage practices of the Ju/'hoansi of the Kalahari Desert. (See EthnoProfile 11.1: Ju/'hoansi [!Kung].) Richard Lee (1992b) notes that all first marriages are set up by means of a long-term exchange of gifts between the parents of a bride and groom. As we saw in Chapter 11, the Ju/'hoansi kinship system is as simple or as complex as people want to make it, and the game of kinship is extended to marriage. A girl may not marry a father, brother, son, uncle, or nephew, or a first or second cousin. A girl may also

IN THEIR OWN WORDS

Why Migrant Women Feed Their Husbands Tamales

Brett Williams suggests that the reasons why Mexican migrant women feed their husbands tamales may not be the stereotypical reasons that outside observers often assume.

Because migrant women are so involved in family life and so seemingly submissive to their husbands, they have been described often as martyred purveyors of rural Mexican and Christian custom, tyrannized by excessively masculine, crudely domineering, rude and petty bullies in marriage, and blind to any world outside the family because they are suffocated by the concerns of kin. Most disconcerting to outside observers is that migrant women seem to embrace such stereotypes: they argue that they *should* monopolize their foodways and that they should *not* question the authority of their husbands. If men want tamales, men should have them. But easy stereotypes can mislead; in exploring the lives of the poor, researchers must revise their own notions of family life, and this paper argues that foodways can provide crucial clues about how to do so.

The paradox is this: among migrant workers both women and men are equally productive wage earners, and husbands readily acknowledge that without their wives' work their families cannot earn enough to survive. For migrants the division of labor between earning a living outside the home and managing household affairs is unknown; and the dilemma facing middle-class wives who may wish to work to supplement the family's income simply does not exist. Anthropologists exploring women's status cross-culturally argue that women are most influential when they share in the production of food and have some control over its distribution. If such perspectives bear at all on migrant women, one might be led to question their seemingly unfathomable obsequiousness in marriage.

Anthropologists further argue that women's influence is even greater when they are not isolated from their kinswomen, when women can cooperate in production and join, for example, agricultural work with domestic duties and childcare. Most migrant women spend their lives within large, closely knit circles of kin and their work days with their kinswomen. Marriage does not uproot or isolate a woman from her family, but rather doubles the relatives each partner can depend on and widens in turn the networks of everyone involved. The lasting power of marriage is reflected in statistics which show a divorce rate of 1 percent for migrant farmworkers from Texas, demonstrating the strength of a union bolstered by large numbers of relatives concerned that it go well. Crucial to this concern is that neither partner is an economic drain on the family, and the Tejano pattern of early and lifelong marriages establishes some limit on the whimsy with which men can abuse and misuse their wives.

While anthropology traditionally rests on an appreciation of other cultures in their own contexts and on their own terms, it is very difficult to avoid class bias in viewing the lives of those who share partly in one's own culture, especially when the issue is something so close to home as food and who cooks it. Part of the problem may lie in appreciating what families are and what they do. For the poor, public and private domains are blurred in confusing ways, family affairs may be closely tied to economics, and women's work at gathering and obligating or *binding* relatives is neither trivial nor merely a matter of sentiment. Another problem may lie in focusing on the marital relationship as indicative of a woman's authority in the family. We too often forget that women are sisters, grandmothers, and aunts to men as well as wives. Foodways can help us rethink both of these problematic areas and understand how women elaborate domestic roles to knit families together, to obligate both male and female kin, and to nurture and bind their husbands as well.

Source: Williams 1984.

---

not marry a boy with her father's or brother's name, and a boy may not marry a girl with his mother's or sister's name. In addition, neither a boy nor girl should marry someone who stands in an avoidance relationship.

Consequently, for the Ju/'hoansi, about three-quarters of a person's potential spouses are off limits. In practice, parents of girls tend to be quite choosy about whom their daughter marries. If they are opposed to a particular suitor, they will come up with a kin or name prohibition to block the match. Because the parents arrange the first marriage, it appears that the girl has very little to say about it. If she has an objection and protests long and hard, however, her parents may well call it off. This clear and insistent assertion of displeasure is not uncommon in the world. Even when a young woman follows the wishes of her parents for her first marriage, that first marriage may not be her last if dissatisfaction persists. Despite the parents' quest to find ideal spouses for their children, close to half of all first marriages among the Ju/'hoansi fail. However, as in many societies, only about 10 percent of marriages that last five years or longer end in divorce (Lee 1992b, 83).

Sometimes the contrast between the formal rules of marriage and the actual performance of marriage rituals can be revealing. Ivan Karp (1978) asks why Iteso women laugh at marriage ceremonies. (See EthnoProfile 11.4: Iteso.) During his fieldwork, Karp was struck by a paradox. The marriage ritual is taken very seriously by the patrilineal Iteso; it is the moment of creation for a new household, and it paves the way for the physical and social reproduction of Iteso patrilineages. But the ritual is carried out entirely by women who are not consanguineal members of the patrilineage! Despite the seriousness of the occasion and although they are carrying out the ritual for the benefit of a lineage to which they do not belong, Iteso women seem to find the ceremony enormously funny.

To explain this apparently anomalous behavior, Karp suggests that the meaning of the marriage ritual needs to be analyzed from two different perspectives: that of the men and that of the women. The men's perspective constitutes the official (or hegemonic) ideology of Iteso marriage. It emphasizes how marriage brings the bride's sexuality under the control of her husband's lineage. It distinguishes between women of the mother-in-law's generation and women of the wife's own generation. It stresses the woman's role as an agent of reproduction who is equivalent, in a reproductive sense, to the bridewealth cattle.

The women's perspective constitutes an unofficial (or counterhegemonic) ideology. For the men and women of a given lineage to succeed in perpetuating that lineage, they must control women's bodies. But the bodies they must control belong to female outsiders who marry lineage men. These same female outsiders direct the two ritual events crucial to lineage reproduction: marriage and birth. And men of the lineage are not allowed to attend either of these rituals. In sum, female outsiders control the continued existence of a patrilineage whose male members are supposed to control them!

Iteso women, Karp says, can see the irony in this: They are at once controlled and controlling. In the marriage ritual itself, they comment on this paradox through their laughter. In so doing, they reveal two things. First, they show that they know the men are dependent on them. Second, even as the men assert their control over women's bodies, the women's ritual actions escape the men's control. The official ideology of male control is subverted, at least momentarily, by the women's laughter. Even as they ensure that lineages will continue, they are able to comment on the paradoxical relation of women to men.

SEXUAL PRACTICES

Some anthropologists seem to regard marriage as an abstract formal system, having little if anything to do with human sexuality. As a result, their discussions tend to ignore its carnal aspects. But sexual intercourse is part of almost all marriages. And because in many societies marriage is the formal prerequisite for becoming sexually active (at least for females), a desire for sex is a strong motivation for getting married (Spiro 1977, 212).

Ranges of Heterosexual Practices

The range of sexual practice in the world is vast. In many Oceanian societies—Tikopia, for example—the young are expected to have a great deal of sexual experience before marriage. (See EthnoProfile 12.8: Tikopia.) Young men and young women begin having sexual relations at an early age, and having several lovers is considered normal for the young. Getting married, as in many societies, is considered the final step (or the beginning of the final step) in becoming an adult. The distinguished British anthropologist Sir Raymond Firth notes that for the Tikopia, marriage represents a great change for both partners in this regard. The woman must abandon sexual freedom, but she replaces it with what Firth calls "a safe and legalized sexual cohabitation" ([1936] 1984, 434). The man is theoretically free to continue to have affairs, but in practice he will "settle down." This pattern is quite common cross-culturally.

The Ju/'hoansi also begin sexual activity at an early age. (See EthnoProfile 11.1: Ju/'hoansi [!Kung].) As a re-

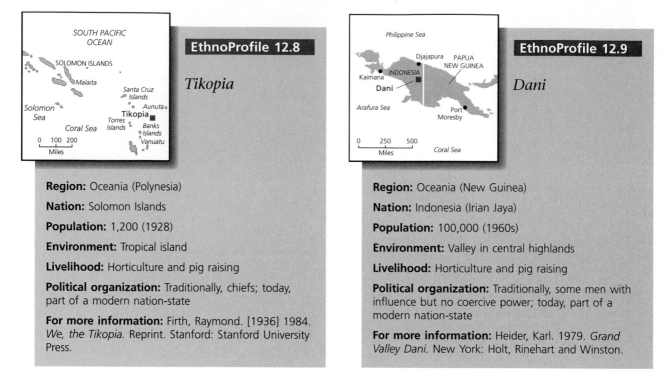

EthnoProfile 12.8

Tikopia

Region: Oceania (Polynesia)

Nation: Solomon Islands

Population: 1,200 (1928)

Environment: Tropical island

Livelihood: Horticulture and pig raising

Political organization: Traditionally, chiefs; today, part of a modern nation-state

For more information: Firth, Raymond. [1936] 1984. *We, the Tikopia*. Reprint. Stanford: Stanford University Press.

EthnoProfile 12.9

Dani

Region: Oceania (New Guinea)

Nation: Indonesia (Irian Jaya)

Population: 100,000 (1960s)

Environment: Valley in central highlands

Livelihood: Horticulture and pig raising

Political organization: Traditionally, some men with influence but no coercive power; today, part of a modern nation-state

For more information: Heider, Karl. 1979. *Grand Valley Dani*. New York: Holt, Rinehart and Winston.

sult, the social and sexual constraints of marriage represent quite a shock at first, especially for young women. Some Ju/'hoansi are strictly faithful to one another, but a significant minority take lovers. The Ju/'hoansi have no double standard; both men and women are free to take lovers, and women are sometimes eloquent about the time they spend with lovers. However, discretion is necessary when taking a lover because both husbands and wives can become very jealous and start fights. Sexual satisfaction is important to the Ju/'hoansi; female orgasm is known, and women expect both husbands and lovers to satisfy them sexually.

Not all societies have the same attitude. Robert Murphy and Yolanda Murphy (1974) note that for the Mundurucu, a group of about 1,250 gardening and hunting people in the Brazilian Amazon, female orgasm is more accidental than expected. Many societies require a woman's virginity at marriage; in some Arab societies, bloodstained sheets must be produced the morning after the consummation of a marriage to demonstrate that the bride was a virgin.

Particularly interesting in this regard is Karl Heider's research (1979) among the Dani, a people of highland New Guinea. (See EthnoProfile 12.9: Dani.) Heider dis-

covered that the Dani have extraordinarily little interest in sex. For five years after the birth of a child, the parents do not have sexual intercourse with each other. This practice, called a *postpartum sex taboo,* is found in all cultures, but in most societies it lasts for a few weeks or months. (In North America, we say that the mother needs time to heal; other societies have other justifications.) In a few cases, the postpartum sex taboo is two years long, which is considered a very long time. Five years is hard to believe. What could explain it?

Heider points out that Westerners assume that the sex drive is perhaps the most powerful biological drive of all, and that if this drive is not satisfied directly in sexual activity, then some other outlet will be found. In fact, some suggest that the Dani's high levels of outgroup aggression may be connected with their low level of sexual intercourse. The Dani are not celibate, and they certainly have sexual intercourse often enough to reproduce biologically. But they do not seem very interested in sex (1979, 78–81). Heider cannot explain why the Dani have such a low level of sexuality, but the implications of this pattern for understanding the range of human sexual behavior are significant. The Dani, who are not abnormal physically or mentally, represent an extreme in the cultural construction of sexuality.

Other Sexual Practices

The traditional anthropological focus on what European Americans call heterosexual relationships is understandable. People in every society are concerned about perpetuating themselves, and most have developed complex ideological and ritual structures to ensure that this occurs. The fact that such elaborate cultural constructions seem necessary to encourage heterosexual practices, however, suggests that human sexual expression would resist such confinement if it were not under strict control. As we saw in the previous chapter, anthropological information about supernumerary sexes and genders undermines the "two-sex model" that is hegemonic in European American cultures. In the same way, cross-cultural information about sexual practices that differ from this heterosexual model provide a vital context for understanding sexual practices that European Americans call *homosexuality* and *bisexuality*.

FEMALE SEXUAL PRACTICES IN MOMBASA Anthropologist Gill Shepherd shows that traditional patterns of male–female interaction among Swahili Muslims in Mombasa, Kenya, make male and female homosexual relationships perfectly intelligible (1987). (See EthnoProfile 12.10: Mombasa Swahilis.) For one thing, men and women in Muslim Mombasa live in very different subcultures. For women, the most enduring relationship is between mothers and daughters, mirrored in the relationship between an older married sister and a younger unmarried sister. By contrast, relationships between mothers and sons and between brothers and sisters are more distant. Except in the case of young, modern, educated couples, the relationship between husband and wife is often emotionally distant as well. Because the worlds of men and women overlap so little, therefore, relationships between the sexes tend to be one-dimensional. Men and women join a variety of sex-segregated groups for leisure-time activities such as dancing or religious study. Within these same-sex groups, individuals compete for social rank.

Of the some 50,000 Swahili in Mombasa, about 5,000 could be called homosexual. The number is misleading, however, because men and women shift be-

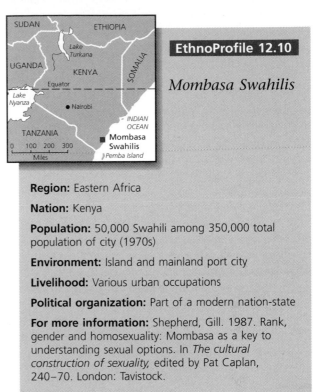

EthnoProfile 12.10

Mombasa Swahilis

Region: Eastern Africa

Nation: Kenya

Population: 50,000 Swahili among 350,000 total population of city (1970s)

Environment: Island and mainland port city

Livelihood: Various urban occupations

Political organization: Part of a modern nation-state

For more information: Shepherd, Gill. 1987. Rank, gender and homosexuality: Mombasa as a key to understanding sexual options. In *The cultural construction of sexuality,* edited by Pat Caplan, 240–70. London: Tavistock.

tween what European Americans call *homosexuality* and *heterosexuality* throughout their lives. Women are allowed to choose other women as sexual partners only after they have been married. Therefore, all such women in Mombasa are married, widowed, or divorced. Both men and women are open about their same-sex relationships, and "nobody would dream of suggesting that their sexual choices had any effect on their work capabilities, reliability, or religious piety" (Shepherd 1987, 241).

Because women in many all-female households do not have sexual relationships with one another, Shepherd uses the term *lesbian* to imply an overt sexual relationship between two women. Lesbian couples in Mombasa are far more likely to live together than are male homosexual couples. In addition to having private, sexual relationships with other women, they also form clublike groups that meet regularly in one another's houses. Each group is composed of an inner circle of relatively wealthy older women who are friends. The rule is that younger, lower-status women visit older, higher-status women. Wealthy lesbian women hold court in the afternoons, when Swahili women have the chance to go visiting. Women in the inner circle compete for status by, for example, trying to outdo one another by dressing their lovers as opulently as possible.

Many women were quite clear about the practical reasons that had led them into sexual relationships with other women. Women with little money are unlikely to marry men who can offer them jewelry, shoes, new dresses, status, or financial security, but a wealthy lesbian lover can offer them all these things. Also, a poor young woman in an unhappy marriage may have no way to support herself if she leaves her husband unless she has a lesbian lover. Very occasionally a wealthy lesbian woman will help a girl who has remained single after all her peers have married. Adult status and freedoms come only with marriage, but a woman who is well-educated or from a high-status family may still be unmarried in her late twenties or early thirties due to her parents' intimidation of potential suitors. A wealthy lesbian who wants to help such a woman finds a man willing to make a marriage of convenience and finances his marriage to the woman. The couple are divorced shortly thereafter, and the girl goes to live with her lesbian benefactress.

According to Islamic law, a wealthy, high-ranking Muslim woman can only marry a man who is her equal or superior. A marriage of this kind brings a great deal of seclusion, and her wealth is administered by her husband. The wealthy partner in a lesbian relationship, however, is freed from these constraints. "Thus if she wishes to use her wealth as she likes and has a taste for power, entry into a lesbian relationship, or living alone as a divorced or widowed woman, are virtually her only options" (Shepherd 1987, 257). Financial independence for a woman offers the chance to convert wealth to power. If she pays for the marriages of other people or provides financial support in exchange for loyalty, a woman can create a circle of dependents. Shepherd points out that a few women, some lesbians, have achieved real political power in Mombasa in this way (1987, 257).

Still, it is not necessary to be a lesbian to build a circle of dependents. Why do some women follow this route? The answer, Shepherd tells us, is complicated. It is not entirely respectable for a woman under 45 or 50 to be unmarried. Some women can maintain autonomy by making a marriage of convenience to a man who already lives with a wife and then living apart from him. Many women, however, find this arrangement both lonely and sexually unsatisfying. Living as

a lesbian is less respectable than being a second, non-resident wife, but it is more respectable than not being married at all. The lesbian sexual relationship does not reduce the autonomy of the wealthy partner "and indeed takes place in the highly positive context of the fond and supportive relationships women establish among themselves anyway" (1987, 258).

Shepherd suggests that the reason sexual relationships between men or between women are generally not heavily stigmatized in Mombasa is because social rank takes precedence over all other measures of status. Rank is a combination of wealth, the ability to claim Arab ancestry, and the degree of Muslim learning and piety. Rank determines marriage partners, as well as relations of loyalty and subservience, and both men and women expect to rise in rank over a lifetime. Although lesbian couples may violate the prototype for sexual relations, they do not violate relations of rank. Shepherd suggests that a marriage between a poor husband and a rich wife might be more shocking than a lesbian relationship between a dominant rich woman and a dependent poor one. It is less important that a woman's lover be a male than it is for her to be a good Arab, a good Muslim, and a person of wealth and influence.

MALE SEXUAL PRACTICES IN NICARAGUA Anthropologist Roger Lancaster spent many months during the 1980s studying the effects of the Sandinista Revolution on the lives of working people in Managua, Nicaragua. While he was there, he learned about *cochónes. Cochón* could be translated into English as *homosexual,* but this would be highly misleading. As Lancaster discovered, working-class Nicaraguans interpret sexual relations between men differently from North Americans, and their interpretation is central to the traditional Nicaraguan ideas about masculinity that have been called *machismo.*

To begin with, a "real man" (or *macho*) is widely admired as someone who is active, violent, and dominant. In sexual terms, this means that the penis is seen as a weapon used violently to dominate one's sexual partner, who is thereby rendered passive, abused, and subordinate. North Americans typically think of machismo as involving the domination of women by men, but as Lancaster shows, the system is equally defined by the domination of men over other men. Indeed, a "manly man" in working-class Nicaragua is defined as one who is the active, dominant, penetrating sexual partner in encounters with women *and* men. A "passive" male who allows a "manly man" to have sexual intercourse with him in this way is called a *cochón*.

A North American gay man himself, Lancaster found that Nicaraguan views of male-male sexual encounters differ considerably from contemporary North American ideas about male homosexuality. In Nicaragua, for example, the people Lancaster knew assumed that men "would naturally be aroused by the idea of anally penetrating another male" (1992, 241). Only the "passive" cochón is stigmatized, whereas males who always take the "active" role in sexual intercourse with other males and with females are seen as "normal." Nicaraguans, moreover, find hate crimes such as gay-bashing inconceivable: Cochones may be made fun of, but they are also much admired performers during Carnival. In the United States, by contrast, the active-passive distinction does not exist, and anal intercourse is not the only form that male homosexual expression may take. Both partners in same-sex encounters are considered homosexual and equally stigmatized, and gay-bashing is a sometimes deadly reality, probably because it is *not* assumed that "normal" males will naturally be aroused by the idea of sex with another man.

In Nicaragua, public challenges for dominance are a constant of male-male interaction even when sexual intercourse is not involved. The term *cochón* may be used as an epithet not only for a man who yields publicly to another man, but also for cats that don't catch mice, or indeed anything that somehow fails to perform its proper function. In Lancaster's view, cochones are made, not born: "Those who consistently lose out in the competition for male status . . . discover pleasure in the passive sexual role or its social status: these men are made into cochones. And those who master the rules of conventional masculinity . . . are made into machistas" (1992, 249).

These ideas about gender and sexuality created an unanticipated roadblock for Sandinistas who wanted to improve the lives of Nicaraguan women and children. The Sandinista government passed a series of New Family Laws, which were designed to encourage men to support their families economically and to discourage irresponsible sex, irresponsible parenting, and familial dislocation. When Lancaster interviewed Nicaraguan men to see what they thought of these laws, however, he repeatedly got the following response: "First the interrogative: 'What do the Sandinistas want from us? That we should all become cochónes?' And then the tautological: 'A man has to be a man.' That is, a man

is defined by what he is not—a cochón" (1992, 274).

SEXUALITY AND POWER

The physical activity that we call sexual intercourse is not just doing what comes naturally. Like so much else in human life, sex does not speak for itself, nor does it have only one meaning. Sexual practices can be used to give concrete form to more abstract notions we have about the place of men and women in the world. They may serve as a metaphor for expressing differential power within a society. This is particularly clear in the sexual practices that embody Nicaraguan machismo, or North American date rape and family violence. That is, sexual practices can be used to enact, in unmistakable physical terms, the reality of differential power. This reminds us that marriages, families, and sexual practices never occur in a vacuum, but are embedded in other social practices such as food production, political organization, and kinship.

Key Terms

marriage	monogamy
affinal	polygamy
consanguineal	polygyny
endogamy	polyandry
exogamy	bridewealth
neolocal	dowry
patrilocal	nuclear family
matrilocal	extended family
avunculocal	joint family

Chapter Summary

1. Marriage is a social process that transforms the status of a man and woman, stipulates the degree of sexual access the married partners may have to each other, establishes the legitimacy of children born to the wife, and creates relationships between the kin of the wife and the kin of the husband.

2. Woman marriage and ghost marriage among the Nuer highlight several defining features of marriage and also demonstrate that the roles of husband and father may not be dependent on the sex of the person who fills it.

3. There are four major patterns of postmarital residence: neolocal, patrilocal, matrilocal, and avunculocal.

4. A person may be married to only one person at a time (monogamy) or to several (polygamy). Polygamy can be further subdivided into polygyny, in which a man is married to two or more wives, and polyandry, in which a woman is married to two or more husbands.

5. The study of polyandry reveals the separation of a woman's sexuality and her reproductive capacity, something not found in monogamous or polygynous societies. There are three main forms of polyandry: fraternal polyandry, associated polyandry, and secondary marriage.

6. Bridewealth is a payment of symbolically important goods by the husband's lineage to the wife's lineage. Anthropologists see this as compensation to the wife's family for the loss of her productive and reproductive capacities. A woman's bridewealth payment may enable her brother to pay bridewealth to get a wife.

7. Dowry is typically a transfer of family wealth from parents to their daughter at the time of her marriage. Dowries are often considered the wife's contribution to the establishment of a new household. Among the Khalapur Rajputs of India, how well a woman marries and how well she is treated by her in-laws depend on the size of her dowry.

8. In some cultures, the most important relationships a man and a woman have are with their opposite-sex siblings. Among the matrilineal Ashanti of western Africa, husbands and wives live with their siblings and other matrilineal kin even after they are married. Even in some patrilineal societies, adult brothers and sisters may see one another often and jointly control lineage affairs.

9. Different family structures produce different internal patterns and tensions. There are three basic family types: nuclear, extended, and joint. Families may change from one type to another over time and with the birth, growth, and marriage of children.

10. Most human societies permit marriages to end by divorce, although it is not always easy. In most societies, childlessness is grounds for divorce. Sometimes nagging, quarreling, adultery, cruelty, and stinginess are causes. In some societies, only men may initiate a divorce. In very few societies is divorce impossible.

11. Families have developed ingenious ways of keeping together even when some members live abroad for extended periods. Gays and lesbians in North America have created families by choice, based on nurturance, which they believe are as enduring as families based on birth.

12. Marriage rules are subject to negotiation, even when they appear rigid. This is illustrated by Iteso marriage. The Iteso depend upon women from the outside to perpetuate their patrilineages, and the women express their ironic awareness of this fact through ritualized laughter at marriage.

13. Sexual practices vary greatly worldwide, from the puritanical and fearful to the casual and pleasurable. In some societies, young men and women begin having free sexual relations from an early age until they are married. Sexual practices that North Americans call *homosexuality* or *bisexuality* may be understood very differently in different societies. They often enact the reality of differential power.

Suggested Readings

Bohannan, Paul, and John Middleton. 1968. *Marriage, family, and residence.* New York: Natural History Press. *A classic collection, with important and readable articles.*

Lancaster, Roger. 1992. *Life is hard.* Berkeley: University of California Press. *A stunning analysis of machismo in Nicaragua, in which sexual practices North Americans consider homosexual are interpreted very differently.*

Sacks, Karen. 1979. *Sisters and wives.* Urbana: University of Illinois Press. *A marxian analysis of the notion of sexual equality. This book includes very important data and analysis on sister-brother relations.*

Shostak, Marjorie. 1981. *Nisa: The life and words of a !Kung woman.* New York: Vintage. *A wonderful book. The story of a Ju/'hoansi (!Kung) woman's life in her own words. Shostak provides background for each chapter. There is much here on marriage and everyday life.*

Suggs, David, and Andrew Miracle. 1993. *Culture and human sexuality.* Pacific Grove, CA: Brooks/Cole. *A collection of important articles from a variety of theoretical perspectives on the nature and culture of human sexuality.*

13 ✳

Beyond Kinship

umorist Garrison Keillor makes the following observation about life in the mythical small town of Lake Wobegon, Minnesota:

When the Thanatopsis Club hit its centennial in 1982 and Mrs. Hallberg wrote to the White House and asked for an essay from the President on small-town life, she got one, two paragraphs that extolled Lake Wobegon as a model of free enterprise and individualism, which was displayed in the library under glass, although the truth is that Lake Wobegon survives to the extent that it does on a form of voluntary socialism with elements of Deism, fatalism, and nepotism. Free enterprise runs on self-interest. This is socialism, and it runs on loyalty. You need a

toaster, you buy it at Co-op Hardware even though you can get a deluxe model with all the toaster attachments for less money at K-Mart in St. Cloud. You buy it at Co-op because you know Otto. Glasses you will find at Clifford's which also sells shoes and ties and some gloves. . . . Though you might rather shop for glasses in a strange place where they'll encourage your vanity, though Clifford's selection of frames is clearly based on Scripture ("Take no thought for what you shall wear. . . .") and you might put a hideous piece of junk on your face and Clifford would say, "I think you'll like those" as if you're a person who looks like you don't care what you look like—nevertheless you should think twice before you get the Calvin Klein glasses from Vanity Vision in the St. Cloud Mall. Calvin Klein isn't going to come with the Rescue

FIGURE 13.1 Locations of societies whose EthnoProfiles appear in Chapter 13.

Squad and he isn't going to teach your children about redemption by grace. You couldn't find Calvin Klein to save your life.

If people were to live by comparison shopping, the town would go bust. It cannot compete with other places item by item. Nothing in town is quite as good as it appears to be somewhere else. If you live there, you have to take it as a whole. That's loyalty. (Keillor 1985, 95–96)

If human beings are social by nature, then no individual can be self-sufficient and autonomous. For many human societies, for most of our history, kinship organized human interdependence within a fairly restricted local arena. Still, every society would risk going bust if its members had no way of establishing links with nonkin. In this chapter we examine some of the ways nonkin loyalties are created and nurtured.

KIN-BASED VERSUS NONKIN-BASED SOCIETIES

In non-Western societies, kinship is central to social organization. As we have seen, an elaborate kinship system can regulate social life and organize behavioral patterns. In the Western world, however, kinship has long been reduced to the realm of personal and family relations. In the nineteenth century, scholars of classical antiquity recognized that kinship groups had played

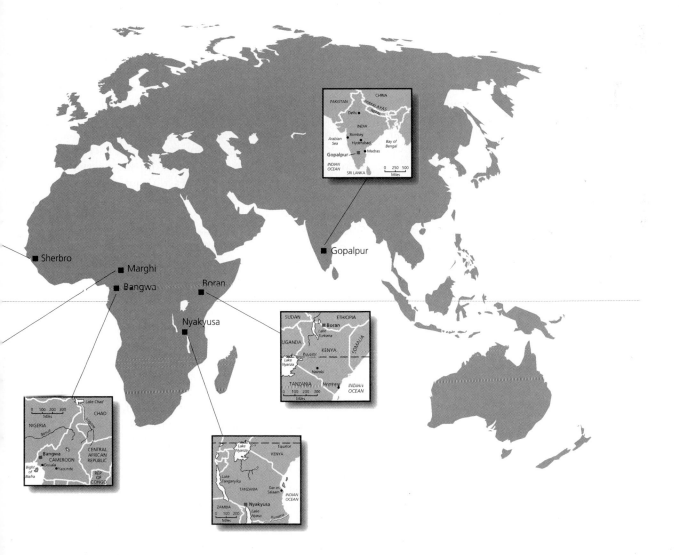

roles in ancient European societies comparable to the role they played in many contemporary non-Western societies. Somehow, over time, those kin-ordered forms of social life had transformed themselves into the large-scale, impersonal, bureaucratically ordered forms of social life typical of a modern nation-state. What was responsible for this transformation?

Status versus Contract Relationships

Sir Henry Maine, an English jurist who studied the roots of Roman law, described the shift as one from status to contract. In ancient societies organized on the basis of **status**, people's relationships with one another were specified by the particular position, or status, that each held within the group. Each status carried with it a bundle of rights and duties, which modern social scientists, using a theatrical metaphor, call a **role.** Statuses (and the roles attached to them) complemented one another: Holders of each status were responsible for particular tasks and could rely on other members of the system to perform different tasks. Ideally, the multiple statuses of the society fit together like pieces of a puzzle, ensuring that all tasks needed for group survival were carried out in an orderly fashion.

Societies organized on the basis of kinship were the prototype of status-based societies. For Maine, the crucial feature of status-based social organization was that people were not free to choose their own statuses, nor could they modify the rights and responsibilities associated with those statuses. Status-based societies contrasted in four major ways with societies organized on the basis of contract, such as modern nation-states. First, at least ideally, the parties to contractual relationships enter into them freely. Second, the contracting parties are equally free to specify the rights and obligations between them for the duration of the contract. Third, the range of possible statuses and roles is limitless, bound only by the imagination and interests of the contracting parties. Finally, once the terms of the contract are met, the parties may choose to terminate their relationship with one another. This would be impossible in a society based exclusively on status.

Mechanical versus Organic Solidarity

French social thinker Emile Durkheim described the shift in terms of the social bonds that held societies to-

gether. For Durkheim, "primitive" societies (ancient and contemporary) were held together on the basis of **mechanical solidarity.** In this view, "primitive" societies assigned the same social tasks to everybody who occupied the same kinship status. This meant that every kinship group—indeed, every family—could carry out the full range of tasks needed for survival. As a result, social solidarity, keeping kin groups together as parts of a larger whole, was problematic. Nothing bound these groups together except "mechanical" similarities in language, mode of livelihood, and so on. Mechanical solidarity, therefore, was brittle. Groups could split off and go their own way without seriously affecting their ability to survive.

"Modern" societies, according to Durkheim, were held together by **organic solidarity,** which was quite different from mechanical solidarity. "Modern" societies were still composed of groups, but each group specialized in a particular task needed for the survival of the larger whole. That is, organic solidarity depended on a highly developed **division of labor.** In societies with mechanical solidarity, the division of labor was limited to the division of kinship roles within each kinship group. Usually, this division was minimal, limited to task specializations based on age and sex. Each kinship group contained the full range of roles necessary to carry out subsistence activities without depending on outsiders. In societies with organic solidarity, however, the division of labor was much more elaborate. Some people specialized in food production, others in trade, others in government, and others in religion. Full-time specialization meant that each group had to depend on other groups to provide it with things it could not provide for itself. Very large societies could be held together on the basis of organic solidarity. Like the separate organs of a living creature, each specialized group had to perform its special tasks if society as a whole were to survive. If any one specialized group were to disappear, the society as a whole would suffer.

Both Maine and Durkheim were asking a question that social thinkers like Hobbes would have understood: What is the social glue that ensures social cooperation? In his 1968 study of North American kinship, anthropologist David Schneider argued that the social glue created by kinship was the feeling of "enduring diffuse solidarity." In many cases, however, human beings seek to establish enduring diffuse solidarity with a wide range of other people who are not formally recognized as kin. Sociologist Zygmunt Bauman argues, in fact, that "All supra-individual groupings are first and foremost processes of collectivization of friends and enemies. . . . More exactly, individuals sharing a common group or category of enemies treat each other as friends" (1990, 152). While a common enemy surely has the effect of drawing people together, however, it is rarely sufficient by itself to produce solidarity that endures.

People in all societies have developed patterned social relationships that aim to bind them together for the long term. In Chapter 11, for example, we discussed the name relationship among the Ju/'hoansi (!Kung) and the Latin American Catholic ritual of co-parenthood, or compadrazgo. What is the status of the people linked through such arrangements? They are not formal kin because they do not fit the prototypes of the formal kinship system, yet they treat one another according to roles associated with the formal kinship system, so they are not nonkin either. Moreover, they often use a kinship idiom to refer to each other and to the expectations each has concerning the other's behavior. Ritual coparents refer to themselves as co-parents (compadres). Members of Catholic monastic orders, who may neither marry nor bear children, nevertheless refer to one another as brother, sister, father, and mother. They also take as the prototype for these interpersonal relationships the formal role obligations of family members.

The plausibility of such extensions of kinship ultimately rests in the fact that the formal kinship system is itself arbitrary. That is, only some of the many links between people are recognized in formal kinship systems, while others are discounted. Changed historical circumstances, however, often draw people's attention to shared aspects of their lives that the formal kinship system ignores or create new common experiences that offer raw material for the invention of new forms of common identity. In this sense, all supra-individual communities are "imagined communities" (Anderson 1983). Although Benedict Anderson devised the term "imagined community" to refer to modern nation-states, he notes that "all communities larger than primordial villages of face-to-face contact (and perhaps even these) are imagined" (1983, 6). This is because the ties that bind such communities are not only the by-product of shared habitual practices, but also the result of symbolic images of common identity promulgated by group members with an interest in making this imagined identity endure.

Nations and nationalism are an important focus of contemporary cultural anthropology, and we will treat them in the following chapter. Here, however, we will consider some other important forms of imagined community that reach beyond the face-to-face relationships organized by kinship. For many people, the bonds of kinship are the prototype of enduring diffuse solidarity. Not surprisingly, nonkin organizations that seek to establish this solidarity among their members often make use of a kinship idiom.

REACHING BEYOND KINSHIP

Friendship

For anthropologist Robert Brain, institutions such as compadrazgo are cases of *institutionalized friendship*. Brain cites a dictionary definition of *friend* as "one joined to another in intimacy and mutual benevolence independent of sexual or family love" (1976, 15). He quickly points out that the Western belief that friendship and kinship are separate phenomena often breaks down in practice. Today, for example, some husbands and wives in Western societies consider each other "best friends." Similarly, we may become friends with some of our relatives while treating others the same way we treat nonrelatives. Presumably, we can be friends with people over and above any kinship ties we might have with them. Thus, *friendship* can be defined as love that is free of bias or self-interest, as "emotional and disinterested love" (28).

---

status A particular social position in a group.
role The rights and duties associated with a status.
mechanical solidarity According to Durkheim, the sense of fellow feeling and interdependence in so-called primitive societies, based on such similarities as language and mode of livelihood.
organic solidarity According to Durkheim, the sense of fellow feeling and interdependence in so-called modern societies, based on specializations of different social groups; like the organs in a body, contributions from each group are necessary for the survival of the society.
division of labor Work specialization within a society based on membership in a given group. The most basic human divisions of labor are by sex and age.

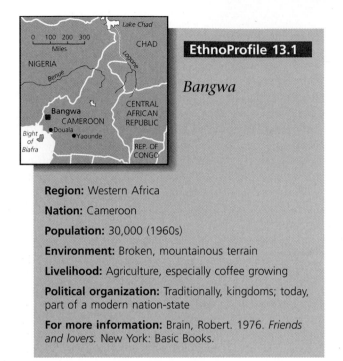

EthnoProfile 13.1

Bangwa

Region: Western Africa

Nation: Cameroon

Population: 30,000 (1960s)

Environment: Broken, mountainous terrain

Livelihood: Agriculture, especially coffee growing

Political organization: Traditionally, kingdoms; today, part of a modern nation-state

For more information: Brain, Robert. 1976. *Friends and lovers.* New York: Basic Books.

BANGWA FRIENDSHIP   How do societies bring strangers together in mutual benevolence? Brain notes that people in many non-Western societies are far less haphazard about this than are Westerners. The Bangwa of Cameroon, among whom Brain did fieldwork, seal friendships with a ritual similar to that of marriage. (See EthnoProfile 13.1: Bangwa.) But the obligations of friendship are not the same as the obligations of kinship that derive from marriage. Friendship limits the risks that follow from close relationships with consanguineal kin.

> The Bangwa spoke of ideal friendship as one of equality and complete reciprocity, backed by moral, rather than supernatural and legal sanctions. He is my friend "because he is beautiful," "because he is good." Although there is in fact a good deal of ceremonial courtesy and gift exchange it is seen as a relationship of disinterested affection. Youths who are friends spend long hours in each other's company, holding hands when they walk together in the market. As they grow older friendships become increasingly valued—elders have little else to do but sit around with their friends, chatting about local politics, disputes over land boundaries, trouble with an obstreperous young wife. . . . Friendship is valued far above kinship; between kin

there are niggling debts and witchcraft fears. Friendship lasts till death; kinship is brittle and involves inequalities of age and wealth and status. Friendship alone can cancel these out. A chief born on the same day as a slave automatically becomes his "best friend" and is bound to treat him in a friendly manner, at least in some contexts. The son who succeeds to a chief's position depends on the friends he made as a child—not his kin—in the crooked corridors of palace politics. (Brain 1976, 35)

Brain recognizes that certain relationships among formal kin may be viewed as prototypes of friendship in some societies. Even for the Bangwa, twins are ideal best friends, and other groups, such as the Kuma of New Guinea, see brothers-in-law as best friends. But friendship can also be seen as a nonkin link that can correct the defects and limitations of formal kinship. If this is assumed, then all social structures above and beyond the boundaries of formal kinship may be viewed as kinds of institutionalized friendship.

AMERICAN COLLEGE STUDENT FRIENDSHIP AND FRIENDLINESS   Between 1977 and 1987, anthropologist Michael Moffatt studied student culture at Rutgers University in New Jersey, where he teaches. Friendship was a central cultural feature for the American college students he knew in the 1980s. Friends were the only freely chosen companions of equal status in their lives; all other social connections—family, religion, work, race, ethnicity—were imposed on the self from the outside. Friends were those with whom you shared "who you really were," your authentic self. But proof of friendship was invisible, which was troubling to the students: "You and I are true friends if and only if both of us consider the other to be a true friend 'in our hearts,' and I am never entirely certain about what you really feel in your heart" (1989, 43). As a result, students spent hours thinking about and discussing the authenticity of their own friendships and those of other people they knew well. Not everyone, of course, could be a friend, but Moffatt found that the students he knew believed that normal Americans should be ready under certain circumstances to extend "real" friendship to any other person. To be otherwise is to be "snobbish," or to "think you are better than other people."

This attitude reflects what Moffatt sees as a central value of American daily life: friendliness. To act "friendly" is "to give regular abbreviated performances of the standard behaviors of real friendship—to look pleased and happy when you meet someone, to put on the all-American friendly smile, to acknowledge the person you are meeting by name (preferably by the first name, shortened version), to make casual body contact, to greet the person with one of the two or three conventional queries about the state of their 'whole self' ('How are you?' 'How's it goin'?' 'What's new?')" (1989, 43–44). Moffatt observed that students were friendly to anyone they had met more than once or twice. This was even more strongly required among students who knew one another personally. "To violate 'friendly' in an apparently deliberate way was to arouse some of the strongest sentiments of distrust and dislike in Rutgers student culture" (1989, 43–44).

Kinship in Nonkin Relationships

The ambiguity between kin and nonkin remains. For the Bangwa, the closest kin—twins—are the best of friends. In many societies, however, kin are not trusted, and friends must be sought outside the kinship group. Nonkin patterns of social relations do not follow the rules of recruitment or enforce the traditional status distinctions and role obligations that are at the heart of kinship. And yet those involved in such nonkin social relations often use a kinship idiom to refer to each other, and to evaluate each other's behavior. Ritual coparents refer to themselves as coparents (*compadres*). They also take as the prototype for these interpersonal relationships the formal role obligations of family members.

Anthropologist David Schneider (1968) argued that the prototypical emotion of kinship is the feeling of "enduring diffuse solidarity." But this definition might just as well apply to friendship, as we discussed it earlier. Perhaps enduring diffuse solidarity is something that human beings regularly seek to establish in their relations with other people—kin or not. The institution of kinship is one traditional means for cultivating such a sentiment. But so are the institutionalized friendships among the Bangwa. Indeed, all customary patterns of human interaction involve enduring diffuse solidarity. As we saw in earlier chapters on kinship and marriage, this is true even for relationships characterized by respect and avoidance or by joking and license. In both cases, the individuals or groups who must avoid one another or joke with one another are people whose co-

operation is essential to orderly social life. Order is preserved if people avoid confrontations with others who might disagree with them. But if it is agreed neither party may take offense at anything that is said or done, then order can be maintained by encouraging such confrontations. "Joking relatives," in particular, are ordinarily said to be the best of friends.

We now turn to some important forms of nonkin social relations. Not surprisingly, nonkin organizations in non-Western societies are often described by their members using a kinship idiom.

SODALITIES

Many societies of foragers, farmers, and herders have developed what anthropologist Elman Service called *pantribal sodalities* (1962, 113). **Sodalities** are "special-purpose groupings" that may be organized on the basis of age, sex, economic role, and personal interest. "[Sodalities] serve very different functions—among them police, military, medical, initiation, religious [Figure 13.2], and recreation. Some sodalities conduct their business in secret, others in public. Membership may be ascribed or it may be obtained via inheritance, purchase, attainment, performance, or contract. Men's sodalities are more numerous and highly organized than women's and, generally, are also more secretive and seclusive in their activities" (Hunter and Whitten 1976, 362). Sodalities create enduring diffuse solidarity among members of a large society, in part because they draw their personnel from a number of "primary" forms of social organization, such as lineages.

Cheyenne Military Societies

Sodalities are not limited to farmers and herders, as shown by the Cheyenne military societies. (See Ethno-Profile 13.2: Cheyenne [c. 1830].) Toward the middle of the nineteenth century, the Cheyenne people of the Great Plains of North America were a foraging people whose main source of meat was the buffalo. They traced descent bilaterally and organized themselves into a

---

sodalities Nonkin forms of social organization; special-purpose groupings that may be organized on the basis of age, sex, economic role, and personal interest.

FIGURE 13.2 The president of the Oruru Devil Fraternity (Bolivia), a sodality organized in honor of the Virgin of Socavon, wears the costume associated with his office, crowned by the devil mask.

number of kindreds. During the winter months, the Cheyenne lived in bands composed of several kindreds. During the summer months, everyone camped together in order to perform important rituals, including the Arrow Renewal and the Sun Dance. Cheyenne identity also rested in the council of 44 peace chiefs, in whom lay supreme authority for the people as a whole.

The Cheyenne had several sodalities whose membership cut across kindreds and bands (Figure 13.3). There were sodalities for women and men, but those for men were more numerous and their organization more complex. The most important of these were the seven military societies. According to E. Adamson Hoebel, Cheyenne military societies "centered on the common experience of the warriors, with rituals glorifying and enhancing that experience, and with duties and services performed on behalf of the community at large" (1960, 33). All seven societies had equal status. A Cheyenne boy who was ready to go to war could join any society he chose and become a full-fledged member immediately. Membership was usually for life. Each society had four leaders, two of whom were war chiefs and two of whom were considered "the bravest men in the society." In addition, each society had ritual paraphernalia, dress, dances, and songs that distinguished it from the other societies.

The military societies were charged with maintaining order during public ceremonies and during the communal buffalo hunt. They were also responsible for carrying out legal decisions of the council of chiefs, such as banishment of murderers from the community. The Cheyenne believed that any member of their community who killed another member began to rot internally and that the stench drove the buffalo away; the expulsion of murderers rid the community of this pollution. The system also prevented feuds between bands and kindreds because any retaliatory killing would only worsen the pollution and undermine the survival of the community as a whole.

The Cheyenne military societies were nonkin voluntary associations that cut across kinship groups. They were dedicated to glorifying and perpetuating the

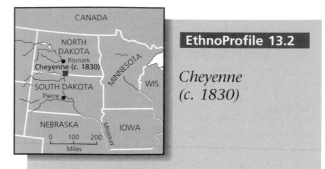

EthnoProfile 13.2

Cheyenne (c. 1830)

Region: North America

Nation: United States (northern Colorado and southeastern Wyoming)

Population: 3,500

Environment: Plains

Livelihood: Originally horticulture, later mounted nomadism

Political organization: Tribal council in the 1800s

For more information: Hoebel, E. Adamson. 1960. *The Cheyennes.* New York: Holt, Rinehart and Winston.

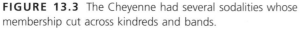

FIGURE 13.3 The Cheyenne had several sodalities whose membership cut across kindreds and bands.

successes of fighting men. And yet they were not totally free of the influence of women and the idiom of
kinship. A mythological female figure, Sweet Medicine,
was believed to have given the Cheyenne the idea of
military societies, together with their rituals. Five of the
sodalities invited four virgin daughters of chiefs "to
participate in their ceremonies and to sit in the midst
of the circle of war chiefs when they meet in common
council." These young girls were similar to mascots.
They represented the sodality as a whole, and its warriors would be successful in battle only as long as these
young women remained chaste. "All the members of a
society call their four maids by the kin term 'sister,' and
they may never marry one of their own maidens"
(Hoebel 1960, 33–34).

Age Sets

All societies recognize in some way that people pass
through stages as they grow from infancy to maturity
to old age. Generational differences are marked in every
kinship system. But some groups emphasize generational
distinctions to an unusual degree and use them as the
basis for forming sodalities. Although age distinctions
were not marked in the Cheyenne military sodalities,
the situation is different in eastern Africa. A number of
societies there assign men from different kinship groups
to sodalities defined in terms of relative age.

Age sets are composed of young men born within
a specific time span (five years, for example). Each age
set is "one unit in a sequence of similar units" that succeed each other in time as their members pass through
youth, maturity, and old age. "Sets are part of the formal social order blessed by tradition and membership
is usually ascribed, and is always obligatory" (Baxter
and Almagor 1978, 4). Age-set systems for women are
not found in these societies. P. T. W. Baxter and Uri Almagor suggest that this may be because women are involved in domestic matters from an early age and
marry shortly after puberty (11).

Age-set systems are like kinship systems in that
they assign people membership in groups on the basis
of generation and age. But age-set systems are built on
two additional assumptions: that generations of fathers
and sons will succeed one another regularly and that
the succession will follow a uniform timetable. Unfortunately, experience belies both assumptions. Members
of age-set systems must continually work to reconcile

age, generation, and the passage of time. "Age systems
which are based on measured units of time are unsuc-
cessful attempts to tame time by chopping it up into
manageable slices" (Baxter and Almagor 1978, 5).

THE EASTERN AFRICAN AGE-SET SYSTEM The classic study of eastern African age sets was by Monica
Wilson (1951), who examined their role among the
Nyakyusa. (See EthnoProfile 13.3: Nyakyusa.) At the
time of Wilson's fieldwork, the Nyakyusa were patrilineal and patrilocal. Their society was divided into
many independent chiefdoms. Nyakyusa age sets initially included a group of boys from about 10 to 15
years old. When the members of this junior set were
about 33 to 35 years old, an elaborate series of rituals
was held to mark their "coming out." At that time, the
reigning senior generation "handed the country over
to them." At any point in time, there were three strata
in the Nyakyusa age system: retired elders, active senior men who carried political and military responsibilities for the entire society, and immature juniors.

In precolonial times, members of junior eastern
African age sets were as flashy as members of Cheyenne
military societies. Each set had distinctive dress and
titles and exhibited flamboyant behavior. According
to Baxter and Almagor, however, it was unusual for junior age sets to take on political or military roles, even
though they most often are found in societies with no
central authority. Baxter and Almagor argue that the
colorful activities of junior sets should not distract observers from recognizing that the seniors run things. If
junior sets act, they usually act as agents of seniors.
Indeed, the wildness of junior sets is conventional in
many societies with age systems. Although this custom
allows juniors to enjoy themselves, it also publicly re-
inforces traditional wisdom that places power and property in the hands of elders.

FOSTERING SOLIDARITY WITH AGE SETS Age-set
systems foster a sense of enduring diffuse solidarity
among their members. This is especially so if membership in a set comes after a rigorous initiation ritual.
That age-mates are supposed to be the best of friends
is illustrated by the widespread rule that forbids age-
mates to accuse one another of adultery and demand
compensation. This means, in practice, that a married
man cannot prevent sexual relationships that might
develop between his wife and his age-mates. This leads

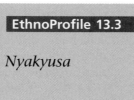

EthnoProfile 13.3

Nyakyusa

Region: Eastern Africa

Nation: Tanzania

Population: 160,000 (1930s)

Environment: Well-watered, fertile valley

Livelihood: Agriculture, especially bananas and millet, and stock raising

Political organization: Traditionally, small chiefdoms; today, part of a modern nation-state

For more information: Wilson, Monica. 1951. *Good company.* Oxford: Oxford University Press.

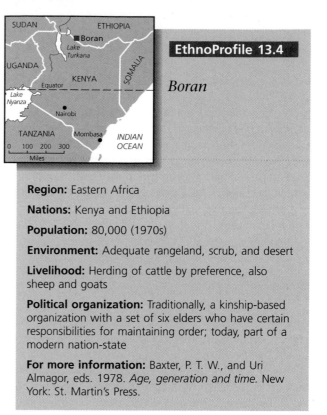

EthnoProfile 13.4

Boran

Region: Eastern Africa

Nations: Kenya and Ethiopia

Population: 80,000 (1970s)

Environment: Adequate rangeland, scrub, and desert

Livelihood: Herding of cattle by preference, also sheep and goats

Political organization: Traditionally, a kinship-based organization with a set of six elders who have certain responsibilities for maintaining order; today, part of a modern nation-state

For more information: Baxter, P. T. W., and Uri Almagor, eds. 1978. *Age, generation and time.* New York: St. Martin's Press.

to a relationship among age-mates similar to that of "joking kin," who are forbidden to take offense at anything they say or do to each other. Here, the refusal to recognize adultery is institutionalized. It emphasizes that nothing, especially not sexual jealousy, must come between age-mates. The rule appears most onerous for the first members of junior sets who marry. Members of senior sets usually all have wives of their own (Baxter and Almagor 1978, 17).

Nyakyusa age sets were able to cultivate an unusual degree of solidarity among their members because each set was required to live in its own village. Indeed, the Nyakyusa believed that the main purpose of age villages was to allow set members to enjoy *ukwangala,* "good company"—the company of friends and equals. Wilson wrote that to attain ukwangala, "men must build not only in villages, rather than in scattered homesteads, but also with contemporaries rather than with kin, since there can be no free and easy intercourse and sharing of food and beer between fathers and sons. Ukwangala implies eating and drinking together frequently and cannot be fully enjoyed by people who do not live close to one another" (1951, 163).

FUNCTIONS OF AGE-SET SYSTEMS Age-set systems may play an important cognitive role in the societies where they are found. For example, Baxter argues that the *gada* age-set system of the Boran of Kenya and Ethiopia provides the idiom the Boran use to describe and debate social and political life. (See EthnoProfile 13.4: Boran.) The complex gada system recognizes five generation sets that succeed one another over a period of 40 years. Every 8 years, a new generation set is formed and the oldest set retires. The retirement of the most senior set is marked by an elaborate culmination ceremony called the *gaadamoji.* "The set organisation is said to be there to ensure that these ceremonies are held. From another point of view the organisation generates a set of men every eight years who, for their own ritual needs, require the opportunity, as they enter the

---

age sets Nonkin forms of social organization composed of young men born within a specified time span, which are part of a sequence of age sets that proceeds through maturity and old age.

condition of *gaadamoji,* to undergo the culmination ceremony" (Baxter 1978, 160).

Other explanations for age-set systems have been offered. Monica Wilson suggested that Nyakyusa age villages played an important role in controlling sexual behavior. Wilson noted that the Nyakyusa themselves argued that young men had to live apart from their fathers to prevent incest between the son's wife and his father. The same arrangement also prevented sexual involvements between a son and his father's wives. Such involvement was a real risk because a son traditionally inherited his father's wives (excluding his own mother) when his father died.

For Baxter, Boran discussions of gada reveal it to be a conceptual system that guides them in political and social matters. But Baxter rejects the suggestion that the gada system ever played a political role in Boran society. "Gada exists primarily . . . the folk view as well as in mine, to ensure the well-being of the Boran and to regulate the ritual growth and development of individuals and to do so in such a way as to permit all men who survive life's full span to achieve responsible and joyful sanctity. It is this last, joyful aspect of *gada* as an institution which performs rituals that has struck intelligent nonprofessional observers . . . and not its political ones" (1978, 156).

Secret Societies in Western Africa

Several neighboring peoples in western Africa use **secret societies** as a way of drawing members of different kinship groups into crosscutting associations. The most famous secret societies are the Poro and Sande, which are found among the Mende, Sherbro, Kpelle, and other neighboring peoples of Sierra Leone, Ivory Coast, Liberia, and Guinea.

MEMBERSHIP AND INITIATION   Poro is a secret society for men; Sande, a secret society for women. Poro is responsible for initiating young men into social manhood; Sande, for initiating young women into social womanhood. These sodalities are secret in the sense that members of each have certain knowledge that can be revealed only to initiated members. Both sodalities are hierarchically organized. The higher a person's status within the sodality, the greater the secret knowledge revealed.

Poro and Sande are responsible for supervising and regulating the sexual, social, and political conduct of all members of the wider society. To carry out this responsibility, high-status sodality members impersonate important supernatural figures by donning masks and performing in public. One secret kept from the uninitiated is that these masked figures are not the spirits themselves.

Membership is automatic on initiation, and all men and women are ordinarily initiated. "Until he has been initiated in the society, no Mende man is considered mature enough to have sexual intercourse or to marry" (Little 1967, 245). (See EthnoProfile 12.5: Mende.) Each community has its own local Poro and Sande congregations, and a person initiated in one community is eligible to participate in the congregations of other communities. Initiates must pay a fee for initiation, and if they wish to receive advanced training and progress to higher levels within the sodality, they must pay additional fees. In any community where Poro and Sande are strong, authority in society is divided between a sodality of mature women and one of mature men. Together, they work to keep society on the correct path. Indeed, the relationship between men and women in societies with Poro and Sande tends to be highly egalitarian.

Anthropologist Beryl Bellman (1984) was initiated into a Poro chapter among the Kpelle of Liberia. (See EthnoProfile 6.5: Kpelle.) He describes initiation as a ritual process that takes place about every 16 to 18 years, about once each generation. One of the Poro's forest spirits, or "devils," metaphorically captures and eats the novices—only for them later to be metaphorically reborn from the womb of the devil's "wife." Marks incised on the necks, chests, and backs of initiates represent the "devil's teeth marks." After this scarification, initiates spend a year living apart from women in a special village constructed for them in the forest. During this period, they carry out various activities under the strict supervision of senior Poro members. Female Sande initiates undergo a similar experience during their year of initiation, which normally takes place several years after the Poro initiation has been completed.

USE OF THE KINSHIP IDIOM   In Kpelle society, the relationship between a mother's brother (*ngala*) and a sister's son (*maling*) describes the formal relationship between kin. There is also a metaphoric aspect to this connection that is used to describe relationships between patrilineages, sections of a town, and towns themselves. "Besides the serious or formal rights and obligations between *ngala* and *maling*, other aspects of the relationship are expressed as joking behavior between kinsmen. . . . The *ngala-maling* relationship is also the basis of labor recruitment, financial assistance, and a general support network" (Bellman 1984, 22–23). This kinship idiom is used within the Poro society to describe the relationships between certain members. For example, two important Poro officials involved in initiation are the *Zo* and the *kwelebah*. The Zo directs the ritual, and the kwelebah announces both the ritual death and the ritual rebirth of the initiates to the community at large. The Zo is said to be the ngala of the kwelebah, and the kwelebah is said to be the maling of the Zo.

THE THOMA SECRET SOCIETY: A MICROCOSM Anthropologist Carol MacCormack (1980) studied secret societies among the Sherbro. (See EthnoProfile 13.5: Sherbro.) In addition to Poro and Sande congregations, the Sherbro have a third secret society called *Thoma,* which initiates both men and women. Members of one society cannot be initiated into the others, and families with several children usually try to initiate at least one child into each.

MacCormack writes: "With Poro and Sande, the contrastive gender categories are split apart and the uniqueness of each gender is emphasized, but always with the final view that the complementarity of the two constitute human society, the full cultural unity. Thoma is a microcosm of the whole. Its local congregations or chapters are headed by a man and a woman, co-equal leaders who are 'husband and wife' in a ritual context but are not married in mundane life" (1980, 97). The Sherbro are concerned with the reproduction of their society. *Reproduction* here means not just production of children but also continuation of the division of labor between men and women. The Sherbro say that the ritual function of the Thoma sodality is to "wash the bush"—that is, "to cleanse the land and the village from evil and restore its fertility and well-being" (98).

The purpose of Thoma initiation is to transform uninitiated, protosocial beings into initiated, fully social, adult human beings. The Thoma society has four masks representing two pairs of spirits: an animal pair and a humanoid pair. The masks, which are considered

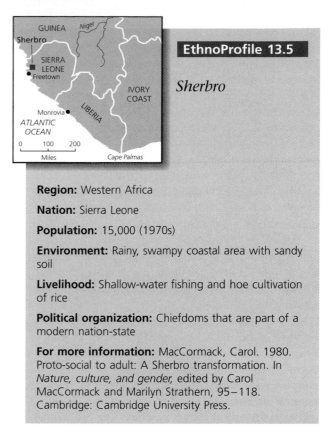

EthnoProfile 13.5

Sherbro

Region: Western Africa

Nation: Sierra Leone

Population: 15,000 (1970s)

Environment: Rainy, swampy coastal area with sandy soil

Livelihood: Shallow-water fishing and hoe cultivation of rice

Political organization: Chiefdoms that are part of a modern nation-state

For more information: MacCormack, Carol. 1980. Proto-social to adult: A Sherbro transformation. In *Nature, culture, and gender,* edited by Carol MacCormack and Marilyn Strathern, 95–118. Cambridge: Cambridge University Press.

very powerful, appear when initiates are nearing the end of their ritual seclusion in the forest. They "symbolize that 'wild,' unsocialized children are being transformed into cultured adults, but will retain the fertile vigour of the animal world" (MacCormack 1980, 100). The humanoid masks represent male and female ancestral spirits who appear when the initiates are about to be reborn into their new, adult status. "Human beings must abide by ancestral rules of conduct if they are to be healthy and fertile. Indeed, they wish to be as healthy and strong as forest animals which give birth in litters. Only by becoming fully 'cultural,' vowing to live by ancestral laws, may they hope to avoid illness and barrenness" (116).

THE MEANING OF SECRECY IN A SECRET SOCIETY Bellman was interested in the secrecy that surrounded

secret societies Nonkin forms of social organization that initiate young men or women into social adulthood. The secrecy concerns certain knowledge that is known only to initiated members.

membership in Poro and other similar sodalities. He argued that Poro (and Sande) initiation rituals are primarily concerned with teaching initiates how to keep a secret. Discretion—knowing when, how, and even whether to speak about various topics—is a prized virtue among the Kpelle and is required of all mature members of their society. So learning how to "practice secrecy" is a central lesson of initiation. "It was always crucial for members to be certain whether they have the right to talk as well as the right to know. The two are not necessarily related. Nonmembers very often know some of the secrets of membership; yet they must maintain a description of the event comparable to that of nonmembers" (1984, 51).

Based on this interpretation of "secrecy" in the secret society he knew, Bellman analyzed what the secret societies meant to outsiders. What do the uninitiated actually believe about these societies? In the case of the Poro, the women speak of devils killing and eating novices as though they believe this to be literally true. Bellman and his informants believe that the women know perfectly well what is "really" happening when Poro novices are taken away into the forest. But women are not allowed to talk about what they know except in the language of ritual metaphor. In the context of the initiation ritual, participation of the "audience" of women and other noninitiates is as important as the participation of the Poro elders and the initiates themselves. In playing their appropriate ritual role, women show respect for traditional understandings concerning which members of society have the right to speak about which topics in which manner and under which circumstances. "The enactment of Poro rituals serves to establish the ways in which that concealed information is communicated. . . . It offers methods for mentioning the unmentionable" (1984, 141).

NONKIN TIES IN STRATIFIED SOCIETIES

Sodalities are most common in **egalitarian societies;** that is, societies where there is no central chief or king who rules over the entire group. People in these societies may gain the esteem of their fellows. Men might even have substantial support groups of wives, children, and retainers. But their status depends entirely on their own personal prowess. They cannot transform what they have achieved into permanent superiority of wealth, power, or prestige.

Permanent hierarchies do exist in other societies. Stratification may be minimal, as in *chiefdoms,* where perhaps only the office of chief is a permanently superior status. Privileges accrue to those who are closely related to the chief, while other members of the society must settle for less. In fully **stratified societies**, by contrast, some members of the society have permanent, privileged access to wealth, power, and prestige, and this privileged access may be inherited.

The stratified society, which can be much larger than tribes or chiefdoms, may be internally divided into a number of groups with their relative status carefully specified. In **caste** societies, membership in each ranked group is closed, and individuals are not allowed to move from one group to another. For anthropologists, India is the prototypical caste society (Figure 13.4). **Class** societies also have internally ranked subgroups, but these groups are open, and individuals can move upward or downward from one class to another. Modern Europe and the United States are classic examples of class societies.

Criteria for Membership in Levels of Society

In stratified societies, different criteria may be used to place people in one or another stratum. Karl Marx argued, for example, that class membership in capitalist society is determined by the relationship people have to the means of production: whether or not they own the tools and raw materials needed for industry. Capitalists who own the means of production make up the ruling class; those who work for capitalists for wages but do not own the means of production make up the proletariat, or subject class. Marx's view of class is clearly different from the view common in the United States, which equates class membership with income. Other criteria can also be important in assigning membership to the various levels in a stratified society. Occupational specialization, one such criterion, appears to be central to caste systems. **Race** and **ethnicity** involve other criteria that are based on biology or culture or both. These may complicate or contradict stratification based on other principles.

The various levels of a stratified society do not in themselves provide ties that link nonkin to one another. The key to social solidarity in stratified societies

FIGURE 13.4 Women like this street sweeper, whose occupations are characterized as polluting, are ranked at the bottom of Hindu caste society.

is the nature of the relationships uniting the levels. Again, in the marxian view of class, the links between capitalists and proletarians are purely economic; both classes must cooperate to produce goods. Their relationship is sealed by the transfer of money, either as wages to workers or as payment for goods. In caste societies, where each caste specializes in one kind of work, money is traditionally less important. Instead, members of different castes are urged to continue to perform their appropriate tasks by a political system that justifies the division of labor in terms of religious doctrines reinforced by strict ritual prohibitions.

Economic or political links between different levels of a stratified society involve groups as wholes. In many of the stratified societies studied by anthropologists, however, levels are also linked by the institution of **clientage.** According to M. G. Smith, clientage "designates a variety of relationships, which all have inequality of status of the associated persons as a common characteristic" ([1954] 1981, 31). It is a relationship between individuals rather than groups. The party of superior status is the patron, and the party of inferior status is the client. For example, clientage is characteristic of compadrazgo relationships, especially when the ritual parents are of higher social status than the biological parents. In fact, the Latin American societies in which compadrazgo flourishes are class societies, and parents often seek social superiors as compadres.

Stratified societies united by links of clientage can be very stable. Often the stratified order is believed to be natural and not questioned. Those of low status believe their security depends on finding someone in a high-status group who can protect them. Clientage links individuals, yet the clients may be unaware that they belong to a group of people who are all similarly underprivileged. In marxian terms, they lack class consciousness. In other stratified societies, underprivileged groups do have a common sense of identity. Sometimes they even have organizations of their own, such as trade unions, that defend their interests in dealings with outsiders. This is also often the case for groups whose memberships depend on race or ethnicity.

Caste Societies

The word *caste* comes from the Portuguese word *casta*, meaning "chaste." Portuguese explorers applied it to the stratification system they encountered in India in the fifteenth century. Each group in society had to remain sexually pure, or chaste: Both sexual and marital links between groups were forbidden. Ever since, the stratification system of India has been taken as the prototype of caste stratification. Some scholars have even argued that caste cannot properly be said to exist

---

egalitarian societies Societies in which no great differences in wealth, power, or prestige divide members from one another.

stratified societies Societies in which there is a permanent hierarchy that accords some members privileged access to wealth, power, and prestige.

caste A ranked group within a hierarchically stratified society that is closed, prohibiting individuals to move from one caste to another.

class A ranked group within a hierarchically stratified society that is open, allowing individuals to move upward or downward from one class to another.

race A social grouping based on perceived physical differences and cloaked in the language of biology.

ethnicity A set of prototypically descent-based cultural criteria that people in a group are believed to share.

clientage The institution linking individuals from upper and lower levels in a stratified society.

outside India. If we take the Indian system as a proto-type, however, we may apply the term *caste* to systems of social stratification that bear a family resemblance. One important non-Indian example, which we examine later in this chapter, comes from Nigeria.

CASTE IN INDIA The word *casta* (*caste*) is the word Portuguese explorers used to translate the Hindi word *jati*. Villagers in the southern Indian town of Gopalpur defined a *jati* for anthropologist Alan Beals. (See Ethno-Profile 13.6: Gopalpur.) They said it was "a category of men thought to be related, to occupy a particular position within a hierarchy of jatis, to marry among themselves, and to follow particular practices and occupations" (Beals 1962, 25). Beals's informants compared the relationship between jatis of different rank to the relationship between brothers. Members of low-ranking jatis respect and obey members of high-ranking jatis just as younger brothers respect and obey older brothers.

Villagers in Gopalpur were aware of at least 50 different jatis, although not all were represented in the village. Because jatis have different occupational specialties that they alone can perform, villagers are sometimes dependent on the services of outsiders. For example, there was no member of the Washerman jati in Gopalpur. As a result, a member of that jati from another village had to be employed when people in Gopalpur wanted their clothes cleaned ritually or required clean cloth for ceremonies.

Jatis are distinguished in terms of the foods they eat as well as their traditional occupations. These features have a ritual significance that affects interactions between members of different jatis. In Hindu belief, certain foods and occupations are classed as pure and others as polluting. In theory, all jatis are ranked on a scale from purest to most polluted. Ranked highest of all are the vegetarian Brahmins, who are pure enough to approach the gods. Carpenters and Blacksmiths, who also eat a vegetarian diet, are also assigned a high rank. Below the vegetarians are those who eat "clean," or "pure," meat. In Gopalpur, this group of jatis included Saltmakers, Farmers, and Shepherds, who eat sheep, goats, chicken, and fish but not pork or beef. The lowest-ranking jatis are "unclean" meat eaters, who include Stoneworkers and Basketweavers (who eat pork) and Leatherworkers (who eat pork and beef). Occupations that involve slaughtering animals or touch-

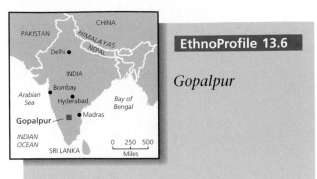

EthnoProfile 13.6

Gopalpur

Region: Southern Asia

Nation: India

Population: 540 (1960)

Environment: Center of a plain, some fertile farmland and pasture

Livelihood: Intensive millet farming, some cattle and sheep herding

Political organization: Caste system in a modern nation-state

For more information: Beals, Alan. 1962. *Gopalpur, a south Indian village*. New York: Holt, Rinehart and Winston.

ing polluted things are themselves polluting. Jatis that traditionally carry out such activities as butchering and washing dirty clothing are ranked below jatis whose traditional work does not involve polluting activities.

Hindu dietary rules deal not only with the kinds of food that may be eaten by different jatis but also with the circumstances in which members of one jati may accept food prepared by members of another. Members of a lower-ranking jati may accept any food prepared by members of a higher-ranking jati. Members of a higher-ranking jati may accept only certain foods prepared by a lower-ranking jati. In addition, members of different jatis should not eat together.

In practice, these rules are not as confining as they appear. In Gopalpur, " 'food' refers to particular kinds of food, principally rice. 'Eating together' means eating from the same dish or sitting on the same line. . . . Members of quite different jatis may eat together if they eat out of separate bowls and if they are facing each other or turned slightly away from each other" (Beals 1962, 41). Members of jatis that are close in rank and neither at the top nor at the bottom of the scale often share food and eat together on a daily basis. Strict observance of the rules is saved for ceremonial occasions.

The way in which non-Hindus have been incorporated into the jati system in Gopalpur illuminates the logic of the system. For example, Muslims have long ruled the region surrounding Gopalpur; thus, political power is a salient attribute of Muslim identity. In addition, Muslims do not eat pork or the meat of animals that have not been ritually slaughtered. These attributes, taken together, have led the villagers in Gopalpur to rank Muslims above the Stoneworkers and Basketweavers, who eat pork. All three groups are considered to be eaters of unclean meat because Muslims do eat beef.

There is no direct correlation between the status of a jati on the scale of purity and pollution and the economic status of members of that jati. Jati membership may be advantageous in some cases. Beals notes, for example, that the high status of Brahmins means that "there are a relatively large number of ways in which a poor Brahmin may become wealthy" (1962, 37). Similarly, members of low-status jatis may find their attempts to amass wealth curtailed by the opposition of their status superiors. In Gopalpur, a group of Farmers and Shepherds attacked a group of Stoneworkers who had purchased good rice land in the village. Those Stoneworkers were eventually forced to buy inferior land elsewhere in the village. In general, however, regardless of caste, a person who wishes to advance economically "must be prepared to defend his gains against jealous neighbors. Anyone who buys land is limiting his neighbor's opportunities to buy land. Most people safeguard themselves by tying themselves through indebtedness to a powerful landlord who will give them support when difficulties are encountered" (Beals 1962, 39).

Although the interdependence of jatis is explained in theory by their occupational specialties, the social reality is a bit different. For example, Saltmakers in Gopalpur are farmers and actually produce little salt, which can be bought in shops by those who need it. It is primarily in the context of ritual that jati interdependence is given full play. Recall that Gopalpur villagers require the services of a Washerman when they need *ritually* clean garments or cloth; otherwise, most villagers wash their own clothing. "To arrange a marriage, to set up the doorway of a new house, to stage a drama, or to hold an entertainment, the householder

must call on a wide range of jatis. The entertainment of even a modest number of guests requires the presence of the Singer. The Potter must provide new pots in which to cook the food; the Boin from the Farmer jati must carry the pot; the Shepherd must sacrifice the goat; the Crier, a Saltmaker, must invite the guests. To survive, one requires the cooperation of only a few jatis; to enjoy life and do things in the proper manner requires the cooperation of many" (Beals 1962, 41).

CASTE IN WESTERN AFRICA Anthropologists often use the term *caste* to describe societies outside India when they encounter one of two features: (1) endogamous occupational groupings whose members are looked down on by other groups in the society or (2) an endogamous ruling elite who set themselves above those over whom they rule. Both these features are present in Indian society. The problem is that, apart from these similarities, caste systems found outside the Indian subcontinent are very different indeed.

Anthropologist James Vaughan (1970; see also Tamari 1991) reviewed the data on western African caste systems. The first feature of non-Hindu castes noted above was common in societies of the Sahara and in the western Sudan (the band of territory between Senegal and Lake Chad that lies south of the Sahara and north of the coastal rain forest). Vaughan also found castes in a second culture area located in the mountain ranges that lie along the modern border between Nigeria and Cameroon. In this region, many societies had endogamous groups of "blacksmiths" whose status was distinct from that of other members of society. These people were not despised, however; if anything, they were regarded with awe or feared.

Vaughan studied such a caste of blacksmiths in a kingdom of the Marghi, whose traditional territory is in the mountains and nearby plains south of Lake Chad in present-day Nigeria. (See EthnoProfile 13.7: Marghi.) Members of the caste, who are called *ngkyagu*, are traditional craft specialists whose major occupation is the smithing of iron (Figure 13.5). They make a variety of iron tools for ordinary Marghi, the most important of which are the hoes used for farming. They also make weapons and iron ornaments of various kinds. They work leather, fashioning traditional items of apparel, leather-covered charms, and the slings in which infants are carried. They work wood, making beds and carving stools. They are barbers, incising traditional tribal markings on Marghi women, and are responsible in some Marghi kingdoms for shaving the head of a newly installed king. They are morticians, responsible for assisting in the preparation of a body for burial, digging the grave, and carrying the corpse from the compound to the grave. They are musicians, playing a distinctive drum played by no one else. Some are diviners and "doctors." And female caste members are the potters of Marghi society.

Vaughan stresses that although regular Marghi and ngkyagu both recognize that ngkyagu are different, in most ways the ngkyagu do not stand out from other Marghi. All the same, Marghi and ngkyagu do not intermarry and will not share the same food. In an interesting parallel to the Indian case described above, ngkyagu can drink beer brewed by Marghi women as long as they provide their own drinking vessel. Marghi, however, will not drink beer brewed by female ngkyagu.

When Marghi described the differences between themselves and ngkyagu to Vaughan, they said that caste members were "different" and "strange." In Vaughan's opinion, this has to do in large part with the fact that ngkyagu do not farm: "To be a Marghi means to be a farmer. . . . A person who does not farm cannot in the Marghi idiom be considered an altogether normal person" (1970, 71). By contrast, ngkyagu attribute the difference between themselves and other Marghi to the division of labor and point out that both groups depend on one another. Marghi do their own smelting, but they require ngkyagu to use their skills as smiths to turn the smelted ore into implements. Thus, Marghi rely on members of the caste for their farming tools, but ngkyagu rely on Marghi for food.

Vaughan suggests that this division of labor and interdependence is not only practical but also part of the Marghi worldview, revealed in the domains of politics and ritual. For example, a curious relationship links ngkyagu to Marghi kings. The most remarkable feature of this relationship is that Marghi kings traditionally take a female member of the caste as a bride, thereby violating the rule of endogamy. Recall the role a member of the caste plays during the investiture of a new king; it is even more common for ngkyagu to bury deceased Marghi kings seated on an iron stool, surrounded by charcoal, which is the way ngkyagu themselves are buried. In addition, of all Marghi clans, only the ngkyagu clans are exempt from participating in the choice of a new Marghi king. Indeed, traditionally they

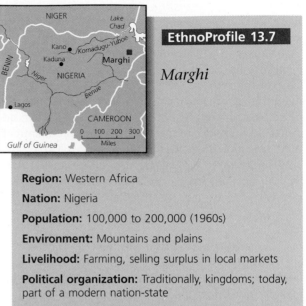

EthnoProfile 13.7

Marghi

Region: Western Africa

Nation: Nigeria

Population: 100,000 to 200,000 (1960s)

Environment: Mountains and plains

Livelihood: Farming, selling surplus in local markets

Political organization: Traditionally, kingdoms; today, part of a modern nation-state

For more information: Vaughan, James. 1970. Caste systems in the western Sudan. In *Social stratification in Africa*, edited by Arthur Tuden and Leonard Plotnikov, 59–92. New York: Free Press.

had their own "king," the *ptil ngkyagu,* who decided disputes among ngkyagu without recourse to the legal advisers of the Marghi king.

All this suggests that the two categories Marghi and ngkyagu form the foundation of Marghi society. They are mutually interdependent. The ritual prohibitions that divide them, however, suggest that this interdependence carries symbolic overtones. According to Vaughan, the caste system allows the Marghi to resolve a paradox. They are a society of farmers who need to support full-time toolmaking nonfarmers in order to farm. Marghi dislike being dependent on others, yet their way of life requires them to depend on ngkyagu. The ritual prohibitions that separate ngkyagu from other Marghi also seem designed to ensure that there will always be some caste specialists around to provide Marghi with the tools they cannot make themselves.

Class, Race, and Ethnicity

We now turn to the role of social class in human society, specifically as it relates to race and ethnicity. Recall that classes are levels in a socially stratified society

FIGURE 13.5 The Marghi *ngkyagu* are traditional craft specialists. The woman on the right holds a basket. The man in the left foreground is hammering a steel knife. The man in the center is making the scabbard for another knife out of crocodile skin. The man on the left (hidden by the child) is fashioning leather loin garments. Three pots in the left rear contain divining paraphernalia. Only members of the ngkyagu caste may perform these tasks.

whose boundaries are less rigid than those of the caste system. Unlike castes, classes are not endogamous, although members of a class often tend to choose other members of their class as spouses. Also unlike castes, the boundaries between classes are fluid enough for people to change their class membership within their lifetimes.

Social stratification is rarely a simple matter in societies as large and complex as nation-states. Social scientists mainly agree that the large-scale societies of the modern world are divided into classes. There is debate over the precise boundaries of the classes, as well as the distinctive features that indicate class membership. Position in the hierarchy depends not only on power, not only on wealth, not only on prestige, but on a mix of all three. In a complex society, hierarchy may also be complicated or contradicted by the presence of non-class groupings based on race or ethnicity. Caste systems are faced with similar contradictions: In the example from Gopalpur, social pressure and physical violence forced the Saltmakers to buy inferior land that was more in keeping with their caste status than their economic status.

NEGOTIATING SOCIAL STATUS: MEXICO 1521–1812
Anthropologist John Chance studied the role of class, race, and ethnicity in the city of Oaxaca, Mexico. (See EthnoProfile 13.8: Colonial Oaxaca [1521–1812].) Oaxaca, known as *Antequera* during the colonial period, is a highland city founded in an area that was densely populated prior to the Spanish conquest by indigenous people who participated in Mexican high civiliza-

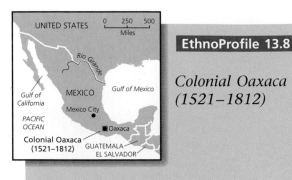

EthnoProfile 13.8

*Colonial Oaxaca
(1521–1812)*

Region: North America

Nation: Mexico

Population: 18,000 (1792)

Environment: High mountain river basin; temperate

Livelihood: Administrative center, clothing and textile industries

Political organization: Colony of Spain

For more information: Chance, John. 1978. *Race and class in colonial Oaxaca.* Stanford: Stanford University Press.

tion. Chance (1978) examined how social stratification changed from the period of Spanish colonial conquest, in 1521, to the early years of the Mexican war of independence, in 1812. He used an anthropological perspective to interpret census records, wills, and other archival materials preserved in Mexico and Spain. As a result, he was able to show that changes occurred both in the categories used to describe social groups and in the meanings attached to those categories.

The Estate System When the Spanish arrived in Mexico in 1521, they found a number of indigenous societies organized into states. The Aztecs, for example, were divided into an upper ruling stratum of nobles and a lower, commoner class. After the conquest, attempts were made to unify the stratification systems of the two societies, Spanish and indigenous. The Spanish conquerors tried to make sense of postconquest society by applying concepts based on the European system of *estates,* legally recognized social categories entitled to a voice in government. European estates prototypically included the nobility, the clergy, and the common people. In New Spain, estate membership was assigned on the basis of race. The clergy and nobility were reserved for the Spanish; conquered indigenous groups became the common people.

There were exceptions to this system, however. Indigenous nobles were given special status in post-conquest society and were used by the colonial administration to control their own people. Moreover, the conquistadors, who brought no Spanish women with them, soon established sexual relationships with local indigenous women. In the early years, if these unions involved marriage, the offspring were usually considered Spanish, but if they were casual or clandestine, the offspring were more likely to be considered indigenous. Thus a population of mixed descent was created. By 1529, African slaves had been brought to New Spain. These slaves ranked at the bottom of the colonial hierarchy. Europeans, indigenous peoples, and Africans interbred, producing their own mixed offspring.

According to the system of estates, people of mixed race were not supposed to exist. By the mid-sixteenth century, however, their numbers and their economic importance made them impossible to ignore. As a result, the rulers of New Spain developed the *sistema de castas,* "a cognitive and legal system of ranked socioracial statuses" used to refer to all people of mixed racial heritage (Chance 1978, viii). The first castas recognized were *mestizos* (people of mixed Spanish and indigenous descent) and *mulattoes* (people who showed evidence of African ancestry).

Whether the Spanish word *casta* should be translated "caste" or "class" or "race" or "ethnic group" is an interesting question. The original "estates" whose interbreeding produced the castas were defined in terms of race. In addition, it was understood that races should not intermarry. That is, each estate was supposed to practice endogamy, like a caste. The sixteenth-century assumption that all people of mixed race were illegitimate demonstrated this belief. Because Spaniards monopolized wealth, power, and prestige in the new colony, they could be viewed as the ruling class—with everyone else making up the subject class. Finally, members of the original colonial estates initially differed from one another not only in terms of race but also in terms of culture. So they might also be seen as constituting separate ethnic groups within colonial society.

As soon as there were enough mestizos and mulattoes to attract attention, the colonial government tried to limit their social mobility by legal means. Yet their status was ambiguous. Mestizos were ranked above mu-

IN THEIR OWN WORDS

The Politics of Ethnicity

Stanley Tambiah reflects on the late-twentieth-century up-surge in ethnic conflict that few people predicted because many assumed that ethnic particularisms would disappear within modern nation-states.

The late-twentieth-century reality is evidenced by the fact that ethnic groups, rather than being mostly minority or marginal subgroups at the edges of society, expected in due course to assimilate or weaken, have figured as major "political" elements and major political collective actors in several societies. Moreover, if in the past we typically viewed an ethnic group as a subgroup of a larger society, today we are also faced with instances of majority ethnic groups within a polity or nation exercising preferential or "affirmative" policies on the basis of that majority status.

The first consideration that confirms ethnic conflict as a major reality of our time is not simply its ubiquity alone, but also its cumulative increase in frequency and intensity of occurrence. Consider these conflicts, by no means an exhaustive listing, that have occurred since the sixties (some of them have a longer history, of course): conflicts between anglophone and francophone in Canada; Catholic and Protestant in Northern Ireland; Walloon and Fleming in Belgium; Chinese and Malay in Malaysia; Greek and Turk in Cyprus; Jews and other minorities on the one hand and Great Russians on the other in the Soviet Union; and Ibo and Hausa and Yoruba in Nigeria; the East Indians and Creoles in Guyana. Add, to these instances, upheavals that became climactic in recent years: the Sinhala-Tamil war in Sri Lanka, the Sikh-Hindu, and Muslim-Hindu, confrontations in India, the Chackma-Muslim turmoil in Bangladesh, the actions of the Fijians against Indians in Fiji, the Pathan-Bihari clashes in Pakistan, and last, but not least, the inferno in Lebanon, and the serious erosion of human rights currently manifest in Israeli actions in Gaza and the West Bank. That there is possibly no end to these eruptions, and that they are worldwide has been forcibly brought to our attention by a century-old difference that exploded in March 1988 between Christian Armenians and Muslim Azerbaijanis in the former U.S.S.R.

Most of these conflicts have involved force and violence, homicide, arson, and destruction of property. Civilian riots have evoked action by security forces: sometimes as counteraction to quell them, sometimes in collusion with the civilian aggressors, sometimes both kinds of action in sequence. Events of this nature have happened in Sri Lanka, Malaysia, India, Zaire, Guyana, and Nigeria. Mass killings of civilians by armed forces have occurred in Uganda and in Guatemala, and large losses of civilian lives have been recorded in Indonesia, Pakistan, India, and Sri Lanka.

The escalation of ethnic conflicts has been considerably aided by the amoral business of gunrunning and free trade in the technology of violence, which enable not only dissident groups to successfully resist the armed forces of the state, but also civilians to battle with each other with lethal weapons. The classical definition of the state as the authority invested with the monopoly of force has become a sick joke. After so many successful liberations and resistance movements in many parts of the globe, the techniques of guerrilla resistance now constitute a systematized and exportable knowledge. Furthermore, the easy access to the technology of warfare by groups in countries that are otherwise deemed low in literacy and in economic development—we have seen what Afghan resistance can do with American guns—is paralleled by another kind of international fraternization among resistance groups who have little in common save their resistance to the status quo in their own countries, and who exchange knowledge of guerrilla tactics and the art of resistance. Militant groups in Japan, Germany, Lebanon, Libya, Sri Lanka, and India have international networks of collaboration, not unlike—perhaps more solidary than—the diplomatic channels that exist between mutually wary sovereign countries and the great powers. The end result is that professionalized killing is no longer the monopoly of state armies and police forces. The internationalization of the technology of destruction, evidenced in the form of terrorism and counterterrorism, has shown a face of free-market capitalism in action unsuspected by Adam Smith and by Immanuel Wallerstein.

Source: Tambiah 1989, 431–32.

---

lattoes because they had no African ancestry but were theoretically ranked below the Spanish because of their "illegitimacy." In cases where indigenous and Spanish people were legally married, their children were called

españoles (creoles). They were distinguished from *españoles europeos* (Spaniards born in Spain). In later years, the term *creole* (*criollo*) was also used to refer to people of presumably "pure" European ancestry who were born in America. Some mestizos managed to obtain elite privileges, such as the right to carry arms. Most mulattoes were classed with Africans and could be enslaved. Yet free mulattoes could also apply for the right to carry arms, which shows that even their status was ambiguous.

During the seventeenth century, the castas were acknowledged as legitimate strata in the system of colonial stratification. A number of new castas were recognized: *castizo* (a person of mixed Spanish and mestizo descent), *mulato libre* ("free mulatto"), *mulato esclavo* ("mulatto slave"), *negro libre* ("free black"), and *negro esclavo* ("black slave"). Perhaps most striking is the castizo category. This seems to have been designed by the colonial elite to stem the tide of ever "whiter" mestizos who might be mistaken for genuine Spaniards. John Chance (1978, 126) points out that racial mixing was primarily an urban phenomenon and that the castas perceived themselves, and were perceived by the elite, as belonging to Hispanic rather than indigenous society (1978, 126). It is perhaps not surprising that lighter-skinned castas became increasingly indistinguishable from middle-class and lower-class creoles. In fact, census records in Oaxaca list creoles as the largest segment of the city's population throughout the entire colonial period.

Other Stratification Systems   As if the sistema de castas were not enough, colonial society recognized three additional systems of classification that cut across the castas. One distinguished groups required to pay tribute to the Spanish crown (indigenous groups, Africans, and mulattoes) from everyone else. The second distinguished *gente de razon* ("rational people," who practiced the Hispanic culture of the city) from *indios* (the rural, culturally distinct indigenous population). And a third distinguished *gente decente* ("respectable people") from *la plebe* (the "common people"). Chance suggests that the last distinction, which made most sense in the urban setting, represented an embryonic division into socioeconomic classes (1978, 127).

Mobility in the Casta System   Throughout the colonial period, the boundaries of the stratification system in Oaxaca were most rigid for those of pure indigenous, African, and European descent. These were the "unmixed" categories at the bottom and top of the hierarchy. Paradoxically, those of mixed background had

the most ambiguous status—and the greatest opportunity to improve it. For example, when a couple married, the priest decided the casta membership of the bride and groom. The strategy for upward mobility called for choosing a marriage partner who was light-skinned enough for the priest to decide that both spouses belonged in a high-ranking casta. Over time, such maneuvering swelled the ranks of the creoles.

The growth of the casta population coincided with the transformation of the colonial economy from one based on tribute and mining to one based on commercial capitalism. The prosperity this transformation brought to Oaxaca was greatest in the eighteenth century, when the city became the center of an important textile and dye-manufacturing industry. Many castas were able to accumulate wealth, which together with a light skin and adoption of the urban culture made it possible for them to achieve the status of creole.

Chance argues that during the late colonial period, racial status had become an achieved, rather than an ascribed, status. By that time, the increasing rate of legitimacy in all castas meant that descent lost its importance as a criterion of group membership. Creole status could be claimed by anyone who was able to show that his or her ancestors had not paid tribute. At the same time, in a dialectical fashion, people's image of what high-status people looked like had changed. As people with indigenous and African ancestry moved up the social scale, their physical appearance, or phenotype, widened the range of phenotypes considered prototypical for people of creole status.

NEGOTIATING SOCIAL STATUS IN OTHER SOCIETIES Processes similar to those Chance describes continue to take place today. In many areas of Latin America where extensive racial mixing has occurred, "racial" status is an achieved status. Benjamin Colby and Pierre van den Berghe (1969) documented the process that occurred in Guatemala during the twentieth century. Members of indigenous groups who left their traditional communities, learned Spanish, dressed like Europeans, and took a "non-Indian" occupation might easily pass as *ladinos* (members of the "white" population) whether they wanted to or not. Colby and van den Berghe write: "A factor which probably contributes to ladinoization is the ambiguity in the ethnic status of the Indian who does not belong to the local majority group. Local Indians will regard him as a stranger, and, of course, unless he speaks the local Indian language, he will be forced to use Spanish as a lingua franca. Ladinoization and 'passing' of Indian 'strangers' are probably more the consequences of marginality than of any conscious desire to become assimilated to the ladinos. Rejection by local Indians makes ladinoization almost inevitable" (1969, 172).

I (Emily Schultz) encountered a similar process at work in Guider, Cameroon. (See EthnoProfile 8.1: Guider.) I found that people born outside the dominant Fulbe ethnic group could achieve Fulbe status within their lifetimes (1984). To do this, they had to be successful in three tasks: They had to adopt the Fulbe language (Fulfulde), the Fulbe religion (Islam), and the Fulbe "way of life," which was identified with urban customs and the traditional high culture of the western Sudan. Many Fulbe claimed that descent from one or another Fulbe lineage was needed in order to claim Fulbe identity. Nevertheless, they seemed willing to accept "Fulbeized Pagans" as Fulbe (for example, by giving their daughters to them as brides) because those people were committed defenders of the urban Fulbe way of life. Those who were "Fulbeizing," however, came from societies in which descent had never been an important criterion of group membership. For those people, ethnic identity depended on the language, customs, and territorial affiliation of the group to which they were currently committed. In becoming Fulbe, they had simply chosen to commit themselves to Fulfulde, Islam, and life in "Fulbe territory," the town.

THE DIMENSIONS OF GROUP LIFE

We have considered some features of the larger imagined communities that human beings have invented to link them into forms of social organization of increasing size and complexity. Many anthropologists would argue that transition to a class-based society marks a qualitative change in the nature of social life. That is, *class organization* marks a threshold where a change in *degree* of complexity is transformed into a change in *kind* of complexity. Thus, the issues that occupied the attention of such figures as Maine and Durkheim are still alive.

But complex forms of social organization do not develop in a vacuum. Many of the social organizational

complexities of the contemporary world, including divisions based on class, race, and ethnicity, developed during the 500 years of European imperial expansion, which came to an end only a few decades ago. European colonial empires may be viewed as attempts to forge imagined communities that would stretch over significant portions of the globe. They attempted to integrate societies with various degrees of precolonial social complexity into a new, unified social system. Some of the results of this process can be seen in the complications and contradictions displayed in the history of Oaxaca.

One of the most important products of European colonial expansion has been the nation-state. Every society in the world today finds itself located within one or another set of state borders, and coping with state power and ideology is a challenge faced by most groups that anthropologists choose to study. In the late twentieth century, the group life of all societies, in one way or another, has taken on global dimensions. Put another way, at the beginning of the twenty-first century, what goes on locally in face-to-face society is everywhere affected by forces that originate elsewhere in the world. These themes are explored in the chapter that follows.

Key Terms

status	egalitarian societies
role	stratified societies
mechanical solidarity	caste
organic solidarity	class
division of labor	race
sodalities	ethnicity
age sets	clientage
secret societies	

Chapter Summary

1. Early social scientists described and explained the differences they saw between "primitive" and "modern" human societies. They thought of "primitive" society as organized in terms of kinship and therefore characterized by personalized, face-to-

face relationships, ascribed statuses, and mechanical solidarity. "Modern" society, by contrast, was characterized by impersonal relationships, achieved statuses, and organic solidarity. In "modern" society, kinship played a much reduced role, and most of the people with whom an individual dealt were nonkin.

2. Every society provides ways of establishing links with nonkin. It is sometimes difficult to draw a neat line between kinship and nonkin relationships because kinship terms may be used between "friends" or kinship roles may be the prototypes for the roles expected of friends—or both. In any case, the relationships cultivate a sentiment of enduring diffuse solidarity.

3. The larger a society is, the more complex its division of labor will be. The more specialized the division of labor is, the more likely institutionalized relationships will exist between nonkin. Such institutions are minimally developed in most band societies but become increasingly important in tribal societies, in the form of sodalities.

4. Cheyenne military societies, eastern African age sets, and western African secret societies are all examples of pantribal sodalities. These institutions tend to be found in nonhierarchical societies. Members of the sodalities, drawn from the various kinship groups, ordinarily take on responsibility for various public functions of a governmental or ritual nature. Membership in such sodalities is often a mark of adulthood and may be connected with initiation rituals.

5. In stratified societies, some groups have permanently privileged access to valued resources, while others have permanently restricted access. The relations between subgroups are carefully specified. Two common patterns of stratification are caste and class. Links between castes or classes may be based on such criteria as the relationship individuals have to the means of production and occupational specialization. These links may be complicated by race or ethnicity. In many stratified societies, individuals from different strata are linked by clientage.

6. In stratified societies, particularly those in which membership in one or another stratum is based on race or ethnicity, group membership is often a matter of negotiation. Data from colonial Oaxaca show how the recognized categories of society and the criteria used to assign membership change over time. These data and examples noted elsewhere demonstrate that individuals can manipulate the rules to advance in status, successfully "passing" as members of groups to which they do not "literally" belong. They illustrate that racial, ethnic, or class prototypes are selective cultural constructions that emphasize certain attributes of individuals while ignoring others.

Suggested Readings

Anderson, Benedict. 1983. *Imagined communities.* London: Verso. *The classic discussion of the cultural processes that create community ties between people—such as citizens of a nation-state—who have never seen one another, producing the personal and cultural feeling of belonging to a nation.*

Brain, Robert. 1976. *Friends and lovers.* New York: Basic Books. *A thorough, highly readable account of friendship taken very broadly, with excellent ethnographic examples. Brain draws provocative lessons for Western society from his research.*

Keillor, Garrison. 1985. *Lake Wobegon days.* New York: Viking. *The best-selling book about kinship and other ties that bind in American small-town life.*

Nash, Manning. 1989. *The cauldron of ethnicity in the modern world.* Chicago: University of Chicago Press. *Nash looks at ethnicity in the postcolonial world and sees more of a seething cauldron than a melting pot. He examines the relations between Ladinos and Maya in Guatemala, Chinese and Malays in Malaysia, and Jews and non-Jews in the United States.*

Smith, Mary F. [1954] 1981. *Baba of Karo.* Reprint. New Haven: Yale University Press. *A remarkable document: the autobiography of a Hausa woman born in 1877. A master storyteller, Baba provides much information about Hausa patterns of friendship, clientage, adoption, kinship, and marriage.*

PART V

From Local to Global

Human beings have used their cultural creativity, together with political and economic resources, to create imagined communities that now encompass the entire world. The last part describes some of the most recent steps in this process, beginning with European colonial conquest. The effects of colonialism have been central to the recent histories of most of the peoples with whom anthropologists have traditionally worked, as indeed they were to the European and North American societies from which most anthropologists have traditionally come. In this part, we explore the ways anthropologists have attempted to explain colonialism and subsequent forces for cultural change, as well as how these factors have impinged upon the lives of particular peoples in particular places and times. We also examine the work of those anthropologists who have tried to do more than record and analyze contemporary cultural change, and have taken on the task of applying anthropological information to the solution of contemporary human social problems.

14

The World System

CHAPTER OUTLINE

Capitalism, Colonialism, and "Modernity"

Views of the Political Economy

Modes of Change in the Modern World

rlando, Claudio, and Leonardo Villas Boas were middle-class Brazilians who took part in an expedition that explored central Brazil in the early 1940s. Their experiences led the three brothers to dedicate their lives to protecting Brazil's indigenous peoples from the ravages of contact with Western society. They were instrumental in persuading the government to create in 1952 the Xingu National Park, a large area in the state of Mato Grosso where indigenous groups could live undisturbed by outsiders. Since that time, they have worked to contact threatened indigenous groups and to persuade them to move to Xingu.

One such group was the Kréen-Akaróre, whose existence was menaced by a highway being built through their traditional territory. In February 1973, after years of avoiding outsiders, the Kréen-Akaróre finally made contact with Claudio Villas Boas, who had been following them in hopes of finding them before the highway builders did. Shortly after this, Orlando Villas Boas gave a press conference in which he forcefully urged that a reserve be created for the Kréen-Akaróre by the Brazilian government. The reserve was not located in traditional Kréen-Akaróre territory, however, and it was bounded by the Santarém-Cuiabá Highway. Within months, the 300 remaining Kréen-Akaróre settled there had abandoned their gardens; sick and in despair, they were begging for food from truck drivers. Finally, in October 1974, the Villas Boas brothers were able to fly the 135 surviving Kréen-Akaróre to the Xingu National Park (Davis 1977, 69–73).

Disease, devastation, and misery have been all too common for indigenous peoples who have encountered Western expansion. Many observers, including anthropologists, have long feared that indigenous Amazonian peoples were destined for extinction. After all, of a population of 5 million in 1500, only 280,000 remain today, and some groups have already died out (Gomes 1996). Recent history, however, suggests a reversal of fortune. During the last 30 to 40 years, the surviving 220 indigenous groups have seen their populations grow. Although some still strive to keep free of outside entanglements, others have been educated and live in cities; one has even been elected to the Brazilian National Congress (Gomes 1996).

This remarkable and heartening turn of events is il-lustrated by recent events involving the Kayapo. In March 1989, the *Anthropology Newsletter* published a report from anthropologist Terence Turner describing how indigenous Amazonians had organized themselves to resist outside encroachment on their traditional lands. They were the people most directly affected by continued destruction of the Amazonian rain forest, but no one could have imagined that they might be leaders in defense of the environment, working successfully with national and international allies. Yet they brought some 28 indigenous nations together in a huge intertribal village built in the path of a proposed hydroelectric dam complex at Altamira, on the Xingu River. The Kayapo leader Paiakan combined traditional indigenous political skills with a knowledge of Portuguese and a keen understanding of the international media. He and other Kayapo chiefs, such as Raoni, toured Europe and appeared publicly with well-known celebrities such as the rock musician Sting, who supported their cause (Figure 14.1). The Brazilian government, moreover, has still not built its dam. As anthropologist Terence Turner observes, "The boldness and global vision of this project are breathtaking; nothing like such a concerted action by even a few, let alone 28 unrelated Indian societies has ever taken place in the Amazon. The Indians are trying to tell us something important; we should listen (T. Turner 1989, 21–22).

Peoples like the Kréen-Akaróre and the Kayapo have struggled with the effects of European contact for over 500 years, but rather than disappear forever, they have now moved out of the forest and into the thick of Brazilian national life. Anthropological research on Amazonian peoples has also changed. Today, Mercio Gomes observes, "one's living objects of research are easy to find, not more than a few hours away by plane, at the most a few days away by boat. They are on the outskirts of cities, in hospitals and medical centers, and even in the corridors of the National Congress. . . . They will also be available in the future" (1996, 19).

In this chapter, we deal directly with how the Western world and the societies visited by anthropologists are interrelated, and how those interrelationships have changed over time. We will be looking at ourselves as much as we look at the traditional subjects of anthropological research. Through this reflexive exercise, we will try to establish a context for contemplating the common fate of humankind.

FIGURE 14.1 To publicize their opposition to a proposed hydroelectric dam complex that threatened to flood their traditional territories, indigenous Amazonian peoples, under the leadership of the Kayapo, engaged in a variety of activities. Here, Kayapo chief Raoni (third from right) and British rock star Sting (third from left) hold a press conference.

CAPITALISM, COLONIALISM, AND "MODERNITY"

The European pursuit of centralized monarchy at home and influence abroad began in the Middle Ages and flourished during the Renaissance and the Age of Discovery. Since the fall of the Roman Empire, Europe had never been politically unified, which meant that, beginning in the fifteenth century, fledgling European states could strike out on their own without being answerable to any central authority (Gledhill 1994, 58–59). At the same time, Europeans were working out a new kind of society with a new kind of economy whose development was aided by trade and conquest—namely, capitalism. The term **capitalism** refers to at least two things: an economic system dominated by the supply-demand-price mechanism called *the market;* and the way of life that grew up in response to and in service to that market. This new way of life changed the face of Europe and transformed other regions as well.

The Key Metaphor of Capitalism

There had been expansive empires before the rise of capitalism, but capitalist exploitation was unique be-

cause it derived from a new worldview. In the words of Eric Wolf, "The guiding fiction of this kind of society—one of the key tenets of its ideology—is that land, labor, and wealth are commodities, that is, goods produced not for use, but for sale" (1969, 277). The world is a market, and everything within the world has, or should have, its price.

The genius of capitalism has been the thoroughgoing way in which those committed to the marketing metaphor have been able to convert anything that exists into a commodity; they turn land into real estate and material objects into inventory. They can also attach price tags to ideas (copyright laws) and even to human beings. The slave in Western society is considered "first and foremost a commodity. He is a chattel, totally in the possession of another person who uses him for private ends" (Kopytoff and Miers 1977, 3). Even human beings who are not slaves are nevertheless reduced to their labor power by the capitalist market and become worth whatever price the laws of supply and demand determine; thus, human beings are also turned into objects, and labor becomes a commodity

---

capitalism An economic system dominated by the supply-demand-price mechanism called *the market;* an entire way of life that grew in response to and in service of that market.

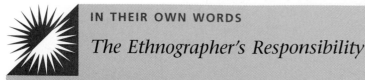

IN THEIR OWN WORDS

The Ethnographer's Responsibility

French ethnographers Jacques Meunier and A. M. Savarin reflect on the role they can play in Europe to affect the policies of Latin American governments toward the indigenous peoples living within their borders.

At the most fundamental level, the history of thought about primitive people—are they human, overgrown children, or replicas of early stages of Western civilization?—provides a summary of the changes that have taken place in our own culture: the West knows that it can no longer hold exclusive power, but it still considers itself the dominant power. Western ignorance follows from this error. Our taste for exoticism and our morality stem from it, as does the deadly intolerance that seems lodged in our hearts. Centuries of culture and well-intentioned unreasonableness, centuries of humanism have led to the most heinous of all crimes: genocide.

Entire communities forced to abandon their lands, children kidnapped, people treated barbarously, degraded mentally and physically, punitive expeditions launched against them. . . . With genocide, with racism, we confront horror itself. We have spoken of the fragility of traditional societies, of the blind intolerance of our civilization toward the Indians, of the lack of understanding that has led the Amazonians—white, creole, and mestizo—to the organized extermination of the Indians. But there is one question that haunts us, that emerges through the pages of this case like the recurring notes of a flute, forcing us to weigh an unpleasant possibility: aren't we just as guilty of exploiting the Indians, aren't

we indulging in a lot of useless discussion? But when we use the word *genocide*, we have no intention of turning ourselves into defenders of a lost cause; we do not see our roles as charity and moralism. We are not writing off the Indians; we do not believe that genocide should be considered an inevitable calamity.

Ethnographers must organize; they must enact plans to safeguard the threatened minorities—this is important. But if they do not capture public opinion, their projects will not produce results. More than anything, ethnographers need to launch an information campaign, a sound and systematic campaign. The general public has the right to know. The right and the duty. To accept this atrocity, to allow these terrible crimes to be committed, is to become an accomplice in them.

Do not misjudge us: our indignation is not mere posturing. We are convinced that it is possible to affect the policy of Latin American governments. Especially since these countries, while dependent on the United States economically, still turn toward Europe culturally. We can say to them without paternalism: the sense Latin Americans have of their countries still comes from Europe. Why shouldn't they learn a respect for their indigenous populations from Europe, just as they have acquired a taste for pre-Colombian antiquities and folklore? In our view, the salvation of the Indian must begin here and now.

Source: Meunier and Savarin 1994, 128–29.

---

along with beans and cotton. Even when people function as buyers in the market, their actions are supposed to be governed by maximizing utility. They should buy cheap, sell dear, and not allow any personal or social considerations to divert their attention from the bottom line.

To be sure, complex commercial activity was not invented by Western capitalists. Long before Western Europe became a world power, stratified state societies in different parts of the world had devised sophisticated socioeconomic systems. In China and India, for example, the use of trade, money, and markets was highly developed by the time the first representatives of Western capitalism arrived on the scene. Elites in

such societies were well prepared to take advantage of new economic opportunities offered by Western entrepreneurs, often helping to establish capitalist practices in their own societies and benefiting as a result. However, the consequences of capitalism were often negative for ordinary members of these societies, who lost many traditional socioeconomic supports.

Capitalism was even more devastating in small-scale societies existing outside the control of these complex states. Members of these societies saw their traditionally inalienable land turned into a commodity for sale on the capitalist market. They experienced the devaluation of their traditional social identities based on descent, alliance, and residence and the ero-

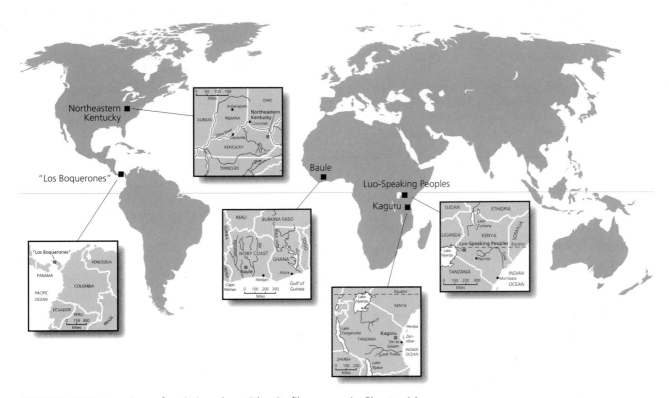

FIGURE 14.2 Locations of societies whose EthnoProfiles appear in Chapter 14.

sion of traditional obligations that protected them from destitution. Before the introduction of capitalism, multipurpose money did not exist, exchanges were hedged about by social restrictions, and there was no single standard according to which anything could be assigned a value. Capitalism changed all this.

What began as trade contracts with European nations was followed nearly everywhere by European conquest. **Colonialism** refers to a social system in which political conquest by one society of another leads to "cultural domination with enforced social change" (Beidelman 1982, 2). Western conquest of non-Western societies created European colonial empires in two historical phases. The first phase, involving Spain, Portugal, and Holland, established tributary empires integrated by merchant capitalism, but the second phase, led by England and France, was based on industrial capitalism (Gledhill 1994, 74). When capitalist practices were imposed on non-Western societies through colonialism, indigenous life was forever altered. To

function intelligibly within the capitalist world order, colonized peoples had to begin to see the world as a storehouse of potential commodities. Much of recent world history can usefully be viewed as a narrative of non-Western responses to this new worldview and the practical actions it encouraged and justified. Some responses were enthusiastic, others were resentful but accommodating, still others were violent in repudiation.

The period of history that includes the rise of European nation-states and colonial empires is traditionally called "modern," and life in European industrial cities has often been seen as the prototype of modernity. The colonial presence was perhaps clearest in colonial cities. To be sure, indigenous civilizations in many parts of the world had produced cities before the arrival of Europeans. But the colonial city in which capitalist transactions centered was "a conquered place"

---

colonialism Cultural domination with enforced social change.

(Gilsenan 1982, 197). Colonial administrators, merchants, and local elites united in such places to defend their joint interests against those who remained in outlying areas.

In the colonial context, however, being modern has often been understood as nothing more than adopting the practices and worldview of Western capitalism. As a result, the so-called backward rural peoples often turned out to be either those who escaped capitalism's embrace or those who actively opposed it. For many of them, the colonial city and the life it represented symbolized everything wrong with the colonial order. At times of crisis in contemporary Muslim societies, for example, "the modern city is itself called in question, taken to symbolize forces of oppression or a non-Islamic way of life. . . . For radical and millennial groups the city is a home of unbelief, not of sober, textual Islam. The true believer should, in an image that has great historical resonance, go out from the city, leave as the Prophet Muhammad did the hypocritical and unbelieving citizens of Mecca" (Gilsenan 1982, 214).

Colonial penetration reshaped conquered territories to serve the needs of capitalist enterprise. Cities were centers of commerce, and rural areas were sources of raw materials for industry. Systems set up by colonial authorities to extract raw materials disrupted indigenous communities and created new ones. The mining towns of Bolivia and South Africa, for example, are outgrowths of this process. Labor for such enterprises was recruited, sometimes by force, from local populations. Little by little, in an effort to streamline the system of colonial exploitation, society was restructured.

The Colonial Political Economy

Because the colonial order focused on the extraction of material wealth, it might be said that its reason for existence was economic. Certainly it linked economically communities and territories that in many cases had led a fairly autonomous existence before colonization. Yet this new economic order did not spring up painlessly by itself. It was imposed and maintained by force. For that reason, many anthropologists describe the colonial order as a **political economy**—a holistic term that emphasizes the centrality of material interest and the use of power to protect and enhance that interest. The colonial political economy created three kinds of

links, connecting conquered communities with one another within a conquered territory; different conquered territories with one another; and all conquered territories with the country of the colonizers. Wolf describes a particularly striking example of this linkage: Silver mined in Spanish colonies in America was shipped to a Spanish colony in Asia—the Philippines—where it was used to buy textiles from the Chinese (1982, 153).

More commonly, colonial enterprises drew labor from neighboring regions, as in South Africa. Here, indigenous Africans were recruited from some distance to work in the mines; money earned in one area was thus remitted for the economic support of families in another area. Again, these linkages did not come about spontaneously. Alverson describes for South Africa a situation paralleled in many other colonies (1978, 26ff.). The British, he argues, could not make a profit in the gold mines of the region without cheap African labor. In the late nineteenth century, however, Africans were still largely able to guarantee their own subsistence through traditional means. They were unwilling to work for wages in the mines except on a short-term basis. Profitability in mining required, therefore, that African self-sufficiency be eliminated so that Africans would have no choice but to work for whatever wages mine owners chose to offer.

This goal was achieved in two ways. First, taxes were imposed on conquered African populations, but the taxes could only be paid in cash. Second, the colonial government deliberately prevented the growth of a cash economy in African areas. Thus, the only way Africans could obtain the cash needed to pay their taxes was by working for wages in the mines. "The Tswana, along with other African populations, comprised a reserve army of potential labor—that is, labor that it was hoped would exist in inelastic supply and cost industry nothing at all when not being used. [Botswana] and the rural, native reserves in South Africa itself were, and from the capitalist viewpoint still are, social security systems that keep labor alive until such time as it is in demand by the money sector" (Alverson 1978, 34–35). (See EthnoProfile 2.1: Tswana.)

Political independence did not remove Botswana from the clutches of the South African political economy. At the time of Alverson's fieldwork, Botswana was still sending more than two workers to South Africa for every one worker it could supply with a job at home. And these workers were not "surplus" migrants whose home communities were eager to get rid of them. "In many ways some Tswana communities have become quasi-societies and quasi-economies, for the absence of men and women abroad has virtually destroyed institutional life and replaced it with nothing except cash" (1978, 62–63). What is true for Botswana became true for ex-colonies elsewhere in Africa, Asia, and the New World.

Accounting for Social and Cultural Change

Anthropology was born as a discipline during the heyday of European colonialism in the nineteenth century. Functional anthropology developed in the context of empire. Anthropologists were hired to provide specific information about particular societies under colonial rule. Colonial governments were preoccupied with day-to-day concerns of administration. From their perspective, social change involved the adjustment of conquered peoples to life under colonial rule. They were interested in research that would let them rule with as little difficulty as possible. As we observed in Chapter 4, European anthropologists often played an equivocal role in the colonial setting; they were valued for the expert knowledge they could provide while they were also viewed with suspicion because their expert knowledge might easily contradict or undermine administrative goals.

A number of North American anthropologists also tried to clarify what their role should be in the expanding world of capitalist colonialism. Two documents (Redfield et al. 1936 and Broom et al. 1954) bracket the period that Bohannan and Plog (1967, x) called the "high period" of the study of culture. The anthropologists involved promoted an impartial and scientific program of research that would discover the laws of culture change. They had a broad view of culture change. They considered situations encountered under colonialism, but they also considered situations where contact and change occurred in the absence of political conquest. The latter cases involved autonomous groups whose members could be freer about what they selected and rejected. The anthropologists did not see themselves supporting any particular political position in advocating that culture change be approached in this way; however, they were sympathetic to the plight of colonial subjects. Melville Herskovits, in particular, was outspoken in his defense of the right of indigenous African peoples to control their own destinies.

In the years following World War II, European colonial powers were increasingly forced to come to terms with colonial subjects who rejected the role they had been forced to play as students of civilization. The colonial order was no longer a given, and its ultimate benevolence was sharply questioned. This critical attitude persisted after independence was granted to most European colonies in the 1950s and 1960s. It became clear that formal political independence could not easily undo the profound social and economic entanglements linking the former colonial territories to the countries that had colonized them. The persistence of these ties in the face of political sovereignty came to be called **neocolonialism.**

The study of neocolonialism led to a new awareness of just how strongly the fate of colonies and the fate of the colonizers have continued to be mutually interdependent. Recognizing the strength of this interdependence, scholars began to offer new explanations for the "underdevelopment" that characterizes the new nations in what came to be known as the Third World.

The Roots of the Neocolonial Order

Coming to terms with the tenacious problems of neocolonialism would seem to require coming to terms with colonial domination itself. The assumption that political independence would allow Latin Americans, Africans, and Asians to become captains of their fate turned out to be premature.

Anthropologist T. O. Beidelman says, "Colonialism is not dead in Africa if, by colonialism, we mean cultural domination with enforced social change. I refer not only to continued economic and political influence by former colonial powers but also to domination of the poor and uneducated masses by a privileged and powerful native elite fiercely determined to make change for whatever reasons" (1982, 2). Defining colonialism

---

political economy A holistic term that emphasizes the centrality of material interest (economy) and the use of power (politics) to protect and enhance that interest.
neocolonialism The persistence of profound social and economic entanglements linking former colonial territories to their former colonial rulers despite political sovereignty.

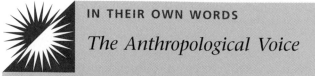

IN THEIR OWN WORDS

The Anthropological Voice

Anthropologist Annette Weiner traces the history of an-thropological challenges to colonialism and Western capital-ism, pointing out why the perspective of anthropologists has so often been ignored.

Colonialism brought foreign governments, missionaries, ex-plorers, and exploiters face-to-face with cultures whose val-ues and beliefs were vastly different. As the harbingers of Western progress, their actions were couched in the rhetoric of doing something to and for "the natives"—giving them souls, clothes, law—whatever was necessary to lift them out of their "primitive" ways. Anthropologists were also part of the colonial scene, but what they came to "do" made them different from those who were carrying out the expectations of missions, overseas trade, and government protectorates. Anthropologists arrived in the field determined to understand the cultural realities of an unfamiliar world. The knowledge of these worlds was to serve as a warning to those in posi-tions of colonial power by charging that villager's lives were not to be tampered with arbitrarily and that changing the lives of powerless people was insensitive and inhumane, un-less one understood and took seriously the cultural meanings inherent in, for example, traditional land ownership, the tech-nologies and rituals surrounding food cultivation, myths, magic, and gender relations.

All too often, however, the anthropologist's voice went unnoticed by those in power, for it remained a voice com-mitted to illuminating the cultural biases under which colo-nialists operated. Only recently have we witnessed the final demise of colonial governments and the rise of independent countries. Economically, however, independence has not brought these countries the freedom to pursue their own course of development. In many parts of the world, Western multinational corporations, often playing a role not too dis-similar from colonial enterprises, now determine the course of that freedom, changing people's lives in a way that all too often is harmful or destructive. At the same time, we know that the world's natural resources and human productive ca-pabilities can no longer remain isolates. Developed and de-veloping countries are now more dependent on one another than ever before in human history. Yet this interdependency, which should give protection to indigenous peoples, is often worked out for political ends that ignore the moral issues. Racism and the practice of discrimination are difficult to de-stroy, as evidenced by the United States today, where we still are not completely emancipated from assumptions that rele-gate blacks, women, Asians, Hispanics, and other minorities to second-class status. If we cannot bridge these cultural dif-ferences intellectually within our own borders, then how can we begin to deal politically with Third World countries— those who were called "primitives" less than a century ago— in a fair, sensitive, and meaningful way?

This is the legacy of anthropology that we must never forget. Because the work of anthropology takes us to the neighborhoods, villages, and campsites—the local level— we can ourselves experience the results of how the world's economic and political systems affect those who have no voice. Yet once again our voices too are seldom heard by those who make such decisions. Anthropologists are often prevented from participating in the forums of economic and government planning. Unlike economists, political scientists, or engineers, we must stand on the periphery of such deci-sion making, primarily because our understanding of cultural patterns and beliefs forces on others an awareness that ulti-mately makes such decisions more formidable.

At the beginning of the twentieth century, anthropolo-gists spoke out strongly against those who claimed that "sav-age" societies represented a lower level of biological and social development. Now, as we face the next century, the an-thropological approach to human nature and human societies is as vital to communicate as ever. We face a difficult, poten-tially dangerous, and therefore complex future. A fundamen-tal key to our future is to make certain that the dynamic qualities of human beings in all parts of the world are recog-nized and that the true value of cultural complexities is not ignored. There is much important anthropology to be done.

Source: Weiner 1990, 392–93.

in this way highlights why political independence in the mid-twentieth century made so little economic dif-ference to the new nations of Africa and Asia. It also helps explain why the Latin American nations that be-came formally independent over a century and a half ago have continued to languish economically. It would seem that political domination is only one option in the growth of a capitalist world system. Cultural domination with enforced social change can occur without political domination if the people of a dominated territory agree to accept the hegemony of an outside power. But they may resist such hegemony or they may lack the means to meet outside needs as fully as the outside power wishes. In either case, the outside power may decide to move in itself, making the changes it sees as necessary, even if local peoples object.

This certainly seems to describe the history of European colonialism in Africa. The major trade routes connecting Africa to Europe had always been across the Sahara to the Mediterranean Sea. However, once Europeans appeared on the Atlantic coast in the fifteenth century, the geography and the nature of African trade was profoundly affected. For example, European traders sought human beings destined for slavery. As African trading partners searched for slaves in the interior of the continent, reverberations were felt far inland by societies who had never seen a European. Then, in the late eighteenth century, the growth of industrialization led Europeans to view African lands as sources of cheap raw materials for industry and African peoples as consumers of European manufactures. By the early nineteenth century, England was the most advanced European industrial power and the nation most interested in trade in nonhuman commodities with Africa. England therefore led the effort to abolish the African slave trade.

Later in the century, competition among England, France, Germany, and Belgium for access to African resources and markets led to a scramble for Africa, as these nations rushed to divide the continent among themselves into mutually exclusive regions of control. Treaties signed with African leaders were the first step to colonial domination, for once a given European power controlled trade within a region, little prevented it from introducing social and cultural changes intended to streamline economic transactions.

Women and Colonization

Colonial administrators were generally convinced that the work of empire would benefit those they dominated—if not now, then in the future. Critics of colonialism deny that any benefits could accrue to a dominated and exploited people. Ethnographic data, however, show that colonial conquest did not affect all groups in the same ways. Women are one such group.

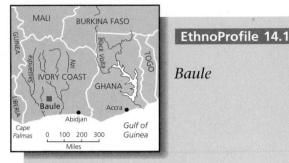

EthnoProfile 14.1

Baule

Region: Western Africa

Nation: Ivory Coast

Population: 2,760,000

Environment: Savanna

Livelihood: Farming (yams in particular) and cloth production

Political organization: In the precolonial period, no state and no clear stratification; today, part of a modern nation-state

For more information: Etienne, Mona. 1980. Women and men, cloth and colonization: The transformation of production-distribution relations among the Baule (Ivory Coast). In *Women and colonization: Anthropological perspectives,* edited by Mona Etienne and Eleanor Leacock, 270–93. New York: Praeger.

As we saw in Chapter 10, Trobriand women suffered no loss of status under colonial rule. (See EthnoProfile 3.4: Trobriand Islanders.) Baule women of Ivory Coast in western Africa were less fortunate. (See EthnoProfile 14.1: Baule.)

In precolonial Baule society, according to Mona Etienne (1980), production centered on two products: yams and cloth. Gifts of yams and cloth consolidated marriages, and both sexes worked together in the production of each. Yet the relations of production assigned men responsibility for yams and women responsibility for cloth. Men's traditional control over yams was an outgrowth of the sexual division of labor; men cleared and prepared farm plots for planting, although the women tended the crops. Similarly, women controlled cloth because they raised the cotton and spun the thread from which it was woven, although the men

FIGURE 14.3 Factory production has displaced traditional household-based production of cloth not just among the Baule of Ivory Coast, but throughout Africa. These women work in a textile factory in Lagos, Nigeria.

did the actual weaving. Both yams and cloth were indispensable for subsistence as well as for exchange in various traditional social contexts. As a result, the balance of power between men and women was highly egalitarian.

Ivory Coast became a colony of France in 1893. In 1923, the French built in Baule territory a textile factory that sold factory-spun thread for cash (Figure 14.3). Baule men with cash could therefore buy their own thread, and they, not their wives, would control any cloth woven from it. French colonial administrators also encouraged Baule farmers to plant new varieties of cotton as a cash crop. Baule women had traditionally raised their cotton on fields that had been planted with yams the previous year, but these plots were now devoted to growing the new cotton. Cash-crop cotton also required new farming techniques, but for a variety of reasons those techniques were taught to Baule men. Consequently, women's cotton production was reduced considerably. Moreover, because women had to work in their husbands' cash-crop fields as well as the traditional yam plots, they also had less time to spin traditional thread.

The colonial government required men to pay their wives' taxes in cash, a move that seemed to justify the right of Baule men to control production of crops that could be sold for cash. Under colonial rule, cash-cropping became increasingly important. As a result, Baule women found that their traditional autonomous rights to use their husbands' land for their own production gradually eroded, and they became increasingly dependent on their husbands' arbitrary generosity.

There is a final irony in this series of developments. By the 1970s, many Baule women had become wage laborers in the textile factory in order to earn cash to buy their own cloth, which they could then control. They were aware of the loss of status and power they had suffered over the years, and their discontent had undermined traditional Baule marriage. Etienne reported that "The wife-husband production relationship has become a constant source of conflict. Because the production relationship has always been the foundation of marriage, and because cloth and cash now tend to be the measure of a husband's affection and respect, the whole personal relationship is also conflict-laden. Inevitably, many women prefer to remain unmarried and all seek to acquire their own cash" (1980, 231). In this way, the traditional Baule mode of production was transformed by contact with the capitalist market. The previously egalitarian relations of production linking women and men (husbands and wives) were destroyed.

VIEWS OF THE POLITICAL ECONOMY

Anthropologists have made use of a variety of theoretical perspectives to explain the relationship between the West and the rest of the world. Of these, probably the most influential have been (1) modernization theory, (2) dependency theory, (3) world system theory, (4) neomarxian theory, and (5) globalization theory.

Modernization Theory

The roots of contemporary **modernization theory** can be seen in the unilineal evolutionism of Herbert Spencer and his followers. In brief, social change in non-Western societies under colonial rule was understood as a necessary and inevitable prelude to higher levels of social development. Europe had passed through the same stages of evolution earlier in its history, and contact with Europe was now shaking other regions out of stagnation. Colonization was thus a positive process because it taught backward peoples the skills they needed to move forward. These were capitalist skills that required Western institutions to work properly. By adopting those skills and institutions, it was argued, conquered societies would eventually become "modern" and prosperous independent nation-states.

Spencerian evolutionism was heavily criticized in anthropology and other social sciences in the early twentieth century. As late as 1960, however, we find Spencerian reasoning in economist W. W. Rostow's book *The Stages of Economic Growth* ([1960] 1971). This book codifies the received wisdom of economics that formed the foundation of U.S. foreign aid policies in the 1960s. It thus offers in a single volume the basic principles of modernization theory.

Rostow surveys the history of the world and decides that, economically speaking, known human societies can be sorted into five categories, each of which represents a stage of development. The first, lowest stage is that of "traditional society," which is defined in neg-

ative terms. Traditional societies are said to have productive techniques that are poorly developed, and their social institutions are viewed as stumbling blocks in the path of economic growth. Progress thus requires that these blocks be removed if prosperity and modernity are to be attained. Stages two through five chart the steps to "modernity," defined as a stage of "high mass-consumption."

Rostow conceives of economic growth as if it were organic growth, from youth to maturity to what he calls *postmaturity*. He describes each new nation-state as if it were an adolescent male undergoing puberty. Young states, like young men, develop according to an inner timetable. They start out ignorant and immature, lacking the knowledge and skills to support themselves properly. In addition, they are unsure of their own identity, and so tend to get involved in fights with one another or with more mature members of the international community. But the passage of time brings wisdom. Rostow has faith that, with sound guidance from their elders, young states will eventually stand beside those elders as self-supporting, even thriving, members of the international community.

Rostow's growth metaphor makes the young state largely responsible for its own success or failure. The only role a mature or postmature outside state can play is that of a wise father. That is, established states can provide the advice and the funding to get development off to a good start. After that, the rest is up to the young state itself. If its leaders follow the advice and take advantage of the opportunities provided, their underdeveloped economy, like an airplane leaving the ground, should eventually "take off" on its own into self-sustaining economic growth.

Rostow's unselfconscious paternalism and ethnocentrism are illustrated by some of his basic assumptions, perhaps most obviously by his belief that modernization is an automatic process operating according to eternal laws unaffected by history. Rostow does not see the colonial past of the developing world as playing an important role in the initial modernization of the West. Equally irrelevant are any contemporary relationships that may bind underdeveloped countries to Western

modernization theory Argues that the social change occurring in non-Western societies under colonial rule was a necessary and inevitable prelude to higher levels of social development that had been reached by the more "modern" nations.

states. There is only one path to modernity, the path blazed by the nations of western Europe and North America. Therefore, if other nations want to share in the same prosperity, they must make history repeat itself and follow the same path.

Dependency Theory

Modernization theory is plausible if you accept a metaphor that equates nations with individual organisms and attributes organismic development largely to innate growth mechanisms beyond the reach of environmental influences. But many observers reject such a view. Once colonialism is considered, some argue, modernization theory appears less and less persuasive. From their perspective, the prosperity of Western nations did not depend on the development of the internal resources of those nations; rather, it was based on the exploitation of cheap raw materials and the captive markets that colonies provided. On this account, the United States differed from European colonial powers only in that the expanding American government did not have to cross oceans to find new resources; it incorporated the lands and resources of indigenous peoples living within its own borders. In both cases, the West would never have prospered if colonial powers had not expropriated the wealth of other people to fuel their own development.

This view challenges the assumption that nations are naturally autonomous and independently responsible for their own success or failure at modernizing. If colonies and other peoples' resources are necessary for a nation to become modern, then countries without colonies, whose own resources were long ago removed by others, can never hope to become modern. The success of a few has required the failure of the many. Indeed, the capitalist nations of the world will be prosperous only as long as others are dependent on them for economic direction. This understanding of development forms the basis for dependency theory.

Dependency theory argues that dependent colonies or nations endure the reshaping of their economic structures to meet demands generated outside their borders. For example, land that could be used to raise food crops for local consumption are planted with flowers or bananas or coffee for export; thus, local needs are pushed into the background. Dependency theorists stress that backward agricultural techniques and careless human overpopulation do not explain why people in many so-called Third World countries cannot feed themselves; rather, the international capitalist economic order is directly responsible for distorting the economies of these nations.

Dependency theory argues that the development of rich capitalist nations requires the underdevelopment of colonies and less powerful trading partners. Indeed, capitalism deliberately creates underdevelopment in formerly prosperous areas that come under its domination. This is the famous **development-of-underdevelopment thesis** of dependency theory. Dependency theorists such as economist André Gunder Frank (1969) argue that the same dependency relationships that link an underdeveloped country to a developed country are found in the underdeveloped country itself. That is, the economically and politically powerful regions of an underdeveloped country dominate the less powerful areas. Local capitalist elites dominate economic transactions and keep peasants and others dependent on them, down to the level of the smallest village. Therefore, until dependent countries are able to take control of their own destinies and to restructure their economies and societies to meet local needs, underdevelopment will persist.

World-System Theory

World-system theory is associated most closely with the work of sociologist Immanuel Wallerstein and his colleagues. Beginning with *The Modern World-System,* published in 1974, Wallerstein sets forth a global framework for understanding problems of development and underdevelopment in the modern world. Like dependency theorists, Wallerstein is concerned with the history of relationships between former colonies and their former masters. He too argues that the exploitative framework of present-day relations between those states took shape historically and was fine-tuned during the colonial era.

Wallerstein rejects the idea that modern nation-states are independent entities engaged in balanced exchange in a free market; quite the contrary. When European capitalism expanded beyond its borders, beginning in the late fifteenth and early sixteenth centuries, it incorporated other regions and peoples into a world economy based on the capitalist mode of production. Wallerstein deliberately chooses to speak of a world *economy,* rather than a world empire or other political entity. This is because a world economy "precisely encompasses within its bounds empires, city-states, and the emerging 'nation-states.' It is a 'world' system, not because it encompasses the whole world, but because it is larger than any juridically defined political unit. And it is a 'world-*economy*' because the basic linkage between the parts of the system is economic" (1974, 15).

Wallerstein points out that when the European world economy took shape, it was not the only world economy in existence. Perhaps its most important competitor centered on China. Nevertheless, the European world economy was able to surpass these other world economies because of capitalism. "The secret of capitalism was in the establishment of the division of labor within the framework of a world-economy that was *not* an empire" (1974, 127). Banking, finance, and highly skilled industrial production became the specialty of western European nations, which became what Wallerstein calls the **core** of the world economy. The core exploited (and continues to exploit) the periphery, draining off its wealth to support highly skilled "free" labor and a high standard of living. The **periphery**, by contrast, practices various forms of coerced labor to produce goods to support core industries, and the standard of living for coerced workers is generally low. Wallerstein also recognizes a **semiperiphery** consisting of states like Mexico and Brazil that have played peripheral roles in the past, but that now have sufficient industrial capacity and other resources to possibly achieve core status in the future.

Wallerstein's model of the world system is functionalist, based on the metaphor that compares a society to a living organism. Functionalism compares various subsystems of society (such as economic and kinship systems) to the various systems of a living organism (such as the digestive and reproductive systems). Wallerstein's search for a social system for which the organic metaphor seemed most apt eventually led him to speak of a world system. Only a world system (and not the individual communities within it) shows the necessary integration and self-sufficiency characteristic of a living organism. Indeed, he often writes of the world system as if it were literally a living organism devouring everything in its path. Wallerstein's analysis can thus be seen as a functionalist analysis raised to a high level. He believes that the world system is the only social entity in which the relationships posited by functionalist theory actually hold.

Nevertheless, Wallerstein has been criticized for setting forth a model of the modern world in which most of the action is over. For him, the periphery has long since been reduced to a series of specialized segments of the capitalist world economy. There remain only two possibilities for future development. First, various units within the system may change roles; for example, a semiperipheral state may move to the core, or vice versa. Second, the system as a whole may be transformed into something else. This could come about, for instance, by a systemwide socialist revolution.

Neomarxian Theory

The work of Karl Marx and his followers has influenced all three of the theoretical perspectives described so far. Dependency theory and world-system theory both are sympathetic to Marx's insights and borrow heavily from marxian theory. By contrast, modernization theory notes Marx's existence only to deny the relevance of his work in explaining social change in the modern world.

The anthropological perspectives we are calling **neomarxian theory** are based on the work of a new generation of marxian scholars. Although inspired by Marx's work, they nevertheless reinterpret or reject aspects of it when necessary. Of particular note are two French neomarxians, Louis Althusser and Etienne Balibar, whose reinterpretation of Marx offered them a new way of understanding social change in the non-Western world.

---

dependency theory Argues that the success of "independent" capitalist nations has required the failure of "dependent" colonies or nations whose economies have been distorted to serve the needs of dominant capitalist outsiders.

development-of-underdevelopment thesis Argues that capitalism deliberately creates "underdevelopment" in formerly prosperous areas that come under its domination.

world-system theory Argues that, from the late fifteenth and early sixteenth centuries, European capitalism began to incorporate other regions and peoples into a world system whose parts were linked together economically but not politically.

core In world system theory, the nations specializing in banking, finance, and highly skilled industrial production.

periphery In world-system theory, those exploited former colonies of the core that supply the core with cheap food and raw materials.

semiperiphery In world-system theory, states that have played peripheral roles in the past, but that now have sufficient industrial capacity and other resources to possibly achieve core status in the future.

neomarxian theory A political economic theory based on the work of a new generation of marxian scholars who, though inspired by the work of Karl Marx, reinterpret or reject certain aspects of his thinking when necessary.

Althusser and Balibar (1971) reexamined the concept of mode of production. They concluded that, in the context of the former colonies, economic activity does not clearly represent any one of the classic modes of production. They saw colonial areas as social formations in which capitalist and noncapitalist modes of production had worked out a mode of coexistence. The capitalist mode of production introduced by the colonial power had linked up with indigenous noncapitalist modes of production, modifying them but not transforming them totally. The capitalist and noncapitalist modes linked up in this fashion are described as **articulating modes of production.**

Following the breakdown of communism in eastern Europe, many neomarxian theorists have developed what some call a *postmarxian* point of view (e.g., Laclau and Mouffe 1985). Ordinary citizens of many so-called underdeveloped societies seem to share this postmarxian perspective. Trying to avoid both traditional capitalist and traditional marxian solutions for their problems, they have created, over the last decade or so, a variety of what are called *new social movements.* From vigilante movements (such as the rondas campesinas of Peru) to squatter movements in cities to movements defending the rights of women and homosexuals to movements defending the rain forests, people have attempted to construct cultural institutions that meet their needs in ways that often bypass national governments or development agencies. (See EthnoProfile 9.6: Northern Peru [Rondas Campesinas].)

Anthropologist Arturo Escobar (1992) argues that the new social movements in Latin America are struggles over meanings as well as material conditions. They challenge the previously unquestioned truths about development and underdevelopment that guided government policies throughout the cold war, whether these concerned the importance of market capitalism or the need for socialist revolution. Escobar sees these new social movements as products of conscious reflection by people who have been marginalized in the development schemes of outsiders and who have begun to build alternative forms of life based on their own values and goals. If some of these alternatives succeed, they could produce less exploitative forms of society in generations to come. That is what Scott (1985) saw as a possible long-term outcome of the everyday forms of peasant resistance he documented in "Sedaka" Village, Malaysia. (See EthnoProfile 9.5: "Sedaka" Village.)

Globalization Theory

Modernization theory, dependency theory, world system theory, and some forms of neomarxian theory all presuppose a world in which geographic and cultural boundaries are relatively clearcut: Only if this is the case does it make sense to distinguish developed from underdeveloped nations, cores from peripheries, or local cultures from global social processes. In recent years, however, a series of worldwide political, economic, and technological changes have caused many social scientists to question the utility of these distinctions. With the end of the cold war, they argue, the cybernetics revolution led to advances in manufacturing, transportation, and communications technology that have dissolved the old polarities. The result has been **globalization:** the reshaping of local conditions by powerful global forces on an ever-intensifying scale.

Globalization is seen in the growth of transnational corporations that relocate their manufacturing operations from core to periphery or appropriate local cultural forms and turn them into images and commodities to be marketed throughout the world (Figure 14.4). It is seen in tourism, which has grown into the world's largest industry, and in migration from periphery to the core on such a massive scale that observers now speak of the "deterritorialization" of peoples and cultures that, in the past, were presumed to be firmly attached to specific geographical locations. Globalization has exacerbated social conflicts and generated new forms of cultural identity, as nation-states try to retain control over citizens living beyond their borders, and as diaspora populations struggle both for recognition in their new homes and for influence in their places of origin. Globalization has drawn the attention of many anthropologists to regions such as the borderland between northern Mexico and the southwestern United States, where struggles with contradictory social practices and ambiguous identities have long been the rule, rather than the exception. Such contexts exhibit a "diffusion of culture traits gone wild, far beyond that imagined by the Boasians" (Kearney 1995, 557). Since borderland conditions are now becoming worldwide, they undermine views of culture that depend upon settled peoples with distinct cultural attributes.

Such heterogeneous and unstable cultural spaces also call into question views like Wallerstein's that portray global processes as part of a world *system.* Anthro-

FIGURE 14.4 One dimension of globalization involves the appropriation of local cultural forms and their use on a variety of widely-sold commodities. For example, the image of "Kokopelli," taken from ancient rock art of the southwestern United States, has been reproduced on many items with no connection to its region or culture of origin, including this doormat, purchased from a mail-order catalog.

pologist Arjun Appadurai claims, to the contrary, that ever-intensifying global flows of people, technology, wealth, images, and ideologies are highly contradictory, generating global processes that are fundamentally disorganized and unpredictable (1990). Moreover, global processes are interpreted and experienced in contradictory ways by different groups and actors. Faye Ginsburg and Rayna Rapp, for example, describe the global process of *stratified reproduction,* in which some categories of people are empowered to nurture and reproduce, while others are not: "Low-income African American mothers, for example, often are stereotyped as undisciplined 'breeders' who sap the resources of the state through incessant demands on welfare. But historically and in the present, they were 'good enough' nurturers to work as childcare providers for other, more privileged class and ethnic groups" (1995, 3).

Ginzburg and Rapp emphasize that their work "focuses on how people act as agents in shaping their own reproductive lives, however constrained their options may be by national and even international power" (11). Globalization has created new opportunities for some groups, like the Kayapo and other indigenous peoples, to build worldwide organizations to defend their interests (Kearney 1995, 560). At the same time, global forces can also intensify old constraints. Evaluating the record of new social movements in Latin America, for exam-

ple, John Gledhill writes that "to date the challenge that popular forces have been able to mount to the remorseless progress of the neoliberal, neomodernization agenda, has remained limited" (1994, 198).

MODES OF CHANGE IN THE MODERN WORLD

Much of modern human history can usefully be interpreted as a struggle by local groups to *maintain* meaningful social life while trying to resist domination or hegemony imposed by outsiders. Increasingly, however, anthropologists are highlighting the struggles that take place within groups, as different factions strive to *create* a sense of meaningful social life—either to construct hegemonic ideologies and practices capable of maintaining social order on permanently unstable ground, or failing that, to impose order through domination alone. The first involves the power of persuasion; the second involves the power of the gun.

The Power of Persuasion

Hegemonic practices that attempt to persuade members of non-Western societies to change their ways can be divided into two main categories: **secular hegemony** (brought by colonial authorities and development experts) and **sacred hegemony** (brought by religious missionaries). Although the messages delivered by both sets of practices had much in common, particularly during the colonial era, they did at times clash. Often they met with success. Nevertheless, both forms of attempted hegemony often generated resistance.

SECULAR HEGEMONY: MODERNIZING THE THIRD WORLD Conquest established the fact of dominance. But to make that dominance profitable, the colonized

---

articulating modes of production An aspect of neomarxian thought that describes the links between capitalist and noncapitalist modes of production in the Third World.

globalization Reshaping of local conditions by powerful global forces on an ever-intensifying scale.

secular hegemony The attempt by Western secular authorities to persuade non-Western societies to change.

sacred hegemony The attempt by Western religious missionaries to persuade non-Western societies to change.

peoples had to be molded into imperial subjects. This took persuasion. The colonial government relied in part on missionaries to win hearts and minds, but missionaries did not always see eye to eye with the colonial government. If we define colonization as cultural domination with enforced social change, then many nonmission projects were also engaged in winning hearts and minds—if not for God, then for capitalism.

Colonial authorities set about restructuring colonized territories in ways that would make those territories pay their way. To do this, they needed the active collaboration of the people. Sometimes this collaboration was not volunteered and forced labor was employed. Yet other times, colonial authorities sought to persuade their subjects of the utility of conforming with colonial aims. For certain classes of the conquered population, conformity brought new wealth and power. They were taught—and they asked to be taught—how to do things in the Western way. Having learned, they took steps to cajole or threaten others to follow their lead.

Foreign aid and development programs in the postcolonial period continue to follow this pattern. New states request help in industrial, agricultural, or social development from Western nations. Implicitly or explicitly, they are offering to do things in a Western manner if the Western powers will but show them how. Even then, however, things do not always go smoothly.

Often, the secular powers are most concerned with economic development, and it is new ways of making a living that the people are urged to adopt. We can call this a form of hegemony to the extent that peasants, for example, are not forced to plant new strains of crops at gunpoint. Of course, to the extent that all other options are beyond their reach as a result of current social, political, and economic arrangements, the element of force is never totally out of the picture.

The Demise of a Peasant Economy For modernization theorists, the replacement of the "insufficiently developed economic techniques" of "traditional society" by market capitalism is a sign of progress. From their perspective, therefore, the demise of a rural economy in an "underdeveloped" country might be cause for cheer. For anthropologist Stephen Gudeman (1978), however, the meaning of such change is highly ambiguous. Gudeman's research allowed him to watch as self-sufficient peasants in the community of "Los Bo-

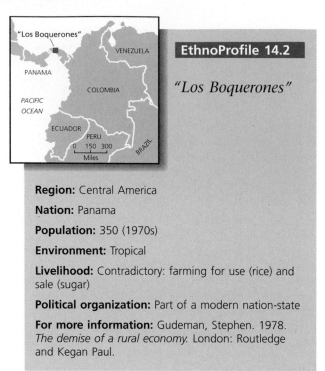

EthnoProfile 14.2

"Los Boquerones"

Region: Central America

Nation: Panama

Population: 350 (1970s)

Environment: Tropical

Livelihood: Contradictory: farming for use (rice) and sale (sugar)

Political organization: Part of a modern nation-state

For more information: Gudeman, Stephen. 1978. *The demise of a rural economy.* London: Routledge and Kegan Paul.

querones" were transformed into a rural labor force at the bottom of the capitalist order in Panama. (See EthnoProfile 14.2: "Los Boquerones.") This economic transformation from production for use (or subsistence production) to production for exchange (or commodity production) was triggered by the introduction of a cash crop: sugarcane (Figure 14.5).

The peasants of "Los Boquerones" were independent producers of subsistence goods—rice and other food crops—and they passed down their knowledge of rice farming to their children. Traditionally, they raised only enough food to tide them over from one harvest to the next, spending much of their remaining time celebrating saints' days commemorated in the Roman Catholic religious calendar. But the land was not the peasants'; it belonged to absentee landlords, who limited what the peasants could do with the land they farmed and who controlled its development.

And so it was with sugarcane production. Wealthy Panamanian families supported the expansion of cane farming in "Los Boquerones" and owned the only two sugar mills to which farmers could sell their cane. There was no turning back, moreover, because sugarcane so alters the local ecology that land once planted

FIGURE 14.5 As soon as peasants become dependent for their livelihood on the sale of cash crops such as sugarcane, shown here being harvested on a Brazilian plantation, they become dependent on the capitalist market.

in cane can never be used again for subsistence crops. In any case, the switch from rice to sugarcane was not an ecological necessity; rather, the local ecology was reshaped to take advantage of opportunities in the world sugar market.

Land reform promised landless peasants title to their own land, but the plots were too small to meet subsistence needs. Consequently, they raised more and more sugarcane to sell for cash to buy what they needed. As this happened, their understandings of labor and time were transformed. Cane cultivation was fitted into the free time they formerly had, the slack period that surrounded the original rice-growing season. In capitalism, time is money, but in subsistence agriculture, time is the surplus left after a person has produced enough food and seed for the next season. Moreover, production for exchange cannot be justified according to the system of values that peasants use to make sense of production for use: "Cane has 'utility' only when the peasant rids himself of it, the reverse of

that which he does with rice" (Gudeman 1978, 121). What is required is a new frame of reference, new understandings about the meaning and end of labor.

The villagers in "Los Boquerones" eventually lost self-sufficiency and became totally dependent on the sale of sugarcane. This made them equally dependent on the capitalist market, which had previously ignored them. The consequences were enormous. By the mid-1970s, most men were working at the mill, where the labor was easier than rice farming and wages were high owing to high world sugar prices. They enjoyed more market goods and had health and pension benefits. Yet these improvements were fragile, sustainable only as long as world sugar prices remained high. When they drop, as they must, these former peasants have little to fall back on.

Peasant Resistance against the Challenge of Capitalism If the situation in "Los Boquerones" were the rule, development in the periphery of the world system promises a dismal future for peasants everywhere. Gudeman describes a peasantry that has been totally captured by the capitalist mode of production, whose capture was facilitated by their acceptance of the hegemonic ideology of capitalism. But some anthropologists question whether that fate is inevitable. Gudeman himself notes that one factor in the demise of peasant production for use in the village was the lack of institutionalized social relationships linking peasant families with one another. His informants thus lacked an established organizational framework on which they might have relied to defend their interests.

Strong suprafamilial social structures still flourish, however, in other societies of the periphery. Indigenous kinship structures, for example, are sometimes strong enough to allow peasants to defend their mode of production in the face of capitalist challenge. This seems to be the case among the Luo speakers of western Kenya, whose mode of livelihood was studied by anthropologist Steven Johnson (1988). (See EthnoProfile 14.3: Luo-Speaking Peoples.) In western Kenya, as in the interior of Panama, land is a crucial force of production both for subsistence and for exchange. All land is now privately owned, but peasants in need of land for production can choose how to obtain access to it: They can purchase it or rent it, or they can approach landowners who are members of their clan and ask that they be granted a plot for cultivation. This last system

EthnoProfile 14.3

Luo-Speaking Peoples

Region: Eastern Africa

Nation: Kenya

Population: 3,250,000

Environment: High plateau

Livelihood: Agriculture; maize, beans, sorghum (formerly, cattle herding)

Political organization: Traditionally, some men with influence; today, elected subchiefs and chiefs, part of a modern nation-state

For more information: Parkin, David. 1978. *Cultural definition of political response: Lineal destiny among the Luo.* New York: Academic Press.

of land allocation does not treat land as a commodity, and use rights are distributed on the basis of traditional generalized reciprocity. Access to other forces of production are equally available in the same two ways. For example, ox-plow teams, seed, and even labor may be purchased on the market for cash, or else one may gain access to them without charge from neighbors or relatives.

Johnson argues that among his informants in western Kenya, "the importance of kinship obligations and generalized reciprocity suggest an association with a noncapitalist mode of production" (1988, 15). He describes his research area as a social formation characterized by two articulating modes of production: one capitalist and one noncapitalist. "The point of articulation between capitalist and noncapitalist modes of production is the peasant household where decisions are made regarding which set of social relationships is to be activated at particular points in the production process" (15). Kinship institutions are strong, and peasants remain committed to their kin as well as to ideas of prestige and autonomy that are apt in a kin-ordered

mode of production. These sociocultural facts, together with the fact that peasants still exercise some control over the forces of production, have allowed them to prevent the demise of their rural economy despite the penetration of western Kenya by the capitalist mode of production.

Doing Things "The Kentucky Way"   Globalization theory claims that in the late twentieth century the distinction between core and periphery is crumbling. As a result, citizenship or residence status no longer guarantees to protect people from the whipsaw effects of global economic forces. Residents of core nations might be as vulnerable to globalizing dislocations as residents of the periphery. As a result, we should not be surprised to find residents of core nations struggling to resist capture by the capitalist market.

Rhoda Halperin did fieldwork in a culturally diverse, racially integrated working-class community in northeastern Kentucky. (See EthnoProfile 14.4: Northeastern Kentucky.) Regionally based family networks, whose members were not always "biological" kin, allow people to defend themselves against powerful economic forces. Members of these family networks practice what they call "the Kentucky way," which Halperin, following Polanyi, identifies as *householding:* a mode of economic integration that involves "provisioning of a group by means of circular flows of resources, goods, and services. . . . Goods move among members of a family network rather than back and forth between two points (reciprocity) or in and out from center to periphery (redistribution)" (1994, 145–46). Householding in northeastern Kentucky is anchored by family-based subsistence farms; like traditional peasant farms in "Los Boquerones," subsistence farmers in rural Kentucky raise food crops using family labor in order to meet consumption needs, not to sell for a profit.

Family members occasionally work for wages in local factories, but they tend to change jobs often and are likely to take odd jobs or engage in economic activities that official employment statistics ignore. Such work makes up an informal economy that contrasts with the formal, governmentally monitored practices of capitalism. Halperin points out, for example, that government statisticians would describe many of the Kentucky householders she knew as "sporadically employed" or even "unemployed," but this is only because the government focuses on what individuals do and ignores the cultural system in which their actions are embedded. Regionally based family networks who do things the Kentucky way coordinate a wide range of formal and informal subsistence- or income-generating activities among their members, who are motivated by the goal of keeping the family network intact in its community of origin, not by the promise of upward social mobility.

Halperin describes the Kentucky way in terms very similar to those Johnson used to describe Luo articulating modes of production; she says that householding "coordinates elements of capitalist and precapitalist economic processes" (1994, 166). Indeed, she says that householding is "designed potentially to handle complexity, change and resistance to political and economic elites in cultural systems where there are constant tensions between the demands of elites and the material and cultural requirements of people who stand on the lower rungs of state stratification systems" (1994, 143). Moreover, she describes the Kentucky way as a form of peasant resistance; "People see themselves as resistant to factory work and their resistance takes many forms" (1994, 161). They criticize fellow factory workers for wasting money on beer and partying instead of investing it in land for gardens or time with family. Although the Kentucky way developed as a response to layoffs and plant closings, Halperin views it as a positive alternative allowing those with some land to be selective about their involvement in the wage economy. "There is a wisdom here . . . a steadfastness and a doggedness that has tremendous resiliency precisely because it is multifaceted and flexible. If people opt out of the family network, they give up householding as a provisioning process and their powers of resistance are weakened considerably" (1994, 165).

SACRED HEGEMONY: MISSIONARIES IN AFRICA The Christian church was a powerful secular institution when young Western states pushed outward across the oceans to make their first territorial conquests. Missionaries of one sort or another accompanied Western expansion in the Americas, in Asia, and in Africa (Figure 14.6).

Anthropologist T. O. Beidelman (1982) examined the nature of missionary activity in Africa. He learned that all missionaries were not alike. Some mission stations were large and well-funded, others were small and run on a shoestring. Catholic missionaries differed from Protestant missionaries, and the Protestants differed among themselves. In fact, different denomina-

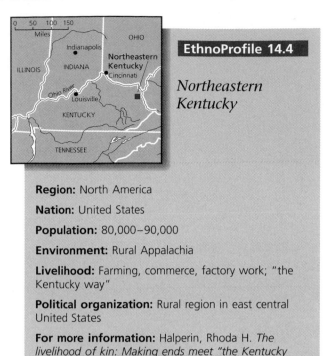

EthnoProfile 14.4

Northeastern Kentucky

Region: North America

Nation: United States

Population: 80,000–90,000

Environment: Rural Appalachia

Livelihood: Farming, commerce, factory work; "the Kentucky way"

Political organization: Rural region in east central United States

For more information: Halperin, Rhoda H. *The livelihood of kin: Making ends meet "the Kentucky way."* 1990. Austin: University of Texas Press.

tions regularly competed over souls to evangelize just as Europeans competed for access to raw materials for industry. Africans found the celibacy of Catholic priests curious. Nevertheless, Catholic missionaries were often able to develop close ties with African converts. Priests were unencumbered by families, well educated, of high status, and often spent their entire careers in a single area. They tended to be more tolerant of African custom, perhaps because they expected to achieve their goals in the long term. By contrast, Protestant missions were eventually staffed by married couples or families. It was thought that those families would present positive role models for converts, yet the presence of women and children in mission stations frequently widened the gulf between missionaries and converts. The missionaries felt the need to protect their wives and families from too-easy contact with Africans.

In Beidelman's opinion, "Christian missions represent the most naive and ethnocentric, and therefore the most thoroughgoing, facet of colonial life. . . . Missionaries demonstrated a more radical and morally intense commitment to rule than political administrators or businessmen" (1982, 5). Beidelman focused his

FIGURE 14.6 Missionary work has been carried out all over the world.

attention on the Church Missionary Society (CMS), who had worked among the Kaguru of Tanzania, people among whom he had carried out fieldwork (See EthnoProfile 14.5: Kaguru). The CMS missionaries were "born-again Anglican Protestants" who first entered Kaguru territory in 1876. Although the CMS missionaries were ostensibly in Africa to save the souls of Africans, "strictly considered the missionaries were in the field to save themselves. . . . Evangelism was thus as much to build character as to convert. Failure to convert, even for decades, was seen as God's will, as a test of faith, and not as a reason either to abandon an area or to reassess methods" (99–100). In more than one instance, CMS missionaries found themselves at odds with secular colonial authorities.

Eventually, the CMS did gain converts and establish congregations. The missionaries introduced certain practices that the Kaguru embraced, the most important being the religious revival. Revival "could occur only after Africans had been converted and then strayed. . . . Revival allowed a congregation to revalidate publicly certain norms which had been threatened; it also allowed readmission of persons who had been judged unfit for mission life, but whose skills were essential" (Beidelman 1982, 106–7). Revivalism was similar to traditional Kaguru witchcraft confessions. It seems likely that converts had, perhaps unwittingly, carried into their new religion practices developed in

the old. Since the 1930s and 1940s, revival has become an important political mechanism among the Kaguru. "Through revival and the resultant assumption of new, superior moral status as 'saved' or 'reborn' Christians . . . local Africans could sometimes compete with local African pastors, catechists, and even European missionaries as the type of Christian most fit to judge and lead others" (108).

CMS missionaries supported revivalism, and yet they were wary of participating fully in revivals with Africans, lest their own admission of sin damage their prestige and authority. The CMS did not want to get involved in secular matters such as education, yet under the colonial regime it either provided the schools demanded by the colonial administration or lost government support. The CMS encouraged Bible study and direct inspiration by the word of God as set forth in the Bible, without the mediation of priests. But African converts who were literate were then able to read stories in the Bible about God redeeming his people from oppression. They began to identify with the oppressed and to see God as on their side. This was particularly disconcerting to the missionaries, who found themselves identified with the oppressors.

Perhaps the greatest irony revealed by Beidelman's study came following the independence of Tanzania, when Kaguru who had rejected the rigorous CMS way of life were asked by the Tanzanian government to live

EthnoProfile 14.5

Kaguru

Region: Eastern Africa

Nation: Tanzania

Population: 100,000 (1960s)

Environment: Varied; about half plateau, some highlands and lowlands, jungle, meadow, savanna, river valley, bush

Livelihood: Agriculture (mostly maize)

Political organization: Traditionally, some men with influence; now, part of a modern nation-state

For more information: Beidelman, T. O. 1971. *The Kaguru.* New York: Holt, Rinehart and Winston.

in much the same way. They were to work hard, deny themselves material comforts, and resist the temptation to deviate from authority. "There are new kinds of missionaries afoot in Ukaguru. Some of the sermons now preached by socialist bureaucrats may appear new, but their tactics and aims are not that different from what has passed away" (1982, 209).

This paradoxical outcome is what Jean and John Comaroff have described as "the colonization of consciousness and the consciousness of colonization" (1991, 4). In their study of the effect of Christian missionizing among the southern Tswana by British Nonconformist evangelists between 1820 and 1920, they encountered similar paradoxes resulting from the struggles between missionaries and their potential converts. (See EthnoProfile 2.1: Tswana.) While evangelists were striving to remake Tswana into Christians that could be incorporated into a global civilization, the Tswana were attracted by tools, goods, and knowledge brought by the missionaries, which they hoped to use to further their own projects. Nevertheless, by having to deal with one another regularly, even if only in the context

of struggle, both parties to the encounter were changed. Missionaries condemned certain Tswana practices, such as rainmaking rituals, as superstitions and yet they ended up creating new prayer services as substitutes for these practices. The Tswana, in turn, found themselves adopting certain Western practices in their very attempts to discredit mission ways. Even to argue with missionaries about whether Christian prayer or Tswana ritual was more effective in bringing rain was to accept some very un-Tswana assumptions about rational argumentation and the testing of hypotheses against empirical facts (1991, 310). In the Comaroffs' view, however, the factor that most transformed Tswana images of themselves was the translation of the Bible into their own language. Whereas traditional Tswana understandings connected language to the breath and the intentions of speakers, the mission version of the language reduced it to a neutral medium of communication in which traditional words were sometimes given new meanings. Yet because the Tswana could see the value of literacy, they adopted the missionized version of their language even when they rejected the gospel message. In the Comaroffs' words, "Colonized peoples like the Southern Tswana frequently reject the message of the colonizers, and yet are powerfully and profoundly affected by its media" (1991, 311).

The Power of the Gun

As with everything else in social life, the plausibility of theories about the destiny of colonized peoples depends on which aspects of their experiences are emphasized. A deterministic view holds that capitalism is bound to triumph, whether for good or for ill. But such a view is challenged by the example of the Luo-speaking peoples of Kenya, among whom capitalism's advance seems either to have stalled or to have veered unexpectedly off its intended course. Even more challenging are cases in which the victims of cultural domination resist the dominators and reject the social changes being forced on them. Specifically, these were indigenous peoples who not only cut political ties to colonial or neocolonial rulers, but also attempted to cut economic ties to the entire capitalist world system. Such dramatic movements often involved the use of military force and might reasonably be called, as Eric Wolf (1969) calls them, *peasant wars.*

Wolf examined six cases of peasant revolution in the

twentieth century: Mexico, Russia, China, Vietnam, Algeria, and Cuba. To understand these revolutions, he argues, requires looking at the historical developments leading up to them. In all six cases, those developments can be traced to the "world-wide spread and diffusion of a particular cultural system, that of North Atlantic capitalism," which was "profoundly alien to many of the areas which it engulfed in its spread" (1969, 276).

The prototypical situation in these cases is colonialism—cultural domination with forced social change. The dominating cultural system in colonialism was capitalism. As a result, forced social change involved getting local peoples to accept the key capitalist metaphor: that land, people, and things can all be treated as objects for sale on the market. Most peasants who tried to live by this capitalist metaphor were ill equipped to withstand the risks and losses it entailed. Some peasants, however, were not only threatened by capitalism but had sufficient resources to try to resist it, by force if necessary. These were "middle peasants" who owned some land or peasants who lived in regions on the fringe of control by landlords. They acted not to usher in a new order but to make the world they knew safe for peasants like themselves. Once successful, however, their revolutionary actions made it impossible to return to the way of life they originally set out to defend.

The revolutions examined by Wolf all were waged by armed bands of peasants, but they probably would not have succeeded had not other indigenously organized groups been fighting with them. Sometimes peasants fought alongside a "paramilitary party organized around a certain vision of what the new society is to be" (Wolf 1969, 296), such as the Bolsheviks in Russia. The Russian revolution was widely viewed as the first successful overthrow of capitalism. It thus became the earliest prototype for revolutionaries seeking to oust capitalists elsewhere. This was the case, for example, in the Chinese and Vietnamese revolutions: "A common Marxist ideology—and especially the Leninist concept of the revolutionary leadership, leading the masses in the interest of the masses—furnished a ready-made idiom in which to cast their own experience of fusion between rebel soldiery and revolutionary leadership" (297).

But revolutionary leaders soon discovered that the Russian example could not be slavishly imitated. Peasant revolutionaries also used traditional group structures to organize their armed resistance. The idiom of socialism meshed nicely with communal idioms characteristic of traditional village organization in China and Vietnam, for example. What was revolutionary, however, was using what had been a village idiom to link villages with one another and with the army.

Indeed, a large part of the subversive power of revolution comes from the way it allows new metaphors to enter social life through armed struggle. That is, it is not enough simply to declare that all people are brothers and sisters nor to preach that peasants, soldiers, workers, and intellectuals are equals. The experience that makes these metaphorical assertions plausible occurs for revolutionaries as they make their revolution. Wolf argues, for example, that by the time they achieved victory in 1949, the citizen-soldiers of the Chinese revolution had lived through a variety of practical experiences that had turned ideological claims into reality: "The experience of war in the hinterland had taken them far from cities and industrial areas; it had taught them the advantages of dispersal, of a wide distribution of basic skills rather than a dense concentration of advanced skills. The citizen-soldiers of the guerrilla army had, in fact, lived lives in which the roles of peasant, worker, soldier, and intellectual intermingled to the point of fusion. . . . In China the relation of the peasant to the citizen-army was immediate and concrete" (1969, 300).

As the twentieth century ends, armed resistance assumes new forms. Ruling elites in nation-states struggling for control in uncertain times have not hesitated to use the power of the gun to assert domination over recalcitrant citizens. Often enough, the citizens they wish to control are viewed as obstacles to development plans made by the elites, and sometimes the citizens fight back. This has been the experience of the Nuer of the southern Sudan. When Evans-Pritchard lived among them in the 1930s, it was the colonial Anglo-Egyptian Condominium government that was struggling to "pacify" the Nuer and their Dinka and Anyuak neighbors. Between 1955 and 1972, however, the Nuer and their neighbors fought a civil war with the northern Sudanese, which finally ended with an agreement that the southern Sudan, in which they lived, would be accorded regional autonomy. Nevertheless, only a decade later, the government of Sudan was again threatening the south because it wanted to control recently discovered oil reserves in western Nuerland. When then-president Gaafar Nimieri announced in 1983 his intention to redivide the south into three parts and to impose Islamic law on the nation as a whole, it was clear that the civil war in the south was about to resume.

Anthropologist Sharon Hutchinson had just completed a period of field research among the Nuer at that time. In the early 1990s, she returned to Sudan, only to find that half a million southern Sudanese had already died as a result of warfare and over 2 million refugees had fled the area, most moving north to Khartoum, the Sudanese capital. Once there, they were harassed by the police and risked being conscripted into the national army—which would send them south to fight their own people. Hutchinson visited again in 1992 to assess the situation of those eastern Nuer who had remained within the war zone. She reports, "I found a people who were physically and emotionally exhausted but undefeated. . . . A truce without hope of equality was unacceptable to them" (1996, 9). Their resilience was remarkable in the face of devastation that showed no signs of ending. The Nuer she knew had been deeply politicized by the earlier civil war and many were now active in military resistance movements. They had become a changed people living in a world very different from the one Evans-Pritchard encountered. As the Nuer reassessed their traditions in the context of their turbulent history, Hutchinson encountered many areas of intersection "between Nuer understandings of their rapidly changing life circumstances and more abstract visions of the encounter between 'global' and 'local' forces of transformation" discussed by anthropologists and other social scientists (1996, 49).

Many of the cases in this chapter demonstrate the human ability to cope creatively with changed life circumstances. They remind us that human beings are not passive in the face of the new, that they actively and resiliently respond to life's challenges. Nevertheless, the example of the Kréen-Akaróre and the current unresolved situation of the Nuer remind us that successful outcomes are never ensured. Modes of livelihood that may benefit some human groups can overwhelm and destroy others. Western capitalism and modern technology have exploded into a vortex of global forces that resist control. A critical self-awareness of our common humanity, together with concerted practical action to lessen exploitation, may be all that can prevent these forces from destroying us all.

Key Terms

capitalism	core
colonialism	periphery
political economy	semiperiphery
neocolonialism	neomarxian theory
modernization theory	articulating modes of
dependency theory	production
development-of-	globalization
underdevelopment thesis	secular hegemony
world-system theory	sacred hegemony

Chapter Summary

1. Modern Western history has been characterized by the rise of capitalism. The achievements of European capitalism were in many cases financed by wealth brought to Europe from other parts of the globe. As a result, other parts of the globe were also transformed.

2. The arrival of capitalism outside the West was often accompanied by the growth of new, commercially oriented cities, which became the focus of intense culture change. Western influence was usually greatest in such cities. The capitalist penetration of non-Western societies was frequently followed by the political conquest of such societies, which were then reshaped to streamline economic exploitation. Indigenous peoples lost their autonomy and were reintegrated as component groups within a larger new society.

3. Colonial empires drew together economically and politically vast and previously unconnected areas of the world. Although colonies were politically controlled by the colonizers, later independence did not free former colonies from deeply entangling economic ties with their former masters. These entanglements have, in some cases, persisted for over 100 years and are called *neocolonialism*.

4. The key metaphor of capitalism is that the world is a market and everything within the world—including land, material objects, and human beings—can be bought and sold. Such a view was unknown in noncapitalist societies before Western

colonialism, even in those with highly developed economic institutions. To function intelligibly within the capitalist world order, colonized peoples had to begin to see the world as a storehouse of potential commodities.

5. Western colonialism triggered a series of profound changes throughout the world. Today, anthropologists choose among five theoretical positions to explain culture change in the non-Western world: modernization theory, dependency theory, world-system theory, neomarxian theory, and globalization theory.

6. Although many varieties of modern social change are backed by force, people attempting to introduce change often rely more on tactics of persuasion. Secular authorities attempted to persuade conquered peoples of the superiority of capitalist economic and political institutions. Many colonized groups embraced these worldviews and institutions, often with unforeseen consequences. Missionaries accompanied Western colonizers wherever they went and attempted to persuade conquered peoples of the superiority of Western religious worldviews.

7. Many anthropologists have assumed that capitalist takeover of traditional societies either has long since occurred or inevitably will occur in the future. Nevertheless, it seems some societies have successfully resisted capitalist takeover, either by maintaining noncapitalist modes of production alongside the capitalist mode or by using military force to eject the capitalists.

Suggested Readings

Bodley, John. 1988. *Tribal peoples and development issues.* Mountain View, CA: Mayfield. *An excellent collection of articles—some recent, some dating back into the nineteenth century—providing examples of the effect of the modern world system on tribal peoples.*

———. 1990. *Victims of progress.* 3d ed. Mountain View, CA: Mayfield. *A very accessible but very depressing documentation of the destruction of tribal peoples throughout the world, all in the name of progress.*

Hobart, Mark, ed. 1993. *An anthropological critique of development.* London: Routledge. *Anthropologists from Britain, Holland, and Germany challenge the notion that Western approaches to development have been successful. They use ethnographic case studies to demonstrate how Western experts who disregard indigenous knowledge contribute to the growth of ignorance.*

Wallerstein, Immanuel. 1974. *The modern world-system.* New York: Academic Press. *A difficult but tremendously influential work that started the world-system approach to understanding and explaining patterns of social change in recent world history.*

Wolf, Eric. 1969. *Peasant wars of the twentieth century.* New York: Harper and Row. *An important, readable study of the commonalities of this century's major wars of revolution.*

15

Anthropology in Everyday Life

CHAPTER OUTLINE

Anthropology beyond the University

Awareness and Uncertainty

Freedom and Constraint

any students say that they have found anthropology interesting—very interesting in fact—and that they have learned a great deal about ethnocentrism, other cultures, and even themselves. But they frequently ask what they can do with it. What is the point of it if they don't go on to university teaching? An appropriate response usually comes in three parts.

ANTHROPOLOGY BEYOND THE UNIVERSITY

The first part addresses the practical concern: Do anthropologists do anything other than teach at universities? The answer is yes. Sir Edward B. Tylor, a founder of anthropology in the early 1870s, called the new field "a reformer's science." The commitment to changing things did not last, however. Anthropology soon concerned itself more with describing and explaining the world than with changing it. Even so, there were always some anthropologists who believed their discipline had a practical side.

Margaret Mead saw anthropology's practical side throughout her long career. Following her first fieldwork in Samoa in the 1920s, she began to speak out on issues of concern in the United States. She suggested that adolescence in the United States did not have to be as stormy as it was and that perhaps we could learn from the Samoans about the nature of adolescence.

In the 1930s and 1940s, several American anthropologists played important roles in attempts to reform the U.S. Bureau of Indian Affairs. During World War II, Mead and other anthropologists were actively involved in the war effort. They developed strategies for boosting morale at home, and as the war ended, they helped draw up terms that would allow the Japanese to surrender with as little turmoil as possible.

After World War II, most anthropologists left government work and went back to their universities, becoming more concerned with the details of anthropological theory than anthropology's practical impact. During this period, the discipline grew at a phenomenal rate, but the growth of its practical applications lagged.

Anthropology in the United States was strongly af-fected by the events of the 1960s. The general distrust of authority at that time was tied to an increasing concern over the uses to which social science data were being put. These concerns increased during the war in Vietnam. For many anthropologists, as for professionals in many other disciplines, the times seemed to demand social action. Since the 1960s, four major trends in anthropology have led to an increasingly prominent role for applied anthropology (Chambers 1985, 9). First, a gradual maturation of the discipline has led to a broader range of concerns, including those associated with regional, national, and even international systems, many of which have applied outcomes.

Second, the peoples with whom anthropologists have traditionally worked have become more sophisticated as they enter into the world system. Consequently, they are increasingly aware of the power imbalance between themselves and anthropologists. In addition, although anthropologists have taken much from the societies they have studied, they have not always given much in return. Some anthropologists feel that the knowledge they have gained and the careers they have established as a result require greater return than a mention in a footnote. In some places, anthropologists have been called on to remedy this imbalance by demonstrating how their work will directly benefit the local community.

Third, more anthropologists have undertaken work in the United States. This trend is due in part to the difficulty of obtaining grants to support fieldwork outside the United States. This trend also stems from a concern about the problems of one's own society and what an anthropological perspective might bring to their solution.

Fourth, over the past 20 years, there have been more new Ph.D. anthropologists and fewer academic jobs. As a result, students and professors realize that "the profession must either shrink or prepare its students for a greater variety of employment possibilities" (Chambers 1985, 10). In answer to this need, applied anthropology programs have multiplied throughout the United States during the last decade. Today, anthropologists can be found in all sorts of areas. A few are psychotherapists, employing the insights of anthropologist Gregory Bateson and others on family systems and family therapy. Others are cross-cultural social workers. Still others are actively involved in international development, sometimes working with the U.S. Agency for

FIGURE 15.1 Applied anthropologists work in a variety of settings. Here, gerontologist Dena Shenk interviews an informant while carrying out a research project for a local social service agency on the status of the rural elderly.

International Development. Their work includes projects dealing with such issues as appropriate technology, fuelwood shortages, agricultural credit, new lands development, feasibility studies for dams and other projects, bilingual education, livestock improvement and range management, and the like (for more examples, see Partridge 1984; van Willigen 1991).

Other anthropologists are in medical anthropology, a new and rapidly growing field. Some are involved in gerontology (Figure 15.1), designing programs for the elderly and doing research on aging in different cultures. Others work in public or community health, medical education, nursing, or hospital planning. Another important area of work is in medical care delivery to distinct ethnic groups. This is related to applied anthropological work in international health, which includes demographics, epidemiology, planning and development of health programs, family planning, environmental health, and the like. Many applied anthropologists are also working on AIDS-related projects.

Some anthropologists have gone into public policy and planning as interpreters, mediators, civil servants, or urban planners. Others have begun to work with indigenous peoples' organizations or with human rights organizations such as Survival International and Cul-tural Survival, itself founded by anthropologists David Maybury-Lewis and Pia Maybury-Lewis. We examine four cases below in greater detail.

Sorghum and Millet in Honduras and the Sudan

Applied anthropologists carry out much work in international development, often in agricultural programs. The U.S. Agency for International Development (AID) is the principal instrument of U.S. foreign development assistance. One new direction taken by AID in the mid-1970s was to create multidisciplinary research programs to improve food crops in developing countries. An early research program dealt with sorghum and millet, important grains in some of the poorest countries in the world. This was the International Sorghum/Millet Research Project (INTSORMIL). Selected American universities investigated one of six areas: plant breeding, agronomy, plant pathology, plant physiology, food chemistry, and socioeconomic studies.

Anthropologists from the University of Kentucky, selected for the socioeconomic study, used ethnographic field research techniques to gain firsthand knowledge of the socioeconomic constraints on the

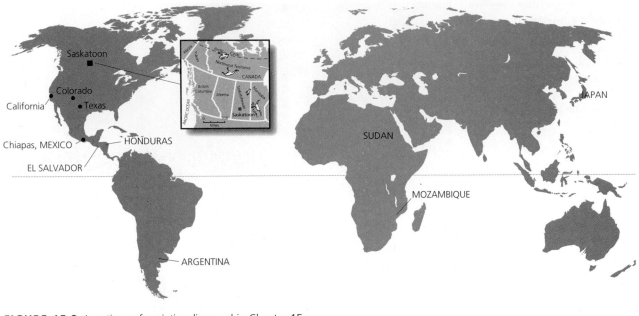

FIGURE 15.2 Locations of societies discussed in Chapter 15.

production, distribution, and consumption of sorghum and millet among limited-resource agricultural producers in the western Sudan and in Honduras. They intended to make their findings available to INTSORMIL as well as to scientists and government officials in the host countries. They believed sharing such knowledge could lead to more effective research and development. This task also required ethnographic research and anthropological skill.

The principal investigators from the University of Kentucky were Edward Reeves, Billie DeWalt, and Katherine DeWalt. They took a holistic and comparative approach, called *Farming Systems Research* (FSR). This approach attempts to determine the techniques used by farmers with limited resources to cope with the social, economic, and ecological conditions under which they live. FSR is holistic because it examines how the different crops and livestock are integrated and managed as a system. It also relates farm productivity to household consumption and off-farm sources of family income (Reeves, DeWalt, and DeWalt 1987, 74). This is very different from the traditional methods of agricultural research, which grow and test one crop at a time in an experiment station. The scientists at

INTSORMIL are generally acknowledged among the best sorghum and millet researchers in the world, but their expertise comes from traditional agricultural research methods. They have spent little time working on the problems of limited-resource farmers in Third World countries.

The anthropologists saw their job as facilitating "a constant dialog between the farmer, who can tell what works best given the circumstances, and agricultural scientists, who produce potentially useful new solutions to old problems" (Reeves, DeWalt, and DeWalt 1987, 74–75). However, this was easier said than done in the sorghum/millet project. The perspectives of farmers and scientists were very different from one another. The anthropologists found themselves having to learn the languages and the conceptual systems of both the farmers and the scientists for the two groups to be able to communicate. The FSR anthropologists had four research goals:

1. To discover what was holding back the increased production of sorghum and millet so that they could identify areas that needed attention from the agricultural researchers

2. To discover which aspects of new technology the farmers thought might benefit them the most

3. To suggest how new crop "varieties and/or technologies might most easily and beneficially be introduced into communities and regions"

4. "To suggest the long-term implications that changing production, distribution, and consumption patterns might have on these communities" (1987, 74)

The anthropologists began research in June 1981 in western Sudan and in southern Honduras. They were in the field for 14 months of participant-observation and in-depth interviewing, as well as survey interviewing of limited-resource farmers, merchants, and middlemen. They discovered that the most significant constraints the farmers faced were uncertain rainfall, low soil fertility, and inadequate labor and financial resources (Reeves, DeWalt, and DeWalt 1987, 80). Equally important were the social and cultural systems within which the farmers were embedded. Farmers based their farming decisions on their understanding of who they were and what farming meant in their own cultures.

As a result of the FSR group's research, it became increasingly clear that "real progress in addressing the needs of small farmers in the Third World called for promising innovations to be tested at village sites and on farmers' fields under conditions that closely approximated those which the farmers experience" (Reeves, DeWalt, and DeWalt 1987, 77). Convincing the scientists and bureaucrats of this required the anthropologists to become advocates for the limited-resource farmers. Bill DeWalt and Edward Reeves ended up negotiating INTSORMIL's contracts with the Honduran and Sudanese governments and succeeded in representing the farmers. They had to learn enough about the bureaucracies and the agricultural scientists so they could put the farmers' interests in terms the others could understand.

As a result of the applied anthropologists' work, INTSORMIL scientists learned to understand how small farmers in two countries made agricultural decisions. They also learned that not all limited-resource farmers are alike. The poorest third of the Sudanese farmers, for example, have to decide during the cropping season whether to weed their own gardens or someone else's for a wage. If they choose the former, they realize a long-term gain but they and their families go hungry. The lat-

ter choice enables them to buy food in the short run but lowers their own harvests later. The decisions farmers make, and the needs they have, are context sensitive.

Together with INTSORMIL, the Honduran and Sudanese governments have increased funding for projects aimed at limited-resource farmers. Staff have been assigned to work with INTSORMIL, new programs have begun, and the research results of the anthropologists are guiding the breeding of sorghum.

Reeves, DeWalt, and DeWalt warn that it is too early to demonstrate gains in sorghum or millet production and use in either country. "Nevertheless, INTSORMIL scientists are clearly coming to accept the farming systems research goals and the value of anthropological fieldwork. The FSR Group has argued that on-site research is both desirable and necessary for the problems of farmers to be correctly identified and that eventually on-farm testing of new plant varieties and technologies will be essential to ensure that farmers are going to accept them" (1987, 79).

The INTSORMIL staff was so impressed by the anthropologists' work that it has begun funding long-term research directed at relieving the constraints that limited-resource farmers face. Rather than trying to develop and then introduce hybrids, INTSORMIL research is now aimed at modifying existing varieties of sorghum. The goal is better-yielding local varieties that can be grown together with other crops.

In summary, Reeves, DeWalt, and DeWalt point out that without the anthropological research, fewer development funds would have been allocated to research in Sudan and Honduras. More important, the nature of the development aid would have been different.

Lead Poisoning among Mexican American Children

In the summer of 1981, a Mexican American child was treated for lead poisoning in a Los Angeles emergency room. When the child's stomach was pumped, a bright orange powder was found. It was lead tetroxide, more than 90 percent elemental lead. Lead in that form is not usually found in lead poisoning cases in the United States. When questioned by health professionals, the mother revealed that her child had been given a folk remedy in powdered form—*azarcón*. Azarcón was used to treat an illness called *empacho*, part of the Mexican American set of culturally recognized diseases. Empacho is believed to be a combination of indigestion and constipation.

This case prompted a public health alert that was sent out nationally to clinics and physicians. The alert turned up another case of lead poisoning from azarcón in Greeley, Colorado. A nurse had read about the Los Angeles case and asked if the mother was treating the child for empacho. She was. Additional questioning in Los Angeles and Greeley turned up what appeared to be widespread knowledge of azarcón in both Mexican American communities. The U.S. Public Health Service decided that an anthropological study of azarcón would be useful.

The Public Health Service in Dallas called Dr. Robert Trotter, who had done research on Mexican American folk medicine. Trotter had never heard of azarcón, and could not find it in south Texas. But a short time later, he received information from the Los Angeles County Health Department, which had discovered that azarcón was not the only name for the preparation. When he asked for *greta,* he was sold a heavy yellow powder that turned out to be lead oxide with an elemental lead content of approximately 90 percent. The shop owners said it was used to treat empacho. Here was confirmation that two related lead-based remedies were being used to treat empacho. Trotter discovered that a wholesale distributor in Texas was selling greta to over 120 herb shops.

Trotter was asked to work in a health education project designed to reduce the use of these lead-based remedies. Because of the complex nature of the problem, he had six different clients with somewhat different needs and responsibilities. The first client was the Public Health Service office in Dallas, which sponsored the first study he did.

The second client was the task force that had been formed to create and implement a health education project in Colorado and California. Task force members wanted to reduce the use of azarcón—but they did not want to attack or denigrate the folk medical system that promoted its use. They knew that attacking folk beliefs would produce strong resistance to the entire health campaign and make people ignore the message, no matter how important it was. The task force hoped Trotter's ethnographic data could help design a health awareness campaign that would encourage a switch to nonpoisonous remedies. The goal of the task force became product substitution—to convince people to switch from greta or azarcón to another, harmless

remedy for empacho that was already part of the folk medical system. This strategy was based on an old advertising technique: It is easier to get people to switch from one product to another when both products perform the same function; it is difficult or impossible to get people to stop using a product they think they need, regardless of its known danger, unless an acceptable alternative is provided.

The Food and Drug Administration (FDA), Trotter's third client, decided it needed basic ethnographic information on the use of greta. The staff wanted to know who used it, what it was used for, how it was used, and where it could be purchased. The FDA had never considered that lead oxide could be a food additive or a drug, and it needed verifiable data that the compound was being used in this way. As a result of Trotter's research, the FDA concluded that greta was a food additive. It issued a Class I recall to ban the sale of greta as a remedy.

Client number four was the Texas regional office of the Department of Health and Human Services. It needed assistance in creating and carrying out a survey along the United States–Mexico border to discover what people knew about greta and azarcón and how many people used them. Trotter's survey indicated that as many as 10 percent of the Mexican American households along the border had at one time used greta or azarcón. The survey also turned up several other potentially toxic compounds that were in use.

Trotter's fifth client was the Hidalgo County Health Care Corporation, a local migrant clinic. It needed a survey that would compare the level of greta and azarcón usage in the local population in general with the level of usage among the people who came to the clinic. Trotter found that the two groups did not differ significantly in their knowledge about and use of the two preparations; however, the clinic population was more likely to treat folk illnesses with folk medicines than was the population at large.

The sixth client was the Migrant Health Service. It needed to know whether it was necessary to design a nationwide lead project. Based on the research that Trotter and others did, it became clear that such a major project was not necessary; rather, health projects were targeted and health professionals notified in the areas of high greta and azarcón use only.

Because Trotter had several clients, his work led to a variety of outcomes. The health education project resulted in considerable media exposure on the dangers of greta and azarcón. Public service announcements were broadcast on Spanish-language radio stations, special television programs aired in Los Angeles county, and information packets were sent to migrant clinics. Trotter commissioned Mexican American students at the Pan American University to design a culturally appropriate poster warning of the dangers of greta and azarcón. The poster, using the culturally powerful symbol of *La Muerte* (a skeleton) to warn of the dangers, has been placed in over 5,000 clinics and other public access sites (Trotter 1987, 152).

The various health education measures may be judged successful by the fact that, two years after the project began, both greta and azarcón were hard to find in the United States. In addition, the various surveys Trotter carried out led to better screening procedures for lead poisoning. Information on traditional medications is now routinely gathered when lead poisoning is suspected, and several other potentially toxic compounds have been discovered. Health professionals were able to learn about the current use of traditional medications in their areas and about the specific health education needs of their clients.

"Perhaps the most important overall result of the project was an increased awareness of the utility of anthropology in solving culturally related health care problems in at least one segment of the medical care delivery system. . . . Our discovery of the use of greta and azarcón and the subsequent discoveries that similar remedies are causing lead poisoning in Hmong, Saudi Arabian, and Chinese communities have finally demonstrated a clear link between anthropological research and the dominant biophysical side of modern medicine. Anthropological knowledge, research methods, and theoretical orientations are finally being used to solve epidemiological problems overlooked by the established disciplines" (Trotter 1987, 154).

Trotter brought to the project the skills of the anthropologist; his principal focus was on culture. He took a holistic, comparative approach, and he was willing to innovate, to look for explanations in areas that investigators from other disciplines had not thought to look.

Doing Business in Japan

Anthropologist Richard Reeves-Ellington (1993) designed and implemented a cross-cultural training program for a North American company doing business in

FIGURE 15.3 Japanese and North American business-people negotiate better when they understand something of each other's culture.

Japan. (See EthnoProfile 11.3: Japan.) He found that many of the traditional methods of anthropology—cultural understanding, ethnographic data, and participant-observation—helped managers conduct business in Japan. Reeves-Ellington began the training program by having employees first gather general cultural information artifacts ("How are things classified or what are the artifacts of an agreed classification system?"), social knowledge ("What are proper principles for behavior? What are the values that drive the categories and artifacts?"), and cultural logic. Social knowledge or values are based on an underlying, taken-for-granted cultural logic. Coming to understand Japanese cultural logic is of great importance to foreigners wishing to live and work in Japan.

The managers at the company decided to learn how to carry out introductions, meetings, leave-taking, dinner, and drinking in Japan (Figure 15.3). Each practice was analyzed according to the framework of artifacts, social knowledge, and cultural logic and was taught by a combination of methods that included the general observations that the managers collected while visiting Japanese museums, theaters, shrines, baseball games,

TABLE 15.1   INTRODUCTIONS AT BUSINESS MEETINGS

Artifacts	Social Knowledge	Cultural Logic
Technology • Business cards • *Meishi* Visual behavior • Presentation of *meishi* by presenting card, facing recipient. • Senior people present *meishi* first. • Guest presents first, giving name, company affiliation, and bowing. • Host presents *meishi* in same sequence. • Upon sitting at conference table, all *meishi* are placed in front of recipient to assure name use.	• Once given a card is kept—not discarded. • *Meishi* are not exchanged a second time unless there is a position change. • Before the next meeting between parties, the *meishi* are reviewed for familiarization with the people attending the meeting. • The *meishi* provides status for the owner.	Human relations • *Meishi* provide understanding of appropriate relations between parties. • *Meishi* take uncertainty out of relationships. Environment • *Meishi* help establish insider/outsider environment. • *Meishi* help establish possible obligations to environment. Human activity • *Meishi* help to establish human activities.

Source: From Reeves-Ellington 1993 (reproduced in Podolefsky and Brown 1997, 236).

and business meetings. The managers analyzed these observations and discussed stories that show how badly things can go when cultural knowledge is not sufficient. For example, one thing Reeves-Ellington's students needed to learn about introductions involved the presentation of the business card (*meishi*). The proper presentation and use of the *meishi* is the central element in the practice of making introductions at business meetings. Reeves-Ellington explained that, to a Japanese businessperson, the meishi is an extension of the self. Damage to the card is damage to the individual. Therefore, mistreatment of a meishi will ruin a relationship. Reeves-Ellington notes that his colleagues did not fully appreciate the consequences of these beliefs until he told them a story: "A major U.S. company was having problems with one of its distributors, and the parties seemed unable to resolve their differences. The president of the U.S. company decided to visit Japan, meet with his counterpart in the wholesaler organization, and attempt to resolve their differences. The two had not met previously and, upon meeting, each followed proper *meishi* ritual. The American, however, did not put the Japanese counterpart's *meishi* on the table; instead he held on to it. As the conversation became heated, the American rolled up the *meishi* in his hand. Horror was recorded on the face of the Japanese businessman. The American then tore the *meishi* into bits. This was more than the Japanese could stand; he excused himself from the meeting. Shortly after-

ward the two companies stopped doing business with each other." Table 15.1 shows the information regarding introductions and the use of the meishi that Reeves-Ellington's students derived from their work based on their analytic framework of artifacts, social knowledge, and cultural logic.

On three critical measures—effective working relationships with Japanese executives, shortened project times, and improved financial returns—the anthropologically based training program that Reeves-Ellington designed was a success. Both employees and their Japanese counterparts felt more comfortable in working with each other. Prior to the program, joint projects required an average of fifteen months to complete; projects run by executives applying the methodologies of the program cut completion time to an average of eight months. Financial returns based on contracts negotiated by personnel who had not participated in the program averaged gross income of 6 percent of sales while those negotiated by personnel applying the anthropological techniques averaged gross income equal to 18 percent of sales.

Urban Social Planning and Restructuring in Canada

Alexander Ervin is an anthropologist in Saskatoon, Saskatchewan, in Canada, who has had considerable experience in collaborative, community-based research in social service and health agencies. (See EthnoProfile 15.1: Saskatoon). In his view, anthropologists seem to be particularly well-suited for this kind of applied work, since they "have been trained conceptually and methodologically to seek linkages among behaviors, institutions, and values, and to attempt to construct integrated overviews of whatever is the phenomenon under investigation" (1996, 324). As government policy makers move to cut costs by downsizing, few policy disciplines are able to provide information about how the different social service providers and their services fit together, nor are they able to listen effectively to grass-roots perceptions of issues, needs, and solutions. Anthropologists, however, are trained to do precisely these things.

To illustrate, Ervin discusses his work with the Saskatoon Social Planning Council. The council was established in 1992 with a push from activists from the approximately 200 human service delivery organizations in Saskatoon. In Canada, social planning councils focus attention on local social issues. They are involved with an extremely wide range of policies and issues and carry out policy research, including needs assessment, program evaluations, and problem-focused investigations. Ervin's main task has been to design a plan for an annual investigation of a specific policy domain or issue to be carried out by the council. The goal of the research would be to provide the data that the human service organizations could use to solve effectively some of the problems the research identified. The pilot investigation has been a multidimensional study of the well-being of children in the city in relation to poverty, hunger, recreation, education, family, native and immigrant issues, substance abuse, and general health concerns. Several organizations collaborated in the project, including the regional health board, the Catholic and public school boards, and the social services district office. A working group of representatives of each organization has been formed to analyze the data, much of which was collected by three anthropology students at the University of Saskatchewan. When the report of the research has been written, the council will call together those organizations and people that are involved with children's issues in Saskatoon to consider the results and discuss possible solutions.

Ervin believes that anthropologists can make important contributions in urban policy contexts, especially in needs assessment, "the process of identifying

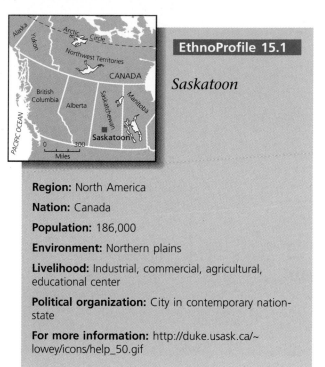

and seeking solutions to problems of particular populations, irrespective of whether programs have already been designed to address them" (330). Anthropologists seem particularly well placed for these projects, given their commitment to participatory research and holism. Indeed, from his point of view, the major need in the kinds of urban policy research that he has been engaged in is for flexible generalists—anthropologists who can move from one policy domain to another and construct integrated overviews of the phenomenon under investigation.

Anthropology and Policy

In all this work—and there is much more—the anthropological perspective illustrated throughout this book has been employed. Applied anthropologists do their work using holism, comparison, relativism, and a concern for particular cases.

Nevertheless, anthropologists are hesitant to make detailed policy recommendations that other professional disciplines make. This may be because anthropologists are particularly aware of the problems in applied work, the problems in trying to make people,

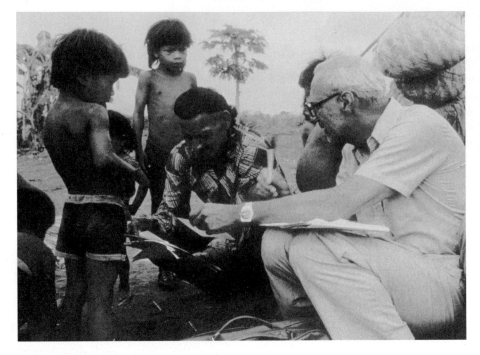

FIGURE 15.4 Anthropologists have become increasingly involved in the defense of human rights. David Maybury-Lewis (pictured here with Xavante informants in Brazil) and Pia Maybury-Lewis founded Cultural Survival, an organization dedicated to helping indigenous peoples and ethnic minorities deal as equals in their encounters with industrial society.

or systems, change. Anthropologists are trained to analyze social and cultural systems, but when they are asked how to change them, they begin to ask questions. These questions are based on an awareness of the enormous complexity of human life when it is viewed from ground level. Anthropologists have developed a keen awareness that not everyone makes the same basic assumptions about the world that planners and officials make. They know that sometimes technical experts providing help in other cultures know less than the people they are advising or give advice that is culturally inappropriate. Anthropologists realize that no change benefits everyone equally, that some gain as others lose. They also understand that even if they get involved in planning a program, implementation depends on external factors over which they have no control: cash flow problems to the AID office, fear over a congressman's response, political issues, elections, budget reductions, lack of interest, and so on.

Anthropologists believe they have much to contribute in helping build a better world, yet they are also highly sensitive to the kinds of issues that arise when dealing with the complex human systems we have discussed throughout this text. Applied anthropologists are well aware of the ambiguities of the human experience.

Anthropology and Human Rights

Recently, anthropologists have been involved in expanding the understanding of human rights and have participated in organizations for the defense of human rights. In particular, they have contributed to the recognition by human rights legal advocates that the collective rights of groups (such as indigenous peoples) deserve as much attention as the rights of individuals. Ellen Messer observes that anthropologists have examined, and continue to examine, the "contexts of human rights abuses, to understand how the political economic conditions that create cultural customs such as infanticide, underfeeding of women and children, and other abuses of women might be improved and make the customs of less evident utility. They also continue to work with interpreters of local traditions, so that through persuasion and contextualization, and by drawing on the authority of multiple traditions, people might be empowered to improve human rights in their own lives" (1993, 24).

Perhaps one of the foremost anthropologically oriented organizations involved with human rights is Cultural Survival, founded in 1972 by anthropologists Pia Maybury-Lewis and David Maybury-Lewis (Figure 15.4)

IN THEIR OWN WORDS

Group Rights and Individual Rights

Citizens of the United States are familiar with the concept of individual human rights, but the concept of group rights is less familiar and may even seem threatening. Marc S. Miller describes what group rights mean and argues that "individual rights mean little without group rights."

The concept of group rights, like those rights themselves, needs defining. Simply, group rights are those rights we enjoy, or are denied, because we are identified in some way with others. For indigenous people (the "target population" for the social scientists who founded Cultural Survival), group rights include the ability of an indigenous society to maintain its language, spiritual practices, economic systems, and so forth. In the absence of these rights, societies die. Group rights also include the rights of women, people of color, elders, and so forth to protection from any discrimination based on their shared membership in a collective identity.

Group rights relate to the rights of individuals, and they involve far more than just a moral assertion that cultures have a right to exist. Rather, group rights are a practical principle involving individuals: without their collective culture to support them, individuals are at risk. As E. P. Thompson and other historians have pointed out, the making of an English working class required the undermining of a previous agrarian, communal culture. For U.S. Indians, Australian Aborigines, and a host of other indigenous peoples, breaking down the patterns of tradition-based human interactions often leads to high rates of unemployment, suicide, alcoholism, and infant mortality.

On a fundamental level individual rights mean without group rights. It is certainly possible, for example, and all-too-common, for individuals to go to court, one after another to defend the same constitutional rights. But even if each plaintiff has a reasonable chance of winning, the process is inefficient, and each case may leave an unjust law standing or a host of criminals untouched. In rare instances, like *Brown vs. the Topeka Board of Education,* the edifice supporting widespread rights violations may be undermined when the plaintiffs marshal the breadth of resources needed to get to the Supreme Court. More often, the next victim of the same injustice has to repeat the fight.

It *is* a praiseworthy endeavor to defend the rights of every oppressed individual. Indeed, most rights advocates choose to highlight the cases of particularly endangered individuals to draw attention to a broader denial. This strategy mobilizes tens or hundreds of thousands of well-meaning people in the United States and Europe to defend the rights of perhaps thousands of wronged individuals, sometimes in their own countries, more often in other states. Such work has yielded many significant victories, but like one person's lawsuit, the approach is inefficient and not up to the enormity of rights violations throughout the world.

The strategy underlying a focus on group rights is to mobilize the same tens of thousands of concerned Americans and Europeans to stop the abuse of millions of people throughout the world—and perhaps to prevent more of these violations from ever occurring.

Source: Marc Miller 1993, 1.

and dedicated to helping indigenous people and ethnic minorities deal as equals in their encounters with industrial society. Anthropologist Carolyn Nordstrom (1993) writes about the efforts of the Ministry of Education in Mozambique and the Mozambican Woman's Organization to begin programs to assist children and women traumatized, raped, displaced, and impoverished by the 16-year war in that country. She discusses how indigenous healers have come to develop specialties in war trauma, "to take the violence out of people," and are being brought into the national health-care system.

Biological anthropologists, most notably Clyde Snow, have also contributed in an important way to the defense of human rights in the world. Snow is a consulting forensic anthropologist who is often called on by police departments, medical examiners, and other law enforcement officials to try to identify human remains and to determine the cause of death. He is helped in this task by his knowledge of (1) human skeletal features to determine sex, age, and population subgroup and (2) the different ways trauma can affect the human skeleton.

In recent years, Snow has been involved in a number of international human rights cases. Beginning in

1984, he worked with the American Association for the Advancement of Science to help the Argentinian National Commission on Disappeared Persons to determine the fate of some of the more than 10,000 people who had vanished during the "dirty war" waged by the Argentine military government against supposed subversives. Snow began his work in Argentina by training a team of medical and anthropology students in the techniques of forensic investigation, both skeletal and archaeological, and then helped them exhume and examine scores of the remains of the *desaparecidos* ("those who have disappeared"). By 1988, only 25 victims had been positively identified, but those identifications helped convict seven members of the former ruling junta and other high-ranking military and police officers (Huyghe 1988).

The Argentine team Snow trained has gone on to investigate sites of massacres in Guatemala, Bolivia, Panama, Iraq, and, most recently, the site of the massacre at El Mozote, El Salvador. Snow himself was in Chiapas in February 1994 to investigate the death of peasants following the Mexican army's battle with the Emiliano Zapata Liberation Army in early January (see Figure 1.4). Snow states, "There are human-rights violations going on all around the world. But to me murder is murder, regardless of the motive. I hope that we are sending a message to governments who murder in the name of politics that they can be held to account" (Huyghe 1988).

AWARENESS AND UNCERTAINTY

Why study anthropology? The second part of our answer is personal.

Studying cultural anthropology brings students into contact with different ways of life. It makes them aware of just how arbitrary their own understanding of the world is as they learn how other people have developed satisfying but different ways of living. In addition, if they are from Western countries that were responsible for colonialism and its consequences, it makes them painfully aware of just how much their own tradition has to answer for in the modern world.

Knowing and experiencing cultural variety gives rise, perhaps inevitably, to doubt. We come to doubt the ultimate validity of the central truths of our own cultural tradition, which have been ratified and sanctified by the generations who preceded us. We doubt because a familiarity with alternative ways of living makes the ultimate meaning of any action, of any object, a highly ambiguous matter. Ambiguity is part and parcel of the human condition. Human beings have coped with ambiguity from time immemorial by means of culture, which places objects and actions in contexts and thereby makes their meanings plain. This doubt can lead to anxiety, but it can also be liberating.

FREEDOM AND CONSTRAINT

Why study anthropology? The third part of our response is, for want of a better word, humanistic.

All human beings, ourselves included, live in culturally shaped worlds, enmeshed in webs of interpretation and meaning that we have spun. It has been the particular task of anthropology and its practitioners to go out into the world to bear witness to and record the vast creative diversity in world-making that has been the history of our species. In our lifetimes, we will witness the end of many of those ways of life—and if we are not careful, of all ways of life. This loss is tragic, for as these worlds disappear, so too does something special about humanity: variety, creativity, and awareness of alternatives.

Our survival as a species, and our viability as individuals, depends on the possibility of choice, of perceiving and being able to act on alternatives in the various situations we encounter during our lives. If, as a colleague has suggested, human life is a mine field, then the more paths we can see and imagine through that mine field, the more likely we are to make it through—or at least to have an interesting time trying. As alternatives are destroyed, wantonly smashed, or thoughtlessly crushed, *our* own human possibilities are reduced. A small group of men and women have for the last century labored in corners of the world, both remote and nearby, to write the record of human accomplishment and bring it back and teach it to others.

Surely our greatest human accomplishment is the creation of the sometimes austerely beautiful worlds in which we all live. Anthropologists have rarely given in to the romantic notion that these other worlds are all good, all life enhancing, all fine or beautiful. They are

IN THEIR OWN WORDS

Into the Warp and Woof of Multicultural Worlds

Changes in the contemporary world are producing what anthropologist George Marcus calls "transcultural 'traditional' peoples," whose members live in many different places and whose sense of cultural identity involves a mix of many cultural elements.

The power of global cultural homogenization in the late twentieth century challenges the conventions and rationales by which anthropology has so far produced its knowledge of other cultures. The reorganization of the world economy through technological advances in communication, production processes, and marketing has thoroughly deterritorialized culture. For example, the Tongan islanders of Polynesia that I studied in the early 1970s now constitute a diaspora of communities in locales around the Pacific rim. As many, if not more, Tongans now live permanently in Australia, New Zealand, and the United States as in the islands themselves. One might fairly ponder where both the cultural and geographical center of the Tongan people resides. Their identity is produced in many locales and through the mix of many cultural elements. And their conditions are similar to those of numerous other peoples that anthropologists have traditionally studied. It is no longer just the most powerful, large-scale, and most modern societies, such as the United States and Japan, that exist in international, transcultural science.

Among such transcultural "traditional" peoples, levels of cultural self-consciousness and alternatives increase. The authenticity of performances, rituals, or apparently deep seated norms like those of kinship cannot be merely assumed, either by locals or by visitors such as anthropologists. To some extent, media documentaries have absorbed anthropology's function of presenting vividly the lifeways of other cultures to Euro-American publics that themselves can no longer be considered as homogeneous or mainstream. And, finally, the subjects of anthropological study independently and articulately translate their own perspectives with sensitivity to the effects of different media.

Peoples who in particular have become classic anthropological subjects, such as the Samoans, Trobriand Islanders, Hopi, and Todas of India, know their status well, and have, with some ambivalence, assimilated anthropological knowledge about them as part of their sense of themselves. A recent example was the visit of a Toda woman to Houston. A trained nurse among her people as well as a cultural broker, she was on tour in the United States, giving talks about the Todas, of the sort that anthropologists might have given in past decades. By chance, she was visiting the home of a colleague just as a British documentary about the Todas appeared on the television—a documentary in which the visitor was featured prominently as the filmmaker's prime source of information. The visitor's comments as she watched the program along with my colleague did not much concern the details of Toda culture, but rather dealt with the ironies of the multiple representations of her people—by herself, by anthropologists, and by the British Broadcasting Corporation.

The lesson of this story is compelling. The penetrations of a world economy, communications, and the effects of multiple, fragmented identities on cultural authenticity, once thought restricted to advanced modernity, have increased markedly among most local and regional cultures worldwide. They have thus engendered an ethnography in reverse among many peoples who not only can assimilate the professional idioms of anthropology but can relativize them among other alternatives and ways of knowledge. This does not mean that the traditional task of anthropology to represent distinctive and systematic cultural forms of life has been fundamentally subverted by its own subjects. Rather, anthropology's traditional task is now much more complicated, requiring new sensibilities in undertaking fieldwork and different strategies for writing about it.

Source: Marcus 1990, 254–55.

not. Ambiguity and ambivalence are, as we have seen, hallmarks of the human experience. There are no guarantees that human cultures will be compassionate rather than cruel, or that people will agree they are one or the other. There are not even any guarantees that our species will survive. But all anthropologists have

believed that these are *human* worlds that have given those who have lived in them the ability to make sense out of their experiences and to derive meaning for their lives, that we are a species at once bound by our culture and free to change it.

This is a perilous and fearsome freedom, a difficult

freedom to grasp and to wield. Nevertheless, the freedom is there, and in this dialectic of freedom and constraint lies our future. It is up to us to create it.

Suggested Readings

Cultural Survival Quarterly. *A committed voice for the survival of indigenous peoples. A magazine with a relatively wide circulation,* Cultural Survival Quarterly *always publishes provocative and important material.*

van Willigen, John. 1993. *Applied anthropology: An introduction.* South Hadley, MA: Bergin and Garvey. *A thorough introduction to applied anthropology, including different applied approaches, ethics, and the job search.*

van Willigen, John, Barbara Rylko-Bauer, and Ann McElroy. 1989. *Making our research useful.* Boulder, CO: Westview. *A collection of valuable articles in applied anthropology.*

Wolfe, Robert, and Shirley Fiske. 1987. *Anthropological praxis.* Boulder, CO: Westview. *An excellent collection of essays by applied anthropologists about their projects. The articles are written in a consistent format, which makes them especially valuable for comparison.*

Bibliography

Abu-Lughad, Lila. 1995. The objects of soap opera: Egyptian television and the cultural politics of modernity. In *Worlds apart: Modernity through the prism of the local,* edited by Daniel Miller, 109–210. London: Routledge.

Adams, Richard Newbold. 1979. *Energy and structure: A theory of social power.* Austin: University of Texas Press.

Ahmed, Syed Zubar. 1994. What do men want? *New York Times,* 15 February.

Akmajian, A., R. Demers, and R. Harnish. 1984. *Linguistics.* 2d ed. Cambridge, MA: MIT Press.

Alland, Alexander. 1977. *The artistic animal.* New York: Doubleday Anchor Books.

Allen, Catherine J. 1988. *The hold life has: Coca and cultural identity in an Andean community.* Washington, DC: Smithsonian Institution Press.

Althusser, Louis, and Etienne Balibar. 1971. *Reading capital.* London: New Left Books.

Alverson, Hoyt. 1977. Peace Corps volunteers in rural Botswana. *Human Organization* 36 (3): 274–81.

———. 1978. *Mind in the heart of darkness.* New Haven: Yale University Press.

———. 1990. Guest editorial in *Cultural anthropology: A perspective on the human condition,* by Emily Schultz and Robert Lavenda, 43. 2d ed. St. Paul: West.

Anderson, Benedict. 1983. *Imagined communities.* London: Verso.

Anderson, Richard L. 1990. *Calliope's sisters: A comparative study of philosophies of art.* Englewood Cliffs, NJ: Prentice-Hall.

Appadurai, Arjun. 1990. Disjuncture and difference in the global cultural economy. In *Global culture,* edited by Mike Featherstone, 295–310. London: Sage.

Aufderheide, Patricia. 1993. Beyond television *Public Culture* 5: 5/9–92.

Autobiografías campesinas. 1979. Vol. 1. Heredia, Costa Rica: Editorial de la Universidad Nacional.

Bakhtin, Mikhail. 1981. *The dialogical imagination.* Austin: University of Texas Press.

Barnes, Barry, and David Bloor. 1982. Relativism, rationalism and the sociology of knowledge. In *Rationality and relativism,* edited by Martin Hollis and Steven Lukes, 21–47. Cambridge, MA: MIT Press.

Bascom, William. 1969. *The Yoruba of southwestern Nigeria.* New York: Holt, Rinehart and Winston.

Basham, Richard. 1978. *Urban anthropology.* Palo Alto, CA: Mayfield.

Bateson, Gregory. 1972. *Steps to an ecology of mind.* New York: Ballantine Books.

Bauman, Zygmunt. 1990. Modernity and ambivalence. In *Global culture,* edited by Mike Featherstone, 143–69. London: Sage.

Baxter, P. T. W. 1978. Boran age-sets and generation-sets: *Gada,* a puzzle or a maze? In *Age, generation and time,* edited by P. T. W. Baxter and Uri Almagor, 151–82. New York: St. Martin's Press.

Baxter, P. T. W., and Uri Almagor, eds. 1978. *Age, generation and time.* New York: St. Martin's Press.

Beals, Alan. 1962. *Gopalpur, a south Indian village.* New York: Holt, Rinehart and Winston.

Beidelman, T. O. 1971. *The Kaguru.* New York: Holt, Rinehart and Winston.

———. 1982. *Colonial evangelism.* Bloomington: Indiana University Press.

Bellman, Beryl. 1975. *Village of curers and assassins: On the production of Fala Kpelle cosmological categories.* The Hague: Mouton.

———. 1984. *The language of secrecy.* New Brunswick, NJ: Rutgers University Press.

Belmonte, Thomas. 1978. *The broken fountain.* New York: Columbia University Press.

Bickerton, Derek. 1981. *Roots of language.* Ann Arbor: Karoma.

Blanchard, Kendall. 1974. Basketball and the culture change process: The Rimrock Navajo case. *Council on Anthropology and Education Quarterly* 5 (4): 8–13.

Blanchard, Kendall, and Alyce Cheska. 1985. *The anthropology of sport.* South Hadley, MA: Bergin and Garvey.

Bledsoe, Caroline. 1993. The politics of polygyny in Mende education and child fosterage transactions. In *Sex and gender hierarchies,* edited by Barbara Diane Miller, 170–92. Cambridge: Cambridge University Press.

Bohannan, Laura, and Paul Bohannan. 1969. *The Tiv of central Nigeria.* 2d ed. London: International African Institute.

Bohannan, Paul, and Fred Plog, eds. 1967. *Beyond the frontier.* Garden City, NY: Natural History Press.

Bourgois, Philippe. 1995. *In search of respect: Selling crack in El Barrio.* New York: Cambridge University Press.

Brain, Robert. 1976. *Friends and lovers.* New York: Basic Books.

Braroe, Niels. 1975. *Indian and White.* Stanford: Stanford University Press.

Brenneis, Donald, and Ronald K. S. Macauley, eds. 1996. *The matrix of language.* Boulder, CO: Westview.

Briggs, Jean. 1980. Kapluna daughter: Adopted by the Eskimo. In *Conformity and conflict: Readings in cultural anthropology,* edited by J. Spradley and D. McCurdy, 44–62. 7th ed. Boston: Little, Brown.

Brooks, Allison, and John Yellen. 1992. Decoding the Ju/Wasi past. *Symbols,* September, 24–31.

Broom, Leonard, Bernard J. Siegel, Evon Z. Vogt, and James B. Watson. 1954. Acculturation: An exploratory formulation. *American Anthropologist* 56:973–1000.

Burch, Ernest S., Jr. 1970. Marriage and divorce among the north Alaska eskimos. In *Divorce and after,* edited by Paul Bohannan, 152–81. Garden City: Doubleday.

———. 1975. *Eskimo kinsmen: Changing family relationships in northwest Alaska.* American Ethnological Society Monograph, no. 59. St. Paul: West.

Carneiro, Robert. 1970. A theory of the origin of the state. *Science* 169:733–38.

Carroll, John B., ed. 1956. *Language, thought and reality: Selected writings of Benjamin Lee Whorf.* Cambridge, MA: MIT Press.

Chambers, Erve. 1985. *Applied anthropology: A practical guide.* New York: Prentice-Hall.

Chance, John K. 1978. *Race and class in colonial Oaxaca.* Stanford: Stanford University Press.

Chomsky, Noam. 1957. *Syntactic structures.* The Hague: Mouton.

———. 1965. *Aspects of the theory of syntax.* Cambridge, MA: MIT Press.

Clastres, Pierre. 1977. *Society against the state.* Translated by Robert Hurley. New York: Urizen Books.

Colby, Benjamin, and Pierre van den Berghe. 1969. *Ixil country.* Berkeley: University of California Press.

Cole, Michael, and Sylvia Scribner. 1974. *Culture and thought: A psychological introduction.* New York: Wiley.

Collier, Jane, and Sylvia Yanagisako. 1987. *Gender and kinship: Essays toward a unified analysis.* Stanford: Stanford University Press.

Colson, Elizabeth. 1977. Power at large: Meditation on "The symposium on power." In *The anthropology of power: Ethnographic studies from Asia, Oceania, and the New World,* edited by R. Fogelson and R. N. Adams, 375–86. New York: Academic Press.

Comaroff, Jean, and John Comaroff. 1991. *Of revelation and revolution.* Vol. I. Chicago: University of Chicago Press.

Cowan, Jane. 1990. *Dance and the body politic in northern Greece.* Princeton: Princeton University Press.

Crick, Malcolm. 1976. *Explorations in language and meaning: Towards a semantic anthropology.* New York: Wiley.

Csikszentmihalyi, Mihalyi. 1981. Some paradoxes in the definition of play. In *Play and context,* edited by Alyce Cheska, 14–25. West Point: Leisure Press.

da Matta, Robert. 1994. Some biased remarks on interpretism. In *Assessing cultural anthropology,* edited by Robert Borofsky, 119–32. New York: McGraw-Hill.

D'Andrade, Roy G. 1992. Cognitive anthropology. In *New directions in psychological anthropology,* edited by Theodore Schwartz, Geoffrey M. White, and Catherine A. Lutz, 47–58. Cambridge: Cambridge University Press.

Danner, Mark. 1994. *The massacre at El Mozote.* New York: Vintage.

Darwin, C. R. 1859. *On the origin of species by means of natural selection.* London: John Murray.

Davis, Shelton. 1977. *Victims of the miracle.* Cambridge: Cambridge University Press.

Deng, Francis Madeng. 1972. *The Dinka of the Sudan.* New York: Holt, Rinehart and Winston.

Dolgin, Janet. 1995. Family law and the facts of family. In *Naturalizing power,* edited by Sylvia Yanagisako and Carol Delaney, 47–67. New York: Routledge.

Douglas, Mary. 1966. *Purity and danger.* London: Routledge and Kegan Paul.

———. 1970. *Natural symbols.* New York: Pantheon.

Douglas, Mary, and Baron Isherwood. 1979. *The world of goods: Towards an anthropology of consumption.* New York: W. W. Norton.

Drewal, Margaret. 1992. *Yoruba ritual.* Bloomington: Indiana University Press.

Dumont, Jean Paul. 1978. *The headman and I: Ambiguity and ambivalence in the fieldwork experience.* Austin: University of Texas Press.

Duranti, Alessandro. 1994. *From grammar to politics.* Berkeley: University of California Press.

Elliot, Alison. 1981. *Child language.* Cambridge: Cambridge University Press.

Ervin, Alexander M. 1996. Collaborative and participatory research in urban social planning and restructuring: Anthropological experiences from a medium-sized Canadian city. *Human Organization* 55 (3): 324–33.

Escobar, Arturo. 1992. Culture, economics, and politics in Latin American social movements theory and research. In *The making of social movements in Latin America,* edited by Arturo Escobar and Sonia Alvarez, 62–85. Boulder, CO: Westview.

Etienne, Mona. 1980. Women and men, cloth and colonization: The transformation of production-distribution relations among the Baule (Ivory Coast). In *Women and colonization: Anthropological perspectives,* edited by Mona Etienne and Eleanor Leacock, 270–93. New York: Praeger.

Evans-Pritchard, E. E. 1940. *The Nuer.* Oxford: Oxford University Press.

———. 1951. *Kinship and marriage among the Nuer.* Oxford: Oxford University Press.

———. 1963. *Social anthropology and other essays.* New York: Free Press.

———. [1937] 1976. *Witchcraft, oracles, and magic among the Azande.* Abridged ed. Oxford: Oxford University Press.

Fagen, Robert. 1981. *Animal play behavior.* New York: Oxford University Press.

———. 1992. Play, fun, and communication of well-being. *Play and Culture* 5 (1): 40–58.

Fernandez, James W. [1966] 1971. Principles of opposition and vitality in Fang aesthetics. In *Art and aesthetics in primitive societies,* edited by Carol Jopling, 356–73. New York: E. P. Dutton.

———. 1977. The performance of ritual metaphors. In *The social use of metaphors,* edited by J. D. Sapir and J. C. Crocker. Philadelphia: University of Pennsylvania Press.

———. 1980. Edification by puzzlement. In *Explorations in African systems of thought,* edited by Ivan Karp and Charles Bird, 44–69. Bloomington: Indiana University Press.

———. 1982. *Bwiti: An ethnography of the religious imagination in Africa.* Princeton: Princeton University Press.

Fiddes, Nick. 1991. *Meat: A natural symbol.* London: Routledge.

Firth, Raymond. [1936] 1984. *We, the Tikopia.* Reprint. Stanford: Stanford University Press.

Forge, Anthony. 1967. The Abelam artist. In *Social organization: Essays presented to Raymond Firth,* edited by Maurice Freedman, 65–84. London: Cass.

Fortes, Meyer. 1950. Kinship and marriage among the Ashanti. In *African systems of kinship and marriage,* edited by A. R. Radcliffe-Brown and Daryll Forde. Oxford: Oxford University Press.

———. 1953. The structure of unilineal descent groups. *American Anthropologist* 55:25–39.

Fox, Robin. 1967. *Kinship and marriage.* Harmondsworth: Penguin.

Frank, André Gunder. 1969. Capitalist underdevelopment or socialist revolution? In *Latin America: Underdevelopment or revolution?* 371–409. New York: Monthly Review Press.

Gamble, David P. 1957. *The Wolof of Senegambia.* London: International African Institute.

Geertz, Clifford. 1960. *The religion of Java.* New York: Free Press.

———. 1973. *The interpretation of cultures.* New York: Basic Books.

Geertz, Hildred, and Clifford Geertz. 1975. *Kinship in Bali.* Chicago: University of Chicago Press.

Georges, Eugenia. 1990. *The making of a transnational community: Migration, development, and cultural change in the Dominican Republic.* New York: Columbia University Press.

Giddens, Anthony. 1979. *Central problems in social theory.* Berkeley: University of California Press.

Gilligan, Carol. 1982. *In a different voice.* Cambridge, MA: Harvard University Press.

Gilsenan, Michael. 1982. *Recognizing Islam: Religion and society in the modern Arab world.* New York: Pantheon.

Ginsburg, F. 1991. Indigenous media: Faustian contract or global village? *Cultural Anthropology* 6 (1): 94–114.

Ginsburg, Faye, and Rayna Rapp, eds. 1995. *Conceiving the new world order: The global politics of reproduction.* Berkeley: University of California Press.

Gledhill, John. 1994. *Power and its disguises.* London: Pluto Press.

Gomes, Mercio. 1996. Indians and Brazil: Holocaust and survival of a native population. Unpublished translation of *Os indios e o Brasil.* 2d ed. Petropolis: Editora Vozes.

Goodwin, M. H. 1990. *He-said-she-said: Talk as social organization among black children.* Bloomington: Indiana University Press.

Goody, J., and S. Tambiah. 1973. *Bridewealth and dowry.* Cambridge: Cambridge University Press.

Gordon, Robert. 1992. *The bushman myth.* Boulder, CO: Westview.

Gottlieb, Alma. 1988. American premenstrual syndrome: A mute voice. In *Talking about people,* edited by William A. Haviland and Robert J. Gordon, 57–58. Mountain View, CA: Mayfield.

———. 1989. Witches, kings, and the sacrifice of identity *or* The power of paradox and the paradox of power among the Beng of Ivory Coast. In *Creativity of power: Cosmology and action in African societies,* edited by W. Arens and Ivan Karp, 245–72. Washington, DC: Smithsonian Institution Press.

Gramsci, Antonio. 1971. *Selections from the prison notebooks.* Translated by Q. Hoare and G. N. Smith. New York: International Publishers.

Greenwood, D. 1984. *The taming of evolution.* Ithaca, NY: Cornell University Press.

Greenwood, David, and William Stini. 1977. *Nature, culture, and human history.* New York: Harper and Row.

Gregory, Richard. 1981. *Mind in science: A history of explanations in psychology and physics.* New York: Cambridge University Press.

———. 1983. Visual perception and illusions: Dialogue with Richard Gregory. In *States of mind,* by Jonathan Miller, 42–64. New York: Pantheon.

Gudeman, Stephen. 1978. *The demise of a rural economy.* London: Routledge and Kegan Paul.

———. 1990. Guest editorial in *Cultural anthropology: A perspective on the human condition,* by Emily Schultz and Robert Lavenda, 458–59. 2d ed. St. Paul: West.

Gutierrez Muñiz, José A., Josefina López Hurtado, and Guillermo Arias Beatón. n.d. *Un estudio del niño cubano.* Havana: Empresa Impresoras Gráficas, MINED.

Halperin, Rhoda. 1990. *The livelihood of kin: Making ends meet "the Kentucky way."* Austin: University of Texas Press.

Handelman, Don. 1977. Play and ritual: Complementary frames of meta-communication. In *It's a funny thing, humour,* edited by A. J. Chapman and H. Foot, 185–92. London: Pergamon.

Hanks, William. 1996. *Language and communicative practices.* Boulder, CO: Westview.

Haraway, Donna. 1989. *Primate visions.* New York: Routledge.

Heider, Karl. 1979. *Grand Valley Dani.* New York: Holt, Rinehart and Winston.

Herdt, Gilbert. 1994a. Introduction. In *Third sex, third gender,* edited by Gilbert Herdt. New York: Zone Books.

———. 1994b. Mistaken sex: Culture, biology, and the third sex in New Guinea. In *Third sex, third gender,* edited by Gilbert Herdt, 419–45. New York: Zone Books.

Herskovits, Melville. 1973. *Cultural relativism.* Edited by Frances Herskovits. New York: Vintage Books.

Herzfeld, Michael. 1987. *Anthropology through the looking glass.* Cambridge: Cambridge University Press.

Hill, Jane, and Judith Irvine. 1992. *Responsibility and evidence in oral discourse.* Cambridge: Cambridge University Press.

Hockett, C., and R. Ascher. 1964. The human revolution. *Current Anthropology* 5:135–47.

Hockett, C. F. 1966. The problems of universals in language. In *Universals of language,* edited by J. H. Greenberg, 1–29. Cambridge, MA: MIT Press.

Hodder, Ian. 1982. *Symbols in action.* Cambridge: Cambridge University Press.

Hoebel, E. Adamson. 1960. *The Cheyennes.* New York: Holt, Rinehart and Winston.

Holm, John. 1988. *Pidgins and creoles.* Vol. 1 of *Theory and structure.* Cambridge: Cambridge University Press.

Horner, M. 1972. Toward an understanding of achievement-related conflicts in women. *Journal of Social Issues* 28:157–75.

Horton, Robin. 1982. Tradition and modernity revisited. In *Rationality and relativism,* edited by M. Hollis and Steven Lukes, 201–60. Cambridge, MA: MIT Press.

Hudson, R. A. 1980. *Sociolinguistics.* Cambridge: Cambridge University Press.

Hunter, David, and Phillip Whitten, eds. 1976. *Encyclopedia of anthropology.* New York: Harper and Row.

Hutchinson, Sharon. 1996. *Nuer dilemmas.* Berkeley: University of California Press.

Huyghe, Patrick. 1988. Profile of an anthropologist: No bone unturned. *Discover,* December.

Hymes, Dell. 1972. On communicative competence. In *Sociolinguistics: Selected readings,* edited by J. B. Pride and J. Holmes, 269–93. Baltimore: Penguin.

Jackson, Michael. 1977. *The Kuranko.* New York: St. Martin's Press.

———. 1982. *Allegories of the wilderness.* Bloomington: Indiana University Press.

Johnson, Steven L. 1988. Ideological dimensions of peasant persistence in western Kenya. In *New perspectives on social class and political action in the periphery,* edited by R. Curtain, N. W. Keith, and N. E. Keith. Westport, CT: Greenwood Press.

Jourdan, Christine. 1991. Pidgins and creoles: The blurring of categories. *Annual Review of Anthropology* 20:187–209.

Kapferer, Bruce. 1983. *A celebration of demons.* Bloomington: Indiana University Press.

Karp, Ivan. 1978. *Fields of change among the Iteso of Kenya.* London: Routledge and Kegan Paul.

———. 1986. Laughter at marriage: Subversion in performance. In *The transformation of African marriage,* edited by David Parkin. London: International African Institute.

———. 1990. Guest editorial in *Cultural anthropology: A perspective on the human condition,* by Emily Schultz and Robert Lavenda, 74–75. 2d ed. St. Paul: West.

Karp, Ivan, and Martha B. Kendall. 1982. Reflexivity in field work. In *Explanation in social science,* edited by P. Secord. Los Angeles: Sage.

Kearney, M. 1995. The local and the global: The anthropology of globalization and transnationalism. *Annual Review of Anthropology* 24:547–65.

Keesing, Roger. 1982. *Kwaio religion.* New York: Columbia University Press.

———. 1983. *'Elota's story.* New York: Holt, Rinehart and Winston.

———. 1992. *Custom and confrontation: The Kwaio struggle for cultural autonomy.* Chicago: University of Chicago Press.

Keillor, Garrison. 1985. *Lake Wobegon days.* New York: Viking.

Kelly, R. 1993. *Constructing inequality: The fabrication of a hierarchy of virtue among the Etoro.* Ann Arbor: University of Michigan Press.

Khazanov, Anatoly. 1993. State and violence in the ex-Soviet Union. Paper read at 92nd annual meeting of the American Anthropological Association, November, Washington, DC.

Kondo, Dorinne K. 1990. *Crafting selves: Power, gender, and discourses of identity in a Japanese workplace.* Chicago: University of Chicago Press.

Kopytoff, Igor. 1986. The cultural biography of things: Commoditization as process. In *The social life of things,* edited by Arjun Appadurai, 64–91. Cambridge: Cambridge University Press.

Kopytoff, Igor, and Suzanne Miers. 1977. Introduction: African "slavery" as an institution of marginality. In *Slavery in Africa,* edited by Suzanne Miers and Igor Kopytoff, 3–84. Madison: University of Wisconsin Press.

Kumar, Nita. 1992. *Friends, brothers, and informants: Fieldwork memories of Banaras.* Berkeley: University of California Press.

Kuper, Adam. 1982. *Wives for cattle: Bridewealth and marriage in southern Africa.* London: Routledge and Kegan Paul.

Kürti, Láslö. 1988. The politics of joking: Popular response to Chernobyl. *Journal of American Folklore* 101:324–34.

Labov, William. 1972. *Language in the inner city: Studies in the Black English Vernacular.* Philadelphia: University of Pennsylvania Press.

Laclau, Ernesto, and Chantal Mouffe. 1985. *Hegemony and socialist strategy: Towards a radical democratic politics.* London: Verso.

Lakoff, George, and Mark Johnson. 1980. *Metaphors we live by.* Berkeley: University of California Press.

Lancaster, Roger. 1992. *Life is hard.* Berkeley: University of California Press.

Lave, Jean. 1988. *Cognition in practice.* Cambridge: Cambridge University Press.

Lee, Richard. 1974. Male-female residence arrangements and political power in human hunter-gatherers. *Archaeology of Sexual Behavior* 3:167–73.

———. 1992a. Art, science, or politics? The crisis in hunter-gatherer studies. *American Anthropologist* 94:31–54.

———. 1992b. *The Dobe Ju/'hoansi.* 2d ed. New York: Holt, Rinehart and Winston.

Lever, Janet. 1983. *Soccer madness.* Chicago: University of Chicago Press.

Levine, Nancy. 1980. Nyinba polyandry and the allocation of paternity. *Journal of Comparative Family Studies* 11 (3): 283–88.

———. 1988. *The dynamics of polyandry: Kinship, domesticity, and population on the Tibetan border.* Chicago: University of Chicago Press.

Levine, Nancy, and Walter Sangree. 1980. Women with many husbands. *Journal of Comparative Family Studies* 11(3) [Special Issue].

Lévi-Strauss, Claude. [1962] 1967. *L'antropologie structurale.* Paris: Plon. Translated under the title *Structural anthropology* by Claire Jacobson and Brooke Grundfest Schoepf. New York: Doubleday Anchor.

Lewellen, Ted. 1983. *Political anthropology.* South Hadley, MA: Bergin and Garvey.

Lewis, I. M. 1967. *A pastoral democracy: A study of pastoralism and politics among the northern Somali of the Horn of Africa.* London: Oxford University Press.

Lienhardt, Godfrey. 1961. *Divinity and experience: The religion of the Dinka.* Oxford: Oxford University Press.

Little, Kenneth. 1967. *The Mende of Sierra Leone.* London: Routledge and Kegan Paul.

Lutz, Catherine. 1988. *Unnatural emotions.* Chicago: University of Chicago Press.

MacCormack, Carol P. 1980. Proto-social to adult: A Sherbro transformation. In *Nature, culture, and gender,* edited by Carol MacCormack and Marilyn Strathern, 95–118. Cambridge: Cambridge University Press.

Macintyre, Martha. 1993. Fictive kinship or mistaken identity? Fieldwork on Tubetube Island, Papua New Guinea. In *Gendered fields: Women, men and ethnography,* edited by Diane Bell, Pat Caplan, and Wazir Jahan Karim, 44–62. London: Routledge.

Malinowski, Bronislaw. 1944. *A scientific theory of culture and other essays.* New York: Oxford University Press.

———. [1926] 1948. *Magic, science, and religion, and other essays.* New York: Doubleday Anchor.

Mandler, George. 1975. *Mind and emotion.* New York: Wiley.

———. 1983. The nature of emotion: Dialogue with George Mandler. In *States of mind,* by Jonathan Miller, 136–52. New York: Pantheon.

Marcus, George. 1990. Guest editorial in *Cultural anthropology: A perspective on the human condition,* by Emily Schultz and Robert Lavenda, 254–55. 2d ed. St. Paul: West.

Martin, E. 1987. *The woman in the body.* Boston: Beacon.

Martin, Laura. 1986. Eskimo words for snow: A case study in the genesis and decay of an anthropological example. *American Anthropologist* 88 (2): 418–19.

Marx, Karl. [1932] 1977. *The German ideology.* Selections reprinted in *Karl Marx: Selected writings,* edited by David McLellan. Oxford: Oxford University Press.

———. 1963. *The 18th brumaire of Louis Bonaparte.* New York: International Publishers.

Mead, George Herbert. 1934. *Mind, self, and society.* Chicago: University of Chicago Press.

Messer, Ellen. 1993. Anthropology and human rights. *Annual Review of Anthropology* 22:221–49.

Meunier, Jacques, and A. M. Savarin. 1994. *The Amazon chronicles.* Translated by Carol Christensen. San Francisco: Mercury House.

Miller, Barbara Diane. 1993. The anthropology of sex and gender hierarchies. In *Sex and gender hierarchies,* 3–31. Cambridge: Cambridge University Press.

Miller, Marc S. 1993. Behind the words. *Cultural Survival Quarterly* (Summer): 1.

Minturn, Leigh. 1993. *Sita's daughters.* Oxford and New York: Oxford University Press.

Miracle, Andrew. 1991. Aymara joking behavior. *Play and Culture* 4 (2): 144–52.

Mitchell-Kernan, Claudia. 1972. On the status of Black English for native speakers: An assessment of attitudes and values. In *Functions of language in the classroom,* edited by C. Cazden, V. John, and D. Hymes, 195–210. New York: Teachers College Press.

Moffatt, Michael. 1989. *Coming of age in New Jersey: College and American culture.* New Brunswick, NJ: Rutgers University Press.

Moll, Luis, ed. 1990. *Vygotsky and education.* New York: Cambridge University Press.

Moore, R. 1992. Marketing alterity. *Visual Anthropology Review* 8 (2): 16–26.

Morgan, Lewis Henry. [1877] 1963. *Ancient society.* Reprint. Cleveland: Meridian Books.

Morgan, Marcyliena. 1995. Theories and politics in African American English. *Annual Review of Anthropology* 23:325–45.

———. 1997. Commentary on Ebonics. *Anthropology Newsletter.* 38(3): 8.

Murphy, Robert, and Yolanda Murphy. 1974. *Women of the forest.* New York: Columbia University Press.

Myerhoff, Barbara. 1974. *Peyote hunt.* Ithaca, NY: Cornell University Press.

Nanda, Serena. 1994. Hijras: An alternative sex and gender role. In *Third sex, third gender,* edited by Gilbert Herdt, 373–417. New York: Zone Books.

Narayan, R. K. 1974. *My days.* New York: Viking.

Nash, June. 1979. *We eat the mines, and the mines eat us.* New York: Columbia University Press.

Nordstrom, Carolyn. 1993. Treating the wounds of war. *Cultural Survival Quarterly* 17 (Summer): 28–30.

Ortner, Sherry. 1973. On key symbols. *American Anthropologist* 75 (5): 1338–46.

Ortony, Andrew. 1979. Metaphor: A multidimensional problem. In *Metaphor and thought,* 1–18. Cambridge: Cambridge University Press.

Oswalt, Wendell. 1972. *Other peoples, other customs.* New York: Holt, Rinehart and Winston.

Parkin, David. 1978. *Cultural definition of political response: Lineal destiny among the Luo.* New York: Academic Press.

———. 1984. Mind, body, and emotion among the Giriama. Paper presented in *Humanity as Creator* lecture series, St. Cloud State University.

———. 1990. Guest editorial in *Cultural anthropology: A perspective on the human condition,* by Emily Schultz and Robert Lavenda, 90–91. 2d ed. St. Paul: West.

———. 1991. *Sacred void: Spatial images of work and ritual among the Giriama of Kenya.* Cambridge: Cambridge University Press.

Partridge, William L., ed. 1984. *Training manual in development anthropology.* Special publication of the American Anthropological Association and the Society for Applied Anthropology, number 17. Washington, DC: American Anthropological Association.

Peletz, Michael. 1995. Kinship studies in late twentieth-century anthropology. *Annual Review of Anthropology* 24:343–72.

Poewe, Karla. 1989. On the metonymic structure of religious experiences: The example of charismatic Christianity. *Cultural Dynamics* 2 (4): 361–80.

Rabinow, Paul. 1977. *Reflections on fieldwork in Morocco.* Berkeley: University of California Press.

Redfield, Robert, Ralph Linton, and Melville Herskovits. 1936. Memorandum for the study of acculturation. *American Anthropologist* 38:149–52.

Redford, Kent H. 1993. The ecologically noble savage. In *Talking about people,* edited by W. A. Haviland and R. J. Gordon, 11–13. Mountain View, CA: Mayfield.

Reeves, Edward, Billie DeWalt, and Kathleen DeWalt. 1987. The International Sorghum/Millet Research Project. In *Anthropological praxis,* edited by Robert Wolfe and Shirley Fiske, 72–83. Boulder, CO: Westview.

Reeves-Ellington, Richard H. 1993. Using cultural skills for cooperative advantage in Japan. *Human Organization* 52 (2): 203–16.

Reichel-Dolmatoff, Gerardo. 1971. *Amazonian cosmos: The sexual and religious symbolism of the Turkano Indians.* Chicago: University of Chicago Press.

Richards, Audrey. 1954. *Chisungu.* London: Methuen.

Ringrose, Kathryn M. 1994. Living in the shadows: Eunuchs and gender in Byzantium. In *Third sex, third gender,* edited by Gilbert Herdt, 85–109. New York: Zone Books.

Rodriguez, Clara. 1994. Challenging racial hegemony: Puerto Ricans in the United States. In *Race,* edited by Steven Gregory and Roger Sanjek, 131–45. New Brunswick, NJ: Rutgers University Press.

Ronan, Colin A., and Joseph Needham. 1978. *The shorter science and civilisation in China. An abridgement of Joseph Needham's original text.* Vol. 1. Cambridge: Cambridge University Press.

Roscoe, Will. 1994. How to become a Berdache: Toward a unified analysis of gender diversity. In *Third sex, third gender,* edited by Gilbert Herdt, 329–72. New York: Zone Books.

Rosen, Lawrence. 1984. *Bargaining for reality: The constructions of social relations in a Muslim community.* Chicago: University of Chicago Press.

Rosman, Abraham, and Paula G. Rubel. 1971. *Feasting with mine enemy: Rank and exchange among northwest coast societies.* New York: Columbia University Press.

Rostow, W. W. [1960] 1971. *Stages of economic growth*. 2d ed. New York: Cambridge University Press.

Ruby, J. 1991. Speaking for, speaking about, speaking with, or speaking alongside—An anthropological and documentary dilemma. *Visual Anthropology Review* 7 (2): 50–66.

Sacks, Karen. 1979. *Sisters and wives*. Urbana: University of Illinois Press.

Sacks, Oliver. 1984. *A leg to stand on*. New York: Summit Books.

Sahlins, Marshall. 1972. *Stone Age economics*. Chicago: Aldine.

———. 1976a. *Culture and practical reason*. Chicago: University of Chicago Press.

———. 1976b. *The use and abuse of biology*. Ann Arbor: University of Michigan Press.

Sapir, Edward. 1921. *Language*. San Diego: Harvest/HBJ.

———. [1933] 1966. *Culture, language, and personality*, edited by David Mandelbaum. Berkeley: University of California Press.

Savigliano, Marta. 1995. *Tango and the political economy of passion*. Boulder, CO: Westview.

Scheper-Hughes, Nancy. 1994. Embodied knowledge: Thinking with the body in critical medical anthropology. In *Assessing cultural anthropology*, edited by Robert Borofsky, 229–42. New York: McGraw-Hill.

Schneider, David. 1968. *American kinship: A cultural account*. Englewood Cliffs, NJ: Prentice-Hall.

Schultz, Emily. 1984. From Pagan to *Pullo*: Ethnic identity change in northern Cameroon. *Africa* 54 (1): 46–64.

———. 1990. *Dialogue at the margins: Whorf, Bakhtin, and linguistic relativity*. Madison: University of Wisconsin Press.

Schultz, Emily, and Robert Lavenda. 1990. *Cultural anthropology: A perspective on the human condition*. 2d ed. St. Paul: West.

Schwartzman, Helen. 1978. *Transformations. The anthropology of children's play*. New York: Plenum.

Scott, James C. 1985. *Weapons of the weak*. New Haven: Yale University Press.

———. 1990. *Domination and the arts of resistance: Hidden transcripts*. New Haven: Yale University Press.

Segalen, Martine. 1986. *Historical anthropology of the family*. Cambridge: Cambridge University Press.

Service, Elman. 1962. *Primitive social organization*. New York: Random House.

Shepherd, Gill. 1987. Rank, gender, and homosexuality: Mombasa as a key to understanding sexual options. In *The cultural construction of sexuality*, edited by Pat Caplan, 240–70. London: Tavistock.

Shostak, Marjorie. 1981. *Nisa: The life and words of a !Kung woman*. New York: Vintage Books.

Silverstein, Michael. 1976. Shifters, linguistic categories, and cultural description. In *Meaning in anthropology*, edited by Keith Basso, and Henry Selby, 11–55. Albuquerque: University of New Mexico Press.

Smith, Andrea. 1994. For all those who were Indian in a former life. *Cultural Survival Quarterly* (Winter): 71.

Smith, G. 1989. Space age shamans: The videotape. *Americas* 41 (2): 28–31.

Smith, M. G. [1954] 1981. Introduction to *Baba of Karo*, by Mary Smith. Reprint. New Haven: Yale University Press, 1981.

Smith, Wilfred Cantwell. 1982. *Towards a world theology*. Philadelphia: Westminster.

Solway, Jacqueline, and Richard Lee. 1990. Foragers, genuine or spurious: Situating the Kalahari San in history. *Current Anthropology* 31:109–46.

Spiro, Melford. 1977. *Kinship and marriage in Burma: A cultural and psychodynamic account*. Berkeley: University of California Press.

Starn, Orin. 1992. "I dreamed of foxes and hawks": Reflections on peasant protest, new social movements, and the *rondas campesinas* of northern Peru. In *The making of social movements in Latin America: Identity, strategy, and democracy*, edited by Arturo Escobar and Sonia E. Alvarez, 89–111. Series in Political Economy and Economic Development in Latin America. Boulder, CO: Westview.

Stearman, Allyn. 1989. *The Yuquí*. New York: Holt, Rinehart and Winston.

Steggerda, Morris. [1941] 1984. *Maya Indians of Yucatán*. Reprint. New York: AMS Press.

Steiner, Christopher. 1994. *African art in transit*. Cambridge: Cambridge University Press.

Stewart, Charles, and Rosalind Shaw. 1994. *Syncretism/anti-syncretism*. London: Routledge.

Strathern, Marilyn. 1972. *Women in between*. London: Academic Press.

———. 1992. *Reproducing the future: Anthropology, kinship, and the new reproductive technologies*. New York: Routledge.

Sutton-Smith, Brian. 1992. Notes towards a critique of twentieth-century psychological play theory. In *Homo ludens: der spieldende Mensch*, vol. 2, edited by Günther G. Bauer, 95–108. München-Salzburg: Musikverlag Emil Katzbichler.

Tamari, Tal. 1991. The development of caste systems in West Africa. *Journal of African History* 32:221–50.

Tambiah, Stanley J. 1989. The politics of ethnicity. *American Ethnologist* 16 (2): 335–49.

Tannen, Deborah. 1990. *You just don't understand: Women and men in conversation*. New York: Ballantine Books.

Taylor, Julie. 1987. Tango. *Cultural Anthropology* 2 (4): 481–93.

Trobriand cricket: An ingenious response to colonialism. 1974. Directed by J. W. Leach and G. Kildea. 60 min. Berkeley: University of California Extension Media Center.

Trotter, Robert. 1987. A case of lead poisoning from folk remedies in Mexican American communities. In *Anthropological praxis*, edited by Robert Wolfe and Shirley Fiske, 146–59. Boulder, CO: Westview.

Turnbull, Colin. 1961. *The forest people*. New York: Simon and Schuster.

Turner, Terence. 1989. Amazonian Indians fight to save their forest. *Anthropology Newsletter* 30 (3): 21–22.

———. 1991a. The social dynamics of video media in an indigenous society: The cultural meaning and the personal politics of video-making in Kayapo communities. *Visual Anthropology Review* 7 (2): 68–76.

———. 1991b. Visual media, cultural politics, and anthropological practice. *The Independent*, January/February, 34–40.

Turner, Victor. 1969. *The ritual process*. Chicago: Aldine.

Valentine, Bettylou. 1978. *Hustling and other hard work*. New York: Free Press.

Valentine, Charles. 1978. Introduction. In *Hustling and other hard work*, by Bettylou Valentine, 1–10. New York: Free Press.

Van Gennep, Arnold. 1960. *The rites of passage.* Chicago: University of Chicago Press.

van Willigen, John. 1991. *Anthropology in use: A source book on anthropological practice.* Boulder, CO: Westview.

van Willigen, John, and V. C. Channa. 1991. Law, custom, and crimes against women. *Human Organization* 50 (4): 369–77.

Vaughan, James. 1970. Caste systems in the western Sudan. In *Social stratification in Africa,* edited by Arthur Tuden and Leonard Plotnikov, 59–92. New York: Free Press.

———. 1973. Engkyagu as artists in Marghi society. In *The traditional artist in African societies,* edited by Warren L. d'Azevedo, 162–93. Bloomington: Indiana University Press.

Voloshinov, V. N. [1926] 1987. Discourse in life and discourse in art. In *Freudianism,* translated by I. R. Titunik and edited in collaboration with Neil H. Bruss, 93–116. Bloomington: Indiana University Press.

———. [1929] 1986. *Marxism and the philosophy of language.* Translated by Ladislav Matejka and I. R. Titunik. Cambridge, MA: Harvard University Press.

Vygotsky, L. S. 1962. *Thought and language.* Cambridge, MA: MIT Press.

———. 1978. *Mind in society: The development of higher psychological processes.* Cambridge, MA: Harvard University Press.

Wallace, A. F. C. 1966. *Religion: An anthropological view.* New York: Random House.

———. 1972. *The death and rebirth of the Seneca.* New York: Vintage.

Wallerstein, Immanuel. 1974. *The modern world-system.* New York: Academic Press.

Wallmann, Joel. 1992. *Aping language.* Cambridge: Cambridge University Press.

Weiner, Annette. 1976. *Women of value, men of renown.* Austin: University of Texas Press.

———. 1980. Stability in banana leaves: Colonization and women in Kiriwina, Trobriand Islands. In *Women and colonization: Anthropological perspectives,* edited by Mona Etienne and Eleanor Leacock, 270–93. New York: Praeger.

———. 1988. *The Trobrianders of Papua New Guinea.* New York: Holt, Rinehart and Winston.

———. 1990. Guest editorial in *Cultural anthropology: A perspective on the human condition,* by Emily Schultz and Robert Lavenda, 392–93. 2d ed. St. Paul: West.

Weismantel, Mary. 1995. Making kin: Kinship theory and Zumbagua adoptions. *American Ethnologist* 22 (4): 685–709.

Wertsch, James. 1985. *Vygotsky and the social formation of mind.* Cambridge, MA: Harvard University Press.

Weston, Kath. 1991. *Families we choose.* New York: Columbia University Press.

———. 1995. Forever is a long time: Romancing the real in gay kinship ideologies. In *Naturalizing power,* edited by Sylvia Yanagisako and Carol Delaney, 87–110. New York: Routledge.

Whorf, Benjamin. 1956. *Language, thought, and reality,* edited by John B. Carroll. Cambridge, MA: MIT Press.

Wilk, Richard. 1996. *Economies and cultures.* Boulder, CO: Westview.

Williams, Brett. 1984. Why migrant women feed their husbands tamales: Foodways as a basis for a revisionist view of Tejano family life. In *Ethnic and regional foodways in the United States,* edited by Linda Keller Brown and Kay Mussell. Knoxville: University of Tennessee Press.

Wilmsen, Edwin. 1989. *Land filled with flies: A political economy of the Kalahari.* Chicago: University of Chicago Press.

———. 1991. Pastoro-foragers to "Bushmen": Transformation in Kalahari relations of property, production and labor. In *Herders, warriors, and traders: Pastoralism in Africa,* edited by John G. Galaty and Pierre Bonte, 248–63. Boulder, CO: Westview.

Wilson, Monica. 1951. *Good company.* Oxford: Oxford University Press.

Winn, Peter. 1992. *Americas.* New York: Pantheon.

Witherspoon, Gary. 1975. *Navajo kinship and marriage.* Chicago: University of Chicago Press.

Wolf, Eric. 1969. *Peasant wars of the twentieth century.* New York: Harper and Row.

———. 1982. *Europe and the people without history.* Berkeley: University of California Press.

———. 1994. Facing power: Old insights, new questions. In *Assessing cultural anthropology,* edited by Robert Borofsky, 218–28. New York: McGraw-Hill.

Woost, M. D. 1993. Nationalizing the local past in Sri Lanka: Histories of nation and development in a Sinhalese village. *American Ethnologist* 20 (3): 502–21.

Yanagisako, Sylvia, and Jane Collier. 1987. Toward a unified analysis of gender and kinship. In *Gender and kinship: Essays toward a unified analysis,* edited by Jane Collier and Sylvia Yanagisako, 14–50. Stanford: Stanford University Press.

Credits

Text and Illustration

Chapter 2 Fig. 2.3, from *Humanity's Descent* by Rick Potts, William Morrow, 1996. Used with permission of the publisher. **Chapter 3** page 41, from *Assessing Cultural Anthropology*, Robert Borofsky, ed. Copyright © 1993 McGraw-Hill, Inc. Reprinted by permission; page 48, excerpt from *Yuqui: Forest Nomads in a Changing World* by Allyn Stearman. Copyright © 1989 by Holt, Rinehart and Winston. Reprinted by permission of the publisher. **Chapter 4** page 60, excerpt from Kent Redford, The ecologically noble savage, *Cultural Survival Quarterly*, vol. 15, no.1, Spring 1991. Used with permission of the publisher; Fig. 4.5, Table 4.2, from *Political Anthropology: An Introduction*, Second Edition, by Ted Lewellen. Copyright © 1983 by Ted Lewellen. Reproduced with permission of Greenwood Publishing Group, Inc., Westport, CT. **Chapter 5** Fig. 5.4, reprinted with the permission of The Free Press, a Division of Simon & Schuster from *The Religion of Java* by Clifford Geertz. Copyright © 1960 by The Free Press; Fig. 5.7, courtesy of the Australian Broadcasting Corp.; page 86, reproduced by permission of the American Anthropological Association from *American Anthropologist* 88:2, June 1986. Not for further reproduction; page 90, copyright © 1996 by Houghton Mifflin Company. Reprinted by permission from *The American Heritage Dictionary of the English Language,* Third Edition; page 96, from Marcyliena Morgan, Theories and politics in African-American English, *Annual Review of Anthropology* 23:325–345, 1995. Used with permission. **Chapter 6** Figs. 6.1, 6.5, 6.8, from *States of Mind* by Jonathan Miller. Copyright © 1983 by the Contributors. Reprinted by permission of Pantheon Books, a division of Random House, Inc.; Figs. 6.3, 6.4, 6.9, from Michael Cole and Sylvia Scribner, *Culture and Thought: A Psychological Introduction.* With permission of the author; page 117, from *Assessing Cultural Anthropology*, Robert Borofsky, ed. Copyight © 1993 McGraw-Hill, Inc. Reprinted by permission; page 122, in *Anthropology Today* 4(6), 1988. Reprinted by permission of Royal Anthropological Institute. **Chapter 7** page 141, reproduced by permission of the American Anthropological Association from *Cultural Anthropology* 2:4, November 1987. Not for further reproduction; Fig. 7.6, from *Human Antiquity: An Introduction to Physical Anthropology and Archaeology* by Kenneth L. Feder and Michael Alan Park. Copyright © 1997 Mayfield Publishing Company; page 146, from Aufderheide, *Public Culture* 5:3, 1993. Copyright © 1993 by The University of Chicago Press. Reprinted by permission of the publisher. **Chapter 8** page 173, from Andrea Smith, For all those who were Indians in a former life, *Cultural Survival Quarterly*, vol. 17, no. 4, Winter 1994. Used with permission of the publisher; page 174, from Roger M. Keesing, *Custom and Confrontation.* Copyright © 1992 by The University of Chicago Press. Reprinted by permission of the publisher. **Chapter 9** page 188, excerpt from "State and Violence in the Ex-Soviet Union" by Anatoly Khazanov, unpublished paper read at 92nd annual meeting of American Anthropological Association, Washington, D.C., November 1993; page 196, from *Americas* by Peter Winn. Copyright © 1992 by Peter Winn and WGBH Educational Foundation. Reprinted by permission of Pantheon Books, a division of Random House, Inc. **Chapter 10** Fig. 10.3, from Guaman Poma de Ayala, Nueva Coronica, c. 1610; page 217, from *Autobiografias campesinas*, 1979, vol. 1, Heredia, Costa Rica: Editorial del la Universidad Nacional, translated from Spanish by Robert Lavenda; page 219, from *Crafting Selves* by Dorinne Kondo. Copyright © 1990 by The University of Chicago Press. Reprinted with permission of the publisher; page 226, from *African Art in Transit* by Christopher Steiner, 1994, Cambridge University Press. Reprinted with permission of the publisher. **Chapter 11** page 245, from What do men want? by Syed Subair Ahmed. Copyright © 1994 by The New York Times Co. Reprinted by permission. **Chapter 12** page 261, excerpts from Chapter 9 of *My Days* by R. K. Narayan. Copyright © 1973, 1974 by R. K. Narayan. Published by Penguin USA. Used by permission of the Wallace Literary Agency, Inc.; page 276, reproduced by permission of the Society for Applied Anthropology from John van Willigen and V. C. Channa, Law, custom, and crimes against women, *Human Organization* 50(4), 1991. **Chapter 13** page 288, "Sumos Quod Sumos" from *Lake Wobegon Days* by Garrison Keillor. Copyright © 1985 by Garrison Keillor. Used by permission of Viking Penguin, a division of Penguin Books USA Inc.; page 307, Reproduced by permission of the American Anthropological Association from *American Ethnologist* 16(2), May 1989. Not for further reproduction. **Chapter 14** page 316, from *The Amazonian Chronicles* by Jacques Meunier and A. M. Savarin. Translation copyright © 1994 Carol Christiansen. Published by Mercury House, San Francisco, CA and reprinted by permission. **Chapter 15** page 347, from Marc S. Miller, Behind the words, *Cultural Survival Quarterly*, vol. 17, no. 2, Summer 1993. Used with permission.

Photo

Chapter 1 CO-1, © William Coupon; Fig. 1.2a, © Barbara Smuts/Anthro-Photo; Fig. 1.2b, courtesy Carol Worthman; Fig. 1.3, © Robert Lavenda; Fig. 1.4, courtesy Lilliana Nieto/Physicians for Human Rights; Fig. 1.5, from *Amazonian Cosmos: The Sexual and Religious Symbolism of the Tukano Indians* by Gerardo Dolmatoff, © 1971 by the University of Chicago Press; Fig. 1.6a, © Kenneth L. Feder; Fig. 1.6b, © Lindsay Hebberd/Woodfin Camp and Associates; Fig. 1.7, courtesy C. K. Brain. **Chapter 2** CO-2, © William

Coupon; Fig. 2.1, © Robert H. Lavenda; Fig. 2.5, © UPI/Corbis-Bettmann; Fig. 2.6, © Reuters/Petar Kujundzic/Archive Photos. **Chapter 3** CO-3, © William Coupon; Fig. 3.1, courtesy Dionisio Rodriguez; Fig. 3.3a, courtesy of the Institute for Intercultural Studies, Inc., New York; Fig. 3.3b, courtesy Sharon E. Hutchinson; Fig. 3.4, © Napoleon Chagnon/Anthro-Photo; Fig. 3.5, © Malkin/Anthro-Photo. **Chapter 4** CO-4, © William Coupon; Fig. 4.2, © The Granger Collection, New York; Fig. 4.3, © Reuters/Corbis-Bettmann; Fig. 4.4, M. W. Sexton, Peabody Museum of Salem; Fig. 4.7, courtesy Arjun Guneratne. **Chapter 5** CO-5, © William Coupon; Fig. 5.1, reprinted with special permission of King Features Syndicate; Fig. 5.3, © Robert H. Lavenda; Fig. 5.6, © Donald Smetzer/Tony Stone Images; Fig. 5.8, © David Madison/Tony Stone Images. **Chapter 6** CO-6, © William Coupon; Fig. 6.7, M. C. Escher's *Relativity* © 1997 Cordon Art-Baarn-Holland. All rights reserved. **Chapter 7** CO-7, © William Coupon; Fig. 7.2, © Robert H. Lavenda; Fig. 7.3, © Reuters/Archive Photos; Fig. 7.4, © Richard Pasley/Stock Boston; Fig. 7.5, courtesy Dr. James W. Fernandez/University of Chicago; Fig. 7.7, © Etter/Anthro-Photo. **Chapter 8** CO-8, © William Coupon; Fig. 8.1, © Robert H. Lavenda; Fig. 8.3, © J. F. E. Bloss/Anthro-Photo; Fig. 8.5, © Motion Picture & Television Photo Archive; Fig. 8.6, © Van Cleve/Tony Stone Images; Fig. 8.7, reprinted from Barbara G. Myerhoff, *Peyote Hunt: The Sacred Journey of the Huichol Indians,* p. 163. © 1974 by Cornell University. Used by permission of the publisher, Cornell University Press; Fig. 8.8, courtesy Dr. James W. Fernandez/University of Chicago. **Chapter 9** CO-9, © William Coupon; Fig. 9.1, © Reuters/Rutilio Enamorado/Archive Photos; Fig. 9.3, © Robert H. Lavenda; Fig. 9.4, © Elizabeth Harris/Tony Stone Images; Fig. 9.5, © Hugh Sitton/Tony Stone Images; Fig. 9.6, courtesy Orin Starn. **Chapter 10** CO-10, © William Coupon; Fig. 10.1, © Dr. Irvin DeVore/Anthro-Photo;

Fig. 10.3a, from Guaman Poma de Ayala, *Nueva Coronica,* c. 1610. Courtesy Thames & Hudson; Fig. 10.3b, from R. W. Keatinge, ed. 1988. *Peruvian Prehistory.* New York: Cambridge University Press. Reprinted with permission of the publisher and the owner of the material, Craig Morris; Fig. 10.5, neg. #441791. Courtesy Department of Library Services, American Museum of Natural History; Fig. 10.6, © Robert H. Lavenda; Fig. 10.7, photo from *The Trobrianders of Papua New Guinea* by Annette B. Weiner, copyright © 1988 by Holt, Rinehart and Winston, reproduced by permission of the publisher. **Chapter 11** CO-11, © William Coupon; Fig. 11.2a, © 1988 G. W. James/Southwest Museum, Los Angeles; Fig. 11.2b, © Jacques Jangoux/Tony Stone Images; Fig. 11.6, Dan Budnik/© 1980 Woodfin Camp and Associates; Fig. 11.14, © AP/Wide World Photos. **Chapter 12** CO-12, © William Coupon; Fig. 12.2, © Robert H. Lavenda; Fig. 12.3, © Dr. Irvin DeVore/Anthro-Photo; Fig. 12.4, from *Sita's Daughters: Coming Out of Purdah: The Rajput Women of Khalapur Revisited* by Leigh Minturn. Copyright © 1993 by Oxford University Press, Inc. Used by permission of Oxford University Press, Inc.; Fig. 12.5, © Robert H. Lavenda. **Chapter 13** CO-13, © William Coupon; Fig. 13.2, © United Nations/DPI Photo; Fig. 13.3, photo by Joseph K. Dixon, Courtesy Museum of New Mexico, neg. #67683; Fig. 13.4, © Alan Sussman/The Image Works; Fig. 13.5, courtesy James H. Vaughn. **Chapter 14** CO-14, © William Coupon; Fig. 14.1, © R. Maiman/Sygma Photos; Fig. 14.3, © Bruno Barbey/Magnum Photos; Fig. 14.4, courtesy Robin Mouat; Fig. 14.5, photo by Nancy Scheper-Hughes; Fig. 14.6, © Marc and Evelyne Bernheim/Woodfin Camp and Associates. **Chapter 15** CO-15, © William Coupon; Fig. 15.1, courtesy Jim Altobell/SCSU Public Relations and Publications; Fig. 15.3, © Larry Dale Gordon/The Image Bank; Fig. 15.4, © Crawford/Anthro-Photo.

Index

Boldface page numbers indicate glossary definitions.